The Soup Book

The Soup Book

770 RECIPES

By

LOUIS P. DE GOUY

DOVER PUBLICATIONS, INC.

NEW YORK

Published in Canada by General Publishing Company, Ltd., 30 Lesmill Road, Don Mills, Toronto,
Ontario.
Published in the United Kingdom by Constable
and Company, Ltd., 10 Orange Street, London WC 2.

This Dover edition, first published in 1974, is an
unabridged republication of the work originally
published in 1949 by Greenberg Publisher.

International Standard Book Number: 0-486-22998-X
Library of Congress Catalog Card Number: 73-88332

Manufactured in the United States of America
Dover Publications, Inc.
180 Varick Street
New York, N. Y. 10014

THIS BOOK IS FONDLY DEDICATED

TO THE MEMORY OF

LOUIS P. DE GOUY

(1876-1947)

BY HIS DAUGHTER

JACQUELINE S. DOONER

CONTENTS

vii

Chapter Seven

BISQUES

Fish Cream Soups—also called Coulis—including
Fresh-Water and Salt-Water Fish and Crustaceans

Chapter Eight

CHOWDERS

Fish, Game, Meat, Poultry, and Vegetable, including
Fish Stews considered as soup, and Bouillabaise

Chapter Nine

MISCELLANEOUS SOUPS

Chapter Ten

BALL GARNISHES FOR SOUPS

Chapter Eleven

CUSTARD GARNISHES FOR SOUPS

Chapter Twelve

DUMPLING GARNISHES FOR SOUPS

Chapter Thirteen

MISCELLANEOUS SOUP GARNISHES

INTRODUCTION TO SOUPS

I F THE TRUE GOURMET FOUND HIMSELF STRANDED ALONE WITH the Druid stones and dolmens on the Ile-aux-Moines, he would dream and expeditiously concoct, for all the curtailed possibilities, something better than 108 long Biblical years with grass. And the lowliest Britanny peasant would do as much. For however limited he may be, the true epicure knows no limitations.

Anyone lucky enough to remember the Britanny, not of the *beau monde*, but of the peasants, must wistfully remember the artistry with which they can draw from their broths and soups and stews flavors that would tempt the gods. It is only the uninitiated who assume that it would take the chef of a king's mistress to serve the soup for a king.

From time immemorial, soups and broths have been the worldwide medium for utilizing what we call the kitchen by-products, or as the French call them, the *dessertes de la table* (leftovers), or *les parties intérieures de la bête*, such as head, tail, lights, liver, knuckles, and feet.

The land of the Stars and Stripes will stand for many a day to come on Hollywood's starshot adjectives as the world's most glamorous, supercolossal, gigantic, stupendous, magnificent, bubbling melting pot. Like the whale who swallowed Jonah, we have engulfed all national dishes known to civilized man, and made them in delight, if not in name, our own. Go, when the clouds lift, ye gourmets, to Russia for bortsch . . . to Italy for minestrone . . . Scotland for broth . . . Holland for *ael soep* . . . Canada for the soup *à l'habitant* . . . China for the bird's-nest soup . . . Spain for cold *gazpacho* soup . . . West Africa for ground peanut soup . . . Hungary for *gombaleves* or mushroom soup . . . Burma for *hingyo* or vegetable and shrimp paste soup . . . Denmark for *honsekodsuppe* or chicken soup . . . Greece for *kottósoupa* or chicken soup . . . Finland for *mustikka soppa* or bilberry soup . . . to Mexico for *sopa de frijoles negros* or black bean soup . . . Germany for *riebele suppe* and *wein suppe* . . . but to America for choice. For within the geography sandwiched between Mexico and Canada there is an international choice of menus that has made here the whole world one.

But the process of selection and adaptation of foods, with new fruits and vegetables and spices and condiments drifting across many boundaries, began centuries before America emerged from its swaddling clothes. That the interchange ever existed has been forgotten by modern Europeans who cling so tenaciously to their now established menus. In the grand melting pot of America, it is a different story.

The prodigal intermarriages of many races have brought strange drinks and dishes from one home to another, and national boundaries, with all their incipient peril, wilt on the platter where French and Russian meet over *zakuska* and vodka or *navarin de mouton* and *vin ordinaire*. As a consequence, an American family with its international implications might reasonably concoct a meal that runs from French onion soup to spaghetti *à l'Italienne*, from fruit cocktail to *shish-kebab*, from chowder to *crêpes Suzette*, from Boston baked beans to *cassoulet*, from smörgasbord to *zeleni paprika* Serbian way. And what are the whys and wherefores of these "foreign" restaurants, cafeterias, coffeepots, burger stands, and nickel-in-the-wall eat-quick shops? The reason for their establishment is the same as that abroad: profit on pleasure of the table. But the result is different. You will see in a popular French restaurant hundreds of faces that never hailed from Paris, and in the myriad of Italian restaurants wandering eyes that may have rested often on the Danube, or the Rhine, the Kremlin, Algeria, Brussels, or the Taj Mahal, but eyes that never saw the Basilica of St. Peter.

Viva America! the melting pot. The prosperous restaurant proprietors agree, by and large, that they set up small shop in the beginning to satisfy the demands of their own countrymen in New York, San Francisco, Chicago, or Boston. Now they depend on the products of American intermarriage for their trade.

On this culinary score, though we have adopted many another land's soup, we have contributed many a famous broth ourselves. There is our glorious clam chowder; there is the famous Philadelphia pepper pot, Creole gumbo, a multitude of fish chowders and fish broths made of oysters, clams, lobsters, and other sea foods, and vegetables. Our cream of corn soup may have little relation to the formidable brew recommended to the settlers by the Iroquois—undoubtedly with deliberate malice, for it was composed of a quart and a half of wood ashes mixed with impossible things—but even that was corn soup too. For soup is the song of the hearth . . . and the home. They may be robust and hearty, such as gumbos, chowders, and minestrones, almost a meal in themselves. They may be light and highly spiced, such as fruit soups, wine soups, beer soups, or consommés. They may be creamed, or made distinctive with a dash of wine, parsley, chives, or some other last touch or finishing flourish, but they must be good.

Soup is cuisine's kindest course. It breathes reassurance; it steams consolation; after a weary day it promotes sociability, as the five o'clock cup of tea or the cocktail hour. Every nation, every forgotten corner of the world has its special soup recipe. Soup has been celebrated in verse and story almost as reverently as the first signs of spring. For there is nothing like a plate or a bowl of hot soup, its wisp of aromatic steam making the nostrils quiver with anticipation, to dispel the depressing effects of a grueling day at the office or the shop, rain or snow in the streets, or bad news in the papers. Soup is to the meal what the hostess's smile of welcome is to the party, a prelude to the goodness to come.

The soup kettle on the fire sings of a well-built home, poor or rich, with sturdy trees to shelter it . . . of a flower bed, plump lilacs purpling near by . . . of rich hearty laughter and children's songs . . . of gentle hands . . . of the red-checked or damask cloth on the table, generous and kind, loaded with things that make life worth living . . . of honest sweat and earnings won . . . of Alleluia to the Creator . . . of Zetes and Calais, sons of the north wind, Zephyrus, the west wind, and Notus, the south wind, who love to bend down and whirl around on the snow, on the dead weeds when they play, dancing to Venus in the sky . . . of quaint charm, mystical perfumes hanging in the atmosphere of the home, so humble be it, just picked up from the herb garden, which are amazed, spellbound, delighted beyond measure to waltz side by side with the vegetables from the garden patch and the fowl from the barnyard, to the tune of joy . . . of the girl named Daphne, long and long ago, the daughter of the old river god Peneus, who, because the sunlight got in her eyes and blinded her, became the first laurel tree, which smells so lively in the soup kettle . . . of birds, butterflies, peace, contentment . . . and love!

That's the song, the beautiful song of the soup kettle.

LOUIS P. DE GOUY

Chapter One

GENERAL
INFORMATION

SOUPS AND SOUP GARNISHES—CLASSIFICATION OF SOUPS
—COLORING THE SOUP—BROWN STOCK—CARAMEL FOR
SOUP COLORING—CHICKEN STOCK—FISH STOCK—GRAVY
STOCK—VEGETABLE STOCK—WHITE OR VEAL STOCK—
CLARIFYING ANY STOCK—COMPOSITION OF BONE, ITS
PART IN SOUP—ROUX—CREAM SOUPS—SOUP GARNISHES—
HERBS AND VEGETABLES USED IN SOUPS—THE BOUQUET
GARNI—CONDIMENTS AND SPICES USED IN SOUPS

*Soup is to the meal what the hostess's
smile of welcome is to the party*

CONVERSION TABLES FOR FOREIGN EQUIVALENTS

DRY INGREDIENTS

Ounces	Grams	Grams	Ounces	Pounds	Kilograms	Kilograms	Pounds
1 =	28.35	1 =	0.035	1 =	0.454	1 =	2.205
2	56.70	2	0.07	2	0.91	2	4.41
3	85.05	3	0.11	3	1.36	3	6.61
4	113.40	4	0.14	4	1.81	4	8.82
5	141.75	5	0.18	5	2.27	5	11.02
6	170.10	6	0.21	6	2.72	6	13.23
7	198.45	7	0.25	7	3.18	7	15.43
8	226.80	8	0.28	8	3.63	8	17.64
9	255.15	9	0.32	9	4.08	9	19.84
10	283.50	10	0.35	10	4.54	10	22.05
11	311.85	11	0.39	11	4.99	11	24.26
12	340.20	12	0.42	12	5.44	12	26.46
13	368.55	13	0.46	13	5.90	13	28.67
14	396.90	14	0.49	14	6.35	14	30.87
15	425.25	15	0.53	15	6.81	15	33.08
16	453.60	16	0.57				

LIQUID INGREDIENTS

Liquid Ounces	Milliliters	Milliliters	Liquid Ounces	Quarts	Liters	Liters	Quarts
1 =	29.573	1 =	0.034	1 =	0.946	1 =	1.057
2	59.15	2	0.07	2	1.89	2	2.11
3	88.72	3	0.10	3	2.84	3	3.17
4	118.30	4	0.14	4	3.79	4	4.23
5	147.87	5	0.17	5	4.73	5	5.28
6	177.44	6	0.20	6	5.68	6	6.34
7	207.02	7	0.24	7	6.62	7	7.40
8	236.59	8	0.27	8	7.57	8	8.45
9	266.16	9	0.30	9	8.52	9	9.51
10	295.73	10	0.33	10	9.47	10	10.57

Gallons (American)	Liters	Liters	Gallons (American)
1 =	3.785	1 =	0.264
2	7.57	2	0.53
3	11.36	3	0.79
4	15.14	4	1.06
5	18.93	5	1.32
6	22.71	6	1.59
7	26.50	7	1.85
8	30.28	8	2.11
9	34.07	9	2.38
10	37.86	10	2.74

GOOD SOUP IS ONE OF THE PRIME INGREDIENTS OF GOOD LIVing. For soup can do more to lift the spirits and stimulate the appetite than any other one dish. Soups challenge us, because an enticing flavorful soup can be as different from the thin watery beverage sometimes erroneously called soup as a genuine green turtle is from the mock turtle.

Perhaps one of the surest tests of a good cook is the choice of soup in relation to the rest of the meal. The purpose of soup in the meal is twofold: first, to stimulate appetite; second, to provide nourishment. Light soups serve as appetizers, heavier ones may be a main course. Men, we notice, have always been partial to soups that "fill you up"—those rich with chunks of meat or chicken, hearty with vegetables, alimentary pastes, barley, or rice.

Brillat-Savarin once made the remark that a woman who couldn't make soups should not be allowed to marry. Soups were important in his world, and they still are important to us all, young or ex-young. Steaming hot soup, sipped in leisurely manner, may be as refreshing on hot days as crisp salads and iced beverages served in cold glasses. From the clear well-seasoned bouillon, or the more herbal consommé, which starts everything off amiably, to the thick vegetable, tomato, bean, or pea soup, or purée, that makes a lunch in itself—all have a place in year-round menus. One whiff of a savory, aromatic soup, and appetites come to attention. The steaming fragrance of a tempting soup is a prelude to the goodness to come. An inspired soup puts family and guests in a receptive mood for enjoying the rest of the menu.

Meals, like everything else, are better when they get off to the right start. The first course is vastly important, for hungry people are apt to notice what they eat. If you begin the repast with a comforting chowder or a pungent consommé, you can relax even if the roast is not as tenderly browned as you had hoped. But if your soup lacks flavor and distinction, the rest of the menu must be superb to distract attention from the bad start. Though many first course favorites, such as canapés, fruit and vegetable juices, and all the gamut of hors d'oeuvres, have strayed from the table to the living room, soup must be served at the table. Consequently, it requires more attention than tidbits nibbled informally. Definitely, the soup is the curtain raiser for the meal and must be good.

3

CLASSIFICATION OF SOUPS   [2]

In planning menus, the cook must reckon with his or her soups. This is especially true if the food budget is to run on economical lines, for there are many ways of using soups and many types of soups which will do much to bolster up an otherwise scanty meal.

All soup recipes may generally be classified in three main groups: (1) thin, clear soups which stimulate appetite—consommé, bouillon, broth; (2) thin, light, delicate cream soups, bisques, vegetable broth; (3) heavy, thick soups or chowders—pepper pot, Scotch broth, minestrone, mulligatawny, thick vegetable soups, thick cream soups.

Bouillon, Consommé, and Broth. Bouillon is the clarified liquid in which meat, poultry, or vegetables have been cooked. Clear consommé, or clarified bouillon, flavored with sherry, bitters, and the like, can almost be regarded as a "cocktail." Broth is the unclarified liquid in which meats, poultry, game, or vegetables are cooked. It, like the consommé, is frequently garnished, but lightly.

Light Cream Soup. This is ideal as the preface to a meal, or as the main supper dish, particularly for growing children.

Heavy Soup. This is the hearty soup, and its general characteristic is that of being a whole meal in itself.

Another group comprises the cold, chilled, or jellied soups, usually called summer soups, of which more further on and in their own chapter.

Then we have the soup stocks of which there are five variants: brown stock, fish stock, gravy stock, vegetable stock, and white stock, which all need to be clarified before using for either soup base or sauce base. Any kind of stock should be well seasoned and well flavored by means of spices, condiments, or herbs.

Aside from its use in soup making, the stock which many cooks keep on hand gives flavor to sauces and to many made dishes. Scraps of meat, bones of chops, outside leaves of lettuce, celery tops, and the water in which vegetables are boiled are only some of the items which go into the soup pot, contributing their savors to the stock. Careful cooks see that bones and trimmings of roasts are sent from the market, also chicken feet, to be scalded and scraped for the soup pot.

Stock forms the basis of all meat or fish soups. It is therefore essential to the success of these culinary operations to know the most complete and economical method of extracting from a certain quantity of meat the best possible stock or bouillon or broth. Fresh uncooked beef makes the best stock, with the addition of cracked bones, as the glutinous matter contained in them renders it important that they should be boiled with the meat, which adds to the strength and thickness of the soup. They are composed of an earthy substance —to which they owe their solidity—of gelatin, and a fatty fluid called marrow. Two ounces of them contain as much gelatin as one pound of meat; but, in them, this is so encased in the earthy substance that boiling water can dissolve only the surface of the whole bones. When there is an abundance of gelatin, it causes the stock, when cold, to become a jelly. The flesh of old animals contains more flavor than the flesh of young ones. Red meats contain more flavor than white.

Some cooks use meat that has once been cooked; this renders little nourishment and destroys the flavor. It might answer for ready soup, but for stock to keep, it is not so good, unless it is roasted meat. This contains higher fragrant properties; so by putting the remains of roasted meat in the stockpot, you obtain a better flavor.

The shinbone is generally used, but the neck or "sticking," as the butchers call it, contains more of the substance that you want to extract and makes a stronger and more nutritious soup than any other part of the animal. Meats for soup should *always* be put on to cook in *cold water*, in a covered soup kettle or pot, and allowed to simmer slowly for several hours, in order that the essence of the meat may be drawn out thoroughly. The cooking stock should be carefully skimmed to prevent it from becoming turbid; *never* allow it to boil fast *at any time*, and if more water is needed, use boiling water from the teakettle; cold or lukewarm water spoils the flavor. Stock will be as good the second, third, fourth, or fifth day, if kept in the refrigerator, as the first day, if heated to the boiling point before using.

COLORING THE SOUP   [3]

Coloring, the chief of which is brown burned sugar, known by French cooks as caramel, is used in some brown soups.

Pounded spinach leaves give a fine green color to certain soups. Parsley or the green leaves of celery put in soup will also serve instead of spinach; or use a few drops of green vegetable coloring. Pound a large handful of spinach in a mortar, then tie it in cheesecloth, and wring out all the juice; add this to the soup you wish to color, 5 minutes before taking it up. Mock turtle, and sometimes lamb or veal soups, should be this color.

To color red, skin 6 red tomatoes, squeeze out the seeds, and put the pulp into the soup with the other vegetables, or take the juice only, as directed for spinach, or use a few drops of red vegetable coloring or cochineal.

BROWN STOCK HOME MANNER   [4]
Makes about 6 quarts

Cut up 2 pounds of shin or neck of beef; break 1 pound of knuckle of veal into small pieces (about 3 or 4 pounds of bones altogether); cover with cold water (about 8 quarts) and add 1 tablespoon of salt. Let stand for an hour, then bring gently to the boiling point, skimming the scum as it rises. When quite clear, add 2 carrots, scraped and cut into inch pieces; 2 medium-sized onions, halved, one half stuck with 2 whole cloves; 1 medium-sized white turnip, peeled and quartered; 1 stalk of celery, well washed and cut into inch pieces; a bouquet garni composed of 2 large bay leaves, 1 large sprig of thyme, 12 sprigs of fresh parsley, all tied together with kitchen thread. Add also 15 whole peppercorns, gently bruised. Again bring to the boiling point, skim well, then cover. Lower the flame and let simmer gently, very gently; let it "smile" for 4½ to 5½ hours without disturbing, except skimming occasionally any fat or scum. Strain through a fine-meshed hair sieve and, when cold, remove the cake of fat from the surface. This can be clarified and used for frying. Store in refrigerator until wanted. If you desire a "second" stock, cover the meat and vegetables with cold water and let it boil down until reduced to half, over a gentle flame, and use as a base for soup or sauce, or to cook vegetables in.

Among the 4 pounds of bones indicated for this stock, you may use the cleaned feet and gizzards of chickens, turkey, or any kind of domestic bird. The above brown stock made according to this recipe, after being cleared, could be used for any clear soup, which would take its name from the garnish served with it. (See also No. 114, Jellied Beef Consommé or Bouillon.)

BROWNING THE STOCK   [5]

The best method of assuring a dark brown stock is to sear the meat and bones in their own fat, or to add a few drops of caramel (No. 6). Or you may add a few drops of Pique Seasoning (see No. 19).

CARAMEL FOR SOUP COLORING   [6]

Boil ½ pound of granulated sugar with ⅓ cup of cold water until it is dark brown, almost black, then add another ⅓ cup of cold water and boil again till it acquires the consistency of thick syrup. Strain, bottle, cork, and use as required. Fine for coloring stews, goulashes, gravies, and sauces.

CHICKEN STOCK [7]

Follow directions for Chicken Broth Parisian (No. 25) for stock, consommé, or bouillon.

FISH STOCK HOME MANNER [8]
Makes about 1½ quarts

Put 2 pounds of any inexpensive white-fleshed fish with bones and trimmings in a saucepan and cover with 2 quarts of cold water. Add 1 medium-sized onion, thinly sliced; 1 blade of mace; 12 white peppercorns, gently bruised; 1 teaspoon of salt; a bouquet garni composed of 1 large bay leaf, 1 large sprig of thyme, and 10 sprigs of fresh parsley, tied together with kitchen thread; 1 medium-sized carrot, scraped and thinly sliced; and 2 whole cloves. Bring to a boil, lower the flame, and let simmer gently for about 1 hour from the time the stock begins to simmer. Further cooking sometimes imparts a disagreeable bitter taste to the stock. Skim carefully through a fine-meshed sieve and, when cold, store in the refrigerator until needed.

GRAVY STOCK HOME MANNER [9]

Crack, rather small, some bones from roast meat, and fry them until well browned in a baking pan with a little meat drippings. Pour off all the fat, and add ⅓ of Pique Seasoning (see No. 19) to the amount of water used, enough to cover the bones generously. Season with a little pepper, but no salt, and let simmer very, very gently 35 to 40 minutes. Strain through cheesecloth and keep in refrigerator until required. This stock will keep several weeks in a good refrigerator when tightly sealed in a glass jar.

VEGETABLE STOCK HOME MANNER [10]
Makes about 2 quarts

Cut 2 medium-sized onions, 3 medium-sized carrots, 1 medium-sized white turnip, 1 stalk of celery, and 1 small head of lettuce into small pieces. Wash quickly, drain, and dry well. Heat ¼ cup of butter or margarine in a soup kettle, stir in the prepared vegetables, and cook very gently, over a low flame, having the kettle covered, for about 25 minutes, stirring frequently with a wooden spoon. Then add 2 large fresh tomatoes, peeled and quartered; a bouquet garni, composed of 1 large bay leaf, 8 sprigs of fresh parsley, and 1 sprig of thyme, tied together with kitchen thread; 1 blade of mace; 10 whole peppercorns, gently bruised; 1 small blade of garlic; 2 whole cloves; and ½ teaspoon of salt. Now stir in 1½ quarts of boiling water and 1 cup of Pique Seasoning (see No. 19), mixing well. Gradually bring to a rolling boil, lower the flame, and allow to simmer very gently, covered, for 1½ hours, skimming as the scum rises to the top. Strain through cheese-cloth, and it is ready for use. If not needed at once, cool, then store in glass jars in the refrigerator until needed. This stock will keep more than two weeks in the refrigerator when kept sealed in a glass jar or jars.

WHITE or VEAL STOCK HOME MANNER   [11]

Cut up the meat from 4 pounds of veal knuckle and break the bones into small pieces. Place in a soup kettle, with the neck and cleaned feet of a chicken. Pour over 1 quart of cold water for each pound of meat and bones, or about 4 quarts in all; cover and let stand in a cool place for a full hour. Then place the kettle over a low flame and bring slowly to a gentle boil, skimming as the scum rises to the surface. Simmer very gently, over a low flame, until quite clear. Now add 2 medium-sized onions, quartered; 2 medium-sized carrots, scraped and cut into inch pieces after being halved lengthwise; 1 medium-sized white turnip, peeled and quartered; 1 stalk of celery, scraped, then cut into inch pieces; a bouquet garni composed of 12 sprigs of fresh parsley, 1 sprig of thyme, 2 large bay leaves, 4 whole cloves, tied to-gether with kitchen thread; 12 peppercorns, freshly bruised; 1 table-spoon of salt; and 1 blade each of mace and garlic. Bring slowly to a boil, skim again as the scum rises to the top, and when clear, cover, and let simmer gently for 4 to 4½ hours, skimming occasionally as the fat and scum rise. Remove from the fire, strain through cheese-cloth, cool, and when cold, remove the cake of fat from the surface. Keep in refrigerator until wanted. This stock will keep two weeks in the refrigerator if stored in a closely sealed container.

CLARIFYING ANY STOCK HOME MANNER   [12]
For each 3 quarts of stock

Wash and cut small ½ medium-sized onion or ½ small leek, 1 small carrot, and 3 sprigs of green celery leaves, first peeling the onion or leek and scraping the carrot. Place the prepared vegetables in a clean saucepan with the 3 quarts of stock to be clarified. Add a small bouquet garni composed of 1 small bay leaf, 1 small sprig of thyme, 2 sprigs or leaflet of tarragon herb, 6 sprigs of chervil or parsley, and

1 whole clove, all tied together with kitchen thread; 6 peppercorns; the white and shell of 1 egg; 1 scant teaspoon of lemon juice; and 1 tablespoon of white wine vinegar. Stir with a wire whisk, and when mixed, add ½ pound of finely chopped or ground lean raw beef, previously moistened with 1 tablespoon of cold water. Gradually bring mixture to a boil while whisking steadily until the boiling point is reached. Then lower the flame, and let simmer very, very gently, uncovered and without stirring for 25 to 30 minutes. Taste for seasoning, strain through a fine-meshed sieve, the sieve covered with cheesecloth. When cold, store in refrigerator, or use at once for clear soup or consommé. This clear stock will keep about two weeks in the refrigerator when kept in a sealed container.

COMPOSITION OF BONE—ITS PART IN SOUP [13]

The valuable nourishing properties of soup have been, and indeed still are, much overlooked in this country. Soup forms the first course of those who dine in the true sense of the term, but its importance as a part of the everyday meal is not sufficiently appreciated by the majority of people. Yet no form of food is more digestible and wholesome, nor does any other method of preparing food afford so many opportunities for utilizing material that would otherwise be wasted. The richness or quality of soup depends more on the proper choice of ingredients, and proper management of the fire in the combination of those ingredients, than on the quantity of solid nutritious matter employed; much more on the art and skill of the cook than on the sum laid out in the market. This remark is as true today as it was two centuries ago. The average cook imagines that the goodness of a soup depends on the weight of meat he or she puts into it and on the size of the fire over which it is boiled.

Let's take the bones of animals or birds which are left over from previous repasts. What is the composition of bone? Bone is composed of a close hard material and a softer reticulated substance called spongy or cancellous tissue. All bone is more or less porous, the difference between the hard and the spongy portions being one of degree only, as may be seen when it is viewed under the lens of a microscope. The surface of bones is the densest portion. The inner parts are more cellular and are filled with a fatty tissue called medulla, or marrow. The vascular connective tissue is interspersed with fat cells which support the fine blood vessels and form the center of nourishment for the inner surface of the bones. The rigidity of bones is due chiefly to the presence of phosphate of lime and carbonate of lime, which constitute about two-thirds of the substance of bone. The remaining one-third consists of animal matter, chiefly gelatin. Hollow cylindrical bones possess the qualities of strength and lightness in a remarkable degree, thus adapting them for their special function in animal life. Bones also possess a certain degree of elasticity as, for example, those of the ribs.

Therefore, bear in mind that the best stock and the best consommé are not necessarily those which, when cold, form a jelly. The properties to which meat, poultry, or venison soups owe their valuable stimulating power are not derived from gelatin, but from the juices of the meat and bones combined.

ROUX   [14]

This is not a sauce, but a mixing of butter and flour used as the foundation of sauces, soups, and so on. Roux is the French name for a mixture usually made by melting 2 tablespoons of butter (or drippings) over a very low flame. Then, when thoroughly melted, add 2 tablespoons of kitchen flour, sprinkling a little at a time, mixing well after each addition. Stir almost constantly over the lowest possible fire until the mixture attains a nice color and is almost dry. It may be stored in a covered glass jar until needed. Nothing could sound simpler than this process, but in reality many cooks go wrong in this initial step. Perhaps it is the very simplicity of the operation that leads them to believe that the roux will automatically be a success, but no roux can be trusted to take care of itself.

This roux is used for thickening soups, such as chowders, cream soups, bisques, gravies, or sauces. There are two kinds of roux. The dark is achieved by letting the mixture darken to the desired hue (taking care not to let it burn), and is used to thicken the more highly seasoned soups and sauces.

For the light roux, *roux blond,* do not leave the mixture too long on the fire, just enough time to get a light golden color. It is used with the more delicately flavored soups and sauces.

It should always be remembered never to pour the roux into the basic liquid, but pour the liquid over the roux, stirring constantly, over a gentle fire. If you are using a roux that has been previously made, be sure to heat it in a double boiler (to prevent burning and darkening) before adding the desired soup or sauce.

If you desire a thinner roux, the amount of butter should be increased to two parts and one part of flour. For instance, for every 2 tablespoons of butter or drippings use 1 tablespoon of flour.

CREAM SOUPS—BASIC STANDARD RECIPES [15]
FOR CREAM SAUCES

Cream soups are fully explained with standard recipes in Chapter
Six.

SOUP GARNISHES [16]

Garnishing and decorating the soup challenges any cook who de-
sires to create something beautiful and appetizing. Inspiration may
come from a colorful array of greens, croutons, tiny dumplings, and
so on. Wherever a woman is in charge of activities in a kitchen, half
the monotony and drudgery is eliminated by allowing her imagination
and natural artistry to have full play in the careful arrangement of
the simplest meal. The keynote to happiness within the four walls
that make any home is plain, wholesome, well-cooked food, attrac-
tively served. A sprig of parsley or a bit of tender celery top garnishing the serving dish, a few delicately golden-browned croutons floating on
top of the soup will go a long way toward raising dejected spirits,
stimulating poor or laggard appetites, and creating an atmosphere of
contentment and well-being. It is surprising and oftentimes amusing
to see how easily a clever cook can train her household into accepting
the most ordinary foods when a little forethought is given to the
serving.

Dress up your soups. Serve them with different garnishes and ac-
companiments, such as croutons, noodles, spaghetti, and vermicelli;
rice or barley; grated cheese; tiny forcemeat balls or dumplings, such
as liver dumplings and bread dumplings; marrow balls; sliced frankfurter, sliced hard-cooked eggs, sieved egg yolk over a slice of lemon;
a poached egg; a round of toasted bread; salted whipped cream, plain
or dusted with a film of paprika or cinnamon; shredded salami; chiffonade (thinly shredded salad greens); vegetable julienne; bread
sticks, Melba toast, crackers, cheese straws, savory cheese puffs, tiny
egg balls; bread crumb dumplings; farina dumplings or tiny corn meal
dumplings; toast floats or cheese and olive floats; toasted popcorn;
shredded toasted almonds; burger balls; baking powder dumplings;
matzoth knoedel, and so on. See Chapters Ten to Thirteen for recipes
of soup garnishes.

HERBS AND VEGETABLES USED IN SOUPS [17]

Of vegetables, the principal ones are asparagus, artichoke, beans
(dry), beets, broccoli, Brussels sprouts, cabbage, carrots, cauliflower,

celery, chard, corn (fresh and dry), cucumber, dandelions, eggplant, endive, green pepper, kale, kohlrabi, leeks, lentils, lettuce, lima beans (fresh and dry), mushrooms (fresh and dry), onions (white, yellow, and scallions), parsnips, peas (dry or fresh), potatoes (white), rutabagas (yellow or Swedish turnips), sauerkraut, okra, sorrel, spinach (fresh or canned), squash, string beans (green and yellow), tomatoes, turnips, and so on.

The herbs generally used in soups are parsley, chervil, common thyme, summer savory, knotted marjoram, and so on, and other seasonings, such as bay leaves, tarragon, allspice, cinnamon, nutmeg, cloves, mace, black, red, and white pepper, lemon peel and juice, orange peel and juice—the latter imparts a fine flavor, and the acid is much milder. These materials, with wine, and with the various catsups combined in different proportions, are with other ingredients made into almost an endless variety of excellent soups and gravies.

Soups that are intended for the principal part of the meal certainly ought not to be flavored like sauces, which are only intended to give relish to some particular dish.

THE BOUQUET GARNI [18]

A bouquet garni is always composed of bay leaf, parsley, and thyme, the whole tied together with kitchen thread. Sometimes green celery leaves (tops) are added, but this is always indicated. However, the size of the bouquet garni may vary, depending on the kind of food to which it is applied. Certain fish are blander than others; consequently, the flavor of the broth used to cook them must be enhanced by the addition of a few more sprigs of parsley. Furthermore, the size of the bouquet garni may be large or small, depending on the amount of liquid used. All this information is given with each particular recipe using a bouquet garni. The bouquet garni is always discarded before the soup is served.

CONDIMENTS AND SPICES USED IN SOUPS [19]

Condiments and spices enter largely into the success of soup making, and therefore it is very important to know the numerous varieties, at least the most generally used, their composition and characteristics.

The history of the spice trade goes back to the distant past. We don't know who first added a peppercorn to a stew nor who added a stick of cinnamon to the pudding, but we do know that the trade in spices and condiments was a profitable, as well as a dangerous and adventurous, business long before the beginning of the Christian era.

Nearly all the spices that we now use daily in our cooking are native to those distant and eternally enchanting lands—India, Ceylon, China, and the Dutch Indies—which geographies sometimes refer to as the Spice Islands. They are all ancient countries, known to venturesome travelers from Egypt and Europe generations before the discovery of America. One of the exceptions to the Eastern origin of spices is allspice, which is native to the West Indies, particularly to the island of Jamaica. Some of the Eastern spices are now successfully cultivated in Europe, although the bulk of them still come from the Orient. Mustard is the chief exception, for much of that spice comes from England and from Holland, and a little is grown in our own United States.

Condiments and spices in themselves supply little nourishment, their effect being mainly of a stimulating character to the nerves of taste or secretion and they are used as an accessory to food. They add flavor to otherwise insipid food and relieve monotony in diet. However, they should not be too much used in children's food.

In the mouth, condiments produce an agreeable taste, with an increased flow of saliva, and the desire for food in the stomach is stimulated. They also increase the secretion of gastric juice.

Allspice. So called because it is thought to combine the flavors of cinnamon, nutmeg, and cloves. It is the berry of a handsome tree that grows to the height of twenty feet in the West Indies and in South America. The fruit is not allowed to ripen, but is gathered while yet green; when dried in the sun it becomes black. It is less expensive than the Orient spices, is agreeably aromatic, and is considered the most mild and harmless of the common spices; hence it is much used in cookery and in certain soups to enhance the flavor. The best allspice comes from Jamaica. The essential oil of allspice is of a deep reddish brown color and is extremely pungent, and a few drops are sufficient to give a flavor to gravy, soups, and the like.

Bay Leaves. The leaves of a large evergreen shrub which sometimes reaches the height of sixty feet. They contain an essential oil, aromatic, tonic, digestive, and stomachic. Bay leaves are extensively used in cookery.

Cayenne Pepper. See Pepper.

Chervil. Belongs to the parsley family and has an aromatic flavor that is much liked. Its uses are similar to those of parsley, which see.

Chili Pepper. Small elongated pods of a plant grown in California, Japan, and Mexico. The scarlet chili pods are seen in northern markets during the fall pickling season, but chili powder, made from this pepper or the green one, is packed in glass and sold the year round.

Greatly used in tamales, chili con carne, pickling, and southern cuisine generally. See also Pepper, further on.

Chives. A member of the lily family, this perennial is allied to the leek and the onion. Chives contain a large amount of mustard oil which gives them their peculiar and delicate taste. Widely used in soups, fish, meats, poultry, vegetables, and salads. It is claimed that they stimulate the appetite and help secrete gastric juice by stimulating the digestive organs. The French call this herb "the beneficial *ciboulette* (chive) which cleans the blood." Chives are also good in cottage and cream cheese, and added to scrambled eggs, they make that familiar breakfast specialty a distinctive dish. Excellent in sandwiches too.

Cinnamon. Also called cassia, cinnamon is the thin aromatic bark of the cinnamon tree grown in India, China, Palestine, and Italy. When peeled off and cleaned, it is known as stick cinnamon. In earliest colonial days, cinnamon and sugar were mixed, put in a special big shaker called an "oomah," and used on waffles, pancakes, coffeecake, and hot buttered toast. Fine in beverages, desserts, soups, fish, meat, pies, pastries, and breads.

Cloves. Cloves come from the Molucca Islands, generally known as the Spice Islands. They are also imported from the East and West Indies. The whole clove is the nail-shaped flower bud of the clove tree. Sold whole and in powder form, cloves are used to flavor soups, eggs, fish, meats, stuffings, sauces and gravies, pickles, chutneys, and so on. French housewives have an ingenious way of eliminating cooking odors. They sprinkle a bit of clove on the stove, or place a little burning clove on a special copper container and carry it from room to room. Oil of cloves is used in medicines, perfumes, and cordials.

Fennel. Of the parsley family, the leaves and tender hollow stems of fennel are used in salads and boiled with fish; they may also camouflage medicines. The stalks are used raw, like celery stalks, when well iced. They add flavor to sauces. The seeds of brownish tone, about a quarter-inch long and concave, are used in soups and breads, with fruits, in pastries, liqueurs, and perfumery.

Filé. A Creole seasoning made from powdered sassafras, filé is the soul of New Orleans gumbos. This powder was originated by the Choctaw Indians in Louisiana and is still prepared by members of the tribe.

Garlic, Onions, and Leeks. Vegetables and condiments at the same time. (See No. 17.) A little about garlic! When you think of garlic, think of the lily of which it is the relative. One of the oldest recorded seasonings, garlic may be eaten raw. For centuries, garlic has been employed by superstitious people to ward off evil spirits, especially the legendary vampires. According to the old tales, vampires were bloodsucking nocturnal reincarnations of the dead that rose from their graves at night, hunted the living, and sucked their blood like the South American vampire bats of real life.

Garlic is widely used in French cuisine, in soups, stews, roasts, poultry, steaks, bread, stuffing, salad dressings, salads, pickles, chutneys, and so on. Until the middle of the eighteenth century, many Siberian villagers paid taxes in garlic: fifteen bulbs for a man, ten for a woman, five for a child.

Mace. The fibrous inner covering of the nutmeg which, when dried in the sun, is used as a spice. When fresh, it is a bright red, but on drying it fades to a brown color. It is very aromatic and widely used in cookery. In olden times, nutmegs were said to contain much medicinal value, but today we use them just for what they seem best fitted, for use in tiny amounts, grated, on custards, puddings, junkets, pies, soups, and gravies. Mace is used in powdered form to give flavor to certain foods.

Marjoram. A perennial plant found all over the United States. Several species are used as a potherb, especially in Canada. The shoots and stems of the sweet or knotted marjoram are gathered and dried and used extensively for flavoring purposes in cookery in soups, sauces, meat loaves, stuffings, mushrooms, and cheese dishes. Marjoram is said to be a stimulant and tonic.

Nutmeg. A thousand years ago, Europeans wandering into the Far East were given food that gave out a rare unusual flavor. And in time they were shown the bewitching little nut which was ground for this use. Travelers brought a few of these nuts back to Europe. Kings and other wealthy people prized them highly. But nobody knew just where the nut was grown. Finally in the early part of the sixteenth century, Europeans found the Molucca Islands, and then the mystery was solved. There they found nutmeg trees which attained a height of about thirty feet. The small fruit is pear-shaped, containing a single seed (nutmeg), which is invested first with a crimson fibrous network (mace) and externally by a thick fleshy coat. The tree begins to bear fruit when eight years old, attains its maximum at twenty-five, and continues profitable for another thirty-five years or so. Nutmeg is extensively used in cookery, almost from soup to nuts, especially in desserts and also in beverages.

Parsley. Parsley is a vegetable universally used as a condiment (see No. 17). It is antiscorbutic and serves to stimulate the digestive secretions and give a fillip to the appetite. When washed in hot water, its flavor is greatly improved, and its chopping made easier. It is one of the best sources of vitamin A, an ounce supplying 30,000 units of that vitamin when cooked with other foods. When fresh and raw, parsley is a large source of vitamin C and is high in iron, calcium, phosphorus, manganese, and copper—all essential food minerals. It will keep fresh for a week if placed in a covered glass jar in the refrigerator, after being thoroughly washed and excess water shaken off.

Paprika. Also called Hungarian pepper, paprika is of general use in cookery all over southwest Europe and on a large scale in America. The dominant and piquant flavor in most of the characteristic Hungarian viands is that of paprika. Paprika is the mildest of the pepper compounds. It is a member of the Capsicum family, and is sweeter than any other species. It is made from the sweet red Turkish peppers which are used in the fresh green state all through the Balkans and the Mediterranean countries. Both sweet and sour cream have a peculiar affinity for paprika. Genuine paprika costs as much as three times the price of the ordinary common paprika.

Pepper. The berry of the Piper negrum, a plant which grows in the West Indies, Sumatra, and other Eastern countries. The whole berry is dried and ground for use. White pepper is made from the same berry by previously soaking off the outer husk in water. About fifteen million pounds of black pepper are consumed annually in the United States. Pepper is often adulterated, and to avoid deception, it may be purchased in corns (peppercorns) and freshly ground at the table.

Cayenne pepper is not a true pepper, but is made from the crushed pod of various species of capsicum. It grows in the tropics, especially along the eastern coast of Africa and in Zanzibar. A variety is employed medicinally and recognized by the Pharmacopoeia.

Chili is the common name given to this pepper in England, and chili sauce is an essence prepared from it. It is the strongest variety of capsicum. Capsicum, called also cayenne pepper or red pepper, like mustard, *is a strong irritant to the skin and the mucous membranes,* and should not be used in food intended for children.

Overdoses of cayenne pepper excite violent local inflammation and gastroenteritis. It stimulates a flagging appetite and produces a feeling of warmth in the stomach. When not abused, it forms an agreeable condiment for many adult persons.

Red pepper, like black, is often adulterated. When pure, it may be partially but not entirely suspended in water. Red lead has occasionally been used as an adulterant.

Piperine, an alkaloid of pepper, stimulates perspiration, thus having a cooling effect on the body if a sufficient amount is eaten. For this reason, pepper is widely used in seasoning food in hot countries. Both black and white peppers are grown in the East Indies, southern India, French Indo-China, and Siam.

Pique Seasoning. A meat-free liquid compound made of vegetable protein derivatives, water, salt, yeast, vegetable extract, spices, and vegetable fat. Widely used in cooking as a flavor amplifier (it is a strong seasoning), its sole purpose is to emphasize the natural richness of the foods you cook. Pique Seasoning is concentrated and should be used sparingly in gravies, sauces, soups, meats, stews, goulashes, hashes, poultry, vegetables, fish and meat loaves, hamburgers, stuffings, game, or cooked salad dressings. It is valuable for replacing the meat or vegetable stocks frequently demanded in good cuisine.

With absolutely no effort on the part of the cook, Pique Seasoning unobtrusively brings out hidden flavors in even the simplest dishes. To emphasize the robust flavors of mutton, beef, or venison, a sauce containing this seasoning is almost traditional, as many chefs and cooks look on Pique as the father of liquid condiments. It has aroma, body, character, flavor, and tang.

For instant broth, bouillon, or consommé, hot or cold, stir 1 teaspoon of Pique Seasoning into each cup of boiling or cold water. For gravies, 1 teaspoon of Pique Seasoning, added to the pan after gravy has boiled 2 or 3 minutes, gives zest and enhances the natural flavor. For instant gravy, use 1 teaspoon of Pique Seasoning with 1 cup of vegetable water or stock to replace meat stock or milk in a gravy recipe.

Rosemary. The leaves of this evergreen mint, noted for its stimulating refreshing fragrance, are used to season chicken, lamb, pork, soups, sauces, and fish stuffings, or may be scattered over salads. There is an old legend about rosemary. When Mary hung the infant Jesus' clothes on a rosemary bush, it flowered at once.

It is said that rosemary never grows higher than Christ stood and that it is only supposed to live for thirty-three years. It has always been symbolical of good friendship and remembrance.

Saffron. Favorite flavoring and coloring for food in early England, saffron was so valuable and expensive that the nobles who grew it kept the special yard under lock and key. It is collected from the stigma of a variety of purple crocus which grows profusely in northern and southern Europe. That does not mean, however, that it is easily obtained, for it requires the stigmas of about 75,000 flowers to produce just one pound of saffron. It is a perennial herb. The grasslike narrow leaves are delicately fringed along the edges and keel. Saffron has a strong aromatic odor and a bitter flavor. It is seldom used in soup making, only where specifically stated. The French, the Italians, and the Spanish use it as a flavoring in curries, sauces, and rice.

The ancient Egyptians called saffron "The Blood of Thoth" and used it in religious ceremonies. They considered it a plant dedicated to the sun. Ladies of ancient Greece used it as a hair dye, the Babylonians as a perfume and cosmetic.

Sage. Seers ages ago believed that, if a household prospered, the sage, with its swartly painted leaves, about it grew strong. It is a mint perennial. Its most common uses are in stuffing, cheese, certain gravies and sauces, soups and meats, including game birds and venison, which, however, prefer the sagebrush, a shrubby plant of the aster family, abundant on the elevated plains of the western United States.

Salt. Common salt, formerly regarded as an elementary substance, is sodium chloride. Salt is important in nutrition. Trade between the Aegean and southern Russia was largely dependent on salt, and salt was considered so vital that one of the oldest roads in Italy was called Via Salaria. Over this road the important commodity was carried from Ostia into the Sabine country.

Cakes of salt have been used for money in Abyssinia and Tibet. Marco Polo mentions its importance in his report on the financial system of the Mongolian emperors. As one might expect, much salt is obtained from the Great Salt Lake in Utah; the ocean water off California also yields great quantities of the commodity by evaporation. A daily portion of salt given as pay to Roman soldiers was often computed for money which was called "salarium." Hence the modern word "salary."

To eat salt with an Arab indicates to him the same responsibility of hospitality that we feel toward anyone who breaks bread with us. It is a tradition that the Arabs feel so strongly about salt that a robber who chances to fall over the family salt block as he enters the house will leave that house untouched. Salt was war material to the ancient Mayans. Quilted cotton jackets filled with salt were worn as body armor. It was as a result of looking for salt that one of Vermont's main industries (granite) was established. Montpelier citizens drilling for salt in 1827 gave it up as a bad job after striking layer on layer of granite; later they decided to mine the granite!

"The Condiment of Condiments," thus Plutarch described salt. The Greeks at one time consecrated salt to the gods. In cookery, there is hardly anything that is not improved by a touch of salt, which, however, should be used discreetly. A good cook will test a dish for seasoning and not depend entirely on measurements.

While it is possible to live without salt, if a large amount of meat is eaten, most of us would find it difficult to take enough food to satisfy us if we had to do without salt entirely. And seldom would we enjoy our meals in its absence. Of course, it is true that many of us use so much salt that we ruin our palate for other flavors. We all know men —and women—who shake the salt shaker over food before they taste it. *This practice is an insult to the cook.* Taste first, and salt afterward, if necessary, or if you think it is.

Tarragon. Tarragon, the very badge of the gourmet, is never in the seedman's catalogues, yet it flavors our bottled capers, and the green herb lends magical charm to salads, French dressing, omelets, aspics, and mousses, to pickles, to vinegars, to mustard, to tartar sauce, to cocktail sauces, to ravigote, to fish chowders, to compounded butter for fish and shellfish dishes and chicken dishes, and is the very soul of sauce Béarnaise. Tarragon herb is a European perennial plant allied to wormwood, cultivated in this country for its aromatic leaves.

Thyme. The Romans administered thyme as a certain remedy for melancholy spirits. A fairy tale of the Irish is that mounds of thyme are much liked by the fairies who choose aromatic flower beds for their hours of dancing. Thyme is one of the major herbs in flavor for stuffings, gravies, sauces, soups, meats, poultry, game meat, fish loaves, and "burgers." Thyme is a woody-based perennial with small gray leaves, a natural flavoring for rabbit or other wild game. Used also in pickles, chipped beef, in onion soup and scalloped onions. It is one of the chief ingredients of the bouquet garni used in soups, which see in No. 18.

Yerba Buena. A wild mint of great strength, which must be used with care. Add a miserly pinch to split pea soup, to butter for basting the boiled potato, to squash purée, to fruit salad, or to "make" an afternoon tea.

Chapter Two

HOT CONSOMMES

BOUILLONS AND BROTHS

Louis XIV of France is responsible for the invention of consommé. This popular concoction had its beginning when Louis XIV ordered his chef to create a perfectly clear soup in which he might see his royal countenance. The result was consommé, accomplished with the white of an egg.

CHEMISTRY RESEARCH RENDERED GREAT SERVICE TO THE science of food in the discovery of the exact nature of osmazome. Osmazome is that eminently sapid part of meat which is soluble in cold water and is distinguished from the extractive part because the latter only renders its juice when subjected to the boiling process. It is osmazome which contributes stamina to good soups. When it has passed into a state resembling caramel it forms the browning of meat, as well as the crisp brown of roast meat; finally, from it the savor of venison and other game arises.

Osmazome is derived, above all, from full-grown animals with dark reddish flesh, such as are called meaty; it is found only in very small quantity or is absent in lamb, suckling pigs, wild fowl, or even in the white meat of the largest poultry—turkey, for instance—for which reason lovers of delicate fare have always preferred the thick part of the thigh: their instinct of taste anticipated the discovery of science.

It is to prevent any waste of this precious substance, which may be compared to the "bouquet" of wine, that all cooks, all good cooks, recognize that in order to produce good soup the pot must merely simmer or "smile." The expression originated in France, and no other word is so adequately significant.

Osmazome, scientifically defined after having been so long instinctively appreciated by our forefathers, may be compared to alcohol, which intoxicated many generations before research and experimentation demonstrated its identity and extraction.

In addition to osmazome, we have in meat what is termed "extractive" matter, which as before stated must be subjected to boiling water. This latter product, combined with osmazome, forms the juices of meat.

The tissue of meat is composed of fibers and what is apparent after cooking. This fibrous tissue is resistant to the boiling process, and although it sheds a part of its covering, does not disintegrate wholly but maintains its substance.

Bones, which are essential to the production of good soups, consist principally of gelatin (also found in the soft and cartilaginous parts), its distinctive quality being that it coagulates at the ordinary temperature of the atmosphere. Phosphate of lime also is present in bones.

Albumen is found in the flesh as well as in the blood. It coagulates at a lower temperature than 104°F., and forms the scum on soups. The blood is composed of albuminous serum, of fibrin, of a little gelatin, and a little osmazome. It coagulates in hot water and is transformed into a very nourishing article of food, that is, black pudding, or bloodwursts.

Man shares in common with the animals all these vital principles. It is therefore not surprising that an animal diet is eminently restorative and strengthening to the human organism, because the particles whereof the food is composed, being similar to man's, may easily become revitalized in the human organism when submitted to the activity of the digestive tract.

Thus to make good soups we need all the ingredients above mentioned.

Basis of All Meat Soups. Consommé, or stock, forms the basis of all meat soups, and also of all the principal sauces. It is therefore essential to the success of these culinary operations to know the most complete and economical method of extracting from a certain quantity of meat the best possible stock or broth or consommé. Fresh raw beef makes the best stock, with the addition of cracked bones, as the glutinous matter contained in them renders it important that they should be boiled with the meat, which adds to the strength and thickness as well as richness of the soup. Two ounces of bones contain as much gelatin as one pound of meat; but this is so encased in the earthy substance that boiling water can dissolve only the surface of whole bones; by breaking the bones, they can be dissolved still further. When there is an abundance of gelatin, it causes the stock, when cold, to become a jelly. The flesh of old animals contains more flavor than the flesh of the young.

The shinbone is generally used, but the neck or "sticking piece," as the butchers call it, contains more of the substance that you want to extract, makes a stronger and more nutritious soup than any other part of the animal.

Meats for soup should *always* be put on to cook in *cold water*, in a covered kettle, and allowed to simmer—to "smile"—slowly for several hours, in order that the essence and juices of the meat may be drawn out thoroughly, and should be carefully skimmed of any scum arising on the surface to prevent the soup from becoming turbid. Never allow it to boil fast at any time, and if more water is needed, use only boiling water from the kettle; cold or lukewarm water spoils the flavor. When the liquid is clear and free from scum, then add the indicated vegetables.

For a real good stock, allow a quart of cold water to a pound of meat and bone, and a teaspoon of salt. When done, strain through a sieve; if for clear stock, strain again through a flannel cloth. When cold, pour into quart preserving jars and place in the refrigerator. *Do not remove* the layer of fat until ready to use the stock. The hardened fat, if unloosened, will make a perfect seal, and the stock will keep in a good refrigerator for almost a whole week. To remove the fat, loosen the edges with a sharp-pointed knife. Small pieces of fat, which may adhere to the top of the stock may be removed with a piece of paper towel or cloth. If the meat, bones, vegetables, and water have been simmered long enough, the broth will be clear, rich, and full-bodied, and have a jellylike consistency when cold. If real bouillon or consommé is desired, the stock should be clarified. The recipes for consommés serve 6 persons unless otherwise indicated.

HOW TO CLARIFY STOCK [21]

When the stock is cold, remove the fat which has hardened on top, and put the quantity to be clarified into a saucepan. For one quart of stock, add one raw egg white and the egg shell cracked in small pieces. Place over a gentle flame and stir constantly until the boiling point is reached. Boil steadily for 2 long minutes, stirring constantly. Lower the flame and let simmer very gently; let "smile" for 20 minutes. *Do not stir* any more. Remove the scum, strain through a double thickness of cloth, and reheat without boiling.

Beef, veal, lamb, mutton, or poultry, or combinations of these may be used and are prepared in the same way.

DOUBLE-STRENGTH CONSOMME [22]

Proceed as indicated for No. 21, adding with the egg white and crushed eggshell, ⅓ pound of freshly chopped lean beef, preferably from the leg.

TO COLOR CONSOMME [23]

Pounded spinach leaves give a fine *green* color to soup. Parsley or the green leaves of celery put in soup will serve instead of spinach. Pound a large handful of spinach in a mortar with a pestle, then tie it in a strong cloth, and wring out all the juice. Put this in the soup you wish to color green, 5 minutes before serving. Mock turtle, and sometimes veal and lamb soups, should be this color. Okra gives a very light green color to soup.

To color soup *red*, skin 6 red medium-sized tomatoes, squeeze out the seeds, and put the pulp into the soup with the other vegetables, or take the juice only, as directed for spinach, if for consommé. Or use a few drops of vegetable coloring, enough to make the desired hue.

Coloring is sometimes used in a brown soup, the chief ingredient of which is burned sugar, known as caramel by cooks. This may be prepared in advance and kept in a corked bottle, as it keeps a very long time and is useful not only for soups, but for gravy and stews.

To give your consommé a rich brown color, you may add for every quart of meat or vegetable stock or boiling water, 1 tablespoon of Pique Seasoning, mixing well.

INSTANT PIQUE CONSOMME   [24]
Hot or cold bouillon or broth

For a valuable time and labor saver, try Instant Pique Consommé to replace meat stock. To each quart of boiling or cold water, add 2 tablespoons of Pique Seasoning; for 1 pint, use 1 tablespoon of Pique; and for each cup of water, 1½ teaspoons of Pique. You may use more if a stronger consommé is desired. It also improves stews, pot roasts, and stuffings, and performs flavor miracles with vegetables, fresh or canned.

CHICKEN BROTH PARISIAN   [25]
For stock, consommé, or bouillon

Clean a 4-4½ pound fowl carefully. If you can get a few extra chicken feet and necks, so much the better; this will reinforce your broth. Place the fowl with feet and necks in a soup kettle; cover with 2 quarts of cold water. Bring to a boil as slowly as possible, skimming off all scum as it rises to the top. When quite clear and there is no more scum on the surface, add a bouquet garni composed of 2 well-washed small leeks, split in two, tied with 1 large bay leaf, 10 sprigs of fresh parsley, 2 sprigs of green celery leaves (the greener the better), 1 sprig of thyme, and 2 whole cloves, using kitchen thread. Add also 1 medium-sized carrot, scraped, then quartered; 1 large onion, peeled and quartered; 1 small white turnip, peeled and quartered; 7 or 8 peppercorns, gently bruised; 2 teaspoons of salt; and a small parsnip, about the size of an egg halved. Bring to a boil, lower the flame, and simmer gently for 3 hours, covered. Strain through fine wet cheesecloth, placed over a strainer, into a bowl. Cool and, when cold, remove carefully all fat from the surface. Reheat and serve with any desired garnish, or use in any recipes which require chicken broth or stock. Use the chicken for an entrée, for croquettes, cutlets, hash, and the like. Keep the broth in a glass jar, hermetically sealed and in the refrigerator until wanted. This broth will keep for two weeks in a good refrigerator.

CHICKEN AND CORN BROTH [26]

Bring to a boil 1½ quarts of Chicken Broth (No. 25 above). Add 1 can of strained corn and 1 teaspoon of finely chopped parsley. Boil once. Season with salt and pepper to taste, and serve.

CLAM BOUILLON [27]
Hot or cold

Wash and scrub with a brush ½ peck of clams, changing the water several times. Put in a kettle with 3 generous standard cups of water, cover tightly, and steam until the shells are well opened (10 minutes or thereabouts) over a hot fire. Strain through a very fine cloth; cool and clear. Serve hot or cold.

CLAM BROTH [28]
Hot or cold

Prepare and cook the same amount of clams as indicated for Clam Bouillon (No. 27). Strain through a fine cloth over another saucepan; reheat to the boiling point; season to taste with salt, pepper, and celery salt. Serve hot or cold with saltine crackers.

CLAM BROTH WITH POACHED EGG [29]

Prepare, cook, and strain as indicated for Clam Broth (No. 28). Reheat to the boiling point, and place a freshly poached egg in each cup just before serving.

CLAM CONSOMME [30]

Wash 2 quarts of clams in their shells. Put in a kettle with ¼ cup of cold water; cover and cook until the shells open. Strain the liquor through a very fine cloth and add 4 cups (1 quart) of clear Beef Consommé or Chicken Broth (Nos. 114 and 25).

CLAM CONSOMME WITH WHIPPED [31]
CREAM

Prepare, cook, and serve as indicated for Clam Consommé (No. 30), adding a tablespoon of whipped cream to each cup just before serving.

CLEAR MULLIGATAWNY [32]
India

Put 2 quarts of clear Beef Stock (No. 114), 2 medium-sized thinly sliced onions, 1 green apple, peeled, cored, and thinly sliced, and 1 tablespoon curry powder, previously diluted in a little cold stock or water, into an enamel soup kettle or saucepan. Cover, and allow to simmer very gently for 1¼ to 1½ hours, without disturbing. Strain through a fine sieve; let cool. When cold, add the eggshells and whites of 2 fresh eggs, the shells crushed, the egg whites stiffly beaten with 1 teaspoon of salt. Let the soup boil up again, then let it simmer for 15 minutes, and strain again through a very fine sieve into a clean enamel saucepan (any other metal may blacken the stock). Heat to the boiling point, stir in the strained juice of 1 medium-sized lemon; taste for seasoning, and serve in hot soup plates with a side dish of plain boiled rice, passed around, or put the rice into the soup, if desired.

Note. In some parts of India, tiny cubes of cooked beef or chicken go into the clear mulligatawny.

CLEAR TURTLE SOUP DROUANT [33]
Potage Tortue Clair Façon Drouant

Soak ½ pound of the best sun-dried turtle in cold water for 3 days, changing the water frequently. Put 5 quarts of rich clear Beef Stock (No. 114), the drained, rinsed piece of turtle, and 1 tablespoon of salt (less if stock is salty), in a large soup kettle. Bring to a boil, and boil steadily for 5 minutes, then skim off all scum as it rises to the surface. When quite clear, add 2 large onions, thinly sliced; 3 medium-sized carrots, chopped; 1 medium-sized white turnip, peeled and quartered; 2 stalks of celery, cut into inch lengths; 10 whole peppercorns, left whole and tied in a spice bag with 3 whole cloves and ½ teaspoon each of marjoram, mace, basil, and dried leaves of fennel. Let simmer gently for 7 to 8 hours—the longer the better—adding more boiling stock as it evaporates. Strain through a fine-meshed sieve, and put the piece of turtle aside. Then strain the stock through fine muslin into a large earthenware or porcelain container. When thoroughly cold, skim off the cake of fat from the surface, transfer the stock to a soup kettle, and let simmer very, very gently while preparing the ingredients to clarify it, as follows:

Put ½ pound of boned lean neck of beef together with ½ pound of lean raw veal through a food chopper 2 or 3 times, using the finest blade; add this to the turtle stock. Bring to a boil, beating with a wire whisk the while, and as soon as boiling, add the crushed shells and the stiffly beaten whites of 3 eggs. Let boil up steadily two or three times. Lower the flame, and let simmer gently for 30 minutes, then strain through fine muslin into a soup kettle. Add the reserved turtle meat, cubed small, and 1 small can (optional) of turtle fat (commercial), ¾ cup of the best sherry wine you can get, 1 tablespoon of strained lemon juice, and simmer gently—but do not actually boil, lest the flavor of the wine be impaired—for 5 minutes, or just enough to heat well, over a low flame. Taste for seasoning, and serve at once in heated bouillon cups or soup plates with a side dish of lemon quarters neatly dressed on a bed of crisp green watercress.

CONSOMME   [34]
Clear

Follow the directions as indicated for Beef Consommé (No. 114), and clear it according to No. 21, How to Clarify Stock.

CONSOMME ALPHABET   [35]

To each quart of Beef Consommé (No. 114), add, when boiling, 1 tablespoon of alphabet paste. Boil for 10 to 15 minutes. Serve after correcting seasoning.

CONSOMME ANDALOUSE   [36]

This consommé is known in France and in the United States as Consommé Madrilene, the difference being as follows. In the French recipe, it is made with Chicken Stock (No. 25), strongly flavored with celery and tomato juice. It is quite clear and when served hot is garnished with small tomato cubes, but when served cold it is ungarnished. In Spain, however, ordinary Beef Consommé (No. 114) is used. The tomato purée thickens it slightly, and it is garnished with 3 or 4 tablespoons of cooked vermicelli.

Bring 1½ quarts of Beef Consommé (No. 114) to a boil; stir in 3 or 4 tablespoons of tomato purée; and 5 minutes before serving, add the vermicelli.

CONSOMME ARGENTEUIL   [37]
Serves 6

Bring to a boil 1½ quarts of Beef Consommé (No. 114). When ready to serve, add ½ cup of asparagus tips, cooked or canned, and taste for seasoning. Serve in heated bouillon cups.

CONSOMME A L'AURORE   [38]
Serves 6 to 8

Put into a saucepan 2 quarts of rich Beef Consommé (No. 114). Bring to a boil, and when at a full rolling boil, let drop in, rainlike, ¼ cup of minute tapioca, being careful that the consommé does not stop boiling. Let boil for about 15 minutes; stir in 2 tablespoons of tomato paste; taste for seasoning, and serve in heated bouillon cups.

CONSOMME WITH BEEF DUMPLINGS   [39]

To each serving of Beef Consommé (No. 114), add 2 Beef Dumplings (No. 709).

CONSOMME BELLEVUE   [40]
Serves 6

Combine 3 cups of rich Chicken Consommé (No. 25) and 3 cups of clear Clam Broth (No. 28); serve in hot bouillon cups, each cup topped with a tuft of whipped cream forced through a pastry bag with a small rose tube. No meat, no chicken, and no clam pieces are used as garnish—that is, for authentic Consommé Bellevue.

CONSOMME WITH BREAD DUMPLINGS   [41]

To each serving of Beef Consommé (No. 114), add 2 Bread Dumplings (No. 712).

CONSOMME CENDRILLON   [42]
Serves 6 to 8

This is a very rich and expensive consommé. Bring 2 quarts of clear Chicken Consommé (No. 25) to a boil. Remove from the fire, and stir in 1 black truffle, previously cooked in Marsala wine, then cut into fine julienne strips (matchlike), and ½ cup of cooked rice. Serve in heated bouillon cups.

CONSOMME AUX CHEVEUX D'ANGE   [43]
Angel's Hair Consommé—Consommé with Vermicelli
Serves 6 generously

Bring to a rolling boil 1¾ quarts of rich **Beef Consommé** (No. 114). When ready to serve, drop in ¼ cup of the smallest vermicelli you can get. Cook 5 minutes, and serve in heated bouillon cups.

CONSOMME WITH CUSTARD CUBES [44]

To each serving of Beef Consommé (Nó. 114), add 3 or 4 custard cubes, any kind desired found in Chapter Eleven, Custard Garnishes.

CONSOMME DIABLOTINS [45]

Make a good rich Chicken Consommé (No. 25), and thicken slightly with minute tapioca, using 1 scant tablespoon for each quart of consommé. When ready to serve, top each cup with 1 round of Diablotins Gourmet (No. 782).

CONSOMME WITH DICED CHICKEN [46]

To each serving of Beef Consommé or Chicken Consommé (Nos. 114 and 25), add 4 or 5 small dices of cooked chicken.

CONSOMME EGG DROP [47]

To a quart of Beef Consommé (No. 114), boiling violently, strain 2 fresh eggs broken over a sieve as indicated for Egg Flakes (No. 784).

CONSOMME EGG DUMPLINGS [48]

To each serving of Beef Consommé (No. 114), add 2 or 3 Egg Dumplings (No. 728).

CONSOMME IVAN [49]
Serves 6

Heat to the boiling point 1½ quarts of Chicken Consommé (No. 25). Stir in ¼ cup of beet juice (fresh or canned), and when ready to serve, stir in ½ cup of boiled rice.

CONSOMME WITH JULIENNE OF CARROT [50]

To each serving of Beef Consommé (No. 114), add 1 tablespoon of cooked, shredded carrot.

CONSOMME WITH LIVER DUMPLINGS [51]

To each serving of Beef Consommé (No. 114), add 2 or 3 small Liver Dumplings (No. 742).

CONSOMME LORETTE [52]
Serves 6

Bring to a boil 1½ quarts of Chicken Consommé (No. 25), and when ready to serve, stir in 1 black truffle, peeled and cut julienne fashion, ¼ cup of asparagus tips (fresh or canned), and a teaspoon of finely chopped chervil or parsley.

CONSOMME LUCETTE [53]
Serves 6 to 8

Bring to a rapid boil 2 quarts of Beef Consommé (No. 114), then gradually, in rainlike fashion, drop in ⅓ cup of alimentary alphabet paste, and cook for 5 or 6 minutes, or until the alphabet paste is tender. When ready to serve, stir in 1 tablespoon of small pieces of raw tomato pulp. Serve in soup plates, with a poached egg in each.

CONSOMME WITH MACARONI DUMPLINGS [54]

To each serving of Beef Consommé (No. 114), add 2 or 3 small Italian Dumplings (No. 740).

CONSOMME MADRILENE [55]

Follow directions for Jellied Consommé Madrilene (No. 128), but omit the gelatin.

CONSOMME WITH MARROW DUMPLINGS [56]

To each serving of Beef Consommé (No. 114), add 2 or 3 small Marrow Dumplings (No. 743).

CONSOMME MIDINETTE [57]
Working Girl Consommé—serves 6

Heat 1½ quarts of Chicken Consommé (No. 25) to the boiling point. Cook in a small saucepan 6 poached eggs, and set them aside. To the consommé brought to a rapid boil, add gradually, in rainlike fashion, ¼ cup of minute tapioca, and cook until tender. Pour the consommé into a heated soup tureen, and float the 6 poached eggs on top. To save time, and for something different, try using Instant Pique Consommé (No. 24).

CONSOMME MILLEFANTI [58]
Serves 4 generously

To 1 quart of hot consommé, chicken preferably (No. 25), add the following mixture. Beat 4 eggs, as for an omelet, adding gradually and slowly 2 generous tablespoons of grated cheese (American, Parmesan, Swiss cheese, or any other kind of your favorite hard cheese), and 1 generous tablespoon of chopped parsley. Pour this slowly and gradually into the consommé, stirring rapidly all the while. Finish with a dash of cinnamon and 2 tablespoons of port wine to taste. Serve immediately.

CONSOMME MILLE-FEUILLES [59]
Leafy Consommé—serves 6 generously

Combine, mixing thoroughly, ⅓ cup of soft bread crumbs and 3 tablespoons of grated Gruyère or Swiss cheese. Add 2 fresh eggs, a dash of nutmeg, salt, and a few grains of cayenne, and beat briskly for at least 2 minutes. Have ready, at a rolling boil, 1¾ quarts of clear Beef Consommé (No. 114). Drop the preparation by means of a small funnel into the boiling consommé, and allow it to simmer gently for 5 minutes. By this time, the broth will become clear again. Serve in heated bouillon cups with toasted, buttered finger strips.

CONSOMME MONTE CARLO [60]

Garnish each serving of hot rich Beef Consommé (No. 114) with small Profiterolles (No. 799), filled with a mixture of equal parts of chicken purée and onions. Use four profiterolles for each serving, to represent the four aces of a deck of playing cards. A chiffonade of parboiled, shredded green pepper also may be added, as well as a pinch of finely minced chervil.

CONSOMME MURAT [61]
Serves 6

Bring to a boil 1½ quarts of Beef Consommé (No. 114), and let simmer. When ready to serve, pour the consommé into a heated soup tureen, and add 12 freshly made or canned raviolis (2 to a serving). Serve with a side dish of grated Parmesan cheese.

CONSOMME NANA   [62]
Serves 6 to 8

This consommé is very substantial and nourishing. Arrange in the
bottom of a heated soup tureen a layer of tiny toasted rounds of long
French bread called *flûte*, or ordinary bread cut with the smallest
cooky cutter and toasted. Cover these rounds with a layer of grated
Gruyère cheese. Add another layer of toasted bread rounds, and spread
with grated Parmesan cheese. Cover these with more small toasted
rounds, and top them with 6 poached eggs (or 8, if needed), neatly
trimmed, with just a narrow border of white. When ready to serve,
pour over very gently and carefully 2 quarts of boiling rich Chicken
Consommé (No. 25).

Note. If desired, serve the poached eggs separately, thus preventing
breaking them when ladling the consommé.

CONSOMME WITH NOODLES   [63]

Whenever Giuseppi Verdi, the famous composer, needed inspiration, he found it in a large bowl of noodle soup. He also rewarded
himself with a bowlful when he completed a composition.

To each serving of Beef Consommé (No. 114), add a scant tablespoon of cooked noodles.

CONSOMME OLGA   [64]
Serves 6 generously

Bring to the boiling point 1½ quarts of rich Beef Consommé (No.
114), but do not let it actually boil. When ready to serve, stir in 1
scant cup of port wine and 2 tablespoons each of celery root, cut
julienne fashion, and caviar previously rinsed in hot stock to remove
the brine. Serve in heated bouillon cups.

CONSOMME PAULETTE   [65]
Serves 6

Bring to a boil 1½ quarts of Chicken Consommé (No. 25), and
serve in heated bouillon cups, each cup garnished with 2 or 3 tiny
cubes of Chicken Custard Garnish (No. 686), and with 4 or 5
pimiento stars, cut from drained canned pimientos with a tiny French
star cutter. Serve in heated bouillon cups with Cheese Pastry Sticks
(No. 776).

CONSOMME WITH RICE   [66]

To each serving of Beef Consommé (No. 114), add 1 tablespoon of plain cooked rice. For a different treat, try the rice in Instant Pique Consommé (No. 24).

CONSOMME SAINT QUENTIN   [67]
Serves 6

Heat 1½ quarts of Beef Consommé (No. 114) to the boiling point, and stir in ¼ cup of sherry wine. Serve in heated cups garnished with 2 Egg Balls (No. 672).

CONSOMME WITH SPONGE DUMPLINGS   [68]

To each serving of Beef Consommé (No. 114), add 2 or 3 Sponge Dumplings (No. 760).

CONSOMME WITH TAPIOCA   [69]
Also called Fin de Siècle—serves 6

To 1½ quarts of violently boiling Beef Consommé (No. 114), drop rainlike 3 tablespoons of minute tapioca. Or use Instant Pique Consommé (No. 24).

CONSOMME TRANSPARENT   [70]
Louis XIV's favorite soup—serves 6

This soup takes a long time to prepare, but it is a revelation when finished. Quite "the thing" for a dinner party. It is taken from *Flowers of the French Cuisine*.

Cut the meat from 4 pounds of knuckle of veal into small pieces; break the bones, and put both into a large soup kettle. Pour over 3 quarts of cold water. Add 2 ounces of blanched almonds, finely chopped or ground, a blade of mace, and salt and pepper to taste. Very slowly bring this to a boil, and let boil violently for 5 minutes. Then lower the heat, and let simmer; *let smile very gently* until reduced to half the original quantity, then strain through a fine muslin cloth. Cool. When quite cold, remove every particle of fat. Return the clear stock to the fire. Bring it to a boil, let fall in ½ cup of crushed vermicelli, lower the heat at once, and simmer gently for 10 to 15 minutes. Then season with salt and white pepper, and stir in 3 table-spoons of good sherry wine. Serve at once in heated soup plates.

CONSOMME WITH VEGETABLE VALENTINES [71]
Serves 6

To 1½ quarts of hot consommé, either Beef, Chicken, or Scotch Mutton Broth (Nos. 114, 25, or 650), add 1 cup of mixed vegetables, cut into small hearts with a tiny French heart-shaped cutter before they are cooked. Allow to boil for 15 minutes over a low fire, or cook separately in salted boiling water. Drain, and add to the consommé just before serving.

Note. You may add, if desired, a few drops of red vegetable coloring to the consommé just before serving for St. Valentine's Day.

CONSOMME VENITIEN [72]
Italian—serves 6

Gradually beat into 1½ quarts of rapidly boiling clear Beef Consommé (No. 114) 4 well-beaten fresh egg yolks, beaten with 1 scant tablespoon of strained lemon juice. Taste for seasoning, and serve at once in heated bouillon cups, each cup floated with a thin slice of toasted roll topped with grated Parmesan cheese.

CONSOMME WITH VERMICELLI [73]

To each serving of Beef Consommé (No. 114), add 1 tablespoon of cooked vermicelli.

MUSHROOM CONSOMME AU SHERRY [74]
Serves 6

Melt 4 tablespoons of sweet butter in a saucepan. Add ½ cup of thinly sliced onions, the rings separated, and cook until they are a light golden brown, stirring frequently, over a very gentle flame. Then add ½ pound of fresh mushrooms, peeled, and thinly sliced, and 1½ tablespoons of lemon juice. Cook until mushrooms are tender, or about 4 minutes, stirring almost constantly. Mushrooms should not be brown. Stir in 1½ quarts of rich double-strength hot Beef Bouillon (No. 114), made by boiling down 3 quarts of beef bouillon to half its original volume. Taste for seasoning, and heat, but do not allow to boil. Just before serving in heated bouillon cups, add 4 tablespoons of good sherry. Serve at once.

SCOTCH BROTH [75]

See Chapter Nine, Miscellaneous Soups (No. 648).

SCOTCH MUTTON BROTH [76]

See Chapter Nine, Miscellaneous Soups (No. 650).

COURT BOUILLON, RED WINE [77]
Short broth for fish

Court bouillon means short broth in French. Combine the following ingredients in a fish kettle: 2 quarts of cold water; ¾ cup of red wine; salt to taste; 2 small carrots, scraped and sliced; 2 small onions, peeled then sliced thin; 1 bouquet garni composed of 1 large bay leaf, 8 sprigs of fresh parsley, 1 sprig of thyme, and 2 whole cloves all tied together with white kitchen thread; and ½ teaspoon of peppercorns, slightly bruised. Bring to a boil, and let simmer gently for a few minutes. Again bring to a boil, add the fish, lower the heat, and simmer or "poach" gently until the fish is done. It is appropriate to cook almost any kind of trout, eel, pike, pickerel, or the like.

COURT BOUILLON, VINEGAR [78]

Proceed as indicated for Court Bouillon, Red Wine (No. 77), substituting vinegar for red wine.

COURT BOUILLON, WHITE WINE [79]

Proceed as indicated for Court Bouillon, Red Wine (No. 77), substituting dry white wine for red wine.

COURT BOUILLON, MILK OR CREAM [80]

Cover a large piece of fish, such as salmon or turbot, with salted cold water in a fish kettle, and add ⅔ cup of milk or cream for each quart of water used. Do not add any vegetables, but add 1 slice of lemon, peeled and seeded.

TOMATO BOUILLON WITH OYSTERS [81]
Serves 6 generously

Place in a soup kettle 1 large No. 2 can of tomatoes, 1½ quarts of Fish Stock (No. 8), 3 tablespoons of butter, 1½ tablespoons of finely chopped onion, a tiny bit of bay leaf, 3 crushed cloves, 1 scant teaspoon of celery seed, and 9 crushed peppercorns. Let boil continuously for 15 minutes. Strain through a very fine sieve, and clear. Just before serving, parboil for 2 minutes 6 large fresh oysters in their own liquor until plump and the gills (edges) curl. Place one in each cup with 1 teaspoon of freshly whipped cream. Serve with a side dish of saltine crackers.

Chapter Three

CHILLED AND JELLIED CONSOMMES AND SOUPS

An inspired soup puts family and guests in a receptive mood for the rest of the menu.

THE NAME "CONSOMME," OR CLEAR SOUP, IS GIVEN TO A concentrated bouillon, which to possess all the qualities must be clear and freshly made. Light soups, such as beef or chicken consommé, as appetizers stimulate the desire for food and also prepare the stomach to take care of the food that follows.

Who could dream of serving a man on a steam-cooked day a piping hot broth of chicken, beef, or vegetable? When the best of thermometers is soaring sky-high and dispositions are dangerously glowering, there is nothing so cheering to the inner gourmet as a cold or jellied *potage*, a bouillon, a consommé. Who, presented with a colorful gay and cooling cup, has not longed to eat soup, cup, and all? You can, if you serve jellied madrilene, chicken, beef, tomato, celery, lettuce soup, consommé, or bortsch in scooped-out oranges or tomatoes, and you'll find that any of these tastes even better than it looks. Jellied soups, cool and sparkling, make an ideal beginning to a hot-weather luncheon or dinner. Their delicate flavor gives an apathetic appetite a lift, and just the sight of them is refreshing. However, jellied cold consommés, bouillons, or soups must be served very cold, and they must be well seasoned. If they have these two qualities when they reach the table, they supply an attractive and invigorating appetizer which is exactly what is needed on warm days.

Essentially, a jellied soup is just a combination of gelatin with a standard rich beef or chicken bouillon, or a pure beef consommé without any gelatin.

The prejudice of some persons against gelatin is erroneous. Gelatin is a substance the potential energy of which is calculated to be even more than that of some fats and albuminates. Yet in the body it is very inferior in the production of strength. It is obtained from bones, ligaments, and other connective tissues.

In early days, homemakers made their own gelatin by boiling calves' feet for half a day, then straining the broth through a flannel cloth, not once but several times, and finally clearing it with the whites of a dozen or so eggs. Later, hartshorn shavings and isinglass made from sturgeons' bladders were used in combination. Still, straining and clearing was a prerequisite. Gelatin then was anything but cheap. At one time, the isinglass cost wholesale almost eighteen dollars a pound, almost as expensive as the famous caviar of Beluga.

The first attempt to prepare a commercial gelatin from bones was made by a French chef in 1681. Nothing came of the idea until after the French Revolution when half of France was starving. Then the government got busy, hoping to make gelatin improve the food of the poor. The French Academy of Medicine was asked to pass judgment on the product; they declared it a nourishing food. Thereupon all public institutions and hospitals served gelatin in soups and broths as well as desserts. But the taste was pretty terrible. People ate it because they had to. It was anything but a delectable dish—a very distant cousin of the appetizing jellies we serve today!

The granulated gelatin that we know is a modern invention, so new that most consumers have only a hazy idea as to how the gelatin is made. To watch a single batch progress from bone to packaged gelatin would take at least three months.

Start in the Argentine at a meat-packing plant where bones of beef and veal are collected and bagged. Why South American beef bones, everyone asks, when the United States is the largest consumer of meat in the world? There is a reason. Here the greatest percentage of meat carries its bone to the butcher shop. South America packs most of her meat, thus having a large bone surplus.

This bone and connective tissue goes to Belgium for special treatment before it comes to factories here. There the bone is boiled at 190°–200° F. for almost a day to remove cartilage, grease, and meat. The cleaned bones are then subjected to a series of hydrochloric acid baths to remove the phosphates—a two-week job. What is left the trade terms ossein, a brownish-looking spinylike stuff, which is shoved into 150-pound bags and shipped to gelatin factories all over the world.

The plain granulated beef-bone gelatin is used for soups and with fresh fruits, coffee, wine, and tomatoes.

Some of the elements in gelatin form pure glycine, one of the fourteen amino acids essential to life. In that constituent of gelatin must lie the remarkable energy power that the Long Island College experimenters found and demonstrated so startlingly a few years ago.

Out of glycine comes creatine, which in the chemist's tube appears as a white crystalline substance, somewhat like salt, and while science still has much to learn about it, the very name stands for a great deal. Creatine means creating substance. And right there probably lies the source of energy found in gelatin.

It is important to emphasize here that the gelatin under discussion is the pure, plain, unflavored granular gelatin, and not a dessert powder gelatin.

A final word of advice—don't get jellied soups stiff as dress shirts. They should be just sufficiently firm to melt readily in the mouth—and very, very cold. As for chilled soups, make the stock during the cool morning hours while doing the kitchen work. Cool, and keep in the refrigerator, and it will be ready to serve in a few hours, or it will remain there to wait for an emergency. The following recipes serve 6 to 8 persons unless otherwise indicated.

CHILLED BEET AND CUCUMBER SOUP   [83]
Ukrainian

Take 6 cups of cold highly seasoned Chicken Bouillon (No. 25). Add 1 large peeled, chopped cucumber; 2 freshly boiled medium-sized potatoes, sieved; 2 medium-sized peeled and freshly grated raw beets; 2 teaspoons of finely chopped parsley; 1½ teaspoons of grated raw onion; and 1½ tablespoons of freshly ground green celery leaves. Season with 2 teaspoons of drained, chopped, prepared horseradish, salt, and a few drops of Tabasco sauce or pepper sauce, and leave in the refrigerator until very cold. When ready to serve, stir well. Serve in chilled cups, each topped with unflavored, salted whipped cream, sprinkled with finely chopped chives.

CHILLED BORTSCH I   [84]
Polish—with flaked fish

Combine 2 cups of chilled heavy cream with 2 cups of chilled buttermilk. Add 1 finely chopped dill pickle; 1 medium-sized, peeled, seeded, and finely chopped chilled cucumber; 2 tablespoons of finely minced chives; 5 medium-sized raw beets, peeled then grated; 2 hard-cooked eggs, shelled and chopped. Season to taste with salt, paprika, and a few grains of cayenne pepper. Add a few drops of red vegetable coloring to accentuate the reddish hue to a deep pink shade. Lastly, stir in ½ pound of cooked, flaked fish filets, carefully boned and skinned. Serve in chilled cups dusted with finely chopped parsley.

CHILLED BORTSCH II   [85]
Polish country style—with veal

Poland has a national cookery, characteristically its own. It dates back hundreds of years over its turbulent and much varied career which characterizes the entire history of the Poles, who are among the most gifted and intelligent peoples of Europe, and whose culture is decidedly that of Western Europe. There is a tradition with certain of the older Poles that enough food must always be kept on hand for the unknown or unexpected guest. Quite often there was an extra plate and chair provided at each meal for the wayfarer who might be the Christ come in disguise.

Beat 1 quart of sour milk until bubbles show on the surface. Do likewise with 2 cups of sour cream and mix together. Then add 1 cup of sour beet juice (in some parts of the country in Poland, dill pickle juice is used instead of sour beet juice); 1 cup of finely chopped, cooked beet tops; a few sprigs of chopped dill; and 2 small cucumbers, peeled and salted and let stand for 30 minutes, then sliced and squeezed. Blend thoroughly. Chill for at least 4 hours, and when ready to serve, add 3 hard-cooked eggs, coarsely chopped, and 1½ cups of cooked lean veal, cubed small. Season to taste with salt and white pepper, and serve in individual chilled earthenware bowls.

CHILLED BORTSCH III   [86]
Also called Barscz, Polish farmer's manner—meatless

This soup used to be the favorite soup of Mme. Helena Paderewski. It is a meal in itself on a sultry day.

Chop 1 can of small red beets or the equivalent of freshly cooked ones very fine. Peel and quarter lengthwise, seed and chop 1 large cucumber. Add it to the chopped beets, placed in a shallow pan or earthenware dish, and add 1½ tablespoons of chopped green onion tops or chives. Pour over 1 quart of heavy sour cream, then put in about 1 tray of ice cubes, and let stand until the ice is melted and makes liquid the beet and cucumber mixture. Season to taste with salt, white pepper, and a dash of nutmeg. Serve in colorful individual earthenware bowls, thoroughly chilled, with a side dish of hot boiled potatoes.

CHILLED BUTTERMILK SHRIMP SOUP   [87]
Swedish

In a large mixing bowl, combine 1½ cups of cooked fresh shrimps, cleaned and coarsely chopped; 1 small cucumber, peeled, seeded, then finely chopped or grated; 1 tablespoon each of finely chopped parsley and chives; 2 teaspoons of prepared mustard; salt and a few grains of nutmeg; and 1 generous teaspoon of sugar. Toss well while pouring in 1½ quarts of chilled buttermilk. Chill for at least 3 hours, and serve in chilled bowls, each bowl sprinkled with paprika, with a side dish of brown bread and butter finger sandwiches.

CHILLED CONSOMME ANDALOUSE   [88]
Spanish

Place in a saucepan 2 quarts of Beef Consommé (No. 114). Add 5 medium-sized fresh, peeled, seeded, coarsely chopped tomatoes; 1 large green pepper, seeded and skinned, and white ribs removed; and 3 large oranges, unpeeled, washed, and coarsely chopped. Bring to the boiling point. Lower the flame, and let simmer gently for 1 long hour. Remove from the fire, season to taste with salt and a few grains of cayenne pepper. Strain through a fine cloth, and chill for at least 3 hours. Serve in chilled cups, each cup garnished with a thin slice of peeled, seeded orange.

CHILLED CONSOMME LISBON   [89]
Portuguese

To each quart of rich Beef Consommé (No. 114), add ¾ cup of tomato paste and ¼ cup of tomato juice. Cover and cook for 20 minutes without letting boil too fast. Strain through a fine cloth, pressing gently so as to extract all pulp possible. Cool, then set in the refrigerator to chill.

CHILLED CREAM OF CHICKEN SOUP   [90]
French

Pour into a large saucepan 2 cups of Chicken Consommé (No. 25), and bring to a boil. Remove from the fire, and stir in 4 fresh egg yolks, adding one at a time, beating briskly after each addition. Return to the fire, and cook over a gentle flame, stirring constantly from the bottom of the pan (this is very important, lest the mixture scorch if you stir on the surface only) till the mixture just begins to coat the spoon. Remove from the fire, and stir in ¾ cup of cold fresh pea soup purée. Rub this through a fine-meshed wire sieve into a mixing bowl, then stir in 2 cups (1 pint) of cold thin cream or undiluted, chilled evaporated milk. Now, and only now, season to taste with salt and white pepper, and when ready to serve in chilled bouillon cups, stir in 2 tablespoons of drained, gently squeezed, then chopped, canned red pimiento. Serve at once with each cup dusted with a tiny pinch of finely chopped parsley, or chervil if it is available.

CHILLED CREAM OF CURRY SOUP   [91]
Egyptian

Scald 1½ quarts of rich milk in the top of a double boiler with 1 large bay leaf, 1 whole clove, 3 thin slices of onion, and salt to taste. Stir in 2 teaspoons of curry powder, diluted in a little cold milk. Then strain through a fine cloth. Stir into the strained milk 4 fresh egg yolks, slightly beaten. Return to the fire, and cook for 2 or 3 minutes, or until the mixture is thickened. Strain again into cold cups, and chill the cups in the refrigerator for at least 3 hours. Serve, topping each cup with a teaspoon of toasted, cooled, grated coconut.

CHILLED CREAM OF MUSHROOM SOUP   [92]
French

Peel, wipe with a damp cloth, and chop, or put through a food chopper, ½ pound of fresh mushrooms, using stems and caps. Cook in 2 tablespoons of butter until tender, but not brown, stirring almost constantly. Gradually stir in 1½ quarts of good Chicken Bouillon (No. 25). Add 2 tablespoons of chopped green celery leaves, 1 teaspoon of onion juice, and 1 teaspoon of finely chopped parsley. Simmer gently for 25 to 30 minutes. Empty the contents of the saucepan into a fine sieve and rub through. Return to the fire, and bring to a boil. Then stir in ½ cup of fresh thick cream, mixed with 3 fresh egg yolks. Continue cooking for 2 minutes longer, over a medium flame, stirring constantly from the bottom of the pan. Season to taste. Cool, then chill for at least 3 hours in the refrigerator. Serve in chilled cups, each topped with a thin slice of seeded, peeled lemon, the slice topped with salted whipped cream.

CHILLED CREAM OF PEA SOUP   [93]
French

Combine 2 cups of Cream of Pea Soup (No. 410), or canned soup, and 1 quart of scalded milk in a saucepan. Season to taste with salt, pepper, and nutmeg, and bring to the boiling point. Remove from the fire and beat with a rotary beater. Taste for seasoning. Cool, then chill for at least 3 hours. Serve in chilled cups, each topped with a tablespoon of whipped sour cream, the cream dusted with paprika.

CHILLED CREAM OF TOMATO SOUP   [94]

Combine in a mixing bowl 1 quart of tomato juice (canned or fresh), 1 teaspoon of celery salt, 1 teaspoon of finely chopped parsley, a few grains of cayenne, and 1½ cups of thin cream. Beat with a rotary beater. Chill for at least 3 hours, and serve in chilled cups, each topped with salted whipped cream.

CHILLED CREAM SOUP VICHYSSOISE   [95]

Cream soup "Vish-ee-swahh" is a peasant soup that got into royal favor from Louis XIV up to the last king of France. The story goes that Louis XIV was so suspicious of his cooks after the revocation of the Edict of Nantes and persecution of the Huguenots that he refused to touch a morsel of food until an *officier de bouche*, or Esquire of Cuisine, an official taster, had tasted it first. The taster of Louis, "the Eldest Son of the Church" as he used to call himself, was an honored person with whom to reckon; he in turn had a taster, and this second taster also had one. Tasting became an exaggerated ceremony, so almost all the food the king ate arrived at long last cold or lukewarm. It was on a hot summer day that creamed leek soup was served to the king, and cold. The king refused it, saying that the soup was not cold enough! The *maître queux* of the royal household, not knowing what to do, chilled it through by crude methods. Crème Vichyssoise was born.

Put through a food chopper the white part of 4 well-washed leeks with 1 medium-sized onion. Melt 4 tablespoons of sweet butter in a saucepan, and add the leek-onion mixture. Cook 2 minutes, stirring constantly; then add 3 large or 5 medium-sized potatoes, peeled and thinly sliced. Moisten with 1 quart of rich Chicken Bouillon (No. 25). Add 1 large bay leaf and 1 whole clove; season to taste with salt and white pepper. Cook for 35 to 40 minutes, stirring occasionally to prevent scorching. Empty the whole contents into a fine sieve and rub through into a clean saucepan. Heat to the boiling point. Add 2 cups of scalded milk with 2 cups of thin cream or undiluted evaporated milk, and bring to a boil. Taste for seasoning, and again rub through a fine sieve. Cool, then chill. When ready to serve, stir in 1 cup of heavy chilled sweet cream, and chill for at least 3 hours. Serve in chilled cups, each cup dusted with finely chopped chives.

CHILLED CREAM OF WATERCRESS SOUP   [96]
When served hot, called *Potage Valois*

Wash carefully 2 bunches of fresh green watercress, and pick it up still more carefully. Blanch it in rapidly boiling water for 2 minutes. Drain well, then put it through a food chopper, using the finest blade. Now mix the ground cress with 2 tablespoons of sweet butter and 3 fresh egg yolks. Empty the contents into a fine sieve, and rub through with a wooden potato masher. In a saucepan, blend 1 tablespoon of butter and 1½ tablespoons of flour, over a gentle flame, but do not let brown. Moisten with 1½ quarts of hot Chicken Bouillon (No. 25), stirring constantly until the mixture just begins to boil. Lower the flame, and let simmer gently for 20 minutes, stirring frequently from the bottom of the pan. Then stir in the watercress mixture. Bring to a boil, stirring constantly. Remove from the fire, and beat with a wire whisk or a rotary beater. Heat well. Season to taste with salt, white pepper, and a dash of nutmeg, and let cool. Chill in the refrigerator for at least 3 hours. Serve in chilled cups, each cup topped with a few fresh leaves of watercress.

For hot cream of watercress soup, proceed as above, and when ready to serve, stir in ½ cup of scalded sweet cream, and serve with Croutons (No. 780).

CHILLED CUCUMBER AND DILL SOUP   [97]

Peel 3 medium-sized cucumbers of about the same size, and slice very thin. Put into a pan with 1 medium-sized onion, thinly sliced; 1 teaspoon of salt; a good dash of pepper; a pinch of cayenne, and one of nutmeg; 1 bouquet garni, composed of 1 large bay leaf, 4 sprigs of fresh parsley, and 1 small sprig of green celery leaves, all tied together with kitchen thread; 1 whole clove; and if liked, a thin slice of garlic. Cover with 1 generous cup of cold water. Cook slowly until very soft, or about 30 minutes, over low heat. Remove from the fire, and stir in ¼ cup of sifted flour mixed with 3 cups of rich Beef Stock (No. 114), or with boiling water blended with 1½ tablespoons of Pique Seasoning. Return to the fire, and cook, stirring constantly until the mixture comes to a boil. Lower the heat, and let simmer gently for 5 minutes. Empty the contents of the pan into a fine-meshed wire sieve, and rub through, adding while rubbing ¾ to 1 cup of heavy cream. Taste for seasoning, stir in 1 tablespoon of finely chopped dill, and cool. Chill thoroughly, and serve in chilled cups.

CHILLED CUCUMBER AND TOMATO SOUP [98]
Norwegian

Peel, seed, and coarsely chop 3 nice ripe fresh tomatoes. Place in a saucepan, and add 3 cups of cold Chicken Broth (No. 25). Bring to a boil, lower the flame, and let simmer gently for 25 minutes. Empty the entire contents of the pan into a sieve and rub through into a clean saucepan. Then add 2 more cups of hot chicken broth.

Season to taste with salt, pepper, a dash of mace, and one of nutmeg, and 1 teaspoon of granulated sugar. Bring to a boil, then add, bit by bit, 1 tablespoon of butter kneaded with 1 tablespoon of flour, and let simmer gently for 15 minutes, stirring occasionally. Remove from the fire, and stir in 1 cup of peeled, seeded, grated cucumber, 2 teaspoons of finely chopped dill, and 2 teaspoons of finely chopped parsley. Stir in ¾ cup of thick sour cream. Cool, then chill for at least 3 hours. Serve in chilled individual pottery cups or soup cups, each sprinkled with a little chopped chives.

CHILLED EGG AND LEMON SOUP   [99]

Heat to the boiling point 5 cups of rich clear Chicken Bouillon (No. 25), or canned. Beat 4 whole fresh eggs with 3 tablespoons of good sherry wine; then beat in ¼ cup of strained lemon juice. Gradually stir the egg mixture into the hot chicken stock, beating briskly after each addition. Season with a few grains of nutmeg and salt and pepper to taste. Strain through a fine-meshed sieve into a container. When cold, store in the refrigerator to chill thoroughly, and serve in chilled bouillon cups.

CHILLED MUSHROOM SOUP   [100]
French

The breath of the soil is captured by the mushroom and transmuted into the dark weird flavor that makes a mushroom the greatest natural delicacy of the food world. On its flavor and on its flavor alone, the mushroom bases its claim to fame. An analysis shows it does contain many elements of nutritive value, but these are so diluted by the liquid in its slight fragile structure that they hardly count. A mushroom exists to give grace and fragrance to plain food. In 500 B.C., Hippocrates asserted that mushrooms were eaten in large quantities and exported in commerce. The first record of the cultivation of mushrooms dates to the gourmet period of Louis XIV in France, where mushrooms were included in almost every dish served to the aristocrats who flourished during that era. France then and still is fortunate in possessing miles of mushroom caves. This natural condition was responsible for the growth of the industry throughout the world, but it was not until the latter part of the nineteenth century that the cultivation of the wild mushroom was begun in America.

Never, absolutely never, wash mushrooms; brush them very gently. Brush ½ pound of fresh mushrooms, peel, and chop the stems and caps. Place in a saucepan, and pour over 1½ quarts of rich Chicken Stock (No. 25), brought to the boiling point with 3 thin slices of onion, 1 small bay leaf, and a thin blade of garlic. Cover, and let stand for 15 minutes to steep. Place on the fire, and slowly bring to a boil; lower the flame, and let simmer gently for 25 minutes. Cool. Place in a clean saucepan, add 1 egg white, slightly beaten with 2 tablespoons of cold water, and also add the crushed eggshell. Very slowly bring to the boiling point, stirring constantly, and let boil 2 minutes. Lower the flame, and simmer for 5 minutes. Strain through a fine-meshed sieve or flannel cloth, or through a strainer lined with double-thick fine cloth. Heat to the boiling point, and cool. Chill for at least 3 hours. Serve in chilled cups, each cup containing sherry wine to taste—about 1 generous teaspoon.

CHILLED POTAGE JACQUELINE   [101]
A variation of the French Vichyssoise

Melt 3 tablespoons of sweet butter in a saucepan. Add carefully 1 large leek, using green and white parts, split in two lengthwise, and washed in several changes of cold water, then put through a food chopper, and 1 small head of lettuce, quartered, washed in several changes of water, and finely chopped. Cook until the vegetables are soft, stirring frequently. Gradually stir in 1½ quarts of hot Chicken Broth (No. 25). Add 2 cups of fresh green peas, cooked and drained, and cook gently, covered for 25 minutes. Empty the entire contents of the saucepan into a fine-meshed sieve, and rub through. Return to the fire, and add 1 small bay leaf and 1 whole clove, and season to taste with salt, pepper, and a dash of nutmeg. Strain again into a mixing bowl, cool, and chill thoroughly. When ready to serve, fold in ¾ cup of whipped cream, seasoned with a few grains of salt and 1 tablespoon of drained, squeezed prepared horseradish. Serve in chilled cups, each sprinkled with finely chopped chives.

CHILLED SOUR CREAM DILL SOUP   [102]
Danish

Cook 3 medium-sized potatoes, pared, and cut into small pieces in salted water until tender, covered. Drain; use only the potato water. Measure 2 cups of the potato water into a clean saucepan, stir in 1½ tablespoons of flour, diluted with a little cold water, alternately with 1 cup of scalded sour cream. Then add 1 large bunch of washed, chopped dill, and cook, stirring constantly, until the mixture boils. Let boil for 2 minutes. Now stir in 2 well-beaten fresh egg yolks, beaten with ½ cup of scalded sour cream, stirring briskly until the mixture boils again. Season to taste with salt and pepper and a dash of nutmeg. Cool, and chill thoroughly in the refrigerator. Serve in cold bouillon cups, each garnished with a fresh sprig of green dill.

CHILLED SOUR CREAM PEA SOUP [103]
Quick method

To a No. 4 can of purée of pea soup, add 1 teaspoon of curry powder, and blend thoroughly. Then add ¾ cup of heavy sour cream and ¼ cup of milk. Chill well, and serve with a dab of whipped sour cream forced through a pastry bag with a rose tube.

CHILLED TOMATO CONSOMME [104]
French—also called Essence of Tomato Consommé

Place in a saucepan 1½ cups of peeled, seeded, chopped fresh tomatoes. Add 5 cups of rich Beef Consommé (No. 114), 1 tablespoon of grated onion, 3 whole cloves, and ¼ teaspoon of celery seeds. Season to taste with salt, pepper, and a dash of nutmeg. Bring to a boil, add 1 small piece of bay leaf. Lower the flame, and simmer gently for 25 minutes. Strain through a fine-meshed sieve into a clean saucepan. Add 1 egg white, beaten slightly with 2 teaspoons of cold bouillon and the crushed eggshell. Bring to the boiling point, stirring constantly, and let boil 2 or 3 minutes, then add 1 small leaflet each of tarragon herb and dill. Lower the flame, and let simmer very gently for 25 minutes. Strain into a clean mixing bowl; cool, and when cold, set in the refrigerator to chill for at least 3 hours. Serve in chilled cups, each garnished with a thin slice of seeded lemon. You may stir in, just before dishing into cups, a teaspoon of Worcestershire sauce.

CHILLED TOMATO SOUR CREAM SOUP I [105]
Russian

Press through a coarse sieve a dozen fresh tomatoes into a clean bowl. Add 5 or 6 fresh scallions, carefully washed, minced fine, washed again, and thoroughly drained. Season with salt (about 1 teaspoon), 1 teaspoon of sugar, a good dash of freshly ground black pepper, same of marjoram and thyme, juice of 1 medium-sized lemon, and 2 teaspoons of grated lemon rind. Mix thoroughly. Chill for at least 3 hours, or still better, overnight. When ready to serve, stir in 1 generous cup of cold sour cream, to which has been added 1 teaspoon of curry powder. Serve in chilled bouillon cups or in chilled soup plates, each serving dusted with a good dash of finely chopped parsley. A side dish of very thin brown bread and butter finger sandwiches is the usual accompaniment.

CHILLED TOMATO SOUR CREAM SOUP II   [106]
Quick method

To 1 cup of heavy sour cream, gradually add a No. 4 can of chilled tomato juice, 1 teaspoon of finely grated lime rind, and ½ cup of thin cream or rich sweet milk. Chill thoroughly, and serve with a dab of whipped sour cream over each serving.

CHILLED TOMATO-VEGETABLE SOUP   [107]
Texas—garden style

Place in a saucepan 1 cup of finely shredded cabbage; 1 grated large onion; 1 cup of finely chopped green celery leaves; ½ medium-sized green pepper, seeded, white ribs removed, and finely chopped; 1 blade of garlic; 1 large bay leaf; 1 small pinch of thyme leaves; and salt and black pepper to taste. Cover with cold water, and slowly bring to the boiling point. Reduce the flame, and let simmer for 15 to 20 minutes. Strain through a sieve, rubbing well to pass the vegetable pulp through. Return to the fire, and add 2 cups of fresh or canned tomato juice, mixed with 1 cup of unsweetened canned grapefruit juice, and season to taste with 1 teaspoon of Worcestershire sauce. Taste for seasoning. Cool, then chill for about 3 hours in the refrigerator. Serve in chilled cups, each garnished with a tuft of whipped cream seasoned with a few grains of salt, the whipped cream sprinkled with a little freshly grated nutmeg.

CONSOMME ROUGE A LA LILLEOISE   [108]
Red Consommé Lille Manner—a kind of chilled clear bortsch

Put into a soup kettle 1½ quarts of rich Chicken Consommé (No. 25); 1 large onion, finely chopped; 2 whole leeks, chopped, and carefully washed in several changes of cold water; 2 extra large peeled, seeded fresh tomatoes, quartered; 1 stalk of celery, scraped, then finely chopped; 1 bouquet garni, composed of 1 large bay leaf, 8 sprigs of fresh parsley, 1 sprig of thyme, and 2 sprigs of marjoram, tied together with kitchen thread; 8 whole peppercorns, gently bruised; and 1 teaspoon of salt. Bring to a boil, and let simmer gently for 45 minutes, half covered; then strain into a large container through a fine sieve.

Peel 5 or 6 young raw beets, and run through a food chopper, saving the juice. Add pulp and juice to the soup tureen along with 1 fresh raw cucumber, also put through the food chopper, and 1 tablespoon each of chopped parsley and chervil. Stir in 3 tablespoons of good sherry wine. Cool, then chill in the refrigerator overnight. Next day, strain the mixture through a fine cloth. Taste for seasoning, and serve well chilled in cold cups, each garnished with a wedge of lemon. Serve a side dish of finger lengths of brown bread and butter sandwiches.

"Appulmoy," a popular soup of the fourteenth century, which contained almond, milk, apples, and honey, is still being eaten in some parts of Germany today. Another of the same period, "Snow Pottage," made of rice and milk was revived in England in 1753 and is still very popular.

CREME SENEGALAISE (Chilled) [109]

Melt 3 tablespoons of butter. Add 2 medium-sized green apples, peeled, cored, and diced small; 2 stalks of celery, finely chopped; and 2 medium-sized onions, grated. Cook until just beginning to take on a yellowish color, stirring constantly; then sprinkle 2 teaspoons of curry powder (more if desired), mixed with 2 teaspoons of flour. Continue cooking for 2 or 3 minutes longer, stirring almost constantly.

Gradually stir in 1 quart of Chicken Bouillon (No. 25), and bring to a boil. Reduce the flame, and let simmer gently for 45 to 50 minutes. Empty the whole contents of the pan into a fine-meshed sieve, and rub through. Cool, after seasoning to taste with salt, pepper, and a dash of nutmeg. When cold, stir in 1 pint of light cream or undiluted evaporated milk and ½ cup of finely diced white meat of chicken. Chill in the refrigerator for 3 long hours, and serve in chilled soup plates, each garnished with a sprinkling of paprika. A side dish of Cheese Pastry Sticks (No. 776) is the usual accompaniment.

ESSENCE OF CLAM BELLEVUE (Chilled) [110]
French

This delicious cold soup is one of the easiest to make. Put 3 cups of freshly made or canned clam juice in a saucepan, and add 3 cups of rich Chicken Bouillon (No. 25). Add 2 small fresh egg whites, beaten lightly with 3 tablespoons of cold chicken stock and the crushed shells of the two egg whites. Gradually bring this to a boil, stirring almost constantly, and let boil 3 minutes. Lower the flame, and simmer gently for 20 minutes, then strain the mixture through a flannel cloth or triple thickness of cheesecloth into a large bowl. Cool, then chill in the refrigerator for at least 3 hours. Serve in chilled cups, each garnished with a tuft of whipped cream forced through a pastry bag with a small fancy tube.

ESSENCE OF CLAM POMIDOR (Chilled) [111]
Italian

Proceed as indicated for Essence of Clam Bellevue (No. 110), substituting tomato bouillon or juice for chicken bouillon or stock. Serve as directed.

ESSENCE OF GAME SAINT HUBERT (Chilled) [112]
French

Make a rich consommé as indicated for Beef Consommé (No. 114), substituting the same weight of any kind of wild birds, or a mixture of them, for beef, and season highly with salt, cayenne, and a good pinch of juniper berries. Strain through a fine flannel cloth, and discard the solid parts. Return the liquid to the fire. Bring to the boiling point, stirring constantly, and stir in 2½ tablespoons of tapioca cooked in a little Chicken Broth (No. 25) and pressed through a fine strong cloth. Taste for seasoning, and strain again through a fine cloth, while very hot, into a container. Cool, and chill in the refrigerator for at least 5 hours. Serve in chilled cups, each garnished with 2 tiny squares of Game Custard Garnish (No. 689).

ESSENCE OF MUSHROOMS   [113]
CHARLES SCOTTO (Chilled)

Put through a food chopper ¾ pound of peeled fresh mushrooms, using stems and caps. Bring 2 quarts of Chicken Broth (No. 25) to the boiling point, then to a rolling boil. Immediately add the ground mushrooms. Remove from the fire, cover, and let infuse until the mixture is almost lukewarm. Strain through a triple thickness of cheesecloth into a saucepan, and boil down until there are 1½ quarts of liquid left in the pan. Taste for seasoning. Cool, then chill in the refrigerator for at least 4 hours. When ready to serve, stir in ⅓ cup of Madeira wine, and serve in chilled cups, each garnished with a sprig of fresh tarragon herb.

If desired, you may top each cup with a tuft of whipped cream, whipped with a tiny pinch of powdered tarragon herb, and forced through a pastry bag with a small fancy tube, the whipped cream dusted with mixed paprika and nutmeg to taste.

JELLIED BEEF CONSOMME OR BOUILLON [114]
Master recipe—called Pot-au-Feu when the soup is served hot with the vegetables

To obtain a really good consommé or *pot-au-feu* (pot on the fire), both time and patience are required. Hours of slow and steady simmering will alone extract all the substance from the meat, bones, and vegetables. The French peasant deliberately refrains from skimming the soup, in the belief that it is more nourishing, and all good French cooks, be they men, women, or chefs, recognize the importance of this, but carefully skim the scum from the top of the boiling liquid before adding the vegetables, which give the indefinable flavor to the bouillon. The meat should never be cut up but left whole and secured with kitchen string.

For a very good French consommé, place in a special earthenware dip pot, with a cover, the following ingredients:

For each quart of cold—remember, cold—water, take 1 pound of beef from the shin and ½ pound of beef bone, cracked, and add salt to taste.

Place the pot on the fire, add the meat and bones, well washed and sponged, then pour in the water. Very, very gently bring to a boil, let it "smile" until the scum rises to the surface, which should be skimmed carefully with the perforated ladle if a clear consommé is desired.

When the scum has all disappeared, then and only then, add:

2 large carrots, scraped and cut in quarters, lengthwise, then into inch pieces;
1 white turnip, peeled, quartered;
1 large onion, peeled, left whole, and stuck with 2 or 3 cloves, heads removed;
1 small clove of garlic (optional), left whole after being peeled;
1 small parsnip, peeled, quartered, core removed;
1 bouquet garni, composed of 1 large or 2 small bay leaves, 2 small leeks, cleaned, quartered lengthwise, carefully washed in several changes of cold water, 2 small parsley roots, scraped, or 8 sprigs of fresh parsley, 1 sprig of thyme, all tied up with kitchen thread;
10 whole peppercorns, gently bruised.

If the meat is to be served at table, as it is in most French households, it is usually removed after 3 hours of simmering; only the bones and vegetables are left in. If its sole purpose is the actual making of a rich consommé which will congeal by itself, the meat is left in to the end of the simmering. Besides the shin of the beef, the *ménagères* also use the thin flank and the brisket, if the meat is to be served at table as *boeuf bouilli*, or boiled beef.

Caution. Never use game, mutton, pork, lamb, or ham for making a real *pot-au-feu*, or consommé. Only beef will do to the exclusion of any other kind of meat, including poultry or poultry trimmings, as when these are added, it is called Petite Marmite (No. 633), with, of course, the marrow bones of the beef.

The vegetables and seasonings being added, gradually bring to the boiling point. Cover, and allow to simmer, to "smile" imperceptibly for 3½ to 4 hours, and without disturbing. The longer, the better the consommé or bouillon will be.

When done, strain the stock through a cloth wrung out in cold water. Keep the stock (until now, it is called stock and not consommé) in a cold place, and the next day remove carefully any fat that has set on the surface.

Following these simple directions, you will have the next day a real consommé in natural jelly without the addition of any gelatin.

If the stock is not sufficiently strong enough to jell well, you may add a little unflavored granulated gelatin softened in a little cold water. *But it is preferable* to omit the gelatin, as the fine delicate flavor of a jellied or hot consommé is a little impaired, unless red, white, sherry, Madeira, or port wine is added.

Important. In these jellied consommés or soups, it is recommended that the jellied soup be not too stiff, and before serving, it should be beaten with a fork.

JELLIED BEET MADRILENE   [115]
Russian

Place 1½ quarts of Beef Consommé (No. 114) in a saucepan. Add ⅓ pound of chopped lean raw beef; 3 large fresh tomatoes, skinned and seeded, and cut into small pieces; and 2 egg whites, slightly beaten with a fork with 1 tablespoon of cold consommé. Gradually bring the mixture to a boil, stirring almost constantly. Lower the flame, and let simmer; let smile gently for 25 to 30 minutes, stirring every 10 minutes with a fork. Strain twice through a fine cloth, wrung in cold water, into a fresh saucepan. Return to the fire, and bring to the boiling point. Remove from the fire, and stir in 1½ teaspoons of plain granulated gelatin softened in a little cold consommé, if the consommé doesn't seem to be rich enough to congeal by itself. Stir until the gelatin is dissolved, then stir in ¾ cup of finely diced cooked beets (fresh or canned). Cool to lukewarm, then gently stir. Taste for seasoning. Fill 6 chilled cups or individual colorful earthenware bowls, and chill in the refrigerator until solid. When ready to serve, break lightly the jellied soup with a fork, and serve immediately.

JELLIED BEET AND SOUR CREAM BOUILLON [116]
Polish

To 1 quart of clear hot Beef Consommé (No. 114), stir in 1 cup of canned beet juice. Heat to the boiling point. Stir in 2 tablespoons of plain gelatin, which has been dissolved in ⅓ cup of sherry wine, and 1 tablespoon of strained lemon juice. Taste for seasoning, and cool. Put 1 teaspoon of caviar in the bottom of each bouillon cup. Pour the consommé over it very gently. Chill until firm, and when ready to serve, scoop out from the center about 1 tablespoon of the jellied mixture, and place in the hole 1 large rosette of whipped sour cream forced through a pastry bag with a rose or star tube. Sprinkle the cream with a film of nutmeg, and serve at once.

JELLIED BORTSCH I [117]
American—unstrained

Pour into a saucepan 1½ quarts of Beef Consommé (No. 114). Add 2 cups of peeled, cored chopped beets, ½ cup of chopped onion, and 1 cup of chopped green cabbage. Cook until the vegetables are tender, adding more beef bouillon as necessary. Remove from the fire, and stir in 2 teaspoons of granulated gelatin, softened in 2 tablespoons of cold water. Stir until the gelatin is dissolved. Taste for seasoning, and cool to lukewarm, stirring occasionally so as to mix the vegetables. Fill 6 chilled cups with the mixture, and chill in the refrigerator for at least 3 hours. When ready to serve, break gently the jellied mixture with a fork, and cover the entire surface of each cup with plain whipped cream, slightly salted, and forced through a pastry bag with a small fancy tube. Serve a side dish of finger lengths of brown bread and butter sandwiches.

JELLIED BORTSCH II [118]

To any one of the Chilled Bortsch (No. 84 to No. 86), add 1 tablespoon of granulated plain gelatin for each quart of bortsch strained or unstrained.

JELLIED CELERY AND BEET CONSOMME   [119]
Russian

Place 3 cups of beet juice (drained from cans), 1 generous cup of minced celery (green leaves and stalks), 1 teaspoon of salt, and ¼ teaspoon of black pepper in a large soup kettle, and bring slowly to a boil, then reduce the flame, and simmer for 30 long minutes. Strain through a fine cloth into a second soup kettle. Add 2 cups of Beef Consommé (No. 114) brought to the boiling point with 1 tablespoon and 1 teaspoon of granulated gelatin, which has been soaked 5 minutes in ¼ cup of cold consommé, and 1½ tablespoons of lemon juice. Put a generous teaspoon of caviar in the bottom of each serving cup. Pour the strained consommé over it. Cool, and then chill in the refrigerator until firm. Serve with a slice of lemon.

JELLIED CELERY AND VEAL BOUILLON   [120]
American

With a clean damp cloth, wipe a 4-pound knuckle of veal, and cut it into small pieces. Put the meat and bone in a kettle with 2 quarts of cold water; 1 bouquet garni, composed of 1 large bay leaf, 3 sprigs of green celery leaves, 1 sprig of thyme, and 2 whole cloves, tied together with white kitchen thread; 6 whole peppercorns, freshly crushed; 1 teaspoon of salt; 1 large onion, cut into eighths; and the chopped outside stalks of a head of celery. Bring gradually to a boil. Lower the flame, and let simmer very gently, covered, for 4 to 4½ hours, adding hot water as the water evaporates. After 2 hours of simmering, add 1 more teaspoon of salt or celery salt. Strain through a fine sieve, and let the bouillon stand until the fat comes to the surface, then skim it off very carefully. Now strain through a double thickness of cheesecloth placed over a colander into a clean saucepan. Bring to the boiling point. Stir in 1 tablespoon of granulated unflavored gelatin, softened in 3 tablespoons of cold water; stir until the gelatin is dissolved, and cool. When cold, stir in ½ cup of scraped celery stalks, cut into small cubes and cooked in a little salted water until tender, then drained. Taste for seasoning, fill 6 chilled cups, and chill at least 3 hours. Before serving, break up the celery jelly with a fork, and place over each cup a scant tablespoon of salted whipped cream.

If by mistake you put too much salt in a soup, chop a raw potato into the pot and boil 12 to 15 minutes. The potato will absorb much of the salt. The more potato you use, the more salt will be taken from the soup or stew. There is no waste in this, as the potatoes can be used for the next meal.

JELLIED CHICKEN BOUILLON   [121]

Dissolve 1½ tablespoons of granulated gelatin in 3 tablespoons of cold Chicken Bouillon (No. 25) for 5 minutes. Stir in 1½ quarts of hot chicken bouillon alternately with 1½ tablespoons of chopped parsley or chives. Cool, and when lukewarm, pour into one or two shallow pans. Chill in the refrigerator for at least 3 hours. When ready to serve, cut into small cubes or break with a fork, and serve piled in chilled cups at once, each cup garnished with a dab of salted whipped cream.

JELLIED CHICKEN SOUP FERMIERE   [122]
French

Wash 8 chicken feet and 1 veal knuckle, split open carefully. Hold the chicken feet over the flame to loosen the skin, and scrape the skin carefully. Place the chicken feet and veal knuckle in a soup kettle. Pour in 1¼ quarts (5 cups) of cold water; season with ¾ teaspoon of salt and 8 whole peppercorns, gently bruised; and bring to a boil. Skim carefully, and when perfectly free of scum, add 1 clove of garlic, left whole; 2 stalks of celery, scraped, then cut into small pieces; 1 medium-sized carrot, scraped, then cut into small pieces; ½ small white turnip, coarsely chopped; 1 small piece of parsnip, peeled and coarsely chopped; 1 bouquet garni, composed of 1 small leek, halved lengthwise, carefully washed in several changes of cold water, and folded in thirds, 1 large bay leaf, 6 sprigs of fresh parsley, and 1 sprig of thyme, all tied together with kitchen thread; and 1 medium-sized onion, stuck with 2 whole cloves, heads removed. Cover, and let simmer very gently, imperceptibly, for 2 hours, skimming occasionally the scum if any. Now stir in 1 cup of strained tomato juice, 2 slices of lemon, seeded. Continue simmering for 15 minutes. Strain through a fine-meshed sieve or muslin cloth into a clean container. Stir in 4 tablespoons of sherry wine, let cool, and when cold, store in the refrigerator overnight. Next day, carefully lift the cake of fat from the surface. When ready to serve, break the jelly with a fork, and serve at once in chilled bouillon cups, each cup topped with 1 tablespoon of whipped sour cream, slightly dusted with a halo of paprika.

JELLIED CHICKEN SHERRIED BOUILLON   [123]
Quick method

Soften 2 tablespoons of granulated gelatin in ¼ cup of cold fresh or canned chicken bouillon for 5 minutes. Bring 1 cup of chicken bouillon to the boiling point, and stir in the softened gelatin, then add to the mixture 5 cups of freshly made Chicken Bouillon (No. 25), or canned to save time. Blend thoroughly, adding while blending 3 tablespoons of good sherry or Madeira wine. When cold, place in the refrigerator for at least 3 hours, or until firm. Break the jellied bouillon with a fork, and serve in chilled bouillon cups with or without a garnish of unsweetened whipped evaporated or coffee cream, seasoned merely with a little salt, and with or without a dusting of minced parsley or chives.

Jellied Chicken and Tomato Sherried Bouillon. Use equal parts of chicken bouillon and tomato bouillon, fresh or canned.

JELLIED CLAM BOUILLON I   [124]
American

Wash 2 quarts of clams in their shells carefully with a brush, and rinse in several changes of cold water. Put them in a kettle with ½ cup of cold water, ¼ cup of finely chopped green celery leaves, and a small piece of bay leaf. Cook until the shells open. Strain the liquor through a fine cloth or a double thickness of cheesecloth placed over a colander and saucepan, and let stand 10 minutes to allow the sand, if any, to settle. Carefully transfer the liquor into a clean saucepan. Stir in 3 cups of rich Beef Consommé (No. 114), and add 1 slightly beaten egg white and the crushed shell of the egg. Slowly bring to the boiling point, stirring almost constantly, and let boil 2 minutes. Lower the flame, and let simmer very gently for 20 minutes without stirring. Strain through a fine cloth into a clean pan. Stir in 1 tablespoon of granulated gelatin, which has been softened in 3 tablespoons of cold consommé, and stir until the gelatin is dissolved. Cool, and then chill in the refrigerator for at least 3 hours. Serve in chilled cups, each cup garnished with a small ring of salted whipped cream and in the center of the ring a half teaspoon of caviar.

JELLIED CLAM BOUILLON II   [125]
French

Proceed as indicated for Jellied Clam Bouillon I (No. 124), using white dry wine instead of water to open the carefully scrubbed clams.

Then go ahead as directed. When the bouillon is lukewarm, stir in 4 tablespoons of sherry wine. When cold, chill as directed, and serve in the same manner.

JELLIED CLAM AND TOMATO BOUILLON [126]
American

Place in a saucepan 3 cups of Clam Bouillon (No. 27). Strain through a fine cloth and let stand 10 minutes. Strain again into a clean saucepan, and add 3 cups of hot Tomato Bouillon (No. 81), or canned tomato bouillon. Heat to the boiling point. Stir in 1½ tablespoons of granulated gelatin, which has been softened in 3 tablespoons of cold water; stir well until the gelatin is entirely dissolved. Strain through a fine cloth placed over a colander and saucepan. Cool, and when cold, stir in 3 tablespoons of sherry wine (optional), and chill. Serve in chilled cups, after breaking the jellied mixture with a fork; or you may pour the mixture into one or two shallow pans, and when chilled, cut in small cubes, and pile the cubes in chilled cups.

JELLIED CONSOMME BELMONT [127]
American

Heat to the boiling point 1½ quarts of Beef Consommé (No. 114). Stir in ½ cup of grated raw carrot, 1 tablespoon of onion juice, and ⅓ cup of finely chopped celery leaves. Soften 1½ tablespoons of granulated gelatin in 3 tablespoons of cold water, and stir into the hot consommé. When the gelatin is completely dissolved, taste for seasoning; cool, then chill for at least 3 hours. When ready to serve, beat with a fork. Into each of six chilled cups, put 1 teaspoon of chopped hard-cooked egg. Then pile up the jellied mixture, and top each cup with another teaspoon of chopped hard-cooked egg.

JELLIED CONSOMME MADRILENE [128]

Consommé Madrilene is served either hot or cold, but it is always liquid. The jellied soup, on the other hand, is made with Consommé Madrilene, in the following manner.

To 1½ quarts of Beef Consommé (No. 114), add ⅓ pound of lean raw beef, freshly chopped; 3 large fresh tomatoes, peeled, seeded, and coarsely chopped; and 2 egg whites and their crushed shells. Bring very slowly to a boil, stirring almost constantly; lower the flame, and let simmer gently for about 35 minutes. Strain through a double thickness of cheesecloth placed over a colander and saucepan. Do not press the mixture, just turn gently with a wooden spoon. Return the strained consommé to the fire. Bring to a boil, and stir in 1½ tablespoons of granulated gelatin, softened in 4 tablespoons of cold consommé. Stir until the gelatin is dissolved. Cool, and then chill in the refrigerator for at least 3 hours. Serve in chilled cups, after breaking the jelly with a fork. No garnish is required, as it would hide the beautiful deep pink hue of this delicious soup.

For hot Madrilene, omit the gelatin; for chilled Madrilene, omit the gelatin, and simply chill in the refrigerator.

JELLIED CONSOMME WITH PORT WINE   [129]
French

Put in a saucepan 1½ quarts of clear Beef Consommé (No. 114), or use the concentrated kind. If the stock is not sufficiently strong to jell well, add 1 tablespoon of granulated gelatin, softened in very little cold consommé or water. (It's preferable to omit the gelatin.) Flavor with ⅓ cup of good port, and season with cayenne pepper and about 5 or 6 drops of tarragon vinegar. Allow to jell thoroughly in the refrigerator. Fill 6 chilled bouillon cups, breaking the jelly slightly with a fork, and serve at once.

JELLIED CONSOMME WITH SHERRY   [130]
French

Proceed as directed for No. 129, substituting sherry for port wine, and serve as directed.

JELLIED CREAM OF CURRY SOUP   [131]
East Indies

Place 1½ quarts of rich creamy milk in the top of a double boiler to scald with 1 large bay leaf, 6 thin slices of a medium-sized onion, 1 thin slice of garlic, 2 whole cloves, and 6 sprigs of fresh parsley. Season to taste with salt and pepper and a touch of nutmeg. Stir in 2 tablespoons of plain gelatin, dissolved in 3 tablespoons of cold milk, together with 1 tablespoon of curry powder. Stir until the gelatin and curry are well blended, then strain the mixture through a fine muslin cloth into a saucepan. Beat in 4 egg yolks, adding one at a time, and beating well after each addition. Return to the fire, and bring near the boiling point, stirring constantly. Remove from the direct flame, season with salt and pepper to taste, and let cool slightly. Then beat with a rotary beater. Fill 6 chilled bouillon cups, sprinkle over each cup 1 tablespoon of freshly grated coconut, and chill for at least 2 hours. Serve at once, sprinkled with a film of paprika for color contrast.

JELLIED FUMET OF CELERY [132]
French

In a soup kettle, put 1½ quarts of Beef Consommé (No. 114) and 1 bunch of celery, chopped, then carefully washed in several changes of cold water. Cook for 45 minutes, or until the celery is tender. Strain through a fine cloth placed over a colander and saucepan, pressing gently but thoroughly. Return the strained beef-celery stock to the fire, and add enough beef consommé to make 6 cups. Bring to a boil, then stir in 1 tablespoon of granulated gelatin, which has been softened in 3 tablespoons of cold consommé or water. Stir until the gelatin is dissolved, and cool after tasting for seasoning. When cold, chill in the refrigerator, and serve in chilled bouillon cups, each cup sprinkled with a little finely chopped chervil.

JELLIED GREEN TURTLE SOUP [133]
American

Simply buy a fine brand of green turtle soup, and place it in the refrigerator to jell. It will jell as soon as it is thoroughly chilled, and the bits of green turtle seem to acquire added flavor with chilling. Serve in chilled bouillon cups without any garnish with a side dish of hot toasted saltine crackers, finger-length sandwiches, or anything which is crunchy.

JELLIED HERB CONSOMME PAYSANNE [134]

To 1½ quarts of Beef Consommé (No. 114), hot but not boiling, add 3 tablespoons each of very finely chopped chervil, parsley, green pepper, and chives. Mix well. Stir in ⅓ cup of Madeira wine, mixed with 1½ tablespoons of gelatin, and dissolve this thoroughly in the hot green consommé. Cool. Chill, and when ready to serve, stir with a fork, and pile in chilled bouillon cups, each containing 1 teaspoon of blanched, shredded, toasted almonds. Cover the entire surface of each cup with whipped sweet cream, flavored with a little curry powder (about 1 teaspoon of curry for each cup of cream, more or less according to taste). Force the cream through a pastry bag with a star design. Serve at once.

JELLIED MADRILENE FROMAGERE   [135]
French—with cheese

Place 2 cans of Madrilene consommé, or some freshly made (No. 128), in the refrigerator overnight so it will jell. Next day, before serving, put the consommé in a large mixing bowl, and break the lumps with a fork. Fold in 3 or 4 ounces of crumbled Roquefort or blue cheese. Serve in chilled cups with a spoonful of whipped sour cream on top of each cup and a sprinkling of finely chopped chives.

JELLIED MINT CONSOMME   [136]
American

Bring to a boil 5 cups of Beef Consommé (No. 114), then stir in ¾ cup of dry white wine, and heat slowly until beads appear on the surface. Remove from the fire, and stir in 1 tablespoon of granulated gelatin, which has been softened in 3 tablespoons of cold water. Stir until dissolved. Remove from the fire, and cool to lukewarm. Pour into chilled cups, each cup containing 1 fresh mint leaf, then chill for 3 hours. Just before serving, break up the jelly lightly with a fork, and place a fresh mint leaf over each cup. Serve immediately.

JELLIED MINTED SHERRY CONSOMME   [137]

To 1½ quarts of Beef Consommé (No. 114), add 1¾ tablespoons of mint-flavored gelatin, and stir until dissolved. Strain through a fine muslin cloth into a clean saucepan. Taste for seasoning. Stir in ⅓ cup of dry sherry wine, and divide among 6 chilled bouillon cups. Place a fresh green mint leaflet on top of each cup, and chill. Serve with a wedge of lemon.

JELLIED MUSHROOM BOUILLON   [138]
French

Put ¾ pound of cleaned, peeled mushrooms through a food chopper, using the stems and cups and saving all the juice, with 3 thin slices of mild onion. Place in a saucepan with 5 cups of Beef Bouillon (No. 114). Bring to a boil, lower the flame, and simmer gently for 15 to 20 minutes. Then stir in 1 tablespoon of granulated gelatin, which has been softened in 3 tablespoons of cold bouillon, and stir until the gelatin is dissolved. Remove from the fire, taste for seasoning, and cool a little. Then stir in 4 tablespoons of sherry wine. Chill thoroughly, and serve in chilled cups, each cup garnished with a puff of whipped cream.

JELLIED SPINACH SOUP FLORENTINE [139]
Italian

No product in the food world, certainly no vegetable, has received more publicity than spinach. It has been praised for its food value and maligned for its flavor by those who happen to dislike it. It has achieved real fame by being made the subject of cartoons and vaudeville jokes.

Soak 1 tablespoon of granulated gelatin in 1 cup of spinach liquor, from fresh or canned spinach. Heat 4 cups of Chicken Bouillon (No. 25) to the boiling point. Stir in the spinach liquor and gelatin mixture, and remove from the fire, stirring until the gelatin is thoroughly dissolved. Strain through a double thickness of cheesecloth into a clean pan, add a few drops of green vegetable coloring to accentuate the color, and 1 teaspoon of Worcestershire sauce. Taste for seasoning. Cool to lukewarm, then stir in 1 cup of cold cooked ground spinach. Mix well, and fill 6 individual chilled bouillon cups. Chill for at least 3 hours. When ready to serve, break the jelly with a fork, and make a ring of whipped cream, forced through a pastry bag with a small fancy tube, around the edges of the filled cups. Serve at once with crisp cheese wafers.

JELLIED TAPIOCA CONSOMME [140]
ESTREMADURA
Spanish

Do not treat oranges commonly. An orange is a precious thing. Anyone who reads *Wind, Sand and Stars*, by the French aviator, Antoine de Saint-Exupéry, will remember forever his tribute to the orange. Two pilots were stranded in the Sahara Desert three days without water. "But, miracle of miracles, Prévost came upon an orange. . . . Stretched out beside the fire I looked at the glowing fruit and said to myself that men didn't know what an orange was. Here we are condemned to death, I said to myself, and still the certainty of dying cannot compare with the pleasure I am feeling. The joy I take from this half of an orange which I am holding in my hand is one of the greatest joys I've ever known."

Use peel for flavoring; save the orange shells to serve fruit salads, ice cream or a cooling jellied soup as follows:

Cook ½ cup of quick-cooking tapioca until it is clear in 2 cups of highly seasoned Beef Consommé (No. 114). Then stir in 1 tablespoon of granulated gelatin and 3 more cups of the same consommé, scalded. Mix thoroughly, remove from the fire, and stir in ¼ cup of good sherry wine. Have ready 6 large orange shells, after carefully scraping the pulp from the insides, each shell containing a large pitted black olive. Pour the broth into the orange shells, and chill in the refrigerator for 2 hours.

JELLIED THREE-COLORED CONSOMME   [141]

Red Part. Heat 1½ cups of tomato juice with 1 teaspoon of onion juice and ½ teaspoon of Worcestershire or Pique sauce to the boiling point. Season highly with ½ teaspoon of paprika, salt to taste, and a few grains of cayenne pepper. Stir in 2 cubes of beef extract, and when dissolved, strain through a double thickness of cheesecloth into a clean saucepan. Then stir in 1½ teaspoons of granulated gelatin, softened in a little cold water for 5 minutes, and 1 tablespoon of good sherry wine. Pour into a shallow pan, and set in the refrigerator to jell.

White Part. Pour into a saucepan 1½ cups of clear fresh Chicken Bouillon (No. 25), or canned, and heat to the boiling point. Season to taste with salt and white pepper. Then stir in 1½ teaspoons of granulated gelatin, softened in a little cold water, and stir until the gelatin is dissolved. Stir in 2 generous tablespoons of shredded Brazil nut meats, and pour into a shallow pan. Set in the refrigerator to jell.

Green Part. Heat 1½ cups of fresh Beef Consommé (No. 114), or canned, with ½ teaspoon of curry powder, dissolved in 2 or 3 tablespoons of white wine. Then stir in 2 teaspoons of granulated gelatin, softened in ¼ cup of strained spinach juice. Blend thoroughly, taste for seasoning, then strain through a double thickness of cheesecloth into a shallow pan. Set in the refrigerator to jell.

To Serve. Empty the three pans of jellied bouillon into three different chilled platters, and beat each with a fork, or still better, cut into tiny cubes. Dress each color separately, unmixed, into chilled cocktail glasses or glass bouillon cups. Serve each cup with a wedge of lemon.

JELLIED TOMATO BOUILLON I   [142]
American

Soften 1 tablespoon of granulated gelatin in 3 tablespoons of Chicken Bouillon (No. 25) for 5 minutes. Pour into a saucepan 5 cups of fresh or canned tomato juice. Add 4 thin slices of onion and a bouquet garni, composed of 1 large bay leaf, 3 sprigs of green celery leaves, 1 sprig of thyme, and 6 sprigs of fresh parsley, all tied together with kitchen thread. Bring to a boil, lower the flame, and let simmer gently for 15 minutes. Then discard the bouquet garni, and stir in the softened gelatin. Stir well, and remove from the fire. Taste for seasoning, adding salt, white pepper, and a dash of mace to taste. Cool to lukewarm. Then stir in 3 tablespoons of good sherry wine. Pour into one or two shallow pans, and set in the refrigerator for 2 hours. When ready to serve, break off the jelly with a fork, fill 6 chilled bouillon cups, and serve at once, each cup topped with a green star cut from green pepper. Serve with toasted wafers.

JELLIED TOMATO BOUILLON II   [143]
French—also called Tomato Bouillon Frappé

Scald 2 pounds of fresh tomatoes, and remove the skins, then rub through a fine strainer. Season to taste with salt, pepper, a dash of mace, the juice of a large lemon, and ½ teaspoon of Worcestershire sauce. Then stir in 2 cups of cold Beef Consommé (No. 114). Turn the mixture into a refrigerator tray, and freeze until the mixture is the consistency of mush. Remove from the refrigerator, and stir briskly, scraping the sides and bottom of the tray, while adding 4 tablespoons of good Madeira wine. Return the tray to the refrigerator, and continue freezing, without disturbing, for 2 hours. When ready to serve, fill 6 individual chilled bouillon cups, and serve at once. To obtain a nice red color, you may add to the mixture, when stirring and scraping, a few drops of red vegetable coloring.

JELLIED TOMATO BOUILLON III   [144]
Belgian

Rub 1 pound of skinned fresh tomatoes through a sieve. Place in a saucepan, and add 1 quart of rich Chicken Bouillon (No 25), 1 tablespoon of grated onion, 3 whole cloves, 1 blade of garlic, ⅓ teaspoon of celery salt, 1 large bay leaf, a dash of cayenne, and a dash of mace. Gradually bring to a boil, lower the flame, and let simmer gently for 25 minutes, stirring occasionally. Remove from the fire, and stir in 1½ tablespoons of granulated gelatin, which has been softened in ¼ cup of cold chicken bouillon for 5 minutes. Mix thoroughly, remove from the fire, and strain through a fine sieve. Cool. When lukewarm, stir in ¼ cup of sherry wine, and taste for seasoning. Pour into one or two wet shallow pans, and chill for 2 hours. Cut into small cubes, and pile in chilled glass bouillon cups, sprinkling each cup with finely chopped parsley, chervil, or chives. Serve immediately.

JELLIED TOMATO BOUILLON IV   [145]
Home manner

Place in a saucepan 7 fresh clean tomatoes; 1 blade of garlic; ¾ cup of chopped celery leaves; 2 tablespoons of chopped green pepper; 1 medium-sized onion, grated; 1 bouquet garni, composed of 1 large bay leaf, 3 whole cloves, 8 sprigs of fresh parsley, 1 sprig of thyme, and 2 dill leaflets, all tied together with kitchen thread; ½ teaspoon of salt; and 1 cup of clear rich Chicken Stock (No. 25). Bring gently to a boil, cover, and let simmer gently for 30 minutes, stirring occasionally. Strain through a fine-meshed sieve into a clean saucepan, gently pressing the vegetables to remove all possible liquid. Sprinkle 2 tablespoons of granulated gelatin over 1½ cups of cold chicken stock, and let soak for 5 minutes. Then gradually stir into the hot strained bouillon, stirring until the gelatin is dissolved. Bring to near the boiling point. Taste for seasoning. Turn the preparation into a shallow pan, containing 1 cup of fresh tomato pulp, free from seeds and skin, and coarsely chopped. When cold, store in the refrigerator for about 2 hours, or until set. Upturn the jellied tomato bouillon on a platter, chop coarsely, and serve at once in chilled bouillon cups, preferably glass cups if available. Serve at once.

JELLIED TOMATO CREAM SOUP   [146]
American

Have ready 5 cups of hot Cream of Tomato Soup (No. 434). Stir in 1½ tablespoons of granulated gelatin, which has been softened in ¼ cup of cold water for 5 minutes. Cool. Chill in the refrigerator for at least 3 hours. Serve in chilled bouillon cups, each sprinkled with finely chopped chives. Serve with a wedge of lemon.

JELLIED TOMATO JUICE   [147]
Mexican

Fresh tomato juice in earthen jugs was sold in Holland for medicinal purposes in the 1860s. A jug containing a little more than a quart cost about a dollar.

Scald 6 large ripe tomatoes, and remove the skins. Put in a saucepan, and mash with a potato masher. Add 1 teaspoon of granulated sugar, 1 teaspoon of salt, ½ teaspoon of celery seeds, and a blade of mace, and simmer gently for 15 minutes. Do not let boil. Strain the juice through a very fine sieve, and keep hot. Soften 1 tablespoon of granulated gelatin in ½ cup of dry white wine (cold water may be used) for 5 minutes. Stir into the hot tomato juice, alternately with 1 cup of hot Beef Consommé (No. 114). Cool. When cold, stir in ½ cup of chopped watercress leaves. Chill, and serve in chilled bouillon cups, sprinkled with finely chopped chives.

JELLIED CREAMED WATERCRESS SOUP   [148]

Wash, clean, and carefully pick 1½ bunches of young green watercress. Drain well, and dry between a towel. Put the cress through a food chopper, collecting all the juice possible. Scald 2 cups of cream together with 2 cups of sweet milk with 1 large bay leaf, 4 thin slices of onion, 6 sprigs of fresh parsley, 1 whole clove, and salt and white pepper to taste. Remove from the fire, and strain over the cress in a bowl. Beat in 3 egg yolks, adding one at a time; then add, stirring well, 2 tablespoons of plain gelatin, which has been soaked 5 minutes in ⅓ cup of cold sweet milk. Stir into the cream soup alternately with ½ teaspoon of finely grated lemon rind. Taste for seasoning. Cool, then chill in the refrigerator until firm, or still better, fill 6 cups with the soup, and chill until firm. When ready to serve, break the soup with a fork, and serve at once with a wedge of lemon hung on each cup. Pass a dish of Melba Toast (No. 791) alongside.

Chapter Four

CHILLED, HOT, AND JELLIED BEER, FRUIT, NUT, AND WINE SOUPS

Hot or cold, thick or thin, soups are the nour-ishing prelude to luncheon, dinner, or supper.

WITH THE FIRST BREATH OF REALLY WARM WEATHER, THE cook starts thinking about new and wonderful cold soups. The refreshing chill and tang of these as a first course or as a "starter" is a wonderful nudge to one's appetite.

The main thing to remember is that cold soup must be *really cold*, just as hot soup must be really hot, to be good. No betwixt-and-between stuff here. Have the plates or bouillon cups chilled too. The beading of moisture that usually forms on the cups adds to the illusion of coolness.

A quick way to get soup very cold is to pour it into the ice tray of the refrigerator. Watch it carefully from time to time so that it does not freeze. When it is just at the point of forming ice crystals, or in the case of a jellied soup, has just jellied, take out the tray, and let it stand in the refrigerator until you are ready to serve the soup in cups or plates. Soups chilled in this way are really cold and also do not have the chance to absorb the odors of other foods in the refrigerator while in the lukewarm stage.

Almost any soup that is good hot is good cold, with the exception of mixed vegetable soups and broths with barley or rice. Black bean soup, with a slice of lemon and some sherry added, is wonderful chilled. So is bortsch, topped with a dab of sour cream. Add a pinch of curry powder to cold cream of asparagus soup, and you'll have an unusual and interesting flavor.

Cold potato soup, made with a little extra sour cream and a good sprinkling of chopped chives, makes that aristocrat of cold soup, the Vichyssoise (No. 95), sit up and take notice.

In the days when our young republic was fathered by General George Washington, beer was a part of almost every meal, as beer was regarded as a liquid food.

"Beer and bread make the cheeks red," runs the Alsatian adage. Another adage describes beer as the "joint oiler," and still another says, "Beer is the best drugstore." There is evidence that beer is a valuable food. The evidence is overwhelming, according to medical authorities. English schoolboys of the seventeenth century were fed beer, bread, and cheese for both breakfast and supper. Their lunch consisted of beef and wheat boiled in beer and egg yolks.

While the food faddist may argue that the slab of Liederkranz and the slice of Bermuda onion and the smear of mustard, all tucked in a bun and washed down with a glass of cold beer, may be a midnight morsel which is contrary to said faddist's ideas of what is good for the tummy, we gourmets maintain that it is good for one's soul.

These soups serve 6 to 8 persons unless otherwise indicated.

ALE LEMON SOUP (Hot)   [150]
English

When is beer an ale? you may ask. Ale was the current name in England for malt beverage before the introduction of the use of hops from Germany about 1524. Then, for a time, the German word *bier* was used to distinguish the hopped liquor from ale, the unhopped. However, accepted English writers now use ale and beer synonymously. Nevertheless, it should be remembered that ale is a top-yeast ferment, and in America it is made with a slightly greater concentration of hops than is used in beer.

Put 1 quart of good ale in a saucepan with the juice of half a lemon; ½ teaspoon of grated lemon peel; 2 whole cloves, heads removed; 2 whole peppercorns, freshly crushed; 4 thin slices of peeled, seeded raw cucumber; an inch stick of cinnamon bark; a dash of freshly grated nutmeg; and ½ teaspoon of salt. Gradually bring to the boiling point, but do not let boil, stirring constantly. Then stir in 1 tablespoon of flour, diluted with a little cold water, stirring from the bottom of the saucepan. Let simmer gently for 5 or 6 minutes. Strain into a clean saucepan. Heat well, but do not let boil. Taste for seasoning, and pour into a soup tureen containing some Melba Toast (No. 791). Serve immediately in hot soup plates, each garnished with a thin slice of seeded and peeled lemon.

ALMOND BUTTERMILK SOUP (Hot)   [151]

Bring to a boil together 3 cups of buttermilk with a 2-inch stick of cinnamon over medium flame, stirring all the time. Gradually stir in 3 tablespoons of rice flour, which has been diluted in 2 cups of cold buttermilk, then strained. Cook until smooth, stirring almost constantly. When boiling, stir in ⅓ cup of blanched, then ground, almonds and 3 tablespoons (more or less, according to taste) of sugar. Let simmer 5 minutes, and just before serving, stir in 1 cup of sweet heavy cream, whipped with salt and white pepper to taste. Serve at once, each plate garnished with Croutons (No. 780). A fine, delicious, and nourishing soup for both children and grownups.

ALMOND MILK (Hot) [152]
Potage au Lait d'Amandes—very appropriate for Lent

Take 1½ pounds of sweet almonds and a dozen or more bitter almonds, both blanched and skinned. Wash quickly, then drain thoroughly, sponging the almonds carefully. Pound the almonds in a mortar, using a heavy pestle, or put through the food chopper several times, using the finest blade. Have ready violently boiling salted water, not more than 1½ quarts, into which a thin lemon peel and ½ scant teaspoon of coriander are dropped. To this water, add the almond paste gradually, stirring constantly with a long-handled wooden spoon. When all the almond paste has been added, allow the mixture to boil for 5 minutes without stirring, making sure that it boils steadily. Strain through a flannel cloth, and keep hot over hot water. When ready to serve, stir in 2 egg yolks, one at a time, stirring briskly after each addition. Correct the seasoning, adding a little white pepper to taste, and salt if needed. To serve, pour over thin Melba Toast (No. 791), placed in hot soup plates.

APPLE AND APRICOT CREAM SOUP [153]
NORMANDY (Chilled)
French

Wash 1 cup of sound dried apricots in several changes of cold water, then soak in hot water to barely cover for 3 hours. Drain, and place the apricots in a clean soup kettle together with 1¾ pounds of sound pared and quartered apples, 1 cup of very clear Beef Bouillon (No. 114), and 1 large bay leaf, tied with 8 sprigs of fresh parsley. Gradually bring to a boil, lower the flame, cover, and let simmer very, very gently, stirring frequently to prevent scorching, for about 20 minutes, or until the fruit is soft. Empty the entire contents into a fine-meshed wire sieve, discard the bay leaf and parsley, and rub through into a clean bowl. Season with salt and white pepper to taste, then, while still hot, stir in 1 quart of rich cold milk. When cold, chill in the refrigerator, and serve in chilled bouillon cups, each garnished with a cooked dried apricot, topped with a puff of whipped cream.

APPLE GINGER SOUP (Hot) [154]
India

As early as 800 A.D., good children in North Africa were treated to apples dipped in honey, somewhat like our own popular "apples on a stick." In India, the home cook has used apples in soup for more than 1000 years.

Peel, quarter, and core 2 pounds of cooking apples, and cut up coarsely. Have ready 2 quarts of rapidly boiling meat stock; drop the apples in all at once, and add 3 whole cloves and ¼ inch of root ginger. Simmer very, very gently until the apples are tender; strain through a fine-meshed sieve. Season to taste with salt and white pepper, reheat, and serve in hot soup plates with a side dish of small Croutons (No. 780).

APPLE AND RED WINE SOUP (Cold) [155]
Polish, Russian, Livonian

Peel, core, and slice thin 6 large apples. Place in a saucepan, barely covered with water. Add ½-inch stick of cinnamon, 2 tablespoons of lemon juice, ½ teaspoon of grated lemon rind, and a few grains of salt, mixed with 2 tablespoons of freshly grated bread crumbs. Cook over a gentle flame until the apples are tender and the liquid almost entirely absorbed or evaporated. Strain through a fine sieve, and cool. Divide the cold applesauce among 6 chilled, colorful earthenware bowls. Combine and mix well 1 quart of chilled red wine, 1 tablespoon of black currant jelly, 3 tablespoons of granulated sugar, 1 tablespoon of unstrained lemon juice, a little salt and cinnamon to taste, and when thoroughly blended, divide among the 6 bowls. Serve immediately with a side dish of cold apple fritters.

APPLE, RED WINE, AND RAISIN SOUP (Hot) [156]
Swiss

Wipe 1½ pounds of sour apples with a damp cloth, and cut into quarters without peeling. Put the quarters in a saucepan, and add 2 thick slices of stale white bread, 1 quart of red wine (4 cups), a 2-inch stick of cinnamon, 3 whole cloves with heads removed, 2 thin slices of lemon, seeded and unpeeled, and very little salt. Cook very slowly until the apples are tender. Empty the whole contents into a fine-meshed sieve, and rub through into a clean saucepan. Stir in 2 tablespoons of butter, ½ to ¾ cup of well-washed seedless raisins, and 3 tablespoons of granulated sugar. Heat slowly to the boiling point, or until a few beads appear on the surface, and let simmer gently for 5 minutes, or until the raisins are plumped. When ready to serve, beat 1 egg yolk with 1 tablespoon of brandy, and very slowly pour into the mixture, stirring constantly. Bring to the boiling point, but do not allow to boil. Serve at once, after adding 18 blanched, toasted, shredded almonds for crunchiness. Serve with a tray of brown bread and butter finger sandwiches made with very fresh bread.

AVOCADO BISQUE SAN FRANCISCO [157]
METHOD (Jellied)

As avocados darken on exposure to air, they should be prepared just before serving. To keep sliced or cubed avocados from discoloring, keep the pit on top of the slices until ready to serve or use. If you like avocados and find one that is not ripe enough, place it in a slow oven (250° F.) for 10 to 12 minutes; turn off the flame, and let it remain in the oven. It will ripen within 20 minutes or sooner, ready to use.

Wipe 2 medium-sized ripe avocados with a damp cloth, split in two, and remove the pit. Peel the avocados, and immediately rub through a fine wire sieve, gradually adding 4 tablespoons of sweet heavy cream, alternating with 2 tablespoons of good sherry wine. Season to taste with salt, white pepper, and a small grating of nutmeg. Chill well. Have ready 1 quart of Jellied Chicken Bouillon (No. 121) in liquid form. Place the avocado mixture in a wooden bowl, stir in the bouillon, beating the whole thoroughly with a rotary beater. Chill again for at least 2 hours, or until jellied. Serve in chilled bouillon cups, each topped with a teaspoon of whipped cream, and sprinkled with a little paprika for a volcanic effect.

AVOCADO SOUP FLORIDA MANNER (Hot) [158]

It was Thoreau who once wrote, "It takes a savage or a wild taste to appreciate a wild fruit." Or it takes a gourmet! For no one will quibble the point that the Indian's avocado—calavo in California, avocado in Florida, midshipman's-butter by the sailors, ahuacatl or buttery fruit by the Aztecs, alligator pear by Texans, alligator meaning worthless because it disappointed those who expected a fresh fruit taste, and pear because of its shape—wilts deliciously on our domestic tongues. And when in August, heat waves assault you with the lasting determination of an uninvited week-end guest, and no one has the energy to stir, a cold fruit or vegetable soup to reduce the soaring of those gently homicidal instincts is the nearest approximation to an ice floe anyone can enjoy. For a sheer scoop of ambrosia, take this avocado soup made in the Florida manner.

Melt 4 tablespoons of butter in a saucepan. Stir in 1 rounded tablespoon of finely chopped onion, as much of finely chopped green pepper and celery leaves and parsley, and 2 well-ripe peeled and pitted avocados, rubbed through a fine sieve. Let simmer very, very gently over a low flame for about 8 to 10 minutes, stirring constantly. Sprinkle over 3 tablespoons of sifted flour, and blend thoroughly. Gradually and slowly stir in 2 cups of hot Chicken Bouillon (No. 25), and cook, stirring constantly until the boiling point and the mixture bubbles. At this point, stir in 2 cups of scalded rich milk, to which have been added 2 fresh egg yolks, slightly beaten; stir briskly from the bottom of the pan. Boil steadily for 3 minutes, stirring constantly. Season to taste with salt, pepper, and a dash of nutmeg. Serve immediately in hot soup plates, each sprinkled with finely chopped chives.

AVOCADO SOUP HOME MANNER (Chilled) [159]

Sift 6 tablespoons of flour mixed with 1 scant teaspoon of salt over 5 cups of rich cold Chicken Bouillon (No. 25), and stir until smooth and free from lumps. Place over a gentle heat. Add 1 large bay leaf, tied with 6 sprigs of fresh parsley, a good dash of cayenne, or a few drops of Tabasco sauce, and gradually bring to a boil, stirring constantly. Remove from the fire, strain through a fine-meshed wire sieve into a bowl, and stir in 2 ripe peeled and pitted avocados, sieved. Return to the fire, bring to a boil, and strain again through a fine-meshed wire sieve. Chill thoroughly. When ready to serve, stir in ¾ cup of chilled sweet cream; 3 black peppercorns, freshly crushed; 3 white peppercorns, also freshly crushed; ⅛ of a teaspoon of crushed coriander; and taste for salt. Garnish each serving with a teaspoon of caviar. Serve at once.

AVOCADO AND POTATO MILK SOUP (Hot) [160]
Ecuador—Ajiaco Sopa

Boil 4 medium-sized peeled potatoes in enough Chicken Stock (No. 25) to cover until soft, then put through a ricer. Add 1 cup of scalded rich milk, and stir in 1 tablespoon of grated onion. Return to the fire, and add 3 more cups of rich scalded milk and ½ cup of grated mild cheese. Bring to a boil and simmer gently for 15 minutes, stirring occasionally. Season to taste with salt and pepper. Beat in 2 whole fresh eggs, beaten with ½ cup of scalded milk, beating briskly to prevent curdling. Cook a few minutes longer, stirring constantly. When ready to serve, place 2 small ripe avocados, peeled, pitted, and thinly sliced, in the bottom of a soup tureen, and pour over the hot soup. Dust with a little paprika, and serve at once.

BANANA LENTIL SOUP (Hot) [161]
Mexican Indian

Lentil soup is a favorite among Mexican Indian cooks, but unless a banana is added or served with it, it is considered poison. However, the banana is really delicious.

Prepare a lentil soup, using your favorite recipe, but do not forget to put in some garlic. When the lentils are tender, strain, and rub through a fine sieve. Return to the fire, and heat well. Taste for seasoning, and when ready to serve, about 5 minutes before, stir in 1 large banana, peeled and sliced.

BEER AND MILK SOUP (Hot)   [162]
Bavarian

Pour into a saucepan 1 bottle of dark beer, add 1 tablespoon of sugar, the juice of a small lemon, 2 whole cloves, a ½-inch stick of cinnamon, salt, and a few, very few, grains of white pepper. Bring to the boiling point. Remove from the fire, and strain into 1 quart of rich milk, scalded with a large bay leaf. Serve in hot soup plates with Croutons (No. 780).

BEER SOUP BREWER'S WAY (Hot)   [163]
French

Bring 6 cups of light beer to a boil, but do not allow to boil; remove from the fire as soon as beads form on the surface. Cream 1 tablespoon of sweet butter with 1 tablespoon of flour, then continue creaming while adding 2 fresh egg yolks, a little at a time, creaming well after each addition. Gradually beat in 2 cups of scalded sour cream, beating briskly to prevent curdling. Then stir the mixture slowly into the hot beer, stirring constantly from the bottom of the pan. Serve in fancy, colorful earthenware individual soup bowls, each bowl sprinkled with 1½ tablespoons of grated Swiss cheese and Croutons (No. 780), substituting rye bread for white bread.

BEER SOUP AFTER THE HARVEST   [164]
FEAST (Cold)

Haymaking is a long way removed from foods, yet during haymaking in France's Lorraine, famous for its clear light beer, the haymakers, after having piled the haystacks, indulge in a drinking bout, with dances and merrymaking; and many a bronzed gentleman of other days was fonder of his "sup" of good beer than he was of wine. Here is a very old recipe for six grand haymakers.

Bring to the boiling point, but do not allow to boil, 3 quarts of light clear beer. Remove from the fire as soon as beads form on the surface. Combine the hot beer with a fifth bottle of dry white wine, heated to the beading stage with a 2-inch stick of cinnamon and ½ scant cup of powdered sugar. The mixture will then become limpid. Chill and serve very cold, topping each portion with a soft freshly poached egg yolk floating in each individual soup bowl, and accompany with a tray of plain dry crackers, such as saltines. It's a cool one, and it's marvelous.

BLACKBERRY SOUP (Cold)   [165]
Polish

Blackberries with any tinge of brown or red in their color are not fully ripe and are best for jelly. In some parts of Chile, blackberries grow so abundantly that they are considered a pest, but not by a good cook who knows how to prepare blackberry soup.

Pick 2 pounds of full ripe blackberries; place in a colander, and let cold water run through, shaking the colander. Drain thoroughly, and place the berries in a saucepan. Add 1 quart of cold water; 3 medium-sized lemons, washed, thinly sliced, and seeded; an inch stick of cinnamon; 2 whole cloves, heads removed; and ½ pound of granulated sugar. Gradually bring to a boil, lower the flame, and let simmer gently for 10 minutes. Drain through a fine sieve, and cool the berries. When cold, chill well. When ready to serve, stir in 3 cups of heavy sour cream and 1 cup of rich sour milk, mixed and well chilled. Serve in chilled soup plates with hot toast.

BLUEBERRY CREAM SOUP (Chilled)   [166]
New England

Pick 3 cups of blueberries (huckleberries may be substituted if a tart soup is desired), and boil in 2 quarts of slightly salted water to which has been added 1 whole clove and a ¼-inch cinnamon stick, 1 cup of sugar, and 2 slices of lemon. Cook until soft. Dilute 1½ tablespoons of flour in 3 tablespoons of cold water. Add to the blueberry soup gradually, stirring while adding, and continue cooking for 10 minutes longer. Taste for seasoning, adding salt as needed, empty the mixture into a fine sieve, and rub through. Cool, then chill. When ready to serve, fold in 1 cup of cream, whipped with 2 drops of lemon extract. Serve at once in chilled cups, each topped with a few nice whole fresh blueberries.

BLUEBERRY SOUP (Chilled) [167]
Polish

Proceed as indicated for Chilled Blueberry Cream Soup (No. 166), substituting sour cream for fresh cream. In some parts of Poland, the fruit is simply drained and not sieved.

BLUEBERRY RED WINE SOUP (Chilled) [168]
French

A generous portion of blueberry and red wine soup with a topping of tiny baby meringues floating over the garnet-hued wine is hard to beat for a summer dinner overture.

Choose berries which are large and plump and have a good color. Beauty usually indicates quality as far as blueberries are concerned. Empty one quart of these beauties on a large flat platter or board. Look them over and discard any berries that are moldy or green. Place the berries in a colander, and let cold water run over them. Place 1 quart of good red wine on ice in the morning to be sure to have the wine thoroughly chilled. When ready to serve, place the well-drained washed berries in a glass bowl. Sprinkle with 1 tablespoon of sugar, and let stand for 15 minutes to draw a little of the juice out, then sprinkle over ¼ cup of good rum. Toss, and immediately pour on the chilled claret. Serve in colorful (Vosges method) individual earthenware bowls, each topped with 2 or 3 tiny snow-white meringues made as follows:

Tiny Meringues Vosges Method. Pour in a shallow pan 1 cup of milk and ¼ cup of rum. Bring to a boil, stirring well, then sweeten with 1 tablespoon of sugar. Beat 4 egg whites to a very stiff froth with a few grains of salt. Have ready a sugar spoon shaped like a scalloped shell; if not available, use an ordinary coffee spoon. Dip the spoon into a little cold milk, then fill it with some of the beaten egg whites, and with a knife, smooth it and give it the shape of a pigeon egg. Drop these, one at a time, in the boiling milk-rum mixture. Cook 1 short minute, turn each "egg" carefully with a fork, and cook for 1 minute longer. Immediately remove with a perforated spoon, and drain; then place in a little cold milk to cool. These meringues may be prepared in advance. Place these tiny cold "eggs" on top of the soup, and serve immediately.

Any kind of berries may be used to make this delicious and cooling soup.

BLUEBERRY SOUP (Hot)   [169]

Combine in a saucepan 1 cup of sugar, the thinly sliced rind of
¼ lemon, 3½ cups of blueberries, and 2 quarts of water. Bring the
mixture to a boil, and cook until the berries are soft. Blend 4 teaspoons of potato flour, or 1 tablespoon of cornstarch, with 2 tablespoons of cold water, a pinch of salt, and a little of the blueberry
liquid. Stir this mixture into the soup, and continue to cook until the
soup is slightly thickened. A dab of whipped cream may be added
on serving, or small macaroons may be floated on the surface.

MINTED BOYSENBERRY SOUP (Jellied)   [170]

The delicious boysenberries are developed by crossing the Cuthbert
raspberry, loganberry, and two varieties of blackberries. The result is
a large berry with an individual piquant flavor. These berries are
greatly used to make jelly and jam.

Pick and wash quickly 1 quart of boysenberries; drain well, and
crush lightly with a potato masher. Stir in ¼ cup of brown sugar,
then 1 quart of good sauterne wine. Gradually bring to a boil, season
with a very little salt, 1-inch stick of cinnamon, 3 whole cloves, and
4 fresh mint leaves, coarsely chopped. As soon as beads appear on the
surface of the soup, remove from the fire; fish out the cinnamon stick
and cloves, and stir in 1 tablespoon of granulated gelatin, which has
been soaked in ⅓ cup of cold water for 5 minutes. Pour the mixture
into a shallow wet pan, cool, then chill for 2½ to 3 hours in the
refrigerator. When ready to serve, cut the jellied soup into tiny cubes
with the point of a sharp knife, and serve these tiny cubes in chilled
bouillon cups, each topped with a fresh mint leaflet.

BUTTERMILK RAISIN SOUP (Hot)   [171]
  Danish

Bring to a boil 1½ quarts of buttermilk, stir in ½ tablespoon of
flour, or if available, rice flour, diluted in a little cold milk alternately
with ¼ to ⅓ cup of sugar, according to taste. Then add 6 tiny pieces
of lemon peel and 1 cup of seeded or seedless raisins, quickly washed
and plumped in boiling water and thoroughly drained. Serve in hot
soup plates or large individual bowls, each topped with a tuft of
salted whipped cream. Pass a tray of crisp *biscottes* alongside.

CHERRY ORANGE SOUP (Ice Cold)   [172]

Sweet cherries combined with orange juice and red wine make a marvelous sauce to serve with wild or domestic duck, but they are at their apogee, their zenith, in cold soup form.

Pit 1 quart of sour cherries. Add 1 quart of dry white wine; 1 quart of clear, absolutely clear, Beef Consommé (No. 114); 1 orange, thinly sliced, the slices cut in two crosswise; and from ½ to 1 cup of sugar, the amount depending on the taste and sweetness of the other ingredients. Season with a dash of salt and a dash of nutmeg, and serve ice cold with Melba Toast (No. 791).

CHERRY SOUP (Hot or Cold)   [173]
Oregon

Pit 1¾ pounds of ripe cherries, reserving the pits. In large kitchens, they have a cherry pitter, but at home, where a cherry pitter cannot be found, I suggest a buttonhook as the handiest tool for this tedious task. Place the fruit in a saucepan, pour over 1 quart (4 cups) of good red wine, and add 1-inch stick of cinnamon bark, 3 whole cloves, and a tiny pinch of salt. Cook until the cherries are tender, or for about 15 to 20 minutes, stirring occasionally. Pound the pits with ⅓ cup of fine bread crumbs, and moisten with 2 tablespoons of brandy. Rub this mixture through a fine wire sieve, then through a fine cloth, and add it to the cherries in the saucepan. Sweeten to taste with about ⅓ to ½ cup of sugar, depending on the sweetness of the fruit. Season with a very little salt and white pepper. If the soup is to be served hot, stir in 3 fresh egg yolks, well beaten, and cook for 2 or 3 minutes longer, stirring almost constantly from the bottom of the pan. If it is to be served cold, omit the egg yolks. Serve in soup plates with small brown bread and butter finger sandwiches.

CHERRY SOUP A LA MONTMORENCY (Hot) [174]

Another cherry delight that will warm the heart of any gourmet.
It is said that this soup used to be the favorite summer soup of la belle Mme. de Récamier when she retired to the Abbaye au Bois in the street of the same name. Chateaubriand, then living at 112 rue du Bac, was of all her most sincere and familiar friend. Along with him came artists, savants, writers, lords, and aristocrats attracted by the charm of this gracious woman. David d'Angers, Delacroix, Lamartine,

Victor Hugo, Sainte-Beuve, Humboldt, Ampère, the Dukes of Montmorency and of Noailles were also her companions at her sumptuous but simple supper, the following cherry soup being frequently served, being, it is said, a creation of Mme. de Récamier in honor of her special admirer, the Duke of Montmorency.

Wash quickly in several cold waters 1 quart of large oxheart cherries, then stem and pit carefully. Toss the cherries in ½ cup of butter melted over a low flame, and heat for 2 or 3 minutes. Then pour over them 1 quart (4 cups) of good red Bordeaux wine, previously sweetened with ¼ cup of sugar (more or less, according to the sweetness of the fruit), and flavored with an inch stick of cinnamon bark. Heat to the boiling point, that is, until beads form on the surface. Allow to simmer, well under the boiling point, for about 10 minutes. In the meantime, toast 6 slices of white bread on both sides. Place the fresh toast in hot individual soup plates, and pour over this the hot cherry mixture, liquid and all. You may, if you desire, add to the cherry mixture, while cooking, 1 or 2 slices of lemon for a little tartness.

CHERRY SOUP A LA VIENNOISE I (Cold) [175]
 Austrian

Stone 1½ pounds of ripe red cherries; stem 1 pound of red currants; place both fruits in a colander, and let cold water run very gently over them. Drain. Place the fruits in a saucepan with 3 slices of peeled and seeded lemon, 1-inch stick of cinnamon, and 2 whole cloves. Sprinkle ¼ to ⅓ cup of granulated sugar over the fruit. Let stand 30 minutes to allow the juice to flow a little, then toss; pour over 1 quart of rich Beef Consommé (No. 114), and bring to a boil. Lower the flame, and simmer 12 to 15 minutes. Then stir in very gently 2 cups of good red wine, and thicken with 1 tablespoon of flour, diluted in 1½ tablespoons of cold water, stirring constantly with a wooden spoon until the mixture just begins to thicken. Cool, then chill for at least 2 hours. Serve in chilled soup plates, each garnished with a tuft of whipped cream dusted with a little nutmeg. Serve with Croutons (No. 780) on the side.

CHERRY SOUP A LA VIENNOISE II (Cold) [176]

Proceed as indicated for Cherry Soup à la Viennoise I (No. 175) using 1 pound of cherries, ½ pound of stemmed red currants, and 1 pound of raspberries. Cook, and serve as indicated.

SOUR CHERRY SOUP I (Jellied) [177]
Austrian—with dumplings

Wash, then pit 1½ quarts of fresh sour cherries. Place in a large soup kettle, cover with 2 quarts of cold water, then add the grated rind of a small lemon, ¾ cup of granulated sugar, and a grating of nutmeg. Boil until the cherries are tender, then drop in small dumplings made as follows:

Crumble 6 slices of bread. Pour over the crumbs ½ cup of cherry liquid, cooled a little, then add 3 eggs, well beaten, and a grating of nutmeg. Drop by teaspoon into the boiling cherry liquid. Cover, and boil for 20 minutes. Now stir in 1 tablespoon of granulated gelatin, soaked in a little cold water for 5 minutes. Boil once, or until the gelatin is entirely dissolved. Pour the mixture into serving cups, having at least 2 dumplings in each cup. When cold, chill in the refrigerator until firm.

SOUR CHERRY SOUP II (Jellied) [178]
German

Heat 1 generous quart of tart cherries, freshly stewed, and when near the boiling point, add 2 generous teaspoons of arrowroot moistened with 2 tablespoons of cold water, stirring very rapidly to prevent lumping. Then add 1 tablespoon of granulated gelatin, which has been soaked in 2 tablespoons of cold water, and boil once. Now add the grated rind of a small lemon. Cool, and when mixture begins to set, stir in rapidly but gently 2 cups of the stewed tart cherries, thoroughly drained. Fill 6 serving cups, and chill in the refrigerator until firm. Delicious!

You may add a little sugar, if desired, when heating the cherry juice. By eliminating the gelatin, you have a cold soup which is also delicious. A cherry floating on each cup is very attractive.

SOUR CHERRY SOUP III (Jellied) [179]
English

Wash, then pit 1 generous quart of fresh sour cherries. Place in a soup kettle or saucepan, and add 2 quarts of cold water, 6 slices of orange, and 1 cup of granulated sugar with ½ teaspoon of nutmeg. Boil until the cherries are soft, about 15 minutes. Now add 1 tablespoon and 1 teaspoon of granulated gelatin, soaked for 5 minutes in a little cold water, and stir until the gelatin is thoroughly dissolved. Cool, and when cold, turn the mixture into a refrigerator tray, and chill until firm.

NEW ENGLAND CIDER SOUP (Hot) [180]

> *I'd rather love one blade of grass*
> *That grows on one New England hill,*
> *Than drain the whole world in the glass*
> *Of fortune, when the heart is still.*
> PHILIP HENRY SAVAGE

In New England, there is an imperishable quality about the home instinct which has continued through generations . . . a heritage from the early sturdy pioneers who braved untold hardships in a new land and hewed homes out of a wilderness; since then and now, New England is renowned for its fine clambakes, clam and fish chowders, and fine soups. Here is one example.

As slowly as possible, bring 3 pints of good cider to a boil, and carefully skim off the beads that will appear on the surface. Stir in ⅓ cup of granulated sugar, or even better, brown sugar. Set this aside, and keep it warm. Cut enough stale bread into small cubes to make 2 generous cups. Brown the cubes in 3 tablespoons of butter, and salt them to taste. Keep the cubes warm too. Beat 3 whole eggs as for making an omelet, and add to them, while beating, 2 tablespoons of sugar and 1½ cups of cream, to which have been added 2 tablespoons of flour, a few grains of allspice, and 3 tablespoons of good dark rum. When the whole is well blended, pour the cream-egg mixture slowly into the hot cider, beating steadily. When ready to serve, sprinkle the fried bread cubes over the soup, and serve immediately.

CLARET SOUP (Hot and Spicy) [181]
French

Bring to a boil 1 quart of rich Beef Consommé (No. 114) with a spice bag containing 6 whole cloves, 1 sprig of tarragon herb, and 1 teaspoon of cinnamon stick, broken into small pieces. Simmer for 20 minutes, discard the spice bag, and when ready to serve, put into a heated soup tureen, and pour 1 cup of good Madeira wine over the hot spicy consommé. Serve in hot bouillon cups.

COCONUT SOUP (Hot) [182]
Brazil

Natives of the Amazon Valley use fish tongues to grate or shred coconut and similar foods. The "grater" fish, pirarucu, has a bony tongue covered with rasplike teeth.

Heat to the boiling point 1 quart of good Chicken Bouillon (No. 25), and add 1 cup of grated fresh coconut and ½ cup of coconut milk. Bring again to a boil, lower the flame, and let simmer gently for 35 minutes, stirring occasionally. Rub the mixture through a fine-meshed sieve into a clean saucepan. Return to the fire, and taste for seasoning. Thicken with a little flour moistened with cold water to the consistency of thin cream, if needed. Continue simmering for 5 minutes longer, and serve in hot bouillon cups, each sprinkled with a little freshly grated fresh coconut, then dusted with a dash of nutmeg. Serve Croutons (No. 780) on the side.

DARK BEER BREAD SOUP (Hot) [183]
Hungarian—a very old Gypsy recipe

Break any kind of bread, such as graham, brown, or whole wheat bread, into small pieces in a bowl, just enough to make 2½ to 3 cups. Pour over 1 pint of dark beer, but not stout, and let soak for 15 minutes, then put through a food chopper. Turn this into a large saucepan. Add 1 quart of dark beer, a tiny dash of powdered ginger, 1 tablespoon of butter, salt to taste, and 1 teaspoon of picked caraway seeds. Mix well, then stir in ½ cup of honey, corn syrup, molasses, or maple syrup, and blend thoroughly. Place over a gentle flame, and gradually bring under the boiling point, but do not let boil, stirring frequently. Serve in hot soup plates, each plate topped with a freshly poached egg yolk. Serve immediately.

DRIED FRUIT SOUP I (Hot) [184]
Finnish

Keats in *The Eve of St. Agnes*, written only a little over a century ago, speaks of the heap of dried and candied fruits, quince, plum, gourd, and dates "from silken Samarcand to cedar'd Lebanon." Sumptuous, those delicacies of faraway lands, heaped in golden dishes and baskets of silver, "filling the chilly room with perfume light." Yet such treasure today is on every hand.

Until a few years ago, most of our dried fruits came from southern

Europe and Asia. The quality was uneven, prices comparatively high, and quantity irregular and always limited. The awakening consciousness of new hygienic standards made *ménagères* question or refuse some of the imported supplies as well as many of the bulk homegrown products. But gradually crops from seeds originally brought into the southern and southwestern part of this country by Spanish and other missionaries as well as immigrants became more abundant. Harvesting and drying methods at the orchards and vineyards were improved constantly under advice of private and government specialists. Today, we have the best dried fruits in the world.

Soak for 4 hours, after washing quickly in several changes of cold water, ½ pound of dried prunes together with ½ pound of dried apricots. Do not drain, but place over a gentle flame, after adding 3 medium-sized green apples, peeled and chopped, 1-inch stick of cinnamon, ½ cup of granulated sugar, and enough cold water to make 6 cups with the water from the soaking fruit. Salt to taste. Gradually bring to a boil. Cover, and let simmer very gently for 1 hour, or until fruit is soft, stirring occasionally. Discard the cinnamon stick, empty the mixture into a fine-meshed sieve, and rub through into a clean saucepan. Heat to the boiling point, then stir in 1 tablespoon of cornstarch, diluted with 2 tablespoons of cold water, stirring constantly until the mixture thickens and is smooth. Taste for seasoning. Serve in hot soup plates, each garnished with a thin slice of lemon, peeled and seeded. Should the mixture be too thick, add a little hot water to the desired consistency, which should be that of thin cream soup.

DRIED FRUIT SOUP II (Hot)   [185]
Swedish

Carefully wash and soak in cold water overnight ½ cup each of the following dried fruits: apples, apricots, prunes, and raisins. Next day cut the fruit into small pieces, and seed the raisins, if needed. Place the prepared fruit in a saucepan, and add cold water to generously cover. Stir in ½ cup of granulated sugar, 1-inch stick of cinnamon, 2 whole cloves, a few grains of salt, and if desired, 2 thin slices of lemon, unpeeled and seeded. Bring to a boil as slowly as possible, then stir in 2 tablespoons of sago, and simmer gently until the fruit is tender and the sago transparent. Then stir in 3 cups of boiling Chicken Bouillon (No. 25). Bring to a boil, taste for seasoning, and serve in hot soup plates.

DRIED FRUIT SOUP III (Hot)   [186]
Norwegian

In Norway, hospitality is simple but lavish. There is no time when a Norwegian does not seem able to eat. It is the result of the climate and the tremendous amount of exercise they take. They make almost a cult of physical culture. That is the kind of life that produces hearty appetites.

Wash, rinse, cover with water, and soak overnight ½ cup of seedless raisins, ½ cup of prunes, and ½ cup of dried apples. Next day, put the fruit, well drained, in a saucepan with 4 tablespoons of uncooked rice or the same amount of pearl tapioca, an inch stick of cinnamon, 2 whole cloves, ½ teaspoon of salt, and 1¼ quarts of cold water. Stir well, then pour in 1 tablespoon of vinegar. Cover the kettle or saucepan, and gradually bring to a boil; lower the flame, and simmer gently for about 1 hour, or until the fruit is tender. Then add 2 cups of fresh red plums, pitted after being washed quickly, saving all the juice possible, or lacking fresh plums, add a No. 2 can of red plums, juice and all. Cover, and continue cooking for 35 to 40 minutes over a low flame, stirring occasionally to prevent scorching. It will be wise to place an asbestos pad under the pan as a precaution. At that stage, the rice or tapioca should be soft. Taste for seasoning, discard the cinnamon stick, then stir in 1 tablespoon of lemon juice and ½ cup of granulated sugar (more or less, depending on the sweetness of the fruit). Serve hot in hot soup plates with a side dish of bread and butter finger sandwiches.

DRIED FRUIT SOUP IV (Hot)   [187]
Danish

Place in a bowl ½ pound of dried apricots, 1 cup of seedless raisins, 1 cup of large Malaga raisins, ½ can of crushed pineapple, and 1 lemon, sliced fine and cut lengthwise, and cover with cold water. Let soak overnight. Add 2 parts of cold water to 1 part of fruit, using the water in which the fruit has been soaked overnight. Add 1 cup of pearl tapioca and 1½ cups of sugar. Cook very slowly for 1 long hour, or until the fruit is soft and the tapioca is clear, stirring once in a while to prevent scorching. Now add a few grains of salt to taste, and serve in bouillon cups with a topping of salted whipped cream and an extra side dish of the same.

DRIED FRUIT SOUP V (Hot) [188]
Scandinavian

Soak 1 cup of prunes and ½ cup of seedless raisins in cold water to cover overnight. In the morning, chop the raisins coarsely, stone the prunes, and cut them into small pieces. Boil the fruit in the very same water in which they were soaked, for 25 long minutes; then add 1 cup of diced apples, a 1-inch cinnamon stick, ½ cup of sugar, 1 lemon, sliced thin, ½ cup of oatmeal, 2 cups of grape juice, a pinch of salt, and 1½ quarts of cold water. Cook slowly for 30 minutes, stirring occasionally. Serve as hot as possible in soup plates, each serving topped with a tablespoon of salted whipped cream. An extra side dish of same whipped cream may be passed around. Serve with bread and butter finger sandwiches made of rye bread.

DRIED FRUIT SAFFRON SOUP DINNER (Hot) [189]
Flemish

Cut 3 pounds of short ribs of beef in pieces, and put in a soup kettle with 3 quarts of cold water and 2 teaspoons of salt. Bring slowly to a boil, skim thoroughly, then add 2 pounds of marrow bones, cut in small pieces of about 2 inches. Add 8 peppercorns, freshly bruised; 1 extra large bay leaf; 1 large carrot, scraped, then cut into inch pieces; and 2 large leeks, carefully washed after being split in two lengthwise and tied together with kitchen thread. Cover, and simmer for 3 to 3½ hours. Meanwhile, soak together ⅔ cup of dried currants, ½ pound of prunes, and ⅔ cup of seedless raisins for 2 hours in hot water, previously washed in several changes of cold water. Remove the pits from the prunes, and add them to the soup with ¾ cup of soft bread crumbs and 1 teaspoon of brown sugar. Cover and simmer for 2 hours. Remove the meat and bones onto a hot platter. Taste the soup for seasoning, discard the bay leaf and leeks, stir in a tiny pinch of saffron, and serve in hot soup plates, the meat alongside, with a saucer of prepared horseradish.

> *For wine is like woman, and, like her, was given*
> *To man on earth as a foretaste of heaven.*
> MARSHALL P. WILDER

FRUIT SOUP BOUL' MICH (Hot) [190]
French

Soak ½ cup of pearl tapioca for at least 3 hours in 1½ quarts (6 cups) of dry white wine, to which has been added the juice of a large lemon, unstrained. Boil rapidly for 25 minutes. Season with salt and a grating of nutmeg, and stir well. Then add ½ cup of washed, drained seedless raisins (white ones, if available); ¼ pound of washed prunes, well drained and pitted; ½ cup of diced green apples, peeled and cored; another cup of dry white wine; and 3 whole cloves. Simmer for 30 to 35 minutes. Season to taste with a few grains of salt and cayenne, and serve in hot bouillon cups, each garnished with a slice of orange and a slice of lemon, both peeled and seeded.

FRUIT JUICE SOUP I (Jellied) [191]

Delicious and cooling, especially in the summer.

Soak 2¾ tablespoons of granulated gelatin in ¼ cup of cold water. Heat to the boiling point, mixed together, 1 cup of pineapple juice, 1 cup of cherry juice, 1 cup of orange juice, and ½ cup of lemon juice, adding 2 cups of water, 6 tablespoons of granulated sugar, a few grains of salt, and a grating of nutmeg. Bring to a boil, and stir in the soaked gelatin. Boil, stirring meanwhile, until the gelatin is thoroughly dissolved. Cool. When cold, chill in a refrigerator tray until firm. Serve in bouillon or punch cups, beating with a fork before filling the cups. Sprinkle a tiny bit of grated lemon rind on top of each cup, and serve with a side dish of saltine crackers. You may stir in, before the mixture congeals, 1 or 2 tablespoons of grated or chopped fine orange rind, if desired.

FRUIT JUICE SOUP II (Jellied) [192]

Soak 2 tablespoons of granulated gelatin in ¼ cup of grape juice, then dissolve over hot water with 1 cup of orange juice. When dissolved, add 1 generous cup of leftover mixed fruit juices from canned fruit and 1 cup of grape juice, less whatever has been used to soak the gelatin. Remove from the fire, and when lukewarm, add 2 oranges, peeled, sections separated and free from seeds and membrane, and 2 tablespoons of good kirsch (grenadine syrup may be substituted if desired), or brandy, or rum. Cool, and when cold, fill 6 chilled bouillon cups or glass cups. Chill thoroughly until firm in the refrigerator. Before serving, break the gelatin with a fork, and garnish the edges of each cup with 3 orange sections, free of seeds and membrane, and top the center with a maraschino cherry.

KOSHER MIXED FRUIT SOUP (Hot or Cold) [193]

The following Jewish fruit soup should be made of fresh fruits.

Chop finely the following fresh fruits: ½ cup of orange, free from seeds and skin; ½ cup of fresh pineapple, free from tough core; ½ cup of peeled, stoned fresh peaches; ½ cup of washed hulled fresh strawberries; and ½ cup of fresh rhubarb, carefully scraped. Place in a saucepan, then add 1 cup of granulated sugar (more or less, according to taste and sweetness of the fruit), ½ teaspoon of salt, an inch stick of cinnamon, 2 whole cloves, head removed, and 2 tablespoons of lemon juice, unstrained. Pour over 2 quarts of cold water. Bring slowly to a boil, lower the flame, and simmer gently for 15 minutes. Then stir in ¾ cup of heavy sour cream as soon as chilled if served cold. Serve with matzoth.

HUCKLEBERRIES   [194]

And what are huckleberries? These are the round, beady, almost black berries which are thicker skinned, more seedy, more acid than blueberries and are tart-flavored.

Proceed as indicated for recipes using blueberries (Nos. 166 to 169), but substituting huckleberries, remembering to add a little more sugar if a tart flavor is not desired.

LEMON AND HONEY SOUP (Chilled)   [195]

Blend 2 tablespoons of cornstarch with ⅓ cup of dry white wine. Gradually stir in 1 cup of hot Chicken Consommé (No. 25) absolutely clear from any particles of fat. Bring to a boil, stirring constantly, and let simmer gently over hot water for 10 minutes, stirring occasionally to prevent forming of lumps. Then gradually stir in 1 cup of heated strained lemon juice, which has been mixed thoroughly with ¼ cup of honey until well mixed. Season to taste with mixed salt and white pepper. Cool, then chill well before serving in chilled bouillon cups, each topped with drained and finely chopped red pimiento. Serve buttered crackers alongside.

MELON, STRAWBERRY, AND   [196]
WHITE WINE SOUP (Chilled)
French

Select 1 large or 2 medium-sized, not too ripe, pink-fleshed cantaloupe, or muskmelon as the native variety is often called; place it in the refrigerator overnight. Do likewise with one quart of nice juicy ripe strawberries. Next day, around noontime, pare the melon, cut it in quarters, discard the seeds and filaments carefully, and cube it small. Place the melon cubes in a large crystal bowl, then sprinkle over 1 rounded tablespoon of granulated sugar, mixed with 1 teaspoon of grated orange rind. Add the washed, picked, hulled, and halved strawberries. Pour over the whole 1 bottle of dry white wine, then 1 pony glass of Calvados or applejack, and toss gently but thoroughly. Return to the refrigerator, and chill for one long hour. Serve, after tossing again, in chilled soup plates, with a side dish of whipped cream and one of Melba Toast (No. 791).

ORANGE SOUP I (Jellied) [197]
Brazil—also called Orange Soup Frappé

Kirschwasser, better known in its abbreviated form as simply kirsch, is a German liqueur, also made in France and Switzerland, but the best variety is that made in the neighborhood of the Black Forest, where cherry trees grow in abundance. The name signifies "cherry water," and the liqueur, which has a wide popularity in Europe, has been highly praised in history and in song. The cherries are gathered as soon as they are full ripe, in midsummer, and deposited in a large trough. When the trough is one-half to three-quarters full, men, women, and even children place themselves around it and proceed to extract the juice by pressing the fruit with their hands and rubbing it against the sides of the trough. The juice runs into the fermenting vat through the interstices of the trough, while skins, stalks, and stones are left behind.

Soak 1½ tablespoons of granulated gelatin in ¼ cup of good red wine, then dissolve over hot water. Add 1 cup of strained orange juice, ¼ cup of strained lemon juice, and ¾ cup of strawberry juice. Blend thoroughly, then stir in as gently as possible 2 medium-sized oranges cut into sections and free from skin and seeds, 1 cup of sauterne, ¼ teaspoon of salt, a tiny pinch of nutmeg, and 2 tablespoons of kirsch. Cover the container, and chill in a large bowl of cracked ice, packing the ice over the top of the container, and sprinkling with 2 tablespoons of rock salt. When ready to serve, break up the jelly with a fork, and serve in chilled consommé cups. Stick a mint leaf on the edge and top each cup with a large ripe strawberry, stemmed and rolled in kirsch. Serve with a side tray of Toasted Coconut Fingers.

TOASTED COCONUT FINGERS [198]

Cut fresh white bread into slices ¾ inch thick. Trim off the crusts, and cut the bread into strips ½ inch wide. Have ready 1 cup of chopped or shredded and toasted coconut and ½ cup of thin cream (or evaporated milk) in separate shallow platters. Quickly dip each bread stick into the thin cream, turning it so that it is soaked on all sides, then roll it in the toasted coconut. Place the fingers on a greased baking sheet, and bake in a moderate oven (325°–350° F.) until the coconut is delicately browned, or for about 8 to 10 minutes. Serve cold or hot after draining on absorbent paper.

ORANGE SOUP II (Jellied)   [199]
California

Golden balls of nectar—that is a phrase used by a writer of poetical frame of mind to describe sweet oranges of the Orient. Just as deserving, perhaps more so, of such high praise are our own oranges which have been so highly cultivated in Florida, California, and Texas.

Romantic young men of eleventh-century Greece proposed marriage by sending their sweethearts two halves of a preserved orange. If a girl bound the halves together and returned them to the sender, the proposal was accepted.

Did you know that the amount of food value in a large orange is equivalent to that found in half a slice of bread . . . and that you should not squeeze oranges until ready to use? The longer the juice stands, the more flavor and vitamin C it loses. And don't chill the juice; instead, chill the oranges thoroughly beforehand.

Soak 2 tablespoons of granulated gelatin in 2 tablespoons of cold Chicken Bouillon (No. 25) for 5 minutes. Bring to a boil 2 cups of the chicken bouillon, then stir in the softened gelatin, stirring until thoroughly dissolved. Remove from the fire, and stir in 2 tablespoons of lime juice and ¾ cup of sugar (more or less, according to the sweetness of the fruit). Then stir in 3 cups of freshly made unstrained orange juice and ½ teaspoon of salt. Cool. When the mixture begins to congeal, beat with a rotary beater. Do this two or three times during the congealing process. Cut a slice from the top of 6 oranges, scoop out the pulp, discarding any seeds or filaments, and chop the pulp fine. Add the pulp to the gelatin mixture, then stir in 2 generous tablespoons of Cointreau or similar liqueur. Spread the mixture over one or more chilled shallow wet platters or trays. After chilling in the refrigerator for at least 2 hours, cut into small cubes, and pile in chilled glass cups, bouillon cups, or the scooped-out orange shells. Garnish each cup with a fresh mint leaf, and serve immediately.

ORANGE SOUP III (Jellied) [200]
Portuguese

Sprinkle 2 tablespoons of granulated gelatin over ½ cup of rich cold Beef Consommé (No. 114), and let stand for 5 minutes. Heat 2 cups of beef consommé to the boiling point, and stir in the gelatin mixture, stirring until the gelatin is thoroughly dissolved. Remove from the fire, and stir in 2½ cups of unstrained orange juice, mixed with 2 tablespoons of grenadine syrup, ½ cup of drained shredded pineapple, 2 tablespoons of lemon juice, and ½ teaspoon of salt. Cool, then when just beginning to congeal, beat briskly with a wire whisk, and repeat this beating twice. Chill in the refrigerator for at least 2 hours. When ready to serve, break the gelatin with a fork, and pile in orange baskets made as follows:

Orange Baskets. With a sharp-pointed knife, cut strips from a large orange shell, ½ to ¾ inch from the top, leaving one inch uncut on opposite sides of the shell. Raise the cut strips as loops, and tie them together with narrow ribbon. One large orange makes two beautiful baskets. Chill thoroughly before filling.

PASSION FRUIT SOUP (Hot) [201]
Brazil

The juice of the passion fruit is greatly used in South America for beverages and cold soups. The fruit has a tough hull, but the small black seeds are surrounded by aromatic yellow pulp which is a rainbow of flavors—a cross between the taste of the peach, the apricot, the pineapple, the guava, and the banana—and underlying the sweetness of these fruits is the slightly acid taste of the lime. A very little of the juice goes far in its penetrating flavor. It may be used in almost any cocktail, in cups, in punches, in fruit desserts, fruit cups, or soups. As a sauce over frozen desserts, it has no equal.

Early French, Spanish, and Italian explorers discovered the flower in South America, and declared it to be symbolic of the Passion of Christ, describing it as follows: It bears the emblems of the Cruci-fixion: the stamen represents the cross; corona, the crown of thorns; five anthers, the five wounds; three stigmas, the three nails which pierced hands and feet; the style represents the sponge which mois-tened His lips; petals represent the twelve disciples, less Thomas and Judas; the bracts represent the resurrection on the third day; and the stalk, the Gospel.

Related species, with edible fruits, are found in the south central part of the United States, and are known as maypops.

Heat 3 cups of rich Chicken Bouillon (No. 25) to the boiling point. Stir in 3 cups of sauterne wine, and taste for seasoning. When ready to serve in hot bouillon cups, stir in ½ to ¾ teaspoon of passion fruit juice. Serve with Melba Toast (No. 791).

PAPAYA SOUP (Chilled or Hot)   [202]
Brazil

Like the soybean, the papaya holds mystery for many—except South American gourmets. The papaya tree grows from a seed to full maturity within a year, and today is flourishing in southern Florida, Texas, and California, and in all Central American countries. A syrup, greatly used in beverages and desserts, hot, cold, and frozen, is made from the whole fruit, seed, pulp, and rind, and is bottled just as it is— no additions, no subtractions. The flesh resembles that of a muskmelon, but much more musky. The papaya melon varies in weight from a few ounces to twenty-five pounds and is greenish yellow with amber-colored flesh. The seeds are small, about the size of a small pea. They contain an enzyme called papain which is powerful in digesting proteins. An extract prepared from the plant and fruit is used in several remedies for dyspepsia. West Indian natives wrap pieces of meat in papaya leaves; after a few hours, the fiber is partially pre-digested, and the steaks, chops, cutlets, and roasts are made amazingly tender. Naturally enough, travelers have enlarged on the phenomenon, and there are sailors' yarns about boots that disappeared when they were left carelessly among the papaya leaves in camp. For a long time, it was commonly known as the pawpaw, and is sold under that name in some markets, but it is unrelated to the common American pawpaw that grows in many of the southern and central states.

Heat 5 cups of rich Beef Consommé (No. 114) to the boiling point with 2 tablespoons of lime juice. Remove from the fire; stir in a 4-ounce bottle of papaya syrup. Serve hot in heated bouillon cups, or chill in the refrigerator for at least 3 hours, and serve in chilled cups, topping each cup with a fresh mint leaf.

PEACH AND RED WINE SOUP (Chilled)   [203]
France

Perhaps the favorite summer soup in the South is peach and claret wine soup. Only two methods will prevent cut peaches from darkening as they stand. The first is to cover them with lemon juice, weighing them down with a plate if necessary to hold them under the surface of the juice covering; the other method is to cover them with sugar syrup and then tightly cover the container. Cut peaches oxidize, or tarnish, when they come in contact with the air, and the only control is to prevent the air from touching them directly. But in the following recipe, there is no danger of the cut peaches oxidizing because they are cut directly over the chilled claret.

Bring to a boil 3 cups of good Bordeaux or Burgundy red wine, but do not let boil; remove from the fire as soon as beads appear on the surface. Bring to a boil 3 cups of rich Beef Consommé (No. 114) with an inch stick of cinnamon and 2 whole cloves, and strain into the wine. Cool, then chill for at least 3 hours. When ready to serve, cut 1 pound or so of fresh peaches, scalded and skin removed, into the chilled mixture. Stir in 3 tablespoons of kirsch liqueur. Serve in soup plates with a side dish of Melba Toast (No. 791).

Note. The addition of ½ cup of blanched, shredded, toasted, then cooled, almonds improves the flavor.

PEACH, WILD STRAWBERRY, AND SAUTERNE WINE SOUP (Chilled)   [204]
France

A peach with a rosy blush may be a thing of beauty, but it is not always a ripe peach. A change in the background color from the original green to a yellowish color means that the peach is ripe.

Scald 6 nice yellowish ripe peaches, and peel, then slice in a dish, and sprinkle with 1 tablespoon of granulated sugar and 2 tablespoons of lime juice. Immediately pour over 3 cups of sauterne wine, and place in the refrigerator to chill. When ready to serve, stir in 2 cups of chilled Beef Consommé (No. 114), then 1 pint of strawberries, picked, carefully rinsed under gently running cold water, then hulled. Mix thoroughly, and serve in chilled bouillon cups with a side dish of Melba Toast (No. 791).

MINTED PINEAPPLE SOUP (Chilled)   [205]

Put through a food chopper 1 medium-sized, pared, cored, fresh pineapple, using the finest blade. Place the ground pineapple in a saucepan, add 5 cups of Chicken Bouillon (No. 25), well cleared of fat, ½ cup of unstrained lemon juice, and 6 sprigs of clean fresh mint. Bring to the boiling point, lower the flame, and let simmer very gently for 15 minutes. Empty the contents into a fine-meshed wire sieve, and rub through into a clean saucepan. Stir in 4 tablespoons of sugar and 2 tablespoons of flour, previously diluted in a little cold water. Season with a few grains of salt to taste, and bring to the boiling point, stirring almost constantly; lower the flame, and let simmer very gently for 15 minutes. Pour into a cold bowl, chill thoroughly in the refrigerator, and serve in chilled bouillon cups, each garnished with 1 teaspoon of finely chopped fresh red cherries. Pass a tray of crisp Melba Toast (No. 791) on the side.

PINEAPPLE SOUP I (Jellied)   [206]
Mexican

Do you know that it would take as long as ten years to raise a pineapple from seed? However, commercially grown pineapples are raised from slips that grow in clusters near the base, suckers in the axils of the leaves, or crowns, leafy tufts at the top of the fruit. But grown from these cuttings, it takes a year to twenty-two months for a pineapple to develop! The pineapple is not one fruit, but actually a cluster of many fruits. Each eye on the rind represents the product of one blossom.

Canned pineapple juice has two advantages over fresh, possibly three. The first, the fruit for juice purposes is picked when it is absolutely dead ripe and at the peak of perfection. The second, the fresh juice doesn't congeal with gelatin so well, and the resulting product doesn't stand up. Therefore, it is necessary to cook the fresh juice, whereas you do not have to cook the canned juice. The possible third advantage is that of convenience.

For the following recipe, use either juice, but cook or boil the fresh.

Sprinkle over 3 cups of fresh or canned pineapple juice 2½ tablespoons (7¼ teaspoons) of granulated gelatin, and let stand for 5 minutes. Bring to a rapid boil 3 cups of rich beef consommé, made by boiling down 6 cups of Beef Consommé (No. 114) to 3 cups over a bright flame with an inch' stick of cinnamon and 2 whole cloves. When the consommé is at the right strength, stir in the pineapple-gelatin mixture, stirring until the gelatin is dissolved. Remove from the fire, cool to lukewarm, and pour into 2 shallow pans. Cool thoroughly, then chill in the refrigerator for at least 3 hours. When ready to serve, cut the jelly mixture into small neat cubes, pile in chilled glass bouillon cups, and serve immediately, each topped with salted whipped cream tufts, colored with a drop or two of red vegetable coloring.

PINEAPPLE SOUP II (Jellied) [207]
Santo Domingo

The sugar-loaf pineapple from Santo Domingo, sweet as its name, is ready to eat while still green and doesn't improve as it turns golden. The smooth Cayenne, from near the famous Devil's Island, on the other hand, should be allowed to become almost entirely yellow to reach its finest flavor. These are round in shape with a large. crown.

In Santo Domingo, a favorite way to serve this fruit is as follows:

Proceed as indicated for No. 206, using Chicken Consommé (No. 25) instead of beef consommé reduced to double strength, adding the pineapple-gelatin mixture. When almost cooled to lukewarm, stir in ¼ cup of good rum, the best you can buy. Chill, and serve as directed for No. 206.

PINEAPPPLE SOUP MIX (Jellied) [208]
Havana

Sprinkle over ¾ cup of pineapple juice, fresh or canned, 2 tablespoons of granulated gelatin, and let stand for 5 long minutes. Meanwhile, put in a saucepan ¾ cup of cherry juice, fresh or canned; ¾ cup of orange juice, strained; ¼ cup of lemon juice, strained; 3 cups of rich Chicken Bouillon (No. 25); ½-inch stick of cinnamon; 2 whole cloves, heads removed; 2 or 3 grains of cayenne pepper; and ½ teaspoon of salt. Bring to a boil, stir in the pineapple-gelatin mixture, and stir until the gelatin is dissolved. Remove from the fire, and stir in 4 tablespoons of brandy. Strain through a fine cloth into a mixing bowl. Cool to lukewarm, then stir in ½ cup of well-drained shredded pineapple, fresh or canned. Cool. Chill for at least 3 hours, and when ready to serve, break the jelly with a fork, and pile in chilled glass bouillon cups. No garnishing is required. Serve immediately.

PLUM SOUP AGEN MANNER (Chilled) [209]

An old English cook book recommends medlars and bullaces as fruits to be eaten in October. A medlar resembles a small acid apple; a bullace is a species of plum.

All the colors of the spectrum are to be found among the more than two score varieties of plums in market during the season. Apparently some sort of plum is native to almost every country. In the sixteenth century in England, there was a law against street hawkers displaying plums in public places, as it was thought their penetrating aroma might tempt servants and apprentices to steal from their masters to buy the luscious fruit.

The California plum, also called prune, is of French origin and was introduced into California from France in 1856, from the town of Agen, famous for its delicious plums and prunes. The skin is smooth and heavy and does not separate readily from its pit. The French prune led the world until the method was improved on by California growers and packers. An average tree now gives from 150 to 300 pounds a year.

Heat 1 quart of Chicken Consommé (No. 25) to the boiling point. Wash, sponge, pit, and prick with a darning needle 1 pound of small plums, such as the beach plum or similar plum, including the yellowish greengage plum. Add to the chicken bouillon, to which has been added a 1-inch stick of cinnamon and 2 whole cloves, and simmer until the plums just begin to burst. Drain over a colander or coarse sieve, and when cold enough, slip off the skins, being careful not to bruise the plums, placing them as you go along in a dish containing 2 cups of dry white wine. Strain the chicken bouillon, in which the plums have been poached (poaching means simmering), into the plum and wine mixture. Cool, then chill. Taste for seasoning. When ready to serve, stir in 1 cup of salted sweet heavy cream. Serve in chilled plates, each sprinkled with finely chopped chives. Very cooling.

PLUM SOUP PARISIAN MANNER (Chilled)　　[210]

Wash thoroughly but quickly 1½ pounds of blue plums, or similar plums, in cold water. Drain, and cook in 5 cups of Chicken Broth (No. 25) until tender, but not mushy. Drain, reserving the broth, then carefully pit the fruit. Return the broth to the fire, and heat to the boiling point. Remove from the fire, and beat in 4 egg yolks, one at a time, beating well after each addition. Season to taste with salt, pepper, and a dash of freshly grated nutmeg; then stir in 2 tablespoons of lemon juice. Pour the broth over the plums. Cool, then chill. Serve in chilled soup plates, each sprinkled with a very little freshly chopped mint. A side dish of *biscottes* is the usual accompaniment.

PLUM SOUP BIARRITZ MANNER (Chilled)　　[211]

Wash 1½ pounds of fresh plums (any kind desired, including greengage plums) and cook in 5 cups of Chicken Bouillon (No. 25) until tender. Empty the saucepan into a fine sieve, and rub through into a clean saucepan. Then beat in, one at a time, 4 fresh egg yolks, beating well after each addition, and adding with the last yolk 2 tablespoons of kirsch liqueur. Season to taste with salt, a few grains each of cayenne and nutmeg, and 2 tablespoons of lemon juice. Sweeten to taste with sugar, the amount depending on the sweetness of the fruit, but about ¼ cup will be sufficient. Return to the fire, and cook over a gentle flame until the mixture just begins to thicken, stirring constantly from the bottom of the pan. Cool, and when cold, chill in the refrigerator. Serve in chilled glass cups, each topped with a tuft of salted whipped cream, sprinkled with a few grains of nutmeg and paprika.

PLUM SOUP CALIFORNIA MANNER [212]
(Chilled)

Bring to a rapid boil 2 cups of Chicken Bouillon (No. 25). When boiling to a roll, drop in gradually, rainlike, 2 tablespoons of sago, and cook until the sago is transparent. In another pan, boil 1½ pounds of fresh plums with 4 cups of chicken bouillon until tender, adding 3 slices of peeled and seeded lemon, ½ teaspoon of salt, and a 1-inch stick of cinnamon. Cook for 15 minutes, or until the fruit is tender. To the sago mixture, add 3 egg yolks, slightly beaten, and cook for 5 minutes, stirring constantly from the bottom of the pan, until the mixture just begins to thicken. Discard the cinnamon stick, and combine the sago mixture with the plum mixture; boil once or twice to blend well, then cool. When cold, chill for at least 2 hours, and serve in chilled soup plates, each sprinkled with a little paprika.

POTAGE LOUISIANE WITH ALMONDS [213]
(Chilled)
American

Blend 2 rounded tablespoons of butter with 2 tablespoons of curry powder (more or less, according to taste) in a saucepan over a low flame, stirring constantly until the mixture is a golden brown. Then add 6 cups of freshly made hot Chicken Bouillon (No. 25), or canned, a little at a time, stirring steadily from the bottom of the pan. Let this boil for 3 or 4 minutes, then strain through a fine cloth into another saucepan. Season with salt, cayenne pepper, 1 teaspoon of Worcestershire or Pique sauce, 2 teaspoons of onion juice, and 1 teaspoon of lemon juice. Let boil up once or twice, remove from the fire, and whisk in 4 egg yolks, well beaten with 3 tablespoons of chilled cream. Return to the fire, and cook slowly until the mixture begins to thicken, stirring constantly with a wooden spoon. Set aside, and allow to cool; then stir in ½ cup of blanched, toasted, and shredded almonds. Chill for at least 2 hours in the refrigerator before serving in chilled bouillon cups, each sprinkled with finely chopped chervil.

RAISIN AND CHEESE SOUP (Hot or Cold) [214]
Mexican

In the early eighteenth century, little strips of salted hard cheese were sold to New York City theater audiences who could eat them or throw them at the actors. They did both.

Place 6 slices of bread, trimmed of crusts, on the bottom of a large earthenware casserole. Cover the bread with thin slices of cheese (any desired kind). On each slice of cheese, arrange a thin slice of large onion, then sprinkle with 2 tablespoons of seedless raisins, previously plumped in boiling water and drained. Place another slice of bread over each, then repeat with onion and seedless raisins, and cover with a third slice of bread.

In another large saucepan, boil together 6 cups of good Beef Consommé (No. 114) with 1 teaspoon of aniseed and ¼ cup of sugar, stirring frequently. Pour this over the bread, cheese, onion, and raisin triple-decked sandwiches. Cover tightly, place over a gentle flame, and cook 8 to 10 minutes without disturbing. Serve hot or cold. Very nourishing.

RASPBERRY SOUR CREAM SOUP (Chilled) [215]
Russian

Pick, then wash thoroughly but carefully 1 quart of ripe raspberries. Drain, and place in a saucepan with 3 cups of Beef Consommé (No. 114), 3 cups of dry white wine, 2 tablespoons of unstrained lemon juice, 1-inch stick of cinnamon, 1 large bay leaf, and 1 small bay leaf. Gradually bring to a boil, lower the flame, and let simmer very gently for 12 to 15 minutes, stirring gently occasionally with a wooden spoon. Empty the contents of the pan into a fine-meshed sieve, and rub through into a clean saucepan. Return to the fire, bring to the boiling point, then stir in 3 egg yolks, slightly beaten with 2 tablespoons of brandy. Cook gently for 3 or 4 minutes, stirring constantly with a wooden spoon. Taste for seasoning, adding salt as needed. Cool, then chill in the refrigerator for 2 hours. Serve in chilled colorful earthenware bowls, each topped with a tablespoonful of whipped sour cream, topped with a fresh mint leaf. A side dish of dark pumpernickel bread and butter finger sandwiches is the usual accompaniment, and a pony glass of brandy is swallowed right after the soup has been eaten.

RASPBERRY WHITE WINE SOUP (Chilled)   [216]

Place 1 quart of picked and washed red raspberries in a saucepan. Pour over 1 cup of dry white wine, and cook until the fruit is tender. Empty the entire contents of the saucepan into a fine-meshed sieve, and rub through into a clean saucepan. Mix 1 tablespoon of flour in 2 tablespoons of cold water, and stir into the hot berry mixture. Return to the fire, bring to a boil, and let simmer gently for 10 minutes, stirring frequently, skimming the scum as it rises to the surface. Then season with ¼ teaspoon of salt, a few grains of white pepper, 3 tablespoons of sugar, and ½ cup of strained orange juice mixed with ½ cup of dry white wine. Bring near the boiling point, stirring constantly, then turn the mixture into a chilled container. When cold, chill in the refrigerator for at least 2 hours. Serve in chilled bouillon cups, each garnished with a fresh mint leaflet.

RED WINE SOUP A LA FRANÇAISE (Hot)   [217]

Combine 3 cups of light red wine with 1 pint (2 cups) of cold water, and stir in until dissolved ½ pound (1 cup) of granulated sugar. Add the grated rind of 1 medium-sized lemon and its juice, 3 whole cloves, and a 1-inch stick of cinnamon. Boil once, and allow to simmer gently for 10 long minutes. Strain through a fine sieve, then add 6 whole eggs, one at a time, while beating rapidly off the fire. Return to the fire, and allow the mixture to reach the boiling point, stirring almost constantly, but do not let it boil. Serve at once with either toast or saltine crackers.

RHUBARB SOUP I (Hot or Cold)   [218]
Danish

By the time the first meadow lark warbles his welcome to spring and the first prairie dog pokes his head from his den, the entire family is looking longingly toward the rhubarb patch, and waiting rather impatiently for the delicacies mother almost magically brings forth from it. Remember it as pieplant? Make your "sass" with a consideration for sugar. Serve as is and very cold, or combine with uncooked strawberries, plumped seedless raisins, fresh or canned pineapple. Rhubarb belongs on snow puddings and custards. It jellies right well —no sweetener needed, if you use a package of gelatin dessert for the base. Make rhubarb shortcake, rhubarb pie, but whatever you do, cook it in a little, very little water, and when nearly done, add the sugar. This makes all the difference. It's rhubarb flavor you want, isn't it? And this is the way to get it all. However, beware of the leaves, as they are not edible. They contain so much oxalic acid in soluble form that they are poisonous. The stalks have a much smaller amount of this acid, mostly in insoluble salts.

Rhubarb is a first cousin to the buckwheat family. Though it is generally regarded as a fruit, it is really a vegetable, brought into this country from the colder parts of Asia, probably Siberia, by way of Italy at the height of the Renaissance. By 1806, it was in general use in the United States.

Put 1 pound of rhubarb, cut into small pieces, in a saucepan with 1 quart of cold water and 1 teaspoon of salt, and cook until soft, stirring occasionally. Empty the contents of the pan into a fine sieve, and rub through into a clean saucepan. Return to the fire, and stir in 1 quart of boiling water and 3 tablespoons of sugar (more or less, according to taste), and bring to the boiling point. Then stir in 1½ tablespoons of cornstarch, diluted in a little cold water, stirring constantly until the mixture begins to thicken. Remove from the fire, and stir in a few drops of red vegetable coloring. Taste for seasoning, and serve hot or cold with Croutons (No. 780) or rusks.

RHUBARB SOUP II (Cold)   [219]
Norwegian

Cook 1 pound of scraped rhubarb, cut into inch pieces, in 1 quart of Beef Consommé (No. 114) over a gentle flame until tender, stirring frequently. Rub the mixture through a fine sieve into a clean saucepan, and beat in 3 fresh egg yolks alternately with 4 tablespoons of granulated sugar (more or less, according to taste), then stir in gradually 1 quart of boiling consommé, stirring briskly from the bottom of pan with a wooden spoon. Taste for seasoning. Boil once, remove from the fire, and stir in 1 scant teaspoon of vanilla extract. Cool, chill, and serve in chilled soup plates with freshly made buttered toast.

ROSE HIP ALMOND SOUP (Cold)   [220]

Clean enough rose hips, removing the blossom ends carefully, to make 2½ cups, and wash in several changes of cold water. Drain well, and cook in 2 quarts of water until the rose hips are tender. Empty the contents into a fine-meshed sieve, and rub through into a clean pan.

Stir in a generous ⅓ cup of sugar, ¾ teaspoon of salt, and a few grains of white pepper. Beat in 4 fresh egg yolks, one at a time, beating briskly after each addition. Bring to a boil, lower the flame, and simmer gently for 5 minutes, stirring almost constantly. Taste for seasoning. When ready to serve, stir in ¼ cup of Madeira wine and ½ cup of blanched, toasted, shredded almonds. Cool. Chill, and serve in chilled bouillon cups, each topped with a little salted whipped cream.

SPARKLING WHITE WINE AND   [221]
BLUEBERRY SOUP (Hot)
Strasbourg manner

Beat 3 fresh whole eggs with 4 tablespoons of brown sugar in a large saucepan until fluffy and light. Add 1 tablespoon of lemon juice and ½ teaspoon of grated lemon rind. Gradually beat in 1 teaspoon of flour, mixed with ⅓ teaspoon of salt and a dash of nutmeg. Gradually stir in 3 cups of cold Beef Consommé (No. 114) alternately with 3 cups of sparkling Moselle wine. Then beat with a rotary beater or wire whisk to blend thoroughly. Place the pan over a very, very low flame, and gradually bring to the boiling point, that is, until beads appear on the surface. Do not allow to boil. Strain through a fine cloth or fine-meshed sieve into a heated soup tureen containing some broken rusks, and serve at once in hot soup plates, each sprinkled with 3 tablespoons of fresh picked and washed blueberries.

SPARKLING WHITE WINE   [222]
FRUIT SOUP (Hot or Cold)
Touraine manner

Pick over, wash, and drain thoroughly 1 cup of fresh red currants and 1½ cups of raspberries. Rub through a fine-meshed sieve into a saucepan, adding, while mashing, 2 tablespoons of sugar. Place the pan over a low flame, and heat to the boiling point to extract the juice thoroughly. Again strain through a fine sieve into a clean saucepan. Add 2 tablespoons of unstrained lemon juice and the grated rind of 1 lemon, and stir in 3 cups of rich Beef Consommé (No. 114) and 3 cups of sparkling white wine. (Rosé sparkling wine of Anjou, if available, may be used.) Bring to the boiling point, but do not let boil. Remove from the fire, and stir in 3 fresh egg yolks, slightly beaten with a generous pinch of salt to taste. Heat well, but do not let boil, stirring constantly from the bottom of the pan with a wooden spoon. Serve hot in heated soup plates, each sprinkled with a fresh grating of nutmeg. Or cool, then chill, and serve in chilled bouillon cups, each topped with a spoonful of salted whipped cream.

> *Waste not your Hour, nor in the vain pursuit*
> *Of This and That endeavor and dispute;*
> *Better be joyful with the fruitful Grape*
> *Than sadden after none, or bitter, Fruit.*
>
>   OMAR KHAYYAM

WATERMELON SOUP A LA CHINOISE (Hot)   [223]

Two centuries ago Yuan Mei, popular writer of modern Chinese literature, said: "There is a difference between dining and eating. Dining is an art. When you eat to get most out of your meal, to please the palate, just as well as to satiate the appetite, that, my friend, is dining."

Cut the top from half of a small watermelon. Remove all the seeds, and scallop the rim. Heat 6 cups of rich Chicken Stock (No. 25). Add ½ cup of canned bamboo shoots, ½ cup of canned Chinese mushrooms, and 2 tablespoons of chopped, cold boiled lean ham. Season to taste with salt and white pepper and 1 teaspoon of white Chinese powder called Gourmet Powder. Add 1 cup of cooked, cubed small chicken meat. When ready to serve, stir in 3 cups of melon cubes. Pour into the melon shell, and serve at once, sprinkled with blanched, shredded, toasted almonds over each serving.

In winter, you may use winter melon, such as Persian or Santa Claus melon.

WHITE WINE BISQUE BOURGUIGNONNE (Hot)   [224]

It is easier by far to reach for the wine bottle than the duck press. Better magic, too. For wine gives an elusive subtle flavor to even the simplest dishes. What you taste is not the flavor of wine. It's an unsuspected goodness that wine discovers for you in the food itself. Wine in cooking acts as a flavoring only, the alcohol evaporates as heat is applied. Remember, too, that the delicate flavor of any wine is reduced by boiling. Dry wines, once opened to contact with air, become perishable, like milk, and should be used within a week—sooner if the weather is warm. Sweet wines are not perishable.

Stem, wash in cold water quickly, and drain enough white grapes to make 3 cups. Place in a saucepan, cover with cold water, and stir in ⅓ to ½ cup of sugar (according to the sweetness of the grapes). Add a 1-inch stick of cinnamon and 2 cloves, and gradually bring to a boil. Lower the flame, and let simmer gently for 20 to 25 minutes. Empty the contents of the pan into a fine-meshed sieve, and rub through into a clean saucepan. Keep hot over hot water.

Cook 2 tablespoons of quick-cooking tapioca in 1 cup of water until clear and transparent; then beat in, one at a time, 3 fresh egg yolks, beating briskly after each addition, adding with the last yolk ½ teaspoon of salt. Combine the tapioca mixture with the grape mixture or purée and beat with a rotary beater to blend thoroughly.

Heat 1 quart (4 cups) of white Chablis wine to the boiling point, that is, until beads appear on the surface, but do not allow the wine to boil. Then stir the wine into the grape-tapioca mixture, beating well. Serve in hot soup plates, each garnished with a dozen seeded and skinned fresh grapes. Serve with rye bread and butter finger sandwiches.

WHITE WINE SOUP GERMAN [225]
METHOD (Hot)
Mosel Wein Suppe

In Germany, this soup is often served in winter at evening parties, balls, and the like. A fine stimulating and nourishing soup.

Bring to a boil 1 bottle of Moselle wine. Dilute 1 tablespoon of cornstarch in a wineglass of extra Moselle wine, and pour it into the boiling Moselle wine, stirring rapidly to prevent lumping, and alternately with 4 tablespoons of granulated sugar (more if desired), the grated rind of 1 large lemon, and a 1-inch stick of cinnamon. Stir. Cover, remove from the fire, and let infuse for 5 long minutes. Strain through a fine sieve or cloth. When ready to serve, beat in, one at a time, 4 egg yolks, beating rapidly after each addition. Serve either in glass cups or bouillon cups with thin slices of well-buttered rye bread.

Chapter Five

CANNED SOUP
COMBINATIONS

CONSOMMES, CREAM SOUPS, BROTHS, AND POTAGES

*Domestic peace can never be
preserved in family jars.*

IT HAS BEEN SAID THAT THE INVENTION OF CANNING FOR FOOD is the greatest invention of modern times, perhaps equaled in its importance for mankind only by the discovery of disease germs by Pasteur.

By virtue of widespread canning facilities all over the world, it now is possible for everyone to have a more varied diet than was available to human beings of previous centuries. Not only is appetite served by this, but the average supply of vitamins, necessary mineral salts, and other important food elements required by the individual is greatly increased.

Study of human reactions to tin have been exhaustively investigated by the government laboratories. These studies show that no toxic action need be feared from the use of tin containers. For that reason, it has been widely stated that foodstuffs need not be removed from the can, after opening, because of any danger from tin poisoning. It must be understood, on the other hand, that products like milk or canned fruits, vegetables, soups, and meats are perishable substances. Once the can is open, they are subject to contamination from bacteria in the air just like any fresh product. For that reason, it is certainly not desirable for perishable foods to be allowed to stand in open containers any appreciable length of time unless they are kept very cold. Furthermore, though cold delays the growth of bacteria, it does not entirely prevent their growth. Hence foods cannot be kept in refrigerators in open containers indefinitely.

Actually, what we call a tin can isn't a tin can at all! It is a steel can, coated inside and out with tin. In other words, the tin plate used by the manufacturer is more than 98 per cent steel and less than 2 per cent tin. This type of can has proved to be the ideal container for foods because it meets all the requirements of both canner and consumer. It does not affect the wholesomeness of its contents. It can be shaped to suit products of various sizes. It can be sealed airtight. It conducts heat rapidly, so that the food it holds may be heated and cooled quickly. It is light in weight, yet strong enough to withstand rough handling. It provides fine foods and a varied diet regardless of season.

Canned soup is good not only in itself as soup, but also as an ingredient in other dishes; this is especially so with condensed soups. You can add them to meat dishes for flavor and extra nourishment. Also, many of the condensed soups, notably tomato and cream of mushroom, make good sauces, heated just as they come from the can.

The labels in nearly all instances state the can size and the over-all weight of the can. Seldom do they give the number of cups in the can. But this short table should help you to determine the size best suited for individual needs.

Can	Cups	Can	Cups
No. 1	1¼	No. 2	2½
No. 300	1¾	No. 2½	3½
No. 1, tall	2	No. 5	5¾ to 6
No. 303	2	No. 10	13

Ask your grocer the size of can, and you can then easily compute the size for your family needs.

Soup Combinations. Can A, plus can B, and even can C equals something professional in soups. Simple mathematics works magic in flavorful combinations. Have you ever tried teaming a couple of cans of soup to see what comes of it? This is often done in first-class restaurants. Because of all the canned soups available in every town in the land, it is very easy for even a busy cook to fix a bowl of delicious soup in a hurry. Some cooks think so highly of many canned soups that they do very little to fancy them up. However, there are some little tricks that make a soup taste as if the cook has spent all afternoon over it. A bit of sherry or claret can be added to a can of meat stock and to some vegetable soups. A dab of smooth sour cream floating in the center of a plate of tomato soup is an addition that has been found successful. A sprinkling of grated cheese (any kind), or some mixed herbs, makes a good canned soup taste like an inspired concoction, be it called soup or potage.

All the following canned soup combinations serve six persons.

AUNT JULIA'S SOUP [227]

Combine 2 cans of cream of celery soup with 1 can of chicken noodle soup. Heat thoroughly, and serve without any garnishing. Taste for seasoning.

BOULA SOUPE [228]

Combine 2 cans of pea soup and 1 can of green turtle soup. Bring to a boil. Taste for seasoning, forcing on black pepper. Stir in 2 generous tablespoons of good sherry wine, and fill 6 individual pottery bowls. Place the bowls on a cooky sheet. Top each bowl with 1 tablespoon of salted whipped cream, sprinkle with grated cheese, and brown slightly under the flame of the broiling oven. Serve at once.

BROTH A L'ECOSSAISE [229]

Heat 3 cans of Scotch broth to the boiling point. Stir in, off the fire, ¼ cup of sherry wine. Serve in hot cups.

CLAM BOUILLON RIVOLI [230]

Heat 3 cans of clam bouillon to the boiling point. Taste for seasoning. Serve in cups, each garnished with 2 teaspoons of cooked or canned tomato pulp bits, 1 tiny clam dumpling, and 1 teaspoon of chopped cooked spaghetti. Serve with a side dish of grated cheese.

CONSOMME ALBERT [231]

Heat 3 cans of chicken consommé or bouillon to the boiling point. Serve in cups, each garnished with 4 or 5 pieces of cooked white meat of chicken, cut julienne fashion. Serve immediately.

CONSOMME ALEXANDRE [232]

Heat 3 cans of chicken consommé or bouillon to the boiling point. Serve in cups, each garnished with ½ teaspoon of cooked minute tapioca, a tiny chicken dumpling, and a few shreds of green lettuce.

CONSOMME BARILLET [233]

Heat 3 cans of clear chicken bouillon or consommé to the boiling point. Serve in cups, each garnished with 1 teaspoon of cooked rice and 4 tiny cubes of cooked chicken.

CONSOMME BOUQUETIERE [234]

Heat 3 cans of clear beef bouillon or consommé to the boiling point. Remove from the fire. Stir in ½ cup of cooked assorted fresh vegetables, cut in tiny fancy shapes.

CONSOMME BRAGANCE [235]

Heat 3 cans of clear beef bouillon or consommé to the boiling point. Serve in cups, each garnished with 1 teaspoon of cooked rice and 2 tiny cubes of Pea Custard Garnish (No. 699).

CONSOMME CARLSBAD   [236]

Heat 3 cans of beef bouillon or beef consommé to the boiling point.
Serve in hot soup plates, each garnished with 3 or 4 pieces of cooked
tongue, cut julienne fashion, and 1 tablespoon of very finely shredded,
blanched green cabbage. Dust with finely chopped parsley or chervil.

CONSOMME CELESTINE   [237]

Heat 3 cans of clear beef bouillon to the boiling point. Serve in hot
plates, each garnished with a small round of ordinary pancake, cut
the size of a silver dollar.

CONSOMME CHARMILLE   [238]

Combine 2 cans of clear beef bouillon or beef consommé with 1 can
of oxtail soup. Heat to the boiling point. Serve in hot plates, each
sprinkled with finely chopped parsley.

CONSOMME CHIHUAHUA   [239]

Heat 3 cans of beef bouillon or beef consommé to the boiling point.
Remove from the fire, and stir in 2 tablespoons each of finely shredded
blanched lettuce, spinach or sorrel, and cabbage. Serve in hot plates,
each sprinkled with paprika.

CONSOMME CINCINNATI   [240]

Heat 3 cans of clear beef bouillon or consommé to the boiling point.
Remove from the fire, and stir in 2 tablespoons each of very tiny balls
of cooked potatoes, carrots, white turnips, and small lima beans. Serve
in plates, each sprinkled with finely chopped parsley or chervil.

CONSOMME CZARINA   [241]

Heat 3 cans of chicken bouillon to the boiling point. Serve in hot
cups, each garnished with a pinch of fresh fennel leaves and ½ teaspoon of Beluga caviar.

CONSOMME DEMIDOFF   [242]

Heat 3 cans of chicken bouillon to the boiling point. Serve in hot
cups, each cup garnished with 1 tiny chicken dumpling, 1 scant tea-

spoon of cooked minute tapioca, ½ teaspoon of small cooked or canned peas, and 3 or 4 shreds of black truffle, and dust each cup with finely chopped parsley or chervil.

CONSOMME DIVA [243]

Heat 3 cans of chicken bouillon to the boiling point. Serve in hot plates, each garnished with 1 tiny chicken dumpling, 1 teaspoon of cooked or canned shrimps, coarsely chopped, and 1 teaspoon of cooked rice. Dust each plate with finely chopped parsley or chervil.

CONSOMME DORIS [244]

Heat 3 cans of chicken bouillon to the boiling point. Stir in 12 (2 for each serving) tiny balls of blanched cucumber. Serve in cups, each dusted with finely chopped parsley or chervil.

CONSOMME DOUGLAS [245]

Heat 3 cans of beef bouillon or consommé to the boiling point. Stir in ½ cup of cooked celery stalk, cut in julienne fashion (matchlike), ½ cup of cooked or canned asparagus tips (buds only), and 12 small cubes of cooked sweetbreads (2 for each serving). Serve in plates, each dusted with finely chopped parsley or chervil.

CONSOMME DUTEIL [246]

Heat 3 cans of beef bouillon or consommé to the boiling point. Serve in cups, each garnished with 2 tiny Spinach Dumplings (No. 701) and dusted with finely chopped parsley or chervil.

CONSOMME EMMANUEL [247]

Heat 3 cans of beef bouillon or beef consommé to the boiling point. Serve in hot plates, each garnished with 4 or 5 matchlike-cut cooked chicken, 1 tablespoon of chopped cooked spaghetti, and sprinkled with grated cheese (any kind). Pass a side dish of Tomato Custard Garnish (No. 702), 2 cubes for each serving.

CONSOMME EPICURE [248]

Heat 3 cans of clear chicken bouillon to the boiling point. Serve in hot soup plates, each garnished with 2 tiny cubes of chicken custard, 6 matchlike-cut cooked celery stalks, 6 matchlike-cut cooked white

meat of chicken, and 4 very tiny truffle pearls, and in the center place
a freshly poached small egg.

CONSOMME FLORENCE   [249]

Bring to a boil 4 cans of beef bouillon or consommé. Add ⅓ cup of
uncooked broken vermicelli, and cook 12 minutes, or till the vermicelli is tender. Serve in hot cups, each garnished with 2 bits of raw
tomato pulp, sprinkled with grated cheese mixed with finely chopped
parsley.

CONSOMME FRANC-COMTOIS   [250]

Heat 3 cans of beef bouillon or consommé to the boiling point. Stir
in ¼ cup each of blanched finely shredded sorrel or spinach, lettuce,
and chopped cooked vermicelli, and 1 teaspoon each of finely chopped
parsley and chervil. Serve in hot plates.

CONSOMME GIRONDIN   [251]

Heat 3 cans of clear beef bouillon or consommé to the boiling point.
Stir in 3 tablespoons of tomato paste, and boil once. Serve in cups,
each garnished with 6 tiny cubes of cooked lean ham.

CONSOMME IMPERIAL   [252]

Into a saucepan empty 6 cans of beef bouillon or consommé, and
reduce to half its original volume over a bright flame. Strain, and
serve in hot soup plates, each garnished with 1 tiny Chicken Dumpling (No. 716), 2 tiny cubes of Chicken Custard Garnish (No. 686),
1 teaspoon of thinly sliced cooked mushrooms (cooked in butter and
well drained), and ¼ teaspoon of finely chopped black truffle.

CONSOMME A L'INDIENNE   [253]

Heat 3 cans of chicken bouillon to the boiling point. Stir in 2 teaspoons of curry powder, diluted in a little cold bouillon, and ¾ cup
of coconut milk, and bring to a boil. Serve in hot cups, each garnished
with 2 tiny cubes of coconut custard and 1½ teaspoons of cooked rice.

CONSOMME JACQUELINE   [254]

Bring to a rapid boil 5 cans of clear chicken bouillon, and let boil
till reduced to half its original volume. Serve in hot cups, each garnished with 1 asparagus tip (bud only), 2 tiny cubes of Pea Custard

Garnish (No. 699), 3 tiny balls (pearl-like) of cooked carrot, and 1 teaspoon of cooked rice, and dust each cup with finely chopped parsley or chervil.

CONSOMME JUANITA [255]

Heat 3 cans of chicken bouillon to the boiling point, and stir in ⅓ cup of cooked vermicelli. Heat well, and serve in cups, each garnished with 2 tiny cubes of Tomato Custard Garnish (No. 702), and dust each cup with finely chopped parsley or chervil.

CONSOMME JULIENNE [256]

Heat 4 cans of beef bouillon or consommé to the boiling point, and let boil steadily for 3 minutes to reduce it a little and give it strength. Serve in hot plates, each garnished with the following vegetables, cut julienne fashion, that is, matchlike, and cooked in chicken or beef bouillon (canned or freshly made): ½ tablespoon each of carrots, using only the red part, white turnips, green pepper, leeks (white part only), mushroom (using large caps), celery, shredded green cabbage, and shredded lettuce. The vegetables should be cooked separately and well drained and hot. Dust each plate with finely chopped parsley or chervil.

CONSOMME LAGUIPIERE [257]

Heat to the boiling point 3 cans of clear chicken bouillon; serve in cups, each garnished with 2 tiny cubes of Game Custard Garnish (No. 689) and one freshly poached pigeon egg.

CONSOMME LARONCIERE [258]

Heat 3 cans of clear beef bouillon or consommé to the boiling point. Serve in hot plates, each garnished with 1 teaspoon of cooked or canned small green peas, 2 tiny cubes of Lobster Custard (No. 833) and 2 cooked or canned asparagus tips (buds only), and dust each plate with finely chopped chervil or parsley.

CONSOMME LEBERKNOEDEL [259]
Alsatian method

Heat 3 cans of clear chicken bouillon to the boiling point. Serve in hot cups, each garnished with 2 tiny Liver Dumplings (No. 742), and ⅓ teaspoon each of finely chopped chives and chervil or parsley.

CONSOMME DE LESSEPS [260]

Heat 3 cans of beef bouillon or beef consommé to the boiling point. Serve in cups, each garnished with 2 tiny cubes of cooked Calf's Brain Custard Garnish (No. 681) and a few shreds of blanched sorrel or spinach, and dusted with finely chopped chervil or parsley.

CONSOMME MARIE STUART [261]

Heat 4 cans of beef bouillon or consommé to the boiling point; add 3 tablespoons each of tiny carrot and turnip balls, the size of a very small marble, and cook 10 to 12 minutes, or until tender. Serve in hot plates, each garnished with 2 tiny Burger Dumplings (No. 716), and dust with finely chopped parsley or chervil.

CONSOMME MESSONIER [262]

Heat 3 cans of beef bouillon or consommé to the boiling point. Serve in plates, each garnished with 4 small cubes of cooked or canned artichoke bottoms, 3 small pieces of cooked or canned tomato pulp, and 1 teaspoon of cooked or canned peas. Dust each plate with finely chopped chervil or parsley.

CONSOMME MIREILLE [263]

Heat 3 cans of chicken bouillon to the boiling point. Serve in hot plates, each garnished with 2 tiny Chicken Dumplings (No. 716), and 1 teaspoon of cooked rice mixed with a little saffron, and dust each plate with finely chopped parsley or chervil.

CONSOMME MOGADOR [264]

Bring 4 cans of chicken bouillon to a boil, and let boil until the bouillon is reduced to 3 cans. Serve in hot cups, each garnished with 2 tiny Pâté de Foie Gras Dumplings (No. 748), 1 teaspoon of cooked beef tongue, cut julienne fashion, and a tiny pinch of finely chopped black truffle. Dust each cup with finely chopped chervil or parsley.

CONSOMME MONTE ALBA [265]

Heat 3 cans of beef bouillon or consommé to the boiling point. Serve in hot soup plates, each garnished with 1 tablespoon each of blanched and shredded nettles, lettuce (green part only), spinach, and green cabbage. Dust each plate with grated Parmesan cheese, and serve a side dish of the same cheese.

CONSOMME MONTE IDALGO [266]

Heat 5 cans of beef bouillon or consommé to the boiling point. Let boil until reduced to 3 cans. Remove from the fire, and stir in ¼ cup of Madeira wine. Serve in hot cups, each garnished with 1 small pitted black olive, sliced, and 1 tiny cucumber ball, olive shaped and blanched in a little beef bouillon. Dust each cup with finely chopped chives.

CONSOMME NEVERS [267]

Heat 3 cans of clear beef bouillon to the boiling point. Serve in hot soup plates, each garnished with 2 small cooked Brussels sprouts, 2 very small (marble size) potato balls, and 1 tiny slice, rind removed, of cervelat sausage. Serve with a side dish of toasted bread sticks, cut the size of the small finger.

CONSOMME NIÇOIS [268]

Heat 5 cans of beef bouillon to the boiling point, and let boil over a bright flame until reduced to 3 cans. Serve in hot soup plates, each garnished with 2 small cubes of Tomato Custard (No. 702) and 6 very small cooked string beans, cut lozenge fashion. Dust the plates with finely chopped chervil or parsley.

CONSOMME A LA NINON [269]

Heat 4 cans of chicken bouillon to the boiling point. Serve in hot soup plates, each garnished with 2 tiny Chicken Dumplings (No. 716), 1 teaspoon each of cooked carrot and turnip, cut in tiny stars, and 4 tiny pearls of black truffle. Dust each plate with finely chopped chervil or parsley.

CONSOMME A LA NOAILLES [270]

Heat 6 cans of clear beef bouillon to the boiling point, and let boil over a bright flame until reduced to half the original volume. Serve in hot soup plates, each garnished with 2 very small cubes of Artichoke Bottom Custard (No. 678), 1 tiny Veal Ball (No. 675), 1 tiny Chicken Dumpling (No. 716), and 6 matchlike pieces of cooked tongue about 1½ inches in length. Dust each plate with finely chopped chervil or parsley mixed with equal parts of finely chopped chives.

CONSOMME D'ORSAY   [271]

Heat 3 cans of clear chicken bouillon to the boiling point. Serve in very hot plates, each garnished with a freshly poached small egg, 4 cooked or canned asparagus tips (buds only), and 2 very tiny Crawfish Dumplings (No. 723). Dust each plate with finely chopped chervil or parsley.

CONSOMME PEPITA   [272]

Heat 6 cans of clear chicken bouillon, and let reduce to half its original volume over a bright flame. Serve in hot cups, each garnished with 3 tiny cubes of Almond Custard (No. 677). Do not use parsley or chervil on this rich consommé.

CONSOMME POLIGNAC   [273]

Heat 6 cans of chicken bouillon, and allow to reduce to half its original volume over a bright flame. Serve in hot cups, each garnished with 2 tiny Crawfish Dumplings (No. 723) and 3 cooked or canned mushroom buttons, cooked in butter and thoroughly drained. Dust each cup with finely chopped chervil, parsley, and chives in equal parts.

CONSOMME PRINCESSE   [274]

Heat 6 cans of clear chicken bouillon, and allow to reduce to half its original volume over a bright flame. Serve in hot soup plates, each garnished with 2 small cubes of Asparagus Custard (No. 679), 1 teaspoon of cooked or canned small peas, ½ teaspoon of cooked barley, and 2 asparagus tips (buds only). Dust each plate with finely chopped chervil or parsley.

CONSOMME REJANE   [275]

Heat 4 cans of clear chicken bouillon, and allow to reduce to ¾ its original volume over a bright flame. Serve in hot cups, each garnished with 2 tiny cubes of Almond Custard (No. 677) and stringed eggs. Dust each cup with finely chopped chervil or parsley.

CONSOMME REMUSAT [276]

Heat 3 cans of clear beef bouillon or consommé to the boiling point. Serve in hot soup plates, each garnished with 2 tiny cubes of Tomato Custard (No. 702), Carrot Custard (No. 682), and Spinach Custard (No. 701). Dust all around the custard cubes with finely chopped chervil or parsley.

CONSOMME RICHELIEU [277]

Heat 6 cans of beef consommé, and let reduce to half its original volume over a bright flame. Serve in hot soup plates, each garnished with 2 tiny Chicken Dumplings (No. 716), filled with the size of a pea of meat glaze or meat extract (commercial), and 1 tablespoon each of blanched shredded lettuce and carrot (red part only), cooked in beef bouillon and cut julienne fashion. Dust the plate with finely chopped chervil or parsley.

CONSOMME ROSSINI [278]

Heat 5 cans of clear beef bouillon or consommé, and allow it to reduce to 3 cans over a bright flame. Serve in cups, each garnished with 2 tiny Profiterolles (No. 799), split and filled with pâté de foie gras purée and 4 or 5 matchlike sticks of black truffle about an inch in length. No parsley or chervil is used in this rich consommé.

CONSOMME RUBENS [279]

Heat 3 cans of beef bouillon or consommé to the boiling point. Serve in hot soup plates, each garnished with 1 teaspoon of cooked minute tapioca, 1 very small fresh egg, poached in beef bouillon and dusted with paprika, and 1 tablespoon of cooked hop shoots. Serve immediately.

CONSOMME SAINT-BENOIT [280]

Heat 5 cans of clear beef consommé to the boiling point, and let it reduce to 3 cans over a bright flame. Serve in hot soup plates, each garnished with 2 Profiterolles (No. 799), split and filled with artichoke bottom purée, 1 tablespoon of blanched shredded green cabbage, and 4 tiny cubes of cooked sweetbreads. Dust each plate with finely chopped chives.

CONSOMME SAINT-SAENS [281]

Heat 4 cans of clear chicken bouillon to the boiling point, and let it reduce to 3 cans over a bright flame. Serve in hot soup plates, each garnished with 1 teaspoon of cooked minute tapioca, 1 teaspoon of cooked barley, 2 tiny cooked potato balls, the size of a small marble, and 2 hot raviolis, cooked in chicken bouillon. Sprinkle each plate with grated Parmesan cheese, and serve a dish of grated Parmesan cheese on the side.

CONSOMME SAVARIN [282]

Heat 4 cans of clear beef bouillon or consommé to the boiling point, and let it reduce to 3 cans. Serve in hot soup plates, each garnished with 2 tiny Chicken Dumplings (No. 716), filled with thick onion purée, and 4 tiny cubes of cooked sweetbreads. Dust each plate with finely chopped chervil or parsley.

CONSOMME SEVILLE [283]

Heat 5 cans of clear chicken bouillon to the boiling point, and let it reduce to 3 cans over a bright flame. Serve in hot soup plates, each garnished with 2 tiny eye-shaped Chicken Dumplings (No. 716), 1 teaspoon of cooked minute tapioca, and 2 tiny cubes of Tomato Custard (No. 702). Do not dust with chervil or parsley.

CONSOMME SULTANE [284]

Heat 4 cans of chicken bouillon to the boiling point, and let it reduce to 3 cans over a bright flame. Serve in hot soup plates, each garnished with 2 tiny Chicken Dumplings (No. 716), 1 teaspoon of cooked rice, mixed with a tiny pinch of saffron, and half a hard-cooked egg white cut into tiny crescents. Top each plate with a tiny piece of freshly made toast, cut crescent fashion.

CONSOMME TALMA [285]

Heat 3 cans of clear chicken bouillon to the boiling point. Serve in hot soup plates, each garnished with 2 tiny cubes of Almond Custard (No. 677), 3 cooked or canned asparagus tips (buds only), and 1 tablespoon of chopped hard-cooked egg white. Dust each plate with finely chopped dried chervil or parsley.

CONSOMME THEODORA   [286]

Heat 6 cans of clear chicken bouillon to the boiling point, and let it reduce to half its original volume over a bright flame. Serve in hot soup plates, each garnished with 2 tiny cubes of Asparagus Custard (No. 679), 1 teaspoon of cooked breast of chicken, cut julienne fashion about an inch in length, and ¼ teaspoon of black truffle, also cut julienne fashion. Do not dust with parsley or chervil.

CONSOMME TOSCANE   [287]

Heat 6 cans of clear beef bouillon to the boiling point, and let it reduce to half its original volume over a bright flame. Serve in hot soup plates, each garnished with 2 small eggplant cubes, cooked in butter and well drained, 1 teaspoon of cooked or canned tomato pulp bits, 2 teaspoons of cooked mushroom cups, coarsely chopped, and 2 teaspoons of chopped cooked macaroni. Serve with a side dish of grated Parmesan cheese.

CONSOMME VALENTINE   [288]

Heat 5 cans of clear chicken bouillon to the boiling point, and let it reduce to 3 cans over a bright flame. Serve in hot soup plates, each garnished with 2 tiny heart-shaped Chicken Dumplings (No. 716), 1 teaspoon of cooked breast of chicken, cut julienne fashion about 1½ inches in length, ½ teaspoon of black truffle, cut julienne fashion, and 2 tiny heart-shaped canned pimientos. Dust each plate with finely chopped dried chervil or parsley.

CONSOMME VINCENT   [289]

Heat 2 cans each of clear beef and chicken bouillon to the boiling point, and let it reduce to about 3 cans over a bright flame. Serve in hot cups, each garnished with 1 teaspoon of cooked pearl-like balls of the red part of carrot and 1 teaspoon of cooked rice. Dust each cup with finely chopped chervil or parsley, mixed with equal parts of finely chopped chives.

CREAM OF CELERY SOUP HOME MANNER [290]

Heat 3 cans of cream of celery soup to the boiling point. Remove from the fire, and stir in 2 or 3 fresh egg yolks, adding one at a time, and beating briskly after each addition. Serve in hot plates, each topped with a generous teaspoon of puffed rice cereal.

CREAM OF MUSHROOM SOUP SAINT-DENIS [291]

Heat 3 cans of cream of mushroom soup to the boiling point. Serve in hot soup plates, each garnished with 1 tablespoon of chopped red pimiento (canned) and 1 tablespoon of tiny Croutons (No. 780) fried in butter.

CREAM OF TOMATO SIGURD   [292]

Heat 2 cans of cream of tomato soup with ⅓ cup of scalded thin cream or undiluted evaporated milk, scalded with ¾ cup of hot mashed potatoes, to the boiling point. Serve in plates, after tasting for seasoning, each plate garnished with 1 tablespoon of cooked small chicken cubes, and 1 teaspoon each of chopped red and green pepper. Dust each plate with finely chopped parsley or chervil and chives.

INDIAN CHOWDER   [293]

Heat 2 cans of corn chowder with 1 can of onion soup to the boiling point. Serve in hot soup plates, each garnished with a Cracker Puff (No. 779), topped with grated cheese.

KNIGHT SOUP   [294]

Heat 2 cans of chicken gumbo creole with 1 can of vegetable soup to the boiling point. Serve in hot soup plates, each garnished with 1 teaspoon of blanched, skinned, shredded, and toasted almonds.

LONDON'S MOCK TURTLE SOUP   [295]

Heat 3 cans of mock turtle soup to the boiling point. Stir in ⅓ cup of blanched shredded green cabbage, 2 tablespoons of blanched chopped green pepper, and 2 tablespoons of cooked rice. When ready to serve in hot soup plates, stir in ¼ cup of Madeira wine.

MISS BETSY'S POTAGE   [296]

Heat 3 cans of cream of tomato soup to the boiling point. When ready to serve, stir in 3 tablespoons of cooked barley and ¾ cup of small apple cubes, sautéed in butter and well drained. Serve in hot soup plates, each dusted with finely chopped dried parsley.

OLD-FASHIONED VELVET SOUP   [297]

Heat 2 cans of cream of mushroom soup with 1 can of cream of tomato soup to the boiling point. Serve in hot soup plates, each sprinkled with grated Swiss cheese.

PITTSBURGH PEPPER POT   [298]

Heat 2 cans of pepper pot soup with 1 can of vegetable soup to the boiling point. Serve in hot soup plates, each garnished with finely chopped chives.

POTAGE AMBASSADOR   [299]

Heat 3 cans of cream of pea soup to the boiling point. Serve in hot soup plates, each garnished with 1 teaspoon each of cooked rice and minute tapioca and 1 tablespoon of blanched shredded sorrel.

POTAGE A L'AMERICAINE   [300]
A thick soup

Heat 2 cans of canned creamed corn and 2 cans of cream of tomato soup to the boiling point. Serve in hot soup plates, each garnished with 1 tablespoon of cooked rice and 1 tablespoon of very small cubes of cooked lean ham.

POTAGE A L'AURORE   [301]

Heat 3 cans of cream of tomato soup with ⅓ cup of scalded heavy cream to the boiling point. Serve in hot soup plates, each garnished with 2 teaspoons of cooked minute tapioca and 1½ tablespoons of cooked chicken, cut julienne fashion. Do not dust the plates with parsley or chervil.

POTAGE BALTHAZAR   [302]

Heat 3 cans of pea soup to the boiling point. Serve in hot soup plates, each garnished with a generous tablespoon of julienne-cut cooked red carrot and tiny Croutons (No. 780), fried in butter and thoroughly drained.

POTAGE CAMERONI [303]

Heat 3 cans of vegetable soup to the boiling point. Serve in hot soup plates, each garnished with 1½ tablespoons of cooked diced macaroni and 1 small cooked chicken liver, finely chopped.

POTAGE CHANTILLY [304]

Heat 3 cans of pea soup to the boiling point. Serve in hot soup plates, each garnished with 2 shredded small fresh mint leaves and 1 tablespoon of puffed rice cereal. Drop in the center of each plate 1 tablespoon of salted whipped heavy cream.

POTAGE CHARTIER [305]

Heat together 2 cans of cream of mushroom soup with 2 cups of hot mashed potatoes, having the potatoes a little soft. Boil once, stirring from the bottom of the pan. Serve in soup plates, each sprinkled with finely minced chervil or parsley.

POTAGE CLAMOLE [306]

Heat together 2 cans of clam chowder and 1 can of chicken gumbo creole to the boiling point. Serve in hot soup plates, each topped with 1 teaspoon of butter creamed with the size of a small pea of anchovy paste. Serve a side dish of brown bread and butter finger sandwiches.

POTAGE CONDE [307]

Rub through a fine sieve 2 cans of red beans, previously heated. Stir in 1 cup of scalded undiluted evaporated milk, to which has been added 2 fresh egg yolks. Taste for seasoning, and serve in hot soup plates, each garnished with small Croutons (No. 780), fried in butter and dusted with finely chopped chervil or parsley.

POTAGE DOYEN [308]

Rub through a fine sieve 3 cans of hot pea soup, adding enough hot milk or thin cream to make it of thin cream consistency. Heat well, and serve in hot soup plates, each garnished with 2 tiny Chicken Dumplings (No. 716) and 1 generous tablespoon of cooked or canned small green peas.

POTAGE DUCHESSE [309]

Heat 2 cans of cream of chicken soup with 1 can of cream of asparagus soup to the boiling point. Serve in hot soup plates, each garnished with 4 asparagus tips (buds only) and 2 small cubes of Cream Custard Garnish (No. 690).

POTAGE DURAND [310]

Combine 1 can of chicken gumbo, 1 can of cream of celery soup, and 1 can of cream of asparagus soup in a saucepan, and heat to the boiling point. Serve in hot soup plates, each garnished with a teaspoon of cooked barley, and dusted with finely chopped chives.

POTAGE EVA [311]

Rub through a fine sieve 2 cans of bean soup with 1 cup of cooked sieved pumpkin. Add enough scalded rich milk or thin cream to obtain a soup of thin cream consistency, and heat to the boiling point. Serve in hot soup plates, each garnished with 1 tablespoon of cooked vermicelli, chopped fine. Dust each plate with finely chopped parsley or chervil.

POTAGE EXCELSIOR I [312]

Heat 3 cans of cream of asparagus soup to the boiling point. Serve in hot soup plates, each garnished with 4 asparagus tips (buds only) and 1 teaspoon of cooked barley. Dust each plate with finely chopped parsley or chervil.

POTAGE EXCELSIOR II [313]

Pour into a saucepan 6 cans of clear beef bouillon, and reduce to half its original volume over a bright flame. Serve in hot soup plates, each garnished with a dozen pieces of cooked ox tongue, cut julienne fashion, ¼ teaspoon of finely chopped black truffle, 2 thin slices of cooked frankfurter, peeled, and ½ teaspoon of shredded, toasted pistachio nuts.

POTAGE FAUBONNE [314]

Heat 3 cans of bean soup, and rub through a fine sieve, adding, while rubbing, enough scalded thin cream or undiluted evaporated milk to make a cream soup of thin consistency. Heat again to the boiling point, and serve in hot soup plates, each garnished with 1 tablespoon of cooked leeks, cut julienne fashion. Dust each plate with finely chopped parsley or chervil.

POTAGE FONTANGE   [315]

Heat 3 cans of pea soup to the boiling point. Remove from the fire, and beat in 3 fresh egg yolks, adding one at a time, and beating briskly after each addition. Heat well, stirring constantly, but do not allow to boil. Serve in hot soup plates, each garnished with 2 tablespoons of blanched shredded sorrel or spinach.

POTAGE GERMINY   [316]

Heat 2 cans of pea soup to the boiling point, and rub through a fine sieve, adding, while rubbing, 1 cup of scalded thin cream or undiluted evaporated milk. Heat again to the boiling point, stirring constantly to prevent scorching. Remove from the fire, and beat in 3 fresh egg yolks, adding one at a time, and beating well after each addition. Heat well without letting boil, and serve in hot soup plates, each garnished with 1 tablespoon each of blanched shredded sorrel or spinach, cabbage, and lettuce. Serve a side dish of toasted finger bread, about 1½ inches long.

POTAGE HOCHEPOT   [317]
Belgian

Heat 3 cans of oxtail soup and 1 can of clear beef bouillon to the boiling point. Serve in hot soup plates, each garnished with 3 slices of cooked skinned frankfurter and 1 teaspoon of tiny cubes of cooked salt pork. This nourishing soup, almost a meal in itself, is usually served in individual colorful fancy bowls or earthenware casseroles.

POTAGE HODGEPODGE   [318]
Scotch

Heat 2 cans of Scotch broth with 1 can of pea soup to the boiling point. Serve in hot soup plates, each garnished with 1½ tablespoons of cooked small cubes of lamb or mutton. Dust each plate with finely chopped parsley.

POTAGE JUBILE   [319]

Heat to the boiling point 6 cans of clear beef bouillon or consommé, and let boil until reduced to half its original volume over a bright flame. Then stir in 1 can of pea soup, and heat thoroughly. Serve in hot soup plates, each garnished with 1 tablespoon each of blanched shredded sorrel or spinach, cabbage, and lettuce. Dust each plate with finely chopped chervil or parsley.

POTAGE KRONSTADT   [320]
Russian

Heat 3 cans of cream of celery soup to the boiling point. Stir in ½ cup of grated Swiss cheese, and heat well till the cheese melts. Serve in hot soup plates, each garnished with 1 teaspoon of finely chopped canned pimiento and 1 teaspoon of blanched shredded almonds, topped with 1½ tablespoons of salted whipped sour cream. Serve with a side dish of small pumpernickel bread and butter finger sandwiches.

POTAGE LAMBALLE   [321]

Heat 3 cans of pea soup to the boiling point. Remove from the fire, and beat in 3 fresh egg yolks, adding one at a time, and beating well after each addition. Taste for seasoning. Heat well, but do not allow to boil. Serve in hot soup plates, each garnished with 1 tablespoon of cooked minute tapioca. Dust each plate with finely chopped chervil or parsley. Small fried Croutons (No. 780) may be served on the side.

POTAGE LONGCHAMPS   [322]

Heat 3 cans of pea soup to the boiling point, and rub through a fine sieve, adding, while rubbing, ½ cup of scalded thin cream or undiluted evaporated milk. Heat again to the boiling point, and serve in hot soup plates, each garnished with 1 tablespoon of cooked chopped vermicelli, and dusted with finely chopped chervil or parsley.

POTAGE LONGUEVILLE   [323]

Heat 2 cans of pea soup to the boiling point, and rub through a fine sieve, adding, while rubbing, ½ cup of scalded thin cream alternately with 3 fresh egg yolks. Heat again to the boiling point, but do not allow to boil. Serve in hot soup plates, each garnished with 1 tablespoon of cooked chopped macaroni, 1 scant tablespoon each of blanched shredded sorrel or spinach and lettuce. Serve dusted with finely chopped chervil or parsley.

POTAGE LOUISIANE   [324]

Heat together 2 cans of cream of oyster soup and 1 can of cream of tomato soup to the boiling point. Taste for seasoning. Serve in hot soup plates, each garnished with toasted oyster crackers, and dusted with finely chopped chervil or parsley.

POTAGE MADELON   [325]

Heat 3 cans of cream of mushroom soup to the boiling point. Serve in hot soup plates, each garnished with 1 rounded teaspoon each of cooked rice and minute tapioca and 1 tablespoon of canned artichoke bottoms, cubed small. Dust each plate with finely chopped chervil or parsley.

POTAGE MALAKOFF   [326]

Heat 2 cans of cream of tomato soup with 1 can of concentrated chicken bouillon and ½ cup of smooth mashed potatoes to the boiling point, stirring almost constantly. Serve in hot soup plates, each garnished with 1 tablespoon of blanched shredded spinach.

POTAGE MARIGNY   [327]

Heat 2 cans of pea soup, and rub through a fine sieve, adding, while rubbing, 1 cup of scalded thin cream or undiluted evaporated milk alternately with 3 fresh egg yolks, slightly beaten. Return to the fire, and heat to the boiling point, but do not allow to boil, stirring almost constantly from the bottom of the saucepan. Taste for seasoning, and serve in hot soup plates, each garnished with 1 scant tablespoon each of cooked Frenched string beans and blanched shredded sorrel or spinach. Dust each plate with finely chopped chervil or parsley.

POTAGE MONGOL   [328]

Heat together to the boiling point 2 cans of pea soup, 1 can of cream of tomato soup, and ⅓ cup of thin cream or undiluted evaporated milk, stirring constantly. Serve in hot soup plates, each garnished with 1 teaspoon each of cooked shredded carrot (red only), celery, green pepper, turnip, and leeks (white part only).

POTAGE MOSCOVITE [329]
Russian

Heat 2 cans of cream of tomato soup together with 1 can of pea soup and ⅓ cup of thin cream or undiluted evaporated milk, flavored with 1½ (or more) teaspoons of curry powder, and let boil once. Serve in hot soup plates, each garnished with 1 tablespoon of whipped sweet cream, dusted with paprika and surrounded with Croutons (No. 780), fried in butter and well drained.

POTAGE MOZART [330]

Heat 2 cans of bean soup to the boiling point, and rub through a fine sieve, adding, while rubbing, 1 can of concentrated beef bouillon. Return to the fire, and heat to the boiling point. Taste for seasoning, and serve in hot soup plates, each garnished with Croutons (No. 780), fried in butter and rolled in paprika.

POTAGE NOURMAHAL [331]

Heat 2 cans of cream of celery soup with 1 can of cream of mushroom soup and 1 can of cream of tomato soup, and let reduce to 3 cans over a bright flame, placing an asbestos pad under the pan to prevent scorching. Taste for seasoning. Serve in hot soup plates, each garnished with 1 tablespoon each of cooked lean ham, cut in tiny lozenges, chicken breast, cubed very small, and blanched, shredded, toasted almonds. Serve with a side dish of Cracker Puffs (No. 779).

POTAGE SAINT-CLOUD [332]
French

Heat 3 cans of pea soup to the boiling point, and rub through a sieve with ⅓ cup of scalded heavy cream. Heat again to the boiling point, and correct the seasoning. Serve in hot soup plates, each garnished with 1 tablespoon each of blanched shredded lettuce and leeks (using only white parts) and 1 tablespoon of cooked or canned small green peas. Dust with mixed chives and parsley, finely chopped.

POTAGE SAINT-GERMAIN [333]
French

Heat 3 cans of pea soup to the boiling point with ¼ cup of heavy cream. Serve in hot soup plates, each garnished with 1 tablespoon of cooked or canned small green peas, and dusted with finely chopped chervil or parsley.

POTAGE SAINT PATRICK [334]

Heat 2 cans of cream of spinach soup with 1 can of cream of mushroom soup to the boiling point. Correct the seasoning, and serve in hot soup plates, each plate garnished with 2 tablespoons each of blanched shredded spinach and green lettuce. Serve with a side dish of small Croutons (No. 780), fried in butter and well drained.

POTAGE SUZETTE [335]

Heat 2 cans of pea soup with 1 can of cream of mushroom soup and ¼ cup of heavy cream. Rub through a fine sieve. Heat again to the boiling point, and correct the seasoning. Serve in hot soup plates, each plate garnished with 1 tablespoon each of cooked or canned green peas, and tiny pearl-like carrot (using only the red part). Top each center with a ring of whipped cream, and on top of the whipped cream, place a freshly poached small egg, dusted with paprika.

POTAGE VICTOIRE [336]

Heat together 1 can of cream of celery soup, 1 can of cream of tomato soup, and 1 can of pea soup to the boiling point. Correct the seasoning. Serve in hot soup plates, each plate garnished with 1 teaspoon each of cooked minute tapioca, cooked rice, and cooked barley. Top each plate with a small round of toasted bread, buttered and sprinkled with grated cheese, and with chopped chives on top of the cheese.

POTAGE WASHINGTON [337]

Heat 3 cans of cream of tomato soup to the boiling point. Serve in hot cups, each garnished with 1 teaspoon of cooked minute tapioca and 1 generous teaspoon of cooked assorted vegetables, cut in tiny fancy pieces. Dust each cup with finely chopped parsley.

SOUPE BRETONNE [338]

Heat 3 cans of bean soup; rub through a fine sieve; heat again to the boiling point and stir in ½ cup of hot milk. Serve in hot soup plates, each plate garnished with 2 tablespoons of cooked or canned tomato pulp, and dust with finely chopped chervil or parsley.

SOUPE BUCHERONNE [339]

Heat 3 cans of vegetable soup to the boiling point. Serve in hot soup plates, each garnished with 6 small cubes of cooked salt pork.

SOUPE CHARMEUSE [340]

Heat 2 cans of chicken gumbo soup with 1 can of cream of tomato soup to the boiling point. Correct the seasoning, and serve in hot soup plates, each garnished with 1 tablespoon of cooked vermicelli. Dust with finely chopped chervil or parsley.

SOUPE EGLANTINE [341]

Heat 3 cans of chicken gumbo soup to the boiling point. Stir in a generous pinch of saffron, diluted in a little cold water. Serve in hot soup plates, each garnished with 1 tablespoon of good Madeira wine.

SOUPE FLAMANDE [342]

Bring to a boil 4 cans of clear beef bouillon. Add ½ cup of raw celery, cut in very fine sticks, and cook 15 minutes, or until the celery is tender. Then drop in a dozen very small pork sausage balls, and continue cooking for 5 minutes longer. Stir in ⅓ cup of cooked rice, and serve in hot soup plates, each sprinkled with finely chopped parsley.

TOMATO ONION SOUP [343]

Cook 3 cups of thinly sliced onions in ¼ cup of butter over a low flame until lightly browned, stirring frequently. Gradually stir in 1 can each of condensed consommé, hot water, condensed tomato soup, and milk, using the soup can as a measure. Cover, bring to a boil, and let simmer very gently for 20 minutes. Uncover, season to taste with salt and black pepper and a dash of Worcestershire sauce (optional), and serve at once, each serving covered with grated cheese.

VEGETARIAN CREAM SOUP [344]

Heat 2 cans of vegetable soup with 1 can of cream of tomato soup to the boiling point. Serve in hot soup plates, each garnished with 3 tiny Spinach Dumplings (No. 701).

Chapter Six

CREAM SOUPS
VEGETABLE, POULTRY, NUT, AND GAME

*One whiff of a savory aromatic soup,
and appetites come to attention.*

C REAM SOUPS MADE WITH FRESH MILK, THIN CREAM, HEAVY cream, butter, flour, and seasonings, and either a cooked and sieved vegetable, meat, fish, crustacean, or shellfish are a substantial, nourishing, and delicious part of any meal, except, of course, breakfast. They should be distinctive in flavor. The vegetables are cooked, strained, then sieved in a kind of purée before being added to the basic sauce, which is the base of almost all cream soups. They must be well seasoned, and the addition of a little onion cooked with the vegetables, meat, or fish, will always enhance the taste and add flavor.

Four kinds of basic standard cream sauces are used in the making of cream soups. These basic cream sauces are used also for sauces to accompany fish, meat, poultry, game, vegetables, crustaceans, and shellfish.

As a rule, any kind of vegetable, legume, meat, fish, fowl—in fact, almost any kind of edible food which may be sieved—may be used for cream soup. Or a combination of two or three foods may be used.

These cream soups serve 6 to 8 persons, unless otherwise indicated.

BASIC STANDARD RECIPES FOR [346]
CREAM SAUCES

THIN

1 tablespoon butter	½ scant teaspoon salt
1 tablespoon flour	⅛ teaspoon white pepper
1 cup milk or thin or heavy cream	1 beaten egg yolk

MEDIUM

2 tablespoons butter	½ scant teaspoon salt
2 tablespoons flour	⅛ teaspoon white pepper
1 cup milk or thin or heavy cream	1 beaten egg yolk

THICK

3 tablespoons butter	½ scant teaspoon salt
3 tablespoons flour	⅛ teaspoon white pepper
1 cup milk or thin or heavy cream	1 beaten egg yolk

Directions. For any one of the three basic sauces, melt the butter, stir in the flour, and blend thoroughly, but do not let brown, over a gentle flame. Add the seasonings, then gradually, while stirring constantly, stir in the milk, thin cream, or heavy cream, previously scalded with 2 thin slices of onion, a bit of bay leaf, 2 sprigs of parsley, and 1 whole clove. Keep stirring, still over a low flame, until the mixture thickens and bubbles. Let it bubble for 3 or 4 minutes. Remove from the fire, and briskly stir in the egg yolk. Do not boil any more, unless you stir briskly and from the bottom of the pan, lest the mixture curdle. This makes 1 cup of cream sauce.

HINTS ON HOW TO MAKE A GOOD　　　[347] BASIC CREAM SAUCE

Just as every good soup maker has little tricks that are all his own, so nearly every dish requires a different technique to bring the basic part tó just the right consistency and flavor. For instance, when making the basic cream sauce for a cream soup, you may fry a little onion—oh, not much!—in the butter before stirring in the flour, or you may use a little finely chopped shallot, or a soupçon of garlic instead of the onion, and let all blend together slowly to get the full flavor. To this, you add the scalded milk, thin cream, or heavy cream, and the seasonings. Or you may use any one of the compounded (creamed) butters corresponding to the food ingredient or ingredients which are to be added to the basic sauce. Above all, a cream soup should be smooth, light without being liquid, glossy to the eye, and definite as to taste.

The ambrosia, which the Greeks and the Romans insisted was the food of their gods, was probably only a clever way with garlic. A little rubbing of a cut clove of garlic in the pan will do. If a cream soup must stand after being made, place it in a double boiler over hot, but not boiling, water. It is absolutely impossible to keep it hot over direct heat without scorching.

Notice that I call the basic sauce for cream soups "cream sauce." "White sauce" (a most unattractive title) usually is badly made, incorrectly served, cool when it should be hot, sticky when it should be creamy, and the less said about it the better—until numerous cooks really learn to make it.

For delicate cream soups, the milk in the basic recipe for cream sauce may be partly replaced by Chicken Stock (No. 25) or Veal Stock (No. 11). And a little—very little—grated cheese added to a basic sauce for cream soup gives it much more flavor than if it is served plain. These basic cream sauces also may be used for creamy chowders.

The garnish is an important part in the serving of cream soup. If the vegetable, meat, or fish which forms the basis of the soup fails to add color, chopped parsley, a sprinkling of paprika, or nutmeg adds interest to the dish.

There is a fourth basic standard cream sauce—a master-key sauce—which may be used for cream soups and compounded sauces, and as a base or a foundation for any kind of rich cream sauce for fish, meat, poultry, game, or vegetables. It is called Béchamel sauce, a velvety, smooth, rich cream sauce, one of the creamiest white sauces. It was named and created by Louis de Béchamel, Marquis de Nointel, Lord Steward and Maître d'Hôtel of the Household at the Court of Louis XIV.

BECHAMEL SAUCE FOR CREAM SOUP [348]

Bring 1 quart of milk to the scalding point with 1 large bay leaf. Meantime, heat ¼ cup of butter, stir in 1½ tablespoons of grated onion, and cook, but do not let it brown, stirring almost constantly over a very low flame. Now stir in ¼ cup of flour; then gradually add the strained scalded rich milk, cooking until smooth and free from any lumps or clots, still stirring constantly. Set over hot water, and keep hot. In another saucepan, heat 2 tablespoons of butter; stir in ¼ pound of coarsely chopped lean raw veal and cook, without letting it take on color, stirring constantly. Season to taste with salt, white pepper, and a dash of nutmeg. Now, slowly, very slowly, pour the scalded milk mixture over the veal, and cook over a very low flame (placing an asbestos pad under the saucepan) for an hour, stirring frequently from the bottom of the pan. Strain this sauce through a fine-meshed sieve, and spread over it, bit by bit, 1 tablespoon of sweet butter, to prevent the forming of a film or thin crust on the top.

For each quart of this hot sauce, have ready 1½ cups of cooked, sieved, and well-drained fish, meat, fowl, game, vegetable, or a combination of vegetables, and when ready to serve, stir in 2 well-beaten egg yolks. Taste for seasoning, and serve as hot as possible.

Note. This sauce will keep for a whole week in a sealed jar in the refrigerator and needs only to be heated over hot water, and the desired purée of food added to make a smooth rich cream soup; or it may be used as a cream sauce.

CREAM OF ALMOND AND CELERY SOUP [349]

Thoroughly wash 1 large bunch of celery, cut in 1-inch pieces, using the leaves and root. Drain, and put in a large saucepan with 6 peppercorns, slightly bruised; a bouquet garni, composed of 1 large bay leaf and 6 sprigs of fresh parsley, tied together with kitchen thread; 1 generous tablespoon of onion juice; 1 thin slice of lemon; 1 teaspoon of salt; 1-inch stick of cinnamon; and 4 cups (1 quart) of cold water. Cook slowly for 50 long minutes, or until the celery is tender. Turn the mixture into a sieve, and rub over a saucepan, forcing a little to obtain as much celery pulp as possible. Blend 1 generous teaspoon of butter and 1 teaspoon of flour, or rather knead together until thoroughly mixed, as for a Roux (No. 14), then stir in 1 cup of thick cream alternately with ¼ cup of pounded blanched almonds. Turn this mixture into the celery mixture, bring to a boil, and boil for 3 minutes. Serve with cheese crackers.

CREAM OF ALMOND SOUP [350]

Heat 1 cup of rich cream and 1 cup of milk together with the rind of 1 lemon, cut in long narrow strips. Add 2 cups of canned soup (chicken or beef), thickened with 1 tablespoon of flour creamed with 1 tablespoon of butter. Season to taste with salt and white pepper, a few grains of cayenne, a blade of mace, and a few grains of allspice. Boil for 5 short minutes, then add ¼ cup of pounded blanched almonds. Boil again for 5 long minutes. Remove the lemon peel, and serve with a side dish of Profiterolles (No. 799).

The ancient Romans had a triple use for milk—as a beverage, a cosmetic, and as bath "water."

CREAM OF ARTICHOKE SOUP [351]
With globe artichokes

When ancient Greece and Rome were at the height of their glory, the globe artichoke, called by the Greeks *kaktos*, by the Italians *articiocco*, and by the French *artichaut*, was a favorite food. Then it suddenly disappeared, to be discovered once again in 1473 by a wealthy merchant of Venice.

The globe artichoke, which by the way is not related to the Jerusalem artichoke, is an inexpensive vegetable, the origin of which is Africa, where legend says it was a favorite of Antony and Cleopatra.

That "strip tease," the artichoke, is a bargain for spring. It is a dining-hall favorite in women's colleges in the East, where it is used like the daisy to tell success in love. The girls play "He loves me, he loves me not" as they pluck away the leaves. They count even the tiniest, and it is only once in a blue moon that it comes out any way except "He loves me not." Can it be that artichoke leaves grow always in pairs?

The artichoke flower is a purple violet and of an odd shape. It looks like one of those enormous tufts on an imaginary military shako, and nothing is more picturesque and pleasing to see than an artichoke field in bloom. When spring has velveted the pale, long, thin, and finely notched leaves, and hoisted all the tufts, it looks like a military parade. It is a sign that soon the globe artichoke will be ready for the vinaigrette, sour cream, and horseradish beaten together into cream cheese and minced chives sauce, or chiffonade dressing, or Russian dressing, or rolled in a smoking omelet, or stuffed with a learned stuffing, or in a learned bisque, made as follows.

You may use canned, freshly cooked, or frozen artichoke bottoms or hearts. The bur is the choke. That's where the name comes from— the Oxford way of saying "attachoke."

Drain 6 artichoke bottoms, and rub through a fine-meshed sieve. Place the pulp in a saucepan with 2 quarts of Chicken Stock (No. 25), 1 large bay leaf, 1 whole clove, 4 thin slices of onion, no salt, but 5 freshly crushed peppercorns, and a tiny pinch of nutmeg. Bring to a boil, and let simmer gently for 25 minutes, covered. Then add ¼ cup of cooked rice and 3 cups of scalded milk, and boil briskly for 2 minutes. Remove from the fire, and strain through a fine sieve into a clean saucepan. Season to taste with salt, and heat to the boiling point. Then stir in briskly 1 cup of thin cream mixed with 2 fresh egg yolks. Taste for seasoning. When ready to serve, stir in 3 table-spoons of sherry wine. Serve in soup plates, each garnished with 4 small cubes of Artichoke Bottom Custard Garnish (No. 678).

Note. Jerusalem artichoke may be substituted for globe artichoke.

CREAM OF ARTICHOKE (JERUSALEM) A LA PALESTINE [352]

Nobody seems to know why the Jerusalem artichoke is so named, for actually it is a perennial sunflower with tuberous roots. The name is neither descriptive nor true. The word "Jerusalem" has for many years been explained as an English corruption of the Italian *girasole*, meaning sunflower; but the English name of Jerusalem was used before there was any possible connection with *girasole*.

At any rate, the Jerusalem artichoke neither tastes nor looks like the green or globe artichoke. It is not related to it botanically or otherwise. In shape, it resembles an irregular potato. "Knotty potato" would have been a better name for it—certainly more descriptive.

Wash 2 pounds of Jerusalem artichokes carefully. Pare thinly or rub off the thin skin with a dry cloth, dropping the artichoke at

once into a pan of water to which has been added 1 tablespoon of
vinegar or lemon juice for each quart of water, to preserve the white-
ness. Cut 2 medium-sized onions, 1 stalk of celery, scraped, and the
artichokes into thin slices. Fry these vegetables in 2 tablespoons of
sweet butter for 12 to 15 minutes, without browning, stirring frequently, over a very gentle flame. Then pour in 1 quart of hot double-
strength Chicken Stock (No. 25) gradually, and cook until the
vegetables are quite tender. Empty the liquid and solid into a fine-
meshed wire sieve, and rub through into a clean saucepan. Bring to
a boil, and taste for seasoning. Stir in 1 pint of sour cream, which
has been scalded with 1 large bay leaf, 8 sprigs of fresh parsley, 1 thin
slice of garlic, and 2 whole cloves, then strained through a fine
muslin cloth. Beat in 3 fresh egg yolks, slightly beaten, and bring to
a boil, stirring constantly from the bottom of the saucepan. Serve
in heated soup plates, each containing ½ teaspoon of finely chopped
chervil, and add to each plate 6 tiny cubes of Passover Matzoth (No.
796).

CREAM OF ASPARAGUS SOUP   [353]

Trim the end butts from a bunch of asparagus. Cut off the tips and
stems, and boil both in 1 quart of salted boiling water until tender.
Drain. Set aside the tips and 2 cups of the asparagus stock. Cook 1
tablespoon of butter and 1 tablespoon of flour together, stirring constantly until cream colored, but not brown. Gradually add 3 cups of
scalded rich milk, mixed with the 2 cups of reserved asparagus stock,
and 1 small ham bone, or its equivalent in cooked lean ham. Cook
gently for 25 to 30 minutes, stirring occasionally. Strain through a
fine sieve. Season to taste with salt, pepper, and a dash of nutmeg.
Again bring to a boil. Remove from the fire, and beat in 2 or 3 slightly
beaten egg yolks. Taste for seasoning, and when ready to serve, add
the reserved asparagus tips and 1 tablespoon of butter.

CREAM OF BARLEY SOUP   [354]

Simmer 1 veal knuckle or leftover chicken or turkey carcass, broken
into pieces, in 2 quarts of slightly salted cold water very gently for
2½ hours, skimming off all scum as it rises to the surface. Strain
through a fine sieve. Wash ½ cup of barley in cold water, and drain.
Add to the strained stock with 1 large bay leaf, 1 whole clove, and
4 thin slices of onion. Cover the kettle, and cook until the barley
is tender. Remove about half of the barley from the soup, and set
it aside. Rub the soup through a fine-meshed sieve. Return the re-

served barley, stir in 1 can of undiluted evaporated milk or thin cream, and season to taste with salt and white pepper. Bring to a boil, and let simmer gently for 20 minutes. Just before serving, stir in 1 tablespoon of butter. Serve in hot soup plates, each garnished with 2 or 3 Burger Balls with Marjoram (No. 667).

CREAM OF BLACK BEAN SOUP [355]
Old-fashioned method

Wash 2 cups of dried black beans. Place in a kettle with 3 quarts of lukewarm water, and let stand overnight. In the morning, turn the beans and water into a larger kettle. Add ½ pound of salt pork, minced, 1 teaspoon of burned onion sauce, ½ cup of minced celery leaves, 1 small bay leaf and 1 small bunch of fresh parsley tied together, and salt and pepper to taste. Cover, and let simmer very gently until the beans can be mashed, adding more hot water as necessary to keep the beans covered. Discard the parsley and bay leaf. Mash. Serve with a side dish of 2 riced hard-cooked eggs, thin slices of 2 lemons, and Croutons (No. 780), passed around.

CREAM OF KIDNEY BEAN SOUP [356]
French manner

Soak 2 cups of carefully picked red kidney beans in cold water overnight. Next day, drain, and place in a soup kettle. Add 1 small cooked leg of lamb bone, cracked; 1 medium-sized onion, stuck with 2 whole cloves; 1 bouquet garni, composed of 6 or 7 sprigs of parsley, 1 large bay leaf, and 1 sprig of thyme, tied together with kitchen thread; 8 whole peppercorns, freshly crushed; 1 teaspoon of salt; 3 cups of cold water; and 3 cups of cold milk. Bring to a boil, and cook very gently until the beans are tender. Empty the whole contents of the soup kettle, except the bone, into a fine-meshed sieve, and rub through into a fresh saucepan. Return to the fire, adding more scalded milk if the mixture is too thick. Taste for seasoning, and bring to the boiling point. Remove from the fire, and beat in 2 well-beaten egg yolks and 1 tablespoon of sweet butter. Serve in soup plates, with a side dish of freshly made Melba Toast (No. 791).

CREAM OF LIMA AND NAVY BEAN [357]
Chowder style

Soak 1 cup of dried lima beans and 1 cup of dried navy beans in 2 quarts of water overnight. Cook in the same water until they can be mashed. Strain, reserve liquor, mash, and set aside. Melt 2 table-spoons of drippings or butter in a soup kettle. Fry 2 minced onions and 1 small bunch of celery leaves (tops) for 3 or 4 minutes. Stir in 2 tablespoons of flour, and when brown, add the reserved bean liquor. Stir well. Add the mashed beans, 1 cup of boiling water, and 4 cups (1 quart) of milk. Simmer gently, stirring occasionally for 20 minutes. Season with salt and pepper to taste. Serve with toasted Cracker Puffs (No. 779).

CREAM OF NAVY BEAN SOUP [358]

Soak 1 cup of navy beans in water to cover overnight. In the morning, clean 2 pounds of brisket of beef, and place in a kettle with 2 quarts of cold water. Bring to a boil, and let simmer very gently, after skimming thoroughly. Add the beans well drained, 2 small onions, sliced, another small onion stuck with 3 cloves, 1 small bay leaf, 1 sprig of thyme, 1 small can (2 cups) of tomatoes, and let simmer for 2 hours. Lift out the meat (to be used later in one way or another). Strain through a colander. Reserve the broth. Rub the beans and vegetables through a fine sieve. Place again on the fire. Season with salt and pepper to taste. Boil once or twice, after adding 1 table-spoon of flour diluted with a little water. Serve with Bread Dumplings (No. 712).

CREAM OF BEET SOUP I [359]

To 3 cups of Medium Cream Sauce (No. 346), add a dash of nutmeg, 2 cups (1 pint) of scalded milk, and 1 cup of boiled beets, sieved. Stir well. Bring to a boil, and just before serving, stir in 2 well-beaten fresh egg yolks and 1 generous tablespoon of butter. Season to taste with salt and pepper. Serve at once with freshly made toast.

CREAM OF BEET SOUP II [360]

Put 1 tablespoon of butter and 1 tablespoon of flour in a saucepan. Stir over the fire until quite smooth, then by degrees add 3 pints of scalded milk, and let boil up. Season with ¼ saltspoon of grated nutmeg and 1 teaspoon of salt. Color with 1½ generous tablespoons of boiled beets, rubbed through a fine sieve, and finish with 1 table-spoon of butter.

CREAM OF BREAD WITH SHERRY SOUP [361]

Break 1 pound of bread crusts into small pieces, place in a bowl, and pour over sufficient hot Beef Stock (No. 114) to barely cover. Cover, and let stand until the bread is quite soft, then beat with a wire whisk until smooth. Heat 1¾ quarts of beef stock, and stir in the bread mixture. Bring to a boil, and let simmer very gently for 12 to 15 minutes. Taste for seasoning, remove from the fire, and beat in briskly 3 slightly beaten egg yolks, beaten with 3 tablespoons of sherry wine. Empty the contents of the pan into a fine-meshed wire sieve, and rub through into a clean saucepan. Bring to the boiling point, and serve in soup plates, garnished with 6 tiny cubes of Cream Custard (No. 690), and sprinkled with ½ teaspoon of finely chopped chives.

CREAM OF BROCCOLI SOUP [362]
Crème de Broccoli Tourangeau

One may well hesitate to deprive Thoreau of the credit accorded to him by Professor Adam of Chapel Hill of having, on a foot tour of Cape Cod in 1849, discovered broccoli grown from seeds salvaged from the wrecked Franklin. Nevertheless, in the *Maryland Historical Magazine* we find that under date of October 29, 1766, Charles Carroll, barrister, included "one ounce of the best Brocoli seed Hardiest Sort," in a diversified and exceedingly interesting merchandise order forwarded from the then metropolitan city of Annapolis, Maryland, to "Mr. William Anderson Merchant in London." Broccoli is a member of the cabbage tribe that once commanded a high price because of its comparative scarcity. Then the French in this country who missed their broccoli, common in France and in Italy, began growing it here. Americans took to broccoli also, and today it's a vegetable greatly relished, either the stalks or the flowerets, or even the centers of large leaves in delicious cream soups.

Wash the leaves from a nice bunch of broccoli, discarding any bruised or discolored ones. Trim the large stems by cutting away the woody outside part, and cut the more tender inside pulp into inch lengths. Put the leaves and trimmed stems in a saucepan with boiling Chicken Bouillon (No. 25), or canned, seasoned to taste with salt, pepper, and a pinch of nutmeg. Add a bouquet garni, composed of 1 large bay leaf, 8 sprigs of parsley, and 1 sprig of thyme, tied with kitchen thread. Cook until tender, or about 40 minutes, covered. Drain off the liquid, reserving it. Put the broccoli through a food chopper, using the fine blade, then rub through a fine sieve.

Heat the reserved stock, and stir in 2 tablespoons of flour, mixed with a little cold water, and let boil 3 or 4 minutes. Remove from the fire, and beat in 3 fresh egg yolks, one at a time, beating well after each addition. Strain into a clean saucepan, add the sieved broccoli, and boil twice, stirring constantly from the bottom of the saucepan. Taste for seasoning. When ready to serve, stir in 2 tablespoons of sweet butter. Serve with freshly made small Croutons (No. 780), fried in butter.

## CREAM OF BRUSSELS SPROUT SOUP					[363]

Wash and trim 1½ pounds (about 1 quart) of Brussels sprouts, and cook them till tender in salted boiling water, to which has been added 1 large bay leaf, 1 thin slice of garlic, 1 whole clove, 6 thin slices of onion, and a 1-inch piece of parsley root. Have the pan covered to preserve the green color. Drain thoroughly, then rub the vegetables through a fine-meshed wire sieve into a clean saucepan. Season with salt, pepper, nutmeg, and marjoram to taste. Stir in 1½ quarts of good Beef Stock (No. 114), and bring to a boil. Remove from the fire, and beat in ½ cup of sweet cream, to which has been added 3 well-beaten egg yolks, beating briskly to prevent curdling. Return to the fire, bring to a boil, but do not allow to boil, lest the mixture curdle, stirring constantly. Serve at once with a side dish of Curry Dumplings (No. 726).

## CREAM OF CABBAGE SOUP I					[364]
Chowder style

Pour 6 cups of liquor from corned beef or ham, or Beef Stock (No. 114), into a large kettle, and bring to a boil. Add 3 sliced onions, 2 large diced potatoes, ½ cup of diced celery, 1 small onion stuck with 3 cloves, 3 cups of chopped cabbage, 1 sprig of parsley, 1 small bay leaf, 1 sprig of thyme, 6 whole peppercorns, and lastly 1 cup of beans (either soaked white, black, navy, or limas, fresh shell, or string beans). When boiling, reduce the heat, and let simmer gently for 1 hour. Season to taste with salt, and serve with a slice of toast for each plate.

## CREAM OF CABBAGE SOUP II					[365]
With sour cream

Shred 1 medium-sized head of fresh green cabbage (Savoy cabbage, if possible) together with 3 large onions in a soup kettle, as for slaw. Mince 1 green pepper very fine, and add. Cover generously with boiling water, and add 2 slices of canned pimiento, chopped, and 1 bouquet garni, composed of 1 large bay leaf, 6 sprigs of fresh parsley, and 1 sprig of thyme, tied together with kitchen thread; no salt, but pepper to taste. Cover, and allow to boil gently until the cabbage is tender, the onions nearly dissolved, and the water boiled down to half. Then add 3 cups of scalded sweet milk, mixed with 1 pint of scalded sour cream. Season to taste with salt and a dash of nutmeg, and thicken with 2 tablespoons of butter kneaded with 2 teaspoons of flour. When ready to serve, add to the soup 3 strips of bacon, broiled crisp and coarsely chopped. Serve with a side dish of grated Swiss cheese.

CREAM OF CALF'S BRAIN SOUP   [366]
Also called Calf's Brain Bisque

Chop 1 small carrot, 1 small leek (white part only), 1 stalk of celery, half a small turnip, and 2 tablespoons of green cabbage, and blanch them in 3 tablespoons of butter for about 3 or 4 minutes, stirring constantly. Drain off the butter. Transfer the vegetables into a soup kettle, and pour over 1¾ quarts of boiling water. Then add 6 sprigs of fresh parsley tied up with 1 large bay leaf and 1 sprig of thyme, 2 whole cloves, and 3 tablespoons of chopped onion, and let come to a boil. Reduce the heat, and let simmer gently for 1 hour. Strain, reserving the broth. Heat 3 tablespoons of butter or margarine, stir in 1 tablespoon of grated onion, and cook one minute, without letting the onion get brown, over a low flame, stirring constantly; then stir in 3 tablespoons of flour, blending well. Add 1 blanched calf's brain, well drained, free from any membrane, and finely chopped. Stir until smooth, adding gradually, while stirring, 4 cups of the hot reserved vegetable broth, stirring almost constantly until the mixture just begins to thicken. Season to taste with salt, white pepper, and a tiny pinch of nutmeg, and let simmer gently for 10 minutes, stirring occasionally. Beat 2 fresh egg yolks into 2 tablespoons of fresh heavy cream, and slowly pour into the bisque. Taste for seasoning, and serve in hot soup plates with Croutons (No. 780).

CREAM OF CARROT SOUP I   [367]
Also called Carrot Bisque

Into a large saucepan, put 2 bunches of young carrots, sliced very thin after being grated, 4 tablespoons of butter or margarine, 1 large bay leaf, 1 whole clove, 2 teaspoons of sugar, and 6 sprigs of fresh parsley. Cover, and cook gently for about 20 to 25 minutes over a gentle flame, stirring occasionally. Add 3 medium-sized potatoes, peeled and thinly sliced, and 5 cups of Chicken Bouillon (No. 25). Cover, and let simmer gently for 25 to 30 minutes, or until the potato slices are cooked. Rub the mixture through a fine sieve into a clean saucepan, and stir in 2 cups of hot chicken bouillon. Let simmer gently for 20 minutes, again strain through a fine sieve, and serve in soup plates with Croutons (No. 780).

CREAM OF CARROT SOUP II   [368]
Family style

Grate 6 or 8 carrots (according to size), mince 1 onion, and place in a soup kettle with 2 diced potatoes, ½ cup of diced celery, 1 bay leaf, and 2 whole cloves. Cover with water. Bring to a boil, and let simmer very gently for 45 minutes. Strain through a colander, and rub the ingredients through a sieve. Return the pulp to the soup kettle, and pour over 1 quart of scalded milk. Boil twice. Remove from the fire. Season to taste with salt and pepper, and stir in 2 well-beaten egg yolks. Finish with 1 tablespoon of butter. Serve with crackers.

CREAM OF CARROT SOUP PAYSANNE   [369]
French peasant manner

Cook together 1½ pounds of carrots, diced or sliced thin; ¾ cup of celery root, thinly sliced; ¼ cup of chopped onions; and a bouquet garni, composed of 1 large bay leaf, 5 sprigs of parsley, and 1 sprig of thyme, tied together with kitchen thread. Generously cover with enough salted water, and cook until tender. Drain. Rub through a fine-meshed sieve, after discarding the bouquet garni. Keep hot. Heat 3 tablespoons of butter; blend in 3 tablespoons of flour, until the mixture bubbles, but do not let it get colored; then stir in 1½ quarts (6 cups) of Chicken Stock (No. 25), and let boil for 5 minutes. Then stir in the sieved vegetables alternately with 1 cup of scalded heavy sweet cream. Bring to a boil, season to taste with salt, pepper, and nutmeg, and when ready to serve, stir in 1½ tablespoons of finely chopped chervil or parsley.

CREAM OF CAULIFLOWER   [370]
WITH ALMONDS

Separate a cauliflower into flowerets and clean, saving the trimmings. Cook in 1 quart (4 cups) of water. Now cook until tender the cauliflower trimmings, the leaves and stalks, with 1 large diced potato, 1 medium-sized onion, sliced, a bouquet garni composed of 1 bay leaf tied with 6 sprigs of parsley, and 2 tablespoons of chopped celery, using the water in which the flowerets were cooked. Discard the bouquet garni, and force through a fine sieve the flowerets (reserving a few for garnishing), trimmings, potato, onion, and celery mixture, adding 2½ cups of scalded milk gradually. Season with ½ generous teaspoon of salt and ¼ teaspoon of white pepper. Return to fire, and let boil once. Then stir in 2 tablespoons of chopped parsley and ½ cup of finely chopped blanched almonds. Garnish each serving with the reserved cauliflower clusters. Serve piping hot.

CREAM OF CAULIFLOWER SOUP [371]
Southern manner

Clean a small head of cauliflower, and separate into small flowerets. Blanch for 3 or 4 minutes in slightly salted boiling water; drain, and reserve the water. Cook the blanched flowerets for 6 to 8 minutes in 2 generous tablespoons of butter over a gentle flame, but do not let brown. Sprinkle with 2 tablespoons of flour, mix well, then gradually stir in the reserved cauliflower water, and cook gently for 25 minutes. Strain through a fine-meshed sieve into a clean saucepan. Return to the fire, stir in 1 quart of scalded rich sweet milk, and continue cooking gently for 10 minutes. Remove from the fire, season to taste with salt, white pepper, and a dash of nutmeg, then beat in 2 slightly beaten egg yolks alternately with ⅓ cup of freshly cooked drained rice. You may reserve a few cauliflower flowerets before rubbing, and add them to the finished soup. Serve as hot as possible.

CREAM OF CELERY SOUP I [372]

Long before celery became a food, it was used as a medicine. Ah-Pang Su, a famous Chinese epicure, declared that he could prepare 326 distinctly different recipes or dishes using only celery, water, and salt.

Boil 1 minced medium-sized onion, 1½ cups of finely diced celery stalk and leaves, 1 small bouquet garni composed of 1 small bay leaf, 4 sprigs of fresh parsley, and 1 sprig of thyme tied together with kitchen thread, and 1 whole clove in cold salted water to cover for about 30 to 35 minutes, or until tender. Cream 1 tablespoon of butter and 1 tablespoon of flour, and stir into 1 pint of scalded milk till thoroughly blended; then add to the celery mixture, and cook 10 minutes longer. Turn all into a fine-meshed sieve, and rub through into a saucepan. Return to the fire, season to taste with salt, pepper, and a dash of nutmeg. Remove from the fire, stir in 1 well-beaten egg yolk, mixed with 2 cups of scalded thin cream or undiluted evaporated milk. Heat to the boiling point, and taste for seasoning. Serve in hot soup plates, garnishing with fried Croutons (No. 780).

CREAM OF CELERY SOUP II [373]
With barley and rice

Wash 1 large stalk of celery, and dice small. Boil together the diced celery, 1 small onion, diced, a bouquet garni composed of 1 bay leaf and 6 sprigs of fresh parsley tied together with kitchen thread, 3 whole cloves, 6 peppercorns, 1 small sprig of thyme, and ½ cup of well-washed barley in 2 quarts of cold water for 45 minutes. Rub through a fine sieve. Return to the fire. Add 1 cup of scalded evaporated milk, and bring to a boil. Remove from the fire, and add 1 egg yolk, stirring well, and 2 tablespoons of butter, and stir again. Just before serving, add ½ cup of boiled rice, and season with salt and pepper to taste. Serve with toasted crackers.

CREAM OF CELERY AND TOMATO SOUP [374]

Wash 1 bunch of celery, the stalks scraped and chopped, the leaves finely chopped also. Cook in a small amount of Chicken Stock (No. 25), free of fat, until tender, and then rub through a fine-meshed wire sieve into a clean saucepan. To this purée, add 2 tablespoons of tomato paste, blending thoroughly. Keep hot over hot water, using a double boiler. Scald 3 cups of sweet milk and 1½ cups of sweet heavy cream with 1 bay leaf, 4 thin slices of onion, 1 whole clove, and 6 sprigs of fresh parsley. Strain through a fine sieve, then add to the celery-tomato purée. Season to taste with salt and white pepper and 1 scant teaspoon of paprika, and bring to a boil. Remove from the fire, and let cool slightly. Then beat in 4 fresh egg yolks, adding one at a time, beating well after each addition. Return to the fire, bring to a boil, and let boil 2 or 3 minutes, stirring constantly. Taste for seasoning, and serve in a heated soup tureen. Pass a dish of fried well-drained Croutons (No. 780).

CREAM OF CHESTNUT SOUP I [375]
French manner

Wipe with a damp cloth 1 small veal knuckle, split in two or three pieces. Place in a large soup kettle, and add 5 or 6 bruised peppercorns, 1 small blade of garlic, a bouquet garni composed of 1 bay leaf tied with 6 sprigs of fresh parsley, 2 teaspoons of onion juice, 2 whole cloves, 1 scant teaspoon of salt, and ⅓ cup of chopped celery leaves, and pour over all 5 cups of cold water. Bring slowly to a boil, then let simmer gently, closely covered, for 1½ to 1¾ hours. Turn the entire contents of the kettle into a fine-meshed sieve placed over a clean saucepan. Discard the veal knuckle and bouquet garni, and rub the remaining ingredients through the sieve. Return to the fire, and let the mixture reduce over a bright flame, until about 1½ cups of liquid are left, then add ¾ cup of Medium White Sauce (No. 346) and 2 cups of boiled, peeled, and chopped chestnuts alternately with 1 can of undiluted evaporated milk, or thin cream, previously scalded. Bring to a boil, empty the contents into a very fine sieve, and rub through into a clean saucepan. Taste for seasoning, and reheat to the boiling point. Remove from the fire, and stir in 2 slightly beaten egg yolks. Serve in heated soup plates, each garnished with a little popcorn lightly toasted.

According to Xenophon, the Greek historian, the children of the Persian nobility ate large quantities of chestnuts and thrived on them.

CREAM OF CHESTNUT SOUP II [376]
Quick method

Boil 1 quart of chestnuts for 20 to 25 minutes. Remove the shells and brown inner skin, then put them in a saucepan with sufficient boiling water to cover. Add 1 piece of lemon rind and 1 teaspoon of salt. When soft, remove the rind, and rub through a sieve. Then pour over them, stirring all the time, 2 quarts of White Stock (No. 11), or milk, ½ cup of cream, 1 generous tablespoon of butter mixed with 2 tablespoons of flour, and salt and pepper to taste. Bring to the boiling point. Serve with toasted salted crackers.

CREAM OF CHICKEN SOUP [377]

> *Alas! My child, where is the Pen*
> *That can do justice to the Hen?*
> *Like Royalty she goes her way,*
> *Laying Foundations every day.*
> *Though not for Public Buildings yet—*
> *For Custard, Cake, and Omelette.*
> *No wonder, Child, we prize the hen*
> *Whose egg is mightier than the Pen.* . . .
> OLIVER HERPID

Heat ¼ cup of butter in a saucepan, stir in 1½ cups of rice flour or barley flour, and cook over a gentle flame until the mixture becomes a golden brown, stirring almost constantly. Gradually stir in 2 quarts of Chicken Broth (No. 25), or half milk and half water (either scalded), 2 extra large leeks, carefully cleaned and chopped, using the white part only, 1 chopped celery stalk, and if milk and water are used, the carcass of a leftover chicken. Cook gently for 2 hours, skimming off all the scum as it rises. Empty the entire contents of the pan into a fine-meshed sieve, discard the bones, and rub through into a clean saucepan. Bring to a boil, season to taste with salt and white pepper, and stir in 2 cups of scalded medium thick cream, combined with 2 well-beaten egg yolks. Do not allow the soup to boil any more, lest it curdle. If too thick, stir in a little more scalded milk, and correct the seasoning. Just before serving, stir in ½ generous cup of cooked white meat of chicken, chopped fine or diced.

CREAM OF CHICKEN SOUP   [378]
A LA REINE FAÇON BOURGEOISE
French home method

Put into a large soup kettle ¼ pound of bacon, cut into small cubes; a 3-pound chicken, cleaned and trussed as for roasting; 1 medium-sized onion, left whole and stuck with 1 whole clove; 1 medium-sized carrot, quartered; 1 bouquet garni, composed of 8 sprigs of fresh parsley, 1 extra large bay leaf or 2 medium-sized ones, 1 sprig of thyme, and 1 sprig of green celery leaves (top), all tied together with kitchen thread; 2 teaspoons of salt; 8 whole peppercorns, gently bruised; and 1 quart of White Stock (No. 11), Chicken Broth (No. 25), or canned chicken bouillon. Bring to a boil, skim very carefully, and when the bouillon is clear, cover, and let simmer as gently as possible until the stock is reduced to about 2 cups, turning the chicken occasionally to prevent the part uncovered by the stock or liquid from becoming dry. Add 2 quarts more of similar hot stock to that used previously, and let simmer gently, skimming frequently until the chicken meat falls from the carcass. Carefully remove the chicken from the kettle, and when cool enough to handle, remove the skin and bones very carefully, and put the white meat alternately with ¼ pound of soft bread crumbs twice through a food chopper, using the finest blade. Then rub the chicken and crumb mixture through a fine-meshed wire sieve. Return this purée to the strained stock. Add 1 ounce of blanched, peeled, then twice-ground almonds, cooked for 2 or 3 minutes in a little milk. Taste for seasoning, adding salt and pepper, if needed, with a tiny dash of nutmeg. Bring to a boil, let boil for 2 minutes, and strain again through a fine-meshed wire sieve. When ready to serve, pour into a heated soup tureen containing a dozen Canadian Chicken Forcemeat Balls (No. 671), 3 tablespoons of freshly cooked green peas, a dozen freshly cooked or canned asparagus tips, and 2 tablespoons of sweet butter.

CREAM OF COCONUT SOUP A L'INDIENNE [379]

Note. If dried coconut is used, it should be previously soaked for 3 hours in a little chicken stock. Freshly grated coconut need not be soaked.

Bring 2 quarts of Chicken Broth (No. 25) to a boil, after adding 4 ounces of grated fresh coconut meat and a blade each of mace and clove, and let simmer gently, covered, for 50 minutes, or till reduced to 1½ quarts. Mix 2 ounces of rice flour smoothly with a little sweet milk, or fresh or dried coconut milk. Gradually stir into the stock, then bring to a quick boil. Lower the heat, and let simmer gently for 8 to 10 minutes. Taste for seasoning. Just before serving, stir in ½ cup of coconut milk, to which has been added ½ teaspoon of curry powder and ¼ cup of scalded sweet cream. Serve in heated soup plates, each topped with a tablespoonful of whipped cream, flavored with a little curry powder to taste.

CREAM OF CORN SOUP I [380]

Chop or put through a food chopper 1½ cups of cooked fresh corn or canned corn, and place in a saucepan. Heat 2 tablespoons of butter, stir in 2 tablespoons of finely chopped onion, and cook over a low flame, stirring almost constantly until the onion just begins to take on color. Then stir in the chopped corn, and continue cooking 3 or 4 minutes longer, stirring frequently. Place over hot water, and stir in 1 quart of scalded milk with a few grains of thyme, nutmeg, and mace, a large bay leaf, and 1 whole clove. Dilute 3 tablespoons of flour in a little cold milk, and gradually add to the mixture, stirring the while. Bring to a boil, let boil for 2 or 3 minutes, then strain into a clean saucepan, and stir in ¼ cup of scalded heavy cream. Let boil once, and serve in hot soup plates, garnished with Croutons (No. 780), and dusted with a few grains of paprika.

Variation. You may add to the mixture, before adding the scalded cream, 1 cup of tomato juice and ¼ teaspoon of baking soda, and you'll have a Corn and Tomato Bisque.

CREAM OF CORN SOUP II   [381]
With corn custard garnish

Slice 1 small onion fine, add 1 sprig of parsley, and cook in 2 tablespoons of butter until tender and light brown. Add ½ can of corn and 5 cups of milk. Let simmer for 20 to 25 minutes. Melt another 2 tablespoons of butter, blend in 2 tablespoons of flour, and mix well together. Then add to the soup, and let it come to a boil. Season with salt and pepper to taste. Serve with individual Corn Custard Garnish (No. 688).

CREAM OF CORN SOUP III   [382]
Farmer style

Melt 2 tablespoons of butter in a saucepan; add 1 tablespoon of flour, and when thoroughly blended, but not brown, stir in 2 cups of boiling water. Cook until the mixture begins to thicken, stirring almost constantly. Now add 1 medium-sized can of corn, cream style, 1 pint of scalded milk, 1 bay leaf, 4 thin slices of onion, 1 whole clove, and a little salt and pepper, and continue cooking for 15 minutes longer. Empty the contents of the saucepan into a fine-meshed wire sieve, and rub through into a clean saucepan. Return this purée to the fire, and stir in 1 cup of sweet cream, previously scalded. Bring to a boil, and taste for seasoning. Serve in hot soup plates, garnishing each with a dozen or so freshly popped kernels of corn.

CREAM OF CORN SOUP IV   [383]
Chowder style

In a saucepan, fry 1 sliced onion in 2 tablespoons of butter until light golden brown. Add 2 cups of boiling water, and stir well. Pour in 1 can of corn. Add 2 diced potatoes and 1 tablespoon of chopped parsley, and cook for 20 minutes. Then add 1 quart of scalded milk with a pinch of soda. Let boil twice. Remove from the fire. Season to taste with salt and pepper, and stir in 2 egg yolks. Finish with 1 tablespoon of butter and 2 egg whites beaten to a stiff froth, dropping a tablespoonful in each serving. Serve with Boston crackers, well buttered and soaked five minutes in hot milk.

Note. For additional Corn Chowders, see Chapter Eight.

CREAM OF CUCUMBER SOUP [384]
WITH SHERRY

Peel 3 small cucumbers, and slice thin. Cook in 2 cups of boiling salted water until tender, about 10 minutes. Rub through a fine sieve, moistening with the liquid. Melt 2 tablespoons of butter in a double boiler, add 1 generous tablespoon of flour, and blend well. Stir in 6 cups (1½ quarts) of milk, and cook until thickened. Add the cucumber purée, a dash of cayenne pepper, and salt to taste. Bring to a boil. Remove from the fire, and add 1 tablespoon of sherry wine and 1 tablespoon of finely chopped red pimiento. Serve with whipped cream and Croutons (No. 780).

CREAM OF CUCUMBER SOUP [385]
WITH ALMONDS

Peel 3 medium-sized cucumbers, and split lengthwise. Remove the seeds, slice very thin, and cook, stirring constantly, but without browning, in 3 tablespoons of butter. Sprinkle 1 tablespoon of flour over, and blend well. Gradually stir in 1½ quarts of scalded sweet milk, bring again to the boiling point, stirring constantly, and let simmer gently for 15 minutes, stirring frequently. Empty the whole contents of the saucepan into a fine-meshed wire sieve, and rub through into another saucepan. Return to the fire, bring once more to a boil, and season to taste with salt, pepper, and a generous dash of freshly ground nutmeg. Remove from the fire, and beat in 2 or 3 beaten egg yolks, one at a time, beating briskly after each addition, and adding with the last egg yolk 1 tablespoon of sweet butter. Finally, stir in ½ cup of blanched, toasted, and shredded almonds, and pass a side dish of fried Croutons (No. 780).

CREAM OF EGGPLANT SOUP [386]

Pare 2 medium-sized eggplants, and cut into small pieces. Put in 1 quart of salted boiling water, and cook for 30 minutes. Remove from the fire, and rub through a fine sieve. Return to the fire, and bring to a boil. Add 1 quart of milk and 1 cup of cream gradually, in which has been diluted 1 tablespoon of flour, stirring meanwhile. Cook slowly for 15 minutes. Remove from the fire. Season to taste with salt and pepper, and stir in 2 well-beaten egg yolks. Finish with 1 tablespoon of butter. Just before serving, add Egg Dumplings (No. 728), 2 for each serving.

CREAM OF GIBLET SOUP [387]
New England style

Note. This soup is very good and very inexpensive. It is an excellent imitation of mock turtle soup.

Melt 2 tablespoons of butter, and stir in 1 medium-sized onion, diced, 1 small carrot, finely chopped, and ½ small white turnip, chopped. Cook until tender and light brown over a medium flame, stirring frequently. Then add the giblets of 4 chickens or 2 turkeys, first carefully washed and dried, then cut in small pieces. Cook for 2 or 3 minutes, stirring constantly, then sprinkle in 1 tablespoon of flour, and stir until thoroughly blended. Turn into a soup kettle. Add 2 quarts of boiling water, or equal parts of water and White Stock (No. 11). Bring to a boil, lower the flame, and let simmer gently for 2½ hours, or until the giblets are tender. Rub through a fine sieve the chicken or turkey giblets, and add them to the contents of the soup kettle together with 1 tablespoon of butter and 1 tablespoon of flour browned together. Bring to the boiling point, and cook for 3 minutes. Season to taste with salt and pepper, and when ready to serve, stir in 3 hard-cooked eggs, coarsely chopped. Serve in hot soup plates with freshly made toast.

CREAM OF GREEN ONION SOUP [388]
Parisian method

The green onion has none of that voluptuousness of the full-grown bulb. It is gentle; it is sweet; it's appealing by refined devices. It will do you proud served in an onion soup made as follows:

Trim about 24 tiny green onions, leaving the little bulbs, half an inch long. Place in a saucepan with enough Chicken Broth (No. 25) to generously cover, and boil until tender and the liquid is nearly evaporated. Rub the remaining liquid and the green onion bulbs through a fine-meshed wire sieve into a clean saucepan. Meanwhile, scald 1 quart of sweet milk with 1 bay leaf, 6 sprigs of fresh parsley, and 2 small white leeks, thinly sliced. Strain, and stir into the onion purée, mixing well. Beat 4 egg yolks with 1 cup of scalded sweet cream in a heated soup tureen, and gradually strain the onion soup over the egg yolk mixture, beating briskly with a wire whisk. Taste for seasoning, and serve at once, after dusting with plenty of finely chopped chervil, or lacking it, with chopped parsley. Serve with finger toasts made by cutting bread into finger length and frying in plenty of butter.

CREAM OF GREEN PEPPER SOUP [389]

Follow the directions for Cream of Pimiento Soup (No. 415), substituting green peppers for the red pimientos.

CREAM OF HARE SOUP [390]
Also called Hare Bisque Saint Hubert

Rabbits, squirrels, and hares all yield delicious, fine-textured meat, much like chicken in flavor. Have your butcher dress them, or do it yourself. Keep them three or four days before using. They may be prepared in many delicious ways. Although ancient warriors would not eat rabbit, fearing the flesh of so timid an animal might make them cowardly, we moderns are very fond of rabbits, squirrels, hares, and even muskrat (or marsh rabbit), especially when prepared in a delicious bisque as follows:

Take half of the front part of an old hare (or rabbit) weighing about 4 pounds, and cut it into small pieces. Place in a soup kettle with 2 quarts of cold water. Add 2 small carrots, scraped, then quartered; 1 large onion, quartered; ½ cup of green celery leaves, well washed; 1 small white turnip, peeled and quartered; 1 leek, halved, carefully washed, then cut into inch pieces; 1 clove of garlic, peeled and left whole; 8 whole peppercorns, gently bruised; salt to taste; 1 bouquet garni, composed of 1 large bay leaf, 3 parsley roots, scraped and left whole, 1 sprig of thyme, 2 whole cloves, and all tied together with kitchen thread; and 1 tablespoon of beef extract (commercial). Slowly bring to a boil, skim off the scum carefully; then boil once, lower the heat, and allow to simmer gently for 3 hours, covered. Remove the pieces of hare and bone carefully. Put the meat through a food chopper, using the finest blade, then rub through a fine-meshed sieve, easing the rubbing with 1 quart of strained hare broth, to which has been added ⅓ cup of cooked rice. Return the mixture to the fire, and let simmer for 15 to 20 minutes. Remove from the fire, and stir in 3 fresh egg yolks, beaten with 1 cup of thin cream or undiluted evaporated milk. Taste for seasoning, and heat well, but do not let boil. Serve in hot soup plates, each garnished with 4 small cubes of Game Custard Garnish (No. 689).

CREAM OF KIDNEY SOUP [391]
Hunter style

Cut 2 large veal kidneys in thin slices, and brown in 2 tablespoons of butter over a low flame, stirring almost constantly. Then stir in

1½ cups of water, or Beef Consommé (No. 114), and cook until the kidneys are tender, or about 10 to 12 minutes, skimming carefully. Turn into a fine-meshed wire sieve, and rub through into a clean saucepan. Return to the fire, and let simmer very gently for 25 minutes. Moisten ½ ounce of freshly ground polished rice with 1 cup of cold milk, and add to the soup alternately with 1 quart of scalded sweet milk and ½ cup of finely chopped fresh raw mushrooms. Season to taste with salt, pepper, and a dash of mace. Cover, and let simmer gently for 20 minutes. Then add 1 tablespoon of butter kneaded with 2 teaspoons of flour. Bring to a boil, cook for 3 or 4 minutes, and remove from the fire. Finally, stir in 2 egg yolks, well beaten with 2 or 3 tablespoons of Madeira wine. Taste for seasoning, and serve in heated soup plates, each containing 2 Egg Balls (No. 672).

CREAM OF LAMB SOUP [392]
Also called Lamb Bisque Liverpool Manner

Cut 3 pounds of lamb neck in small pieces, and remove the fat carefully. Put into a soup kettle with 2 quarts of cold water; 1 large onion, peeled and quartered; 2 small carrots, scraped, then quartered; 1 small white turnip, peeled and quartered; ½ cup of well-washed raw rice; 1 cup of fresh quartered tomatoes, or canned; 1 bouquet garni, composed of 1 large bay leaf, 6 sprigs of parsley, 1 sprig of thyme, 2 whole cloves, and tied together with kitchen thread; 6 freshly crushed peppercorns; and 1 teaspoon of salt. Very gently bring this to a boil, skim off the scum carefully, lower the heat, and let simmer gently for 4 hours, covered. At the end of that time, add 1 tablespoon of butter and 1 tablespoon of flour rubbed to a cream. Strain through a fine-meshed sieve. Return the liquid to the fire, and bring to the boiling point, with a small leaflet of fresh mint. Remove the mint leaflet at once. Stir in 2 cups of scalded milk, to which has been added 2 fresh egg yolks, stirring briskly the while. Taste for seasoning, and serve in hot soup plates, each garnished with 2 tiny Watercress Dumplings (No. 763).

CREAM OF LEEK, MUSHROOM, [393]
AND POTATO SOUP
Belgian Potage Pastourelle

The cookery of the Walloons, or the French-speaking part of Belgium, is absolutely the same as French cookery. The Flemish have a cookery which is a mixture of French and Dutch.

Cook in ¼ cup of butter the white parts of 5 large leeks, thinly sliced, carefully washed in several changes of cold water, and well drained, together with ⅓ pound of fresh mushrooms, peeled and thinly sliced, for 5 minutes, stirring almost constantly. Do not let brown. (The original recipe calls for a kind of mushroom called *mousseron*, which is unknown in this country. Fresh mushrooms are substituted for them.) Transfer the well-drained mixture into a soup kettle. Pour over 1 quart of rich Veal Stock (No. 11) or Chicken Broth (No. 25). Add 1 bouquet garni, composed of 1 large bay leaf, 8 sprigs of fresh parsley, 1 sprig of thyme, and 8 or 10 chives, tied together with kitchen thread, and salt and white pepper to taste. Bring to a boil. Then add 1 pound of pared and cubed small raw potatoes. Let simmer gently for 30 minutes. Rub the entire contents of the kettle through a fine sieve into a clean kettle. Bring to a boil, then stir in 1 pint of rich scalded milk, to which has been added 3 fresh egg yolks, well beaten. Taste for seasoning, and pour the mixture into a heated soup tureen. Add ⅓ cup of peeled, thinly sliced fresh mushrooms, cooked in butter and well drained, even sponged, and ½ cup of very tiny raw potato cubes, cooked in butter till browned on all sides and well drained. Serve at once.

CREAM OF LEEK AND POTATO SOUP A LA FRANÇAISE [394]

Sometimes called *l'asperge des pauvres*—poor man's asparagus— the leek, celebrated by writers of antiquity, lends itself to most asparagus recipes, so that we can have "asparagus" even in winter. Unfortunately, it is too often overlooked today for its more sturdy brothers, the onions, or the over-refined shallot. Leek soup was one of Nero's more agreeable weaknesses, which earned him the name of Porrophagus from the Latin name for the leek, *porrum*. From this came the *porée* of France in the Middle Ages, and finally the present French name *poireau*.

Cut 4 leeks into inch pieces, and wash thoroughly, using the white and green parts. Peel, and cut up 3 large potatoes and 1 onion. Pour 3 cups of boiling water over all. Let boil for 35 minutes. Mash through a sieve. Return to the fire, and season to taste with salt and pepper, and if desired, 1 scant teaspoon of marjoram. Add 3 cups of scalded milk, previously combined with 1 cup of undiluted evaporated milk. Let boil once. Finish with 1 generous tablespoon of butter. Serve with toast or crackers.

CREAM OF LEEK AND POTATO SOUP   [395]
A L'ITALIENNE

Cut 4 leeks into inch pieces, using the white and green parts, and
wash in several waters thoroughly. Drain well, and cook in 2 tablespoons of butter for 10 minutes. Do not brown. Add 2 cups of boiling water, 2 large potatoes, peeled and cut in small pieces, 1 bay leaf,
and 1 clove, and let simmer gently for 30 minutes. Then add 1 quart
of scalded milk, and continue cooking for 10 minutes. Season to taste
with salt and pepper, and mash through a sieve. Return to the fire,
bring rapidly to a boil, and add all at once ½ cup of vermicelli. Cook
for 15 minutes. Correct the seasoning, and finish with 1 tablespoon
of butter.

CREAM OF LENTIL SOUP I   [396]
With egg dumplings and variations

Soak 1 cup of washed dry lentils overnight in 3 cups of lukewarm
water. In the morning, turn all into a soup kettle with 1 ham bone
or an equivalent of 1 cup of ham trimmings. Add 1 onion stuck with
2 cloves, ½ cup of celery leaves, finely minced, 2 small diced carrots,
and 2 thinly sliced potatoes, and pour over 1 quart of warm water.
Cover, and let simmer for 1½ hours. Remove the bone, if used, and
mash the other contents through a sieve. Add 1 quart of scalded
milk. Season with salt and pepper to taste. Just before serving, add
Egg Dumplings (No. 728), 2 for each serving.
Variations. Substitute sliced frankfurters for egg dumplings, well
heated for 3 minutes in the soup before serving.
Substitute meat dumplings, such as Beef, Ham, Liver, Pork, or
Sausage Dumplings (Nos. 709, 737, 742, 751, 756) for egg dumplings.
Substitute ½ cup of cooked rice for egg dumplings just before
serving.

CREAM OF LENTIL SOUP II   [397]
Farmer style

Wash ½ cup of lentils, and soak overnight in 1 quart of warm
water. In the morning, combine the lentils with 1 onion, quartered,
1 cup each of diced potatoes and carrots, and ½ cup of shredded
cabbage. Cook for 1½ hours in the same quart of water, adding
more water if necessary. Mash through a sieve, and return to the
fire, adding 2 cups (1 pint) of rich milk and 1 cup of cream. Bring
to the boiling point, but do not let boil. Season with salt and pepper

to taste. Finish with 2 tablespoons of butter. Sprinkle each serving with grated American cheese.

CREAM OF LETTUCE SOUP [398]

Because the Greeks believed that lettuce induced sleep, they served it at the end of a meal. This custom was followed by the Romans, but the cruel Emperor Domitian reversed the custom, serving lettuce and eggs at the beginning of a feast, intending to torture the guests by forcing them to keep awake in the presence of the emperor.

Wash 2 heads of crisp lettuce, the greener the better, first picking carefully and discarding any wilted leaves. Shred very fine, wash again, and drain; then dry by patting between 2 dry towels. Blanch in 2 cups of slightly salted water. Blend 2 tablespoons of butter and 1 tablespoon of flour over a gentle flame. When beginning to bubble, stir in 1 quart of sweet milk, which has been scalded with 3 thin slices of onion, 3 sprigs of fresh parsley, 1 whole clove, and 1 small bay leaf, and then strained. Stir almost constantly over a low flame until the mixture boils and thickens slightly. Then add the shredded lettuce, and continue simmering gently for 30 to 35 minutes, stirring occasionally. Season to taste with salt, pepper, and a dash of nutmeg. Turn into a fine-meshed wire sieve, and rub through into a clean saucepan. Return to the fire, and bring again to a boil. Stir in 2 egg yolks, beaten with 1 cup of thin cream or undiluted evaporated milk. Finally, stir in 1 tablespoon of sweet butter. Taste for seasoning, and serve in heated soup plates, garnishing each with a sprinkling of chopped parsley or chervil. Serve with Croutons (No. 780).

CREAM OF LETTUCE SOUP AMANDINE [399]
Also called Almond Cream of Lettuce Soup

Proceed as indicated for Cream of Spinach Soup (No. 428), substituting lettuce for spinach, and cooking in exactly the same manner. When ready to serve, stir in ⅓ cup of blanched and thinly sliced toasted almonds. Serve hot.

CREAM OF MUSHROOM SOUP [400]
WITH SHERRY

". . . Oddly fashioned, quaintly dyed,
In the woods the mushrooms hide;
Rich and meaty, full of flavor,
Made for man's delicious savor. . . ."

Think what can be done with mushrooms. Add them to a plain omelet, and it becomes a dream. Eat them raw, and they are a sensation. Add them to a casserole dish, and they distribute their delicious perfume throughout the dish. Dry them, and they still retain their fragrance and will impart it lavishly to whatever dish they find themselves a part of. Canned, they are conveniently available in emergencies, ever ready for a gala occasion. Serve a soup of them, such as the following, and the meal invariably is a success. They are a natural for soup, of course.

Remove the stems from ¾ pound of fresh mushrooms; peel the caps, and chop them fine, reserving the stems for other use. Heat 3 tablespoons of butter, and cook the chopped mushrooms for 2 minutes, stirring constantly. Sprinkle over 3 tablespoons of flour, blend well, and stir in 1 cup of rich Chicken Consommé (No. 25). Cook for 3 or 4 minutes longer, then squeeze the mixture through a strong kitchen cloth into a saucepan. To this mushroom liquid, add ½ cup of cooked rice. Let boil once, then rub through a fine-meshed sieve into a clean saucepan. Add 3 cups of scalded milk and 1 cup of thin cream, and bring to a boil. Season to taste with salt, pepper, a few grains of nutmeg and cayenne, and a good pinch of dry mustard. Allow to simmer gently for 15 minutes. Then stir in 3 fresh egg yolks, beaten with 3 tablespoons of good sherry wine, stirring briskly while pouring the egg mixture. Taste for seasoning, and serve in hot soup cups, each topped with a little whipped cream dusted with paprika.

CREAM OF MUSHROOM SOUP [401]

Peel 1 pound of fresh mushrooms; cut off the rough ends of the stems, and chop coarsely, then put through a food chopper. Melt ¼ cup of butter in the top of a double boiler. Add 1 medium-sized onion, finely chopped, also the ground mushrooms, and cook for 5 minutes over direct flame, stirring frequently. Sprinkle in 1½ tablespoons of flour, and blend well. Gradually stir in 1½ quarts of sweet milk (previously scalded with 1 large bay leaf, 4 sprigs of fresh parsley, and 1 whole clove, then strained), and cook, stirring almost constantly, until the mixture thickens and boils. Season to taste with salt, pepper, a dash of cayenne, and one of mace, stirring frequently. Turn into a fine-meshed wire sieve, and rub through into a clean saucepan. Return to the fire, taste for seasoning, and stir in ½ cup of scalded heavy sweet cream, to which has been added 2 well-beaten egg yolks. Stir briskly. Serve in heated soup plates with Croutons (No. 780).

CREAM OF PECAN SOUP [402]

Beat 3 unseparated eggs together. Scald 1½ quarts of milk. Blend 1 tablespoon of butter and 1 tablespoon of flour. Grind 1 cup of halved and skinned pecans. Moisten the flour and butter mixture gradually with the scalded milk, stirring meanwhile. Add the ground pecans, and let simmer very gently for 25 minutes. Strain through a fine sieve. Return to the fire, and let boil once. Season to taste with salt and white pepper. Stir in 2 well-beaten egg yolks. Serve with a tablespoon of whipped cream for each serving.

CREAM OF ONION AND LEEK SOUP [403]
Welsh manner

Every year, on March first all good Welshmen wear leeks in their hats. According to the legend, Saint David was the uncle of King Arthur, king of the Silures, who has been the theme of much romantic fiction concerning his heroic deeds in waging war against the Saxons, Scots, and Picts. He married the celebrated Guinevere, of the house of Cornwall, established the famous order of the Round Table, and made many a favorite meal on leeks. He is supposed to have lived with a contented mind to the age of 146 years. We are not told whether his consumption of leeks had anything to do with either his serenity or his long life. At any rate, the Welsh make a delicious cream soup with the first cousin of the onion.

For six generous servings, melt 2 tablespoons of butter in a soup kettle, and add 6 medium-sized onions, thinly sliced, and 6 medium-sized leeks, finely chopped and well washed, using only the white parts, and sauté until light golden brown. Add 4 large potatoes, cubed small, mix thoroughly, and moisten with 1 quart of Chicken Broth (No. 25). Season to taste with salt, white pepper, and a pinch of nutmeg and mace. Cook covered for 35 to 40 minutes, stirring occasionally. Empty the entire contents into a fine-meshed sieve, and rub the mixture into a clean soup kettle. Then add 1 cup of heavy cream and 3½ cups of rich milk, both scalded and mixed. Bring to a rapid boil, stirring frequently. Remove from the fire, and stir in 3 tablespoons of sweet butter alternately with 2 well-beaten egg yolks. Taste for seasoning, and pour into a hot soup tureen.

Sprinkle the top with grated cheese, using about ¼ cup and spreading the cheese as evenly as possible. Glaze quickly under the flame of the broiling oven until the cheese bubbles and becomes a golden brown. Serve immediately.

CREAM OF ONION SOUP   [404]
A LA PARISIENNE

Elegance and the onion . . . they don't sound compatible, do they? Yet of all the foods known to man, probably none can boast a history so filled with romance and legend. And never forget that the onion is a member of the elegant lily family, and extends so far back that it antedates written records. The name itself is interesting. It is derived from the city of Onias, built long before the Christian era. In the sacred writings, we find the onion mentioned as one of the things for which the Israelites longed when in the wilderness. They complained to Moses because they were deprived of their leeks, onions, and garlic, of which, said the murmurers, "We remember we did eat in Egypt freely." To show how much the onion was esteemed by the ancient Egyptians, we need only mention that Herodotus says in his time (450 B.C.) that there was an inscription on the Great Pyramid, stating that a sum amounting to 1600 talents had been paid for onions, radishes, and garlic which had been consumed by the slaves during the progress of its erection.

Under the term "enneleac," "leac-tun," or leek, all the members of the onion family were grouped in Old England until the Normans arrived and brought the French term which anglicized became onion, from the French *oignon*.

Mince fine 3 medium-sized onions. Brown in 1 tablespoon of butter over a very low fire. Sprinkle 1 tablespoon of flour over the onions. Stir with a wooden spoon, and blend well. Moisten with 2 cups (1 pint) of scalded milk, while stirring constantly. Bring to a boil. Add 2 cups (1 pint) of scalded cream, and let simmer very gently for 20 minutes. Place bread sticks (French bread cut in small sticks) into a soup tureen. Sprinkle about ½ cup of freshly grated Swiss cheese over, and pour the soup on this. Just before serving, sprinkle with freshly ground pepper to taste. Serve piping hot.

This delicious onion soup may be served au gratin. In that case, it is usually served in individual tureens. Cover with grated Swiss cheese, and brown in a hot oven. Meat stock may be substituted for milk and cream.

CREAM OF ONION SOUP YANKEE, [405]
CHEESE TOPPING

Sauté 4 cups of thinly sliced onions in 4 tablespoons of fat over a gentle heat until tender, but not brown, stirring almost constantly with a wooden spoon. Add ½ cup of hot Beef Stock (No. 114). Cover, and let steam until tender and the stock has evaporated. Sprinkle over this 2½ to 3 tablespoons of flour, and season with 2 teaspoons of salt, a generous dash of black pepper, and 1 teaspoon of Worcestershire sauce, and blend well. Gradually stir in 5 cups of scalded rich creamy milk, or 4 cups of milk and 1 cup of cream, and cook until thickened. Add a little hot soup to 2 well-beaten egg yolks, and stir into the onion soup. Pour into hot soup bowls, and sprinkle each bowl with grated American cheese, using about a generous ½ cup in all. Serve immediately.

CREAM OF ONION SOUP [406]
Dutch style

Melt 3 tablespoons of butter in a deep frying pan, and fry 4 large sliced onions, stirring often with a wooden spoon until tender, but not brown. Add 1 quart of scalded milk. Stir. Dilute 1 tablespoon of flour in a little cream, and add the rest of 1 cup of cream. Pour into the soup, and cook for 20 minutes on a low fire. Season to taste with salt and white pepper. Remove from the fire. Stir in 4 well-beaten egg yolks. Serve with fried Croutons (No. 780).

CREAM OF PARSNIP SOUP [407]

Scrape 2 large parsnips, and cut into small pieces. Boil in salted water, enough to cover, until tender. Drain. Reserve 1 cup of liquor. Discard the remainder. Put the parsnips through a potato ricer, then rub through a fine sieve, moistening with the reserved cup of liquor and alternating with 1½ quarts of scalded milk. Return to the fire. Bring to a boil, and let simmer very gently for 15 minutes. Season to taste with salt and pepper. Finish with 1 tablespoon of butter. Serve at once with 1 tablespoon of whipped cream, sprinkled with paprika for each serving.

CREAM OF PEA SOUP I [408]
French method—with green or yellow split peas

Did you know that licorice and peas belong to the same plant family, and that garavances or calavances were words used in colonial recipes for peas, beans, and lentils?

In France in 1600, peas were the food of royalty alone. They sometimes marketed for 50 crowns a litron, which would be about equal to $62.50 for a good-sized dish of canned peas. The price, however, was no obstacle to the wealthy French. Madame de Maintenon wrote in a letter dated May 10, 1696: "The subject of peas continues to absorb all others. The anxiety to eat them, the pleasure of having eaten them, and the desire to eat them again are the three great matters which have been discussed by our Princes for four days past. Peas are both a fashion and a madness."

Lima beans, marrow beans, any kind of beans and lentils may be used instead of the peas in this fine bisque.

Soak 1 pint of dried green or yellow split peas overnight in cold water to cover after washing them in several changes of cold water. In the morning, add sufficient water to make 4 quarts. Place on the fire with 2 thinly sliced onions; 1 medium-sized green pepper, chopped; 1 bouquet garni, composed of 1 large bay leaf, 3 sprigs of fresh parsley, 1 sprig of thyme, 2 whole cloves, and tied with kitchen thread; 6 freshly crushed peppercorns; salt to taste; and also 1 ham bone. Bring to a boil, lower the flame, and let simmer very gently for 3 hours, stirring occasionally from the bottom of the kettle. Empty the contents of the kettle into a fine sieve, discard the ham bone and the bouquet garni, and rub through into a clean kettle. Bring to a boil, and stir in 1 cup of sweet milk and 1 cup of thick cream, scalded together. Continue simmering for 15 minutes. Stir in ⅓ cup of cooked chopped vermicelli. Remove from the fire, and stir in 3 tablespoons of sherry wine. Serve in hot soup plates, each garnished with 3 or 4 small cubes of Pea Custard Garnish (No. 699).

CREAM OF PEA SOUP II [409]
Flemish method—with green or yellow split peas

Proceed as indicated for Cream of Pea Soup I, above, using only 1 cup of dried green or yellow split peas and 2 quarts of water. When the soup is ready to serve, stir in 2 cups of rich Chicken Consommé (No. 25), which should be very hot and in which 3 fresh egg yolks have been beaten. Place in a heated soup tureen ½ cup of freshly made Croutons (No. 780) and ¾ cup of boiled chopped white part of young leeks. After tasting for seasoning, pour the bisque hot over the mixture in the soup tureen. Serve immediately in hot soup plates.

CREAM OF PEA SOUP III [410]
Quick method

Open 1 large can of peas, and pour the contents into a strainer with 2 cups of boiling water, 1½ teaspoons of sugar, and 2 pork sausages, and rub the mixture through thoroughly. Make a cream sauce by blending 2 tablespoons of butter with 2 tablespoons of flour and 2 cups of milk. Add this to the first mixture, and cook slowly for 10 minutes. Season with salt to taste, and serve with Croutons (No. 780).

CREAM OF PEA SOUP IV [411]
With fresh peas

Shred 1 coarse leaf of lettuce, and cook with 2 pounds of fresh shelled peas, 6 very tender pea pods, salt, and 2 cups of boiling water for 15 minutes. Remove the pods, and rub through a sieve, moistening once in a while to ease the rubbing. Cook 2 tablespoons of butter, ½ teaspoon of grated onion, and 2 tablespoons of flour together until well blended. Stir in 1½ quarts of rich scalded milk. Cook gently for 10 minutes. Combine with the pea mixture. Bring to a boil. Remove from the fire. Add a small pinch of sugar, and stir in 2 well-beaten egg yolks. Add salt and pepper, if necessary. Serve at once with Croutons (No. 780). Instead of croutons, you may serve a slice of tomato garnished with whipped cream for each serving.

CREAM OF PEA PODS SOUP [412]

Wash 1 pound of fresh peas in their pods quickly but thoroughly in cold water; snap off the stem ends and put the peas in a saucepan, the pods in a soup kettle. To the pods, add 1 pint of cold milk, 1 small bay leaf, 2 tablespoons of grated onion, 1 small fresh mint leaflet, washed, salt and pepper to taste, and cook until tender but not too soft.

Cook the peas in as little water as possible for 6 or 7 minutes, and combine with the pea pods. Bring the mixture to a rapid boil; empty the contents of the kettle into a fine sieve, and rub through into a clean kettle. Return to the fire; stir in 1 cup of thin cream scalded with 2 cups of milk; boil once, then beat in 3 fresh egg yolks, beaten with 3 tablespoons of Madeira wine, beating briskly and from the bottom of the kettle. Remove from the fire; taste for seasoning; stir in 2 tablespoons of sweet butter; and serve at once in hot soup plates, each garnished with 2 tiny Farina Dumplings (No. 730), or Bran Dumplings (No. 710).

CREAM OF PEANUT BUTTER SOUP [413]

Add 1 generous teaspoon of grated onion and ½ cup of peanut butter to 5 cups of rich creamy milk, which has been scalded with 1 large bay leaf, 2 whole cloves, a tiny blade of garlic, and 4 sprigs of parsley, and then strained. Beat 3 egg yolks slightly, add ½ teaspoon of flour, and beat vigorously, then gradually stir this into the rapidly boiling soup, stirring briskly and from the bottom of the pan to prevent scorching and curdling at the same time, and boiling gently for a minute or two. Remove from the fire; taste for seasoning; and serve at once in heated soup plates, each garnished with 6 toasted halved peanuts.

CREAM OF PEANUT SOUP [414]

Grind 1 cup of shelled and skinned peanuts twice until very fine. Scald 1½ quarts of milk. Add the peanuts, and bring to a rapid boil, stirring constantly. Season to taste with salt and pepper, and let simmer very gently for 15 minutes. Rub through a very fine sieve. Return to the fire. Boil once, and remove from the fire. Then add 2 well-beaten egg yolks, stirring rapidly and constantly while pouring slowly. Finish with 1 tablespoon of butter and 2 tablespoons of finely chopped well-drained red pimiento. Serve very hot with 1 tablespoon of whipped cream to each serving.

CREAM OF PIMIENTO SOUP [415]

The green peppers which we use as a vegetable are the products of a mild type of capsicum shrub which is known also as pimiento. The word "pimento" often used in reference to the canned sweet red peppers that we use for the sake of color, flavor and garnishing, actually belongs to the berry of the pimento tree, which we know as allspice.

Bring 1 quart of Chicken Broth (No. 25) to a brisk boil, and when rapidly boiling, drop in, rainlike, ½ cup of well-washed rice and add 1 large bay leaf, 3 sprigs of parsley, and 2 whole cloves. Cook until the rice is tender, and stir in 4 canned red pimientos, drained and chopped. Rub the contents of the kettle through a fine-meshed sieve, after discarding the bay leaf, parsley, and cloves, into a clean kettle. Season to taste with salt, pepper, nutmeg, and a few grains of cayenne. Boil once, then stir in ¾ cup of heavy cream, scalded and mixed briskly with 2 fresh egg yolks. Serve in hot soup cups, each garnished with 1 tiny Spinach Dumpling (No. 759).

Note. Green peppers may be substituted for the red pimientos.

CREAM OF POTATO SOUP I [416]
Home style

Cook 4 medium-sized cubed potatoes, 1 medium-sized sliced onion, and 1 small bunch of celery until tender (about 25 minutes) in sufficient water to cover. Add 1 small can of corn and 2 tablespoons of butter, and season to taste with pepper and salt. Rub through a sieve. Return to the fire. Add 1½ quarts of scalded milk. Bring to a rapid boil, and finish just before serving with 1 tablespoon of finely chopped parsley.

CREAM OF POTATO SOUP II [417]
Using mashed potatoes

A very economical way to use leftover mashed potatoes.

Melt 2 tablespoons of butter in a saucepan. Add 1 small onion, grated, and 2 tablespoons of flour, and blend well. Stir in 1½ quarts of scalded milk gradually, and heat thoroughly. Season to taste with salt and pepper. Add 2 cups of mashed hot potatoes, 1 tablespoon of grated carrot, and ½ teaspoon of nutmeg. Boil once, and let simmer very gently for 15 minutes. Finish with 1 tablespoon of butter. Serve with Croutons (No. 780).

CREAM OF POTATO SOUP III [418]
London style

Combine 3 large diced potatoes and 2 large onions, chopped fine, in a saucepan, and cover with boiling water. Cook for 15 minutes, then add 1 bay leaf, 1 clove, and 2 tablespoons of celery leaves, chopped fine. Cook for 15 minutes longer. Rub through a fine sieve, moistening once in a while with the cooking liquor. Add 1½ quarts of scalded milk gradually, and stir well. Return to the fire, and let simmer for 10 minutes. Season with salt and pepper to taste, and add 2 tablespoons of butter, 2 tablespoons of blanched chopped green pepper, and a small pinch of nutmeg. Remove from the fire, stir in 1 well-beaten egg yolk, and serve at once with Croutons (No. 780).

CREAM OF POTATO AND LEEK SOUP   [419]
Scotch style

Melt 2 tablespoons of butter in a large saucepan. Add 1 cup of minced leeks (white and green tops), 1 cup of minced celery leaves (tops), and cook for 5 minutes, stirring once in a while. Add 1½ quarts of scalded milk, and let simmer very gently for 15 minutes uncovered. Cook 3 cups of diced potatoes in 2 cups of boiling water until almost soft. Turn into the hot milk mixture, and rub through a sieve. Return to the fire. Let simmer while blending 2 tablespoons each of butter and flour, and add to the soup. Cook gently for 15 minutes longer. Season with salt and pepper to taste and a dish of paprika. Remove from the fire, stir in 2 well-beaten egg yolks, and serve at once with Croutons (No. 780).

CREAM OF PUMPKIN SOUP I   [420]
French style

Of the honesty and sincerity of our sentimental fondness for the pumpkin, there is no doubt. It is possible, indeed, that the aura of sanctity with which we have surrounded that gourd has limited our desire to find new culinary uses for it, for the French, who have no emotion one way or the other about the pumpkin, which they call *potiron*, have gone far beyond pumpkin pie. On a cold winter night, for instance, warmth and comfort that penetrate to the soul can be yours when a rich creamy pumpkin soup is on the table.

Cook 3½ pounds of peeled and diced pumpkin in 1½ quarts of salted water until the pumpkin is tender. Empty the entire contents of the kettle into a fine-meshed wire sieve, and rub through into a saucepan. Stir in 1 quart of milk, which has been boiled with 1 bay leaf, 4 thin slices of onion, and 3 sprigs of fresh parsley, and then strained. Return to the fire, and stir in 1 teaspoon of sugar (more or less, according to taste) and a pinch of freshly grated nutmeg. Keep the mixture over hot water. Then cook until tender 3 tablespoons of quick-cooking tapioca in 2 cups of Chicken Broth or Beef Consommé (Nos. 25 and 114), and add to the soup. Taste for seasoning, and when ready to serve, stir in 1 pint of scalded fresh sweet cream. Serve with Croutons (No. 780).

CREAM OF PUMPKIN SOUP II [421]
Quick method

Combine 3 cups of cooked pumpkin and 1 tablespoon of butter with 1 quart of scalded milk, and bring to a rapid boil. Season to taste with salt and, if desired, with a little white pepper. Stir in 1 well-beaten egg yolk, and finish with 1 tablespoon of butter. Stir well, then serve with Croutons (No. 780).

CREAM OF PUMPKIN SOUP PROVENÇALE [422]

It takes only the wave of a wand, or the cook's knife, to change a pumpkin into something quite different: pumpkin chips for garnishing the grilled steak, the orange flesh for a true American pie, the skin for a coach for Cinderella or a jack-o'-lantern for Halloween, an utterly zaza bit of nonsense that outsells every cocktail niblet— the toasted or grilled pumpkin seed—pumpkin doughnuts, pumpkin custard, and this ultra delicious soup.

Put 3 cups of raw diced pumpkin into a saucepan. Add 2 cups of Chicken Consommé (No. 25), 1 large bay leaf, 4 thin slices of onion, a small piece of grated parsley root, 2 cloves, and salt and pepper to taste; also, if liked, a thin slice of garlic, mashed. Cook until the pumpkin is tender, or about 25 minutes. Empty the entire contents of the pan into a fine-meshed sieve, and rub through into a clean pan.
Cook enough fresh or canned string beans until tender, rub through a fine sieve, and add to the pumpkin mixture. Stir in 2 cups of scalded milk with 2 tablespoons of grated onion, and bring to a boil. Let simmer for 10 to 15 minutes over a very gentle flame, stirring occasionally; then stir in 2 cups of rich scalded milk, to which has been added 3 fresh egg yolks, well beaten. Taste for seasoning, and when ready to serve, stir in 2 tablespoons of sweet butter. Just before pouring into hot soup plates, stir in ¼ cup of Madeira wine. Garnish each plate with 3 thin slices of frankfurters, skinned and heated in a little of the chicken consommé.

CREAM OF QUAIL SOUP [423]
Also called Quail Bisque

Clean 2 plump quails after removing the heads. Place the birds in a soup kettle with 1 medium-sized carrot, grated, then sliced thin; 1 branch of celery, grated, then chopped fine; 1 medium-sized onion, peeled, left whole, and stuck with 1 whole clove; and 1 bouquet garni, composed of 1 large bay leaf, 6 sprigs of fresh parsley, 1 sprig of green celery top, 1 sprig of thyme (wild, if available), and 1 small leek, split in two lengthwise and carefully washed, using the green and white parts, the whole tied together with kitchen thread. Add also 6 peppercorns, freshly and coarsely ground, 1 juniper berry, crushed, a blade of freshly grated nutmeg, and ½ cup of lentils, previously soaked in cold water overnight and well drained. Do not salt as yet. Bring to the boiling point, and let boil for 5 minutes, after pouring over 1½ quarts of Chicken Consommé (No. 25). Now salt to taste, about 1 scant teaspoon of salt. Lower the flame, and let simmer very gently for 1½ to 1¾ hours, half covered. The cooking time depends on the age of the birds; if young quails are used, 1½ hours is sufficient.

Remove the birds, discard the bouquet garni, and strain the liquid through a sieve, pressing well to pass through the vegetables and lentils. Return the liquid to the fire, and let simmer gently while boning the birds carefully and pounding or putting the meat through a food chopper, using the finest blade. Add the ground meat to the liquid, boil for 2 or 3 minutes, then pass through a fine sieve again. Return the bisque to the fire, and let boil once. Remove from the fire, and stir in, little by little, a mixture made of 3 tablespoons of heated heavy cream, 3 tablespoons of Madeira wine, and 2 fresh egg yolks, beaten together until thoroughly blended, stirring constantly. Heat well without letting boil, taste for seasoning, and serve at once with a side dish of small cubes of Boston brown bread, fried in butter.

CREAM OF RABBIT SOUP   [424]

Proceed as indicated for Cream of Hare Soup (No. 390), substituting rabbit (domestic or wild) for hare, and cook and serve as directed.

CREAM OF CURRIED RICE SOUP   [425]
SINGAPORE

Pour 4 cups (1 quart) of Chicken Broth (No. 25) into a kettle. Add 1 cup of freshly ground apple, 1 cup of grated onion, 1 large bay leaf, 2 whole cloves, and 2 grated parsley roots, and cook over a bright flame to the boiling point. Lower the flame, and allow to simmer gently for 15 minutes. Stir in 1 teaspoon of curry powder, diluted in a little cold milk; season to taste with salt and a few grains of cayenne pepper; and add ⅓ cup of cooked rice. Turn the contents of the kettle over a fine-meshed sieve, and rub through into a clean saucepan. Return to the fire, bring to the boiling point, then stir in ½ cup of heavy cream, which has been scalded with 2 well-beaten egg yolks. Taste for seasoning, and serve in hot cups without garnish.

CREAM OF SAUERKRAUT SOUP [426]
German style

Cook 2 pounds of sauerkraut in 3 quarts of unsalted water for about 30 minutes on a very hot fire and covered. Remove from the fire. Strain, and discard the water. Cut the sauerkraut coarsely, and place it in a kettle. Cover with 2 quarts of Beef Consommé (No. 114), add 8 peppercorns, and let simmer over a low fire for 2 hours. Meanwhile, blend 2 tablespoons of butter with 2 tablespoons of flour, and moisten with 1 wineglass of white wine for each quart of soup. Bring to a boil, and add to the soup. Let simmer gently for 15 minutes. Remove from the fire. Stir in 3 well-beaten egg yolks, beaten with 3 tablespoons of slightly melted butter. Correct the seasoning, adding salt if necessary. Serve with toasted bread.

CREAM OF SORREL SOUP [427]

Wash and sponge a bunch of sorrel, and put it through a food chopper with 1 medium-sized onion and 12 sprigs of parsley, stemmed. Place in a soup kettle, and pour over 2 cups of water. Cook for 35 minutes over a medium fire, or until the sorrel is tender. Then add 1 quart of rich milk which has been scalded, and stir in ½ scant cup of flour made into a paste with a little cold milk. Let simmer very gently for 1 hour, stirring occasionally, or still better, turn the mixture into a double boiler, but stir occasionally. When ready to serve, season with salt and pepper, and beat in, one at a time, 3 egg yolks. Serve very hot with a side dish of Croutons (No. 780).

CREAM OF SPINACH SOUP I [428]
Home style

For twenty-four centuries, spinach, an ancient vegetable, has enjoyed prestige as a bodybuilder. Traced from its early origin in Persia, it has remained a favorite from King Nebuchadnezzar of Babylon down to the present. Twelfth-century Spaniards called it "the prince of vegetables." A fourteenth-century cook book used by King Richard II of England gives a recipe for "spinoches." Even the famous

Boswell's *Life of Samuel Johnson* refers to the green grass: "To eat it guarantees curly hair, great height, and bulging muscles." But a nutritional chemist from Columbia University recently issued a statement that spinach is a highly overrated food! *Qui croire?* (Who to believe?)

Wash, pick, and chop 2 quarts of spinach. Wash once more, and cook in a large soup kettle without water, cooking gently and slowly until the juice is drawn out; then boil until tender, and chop. Rub the spinach through a fine-meshed wire sieve into a saucepan. Stir in 1 quart of Chicken Stock (No. 25), and set over a hot fire. When boiling, lower the flame, and let simmer gently for about 15 minutes. Blend 1 tablespoon each of butter and flour over a low flame. Stir in 1 cup of heavy cream, which has been scalded with 1 small bay leaf, 4 thin slices of onion, 3 sprigs of parsley, and 1 whole clove, and then strained. Cook gently for 10 minutes, stirring frequently. Season to taste with salt and pepper, and boil up once. Remove from the fire, and beat in 2 egg yolks, adding one at a time, beating well after each addition. Serve very hot in heated soup plates, each topped with a spoonful of whipped cream dusted with finely chopped parsley and a film of paprika.

CREAM OF SPINACH SOUP II   [429]
Farmer style

Fry 4 strips of bacon, diced, until crisp in a soup kettle. Remove, and keep warm. Add 2 tablespoons of butter to the fat, and cook 1 diced onion in it. Stir in 2½ tablespoons of flour, and blend well over a low flame for 2 minutes. Add 2 cups of cooked sieved spinach to the fat and cooked onion. Mix well, and cook for 2 minutes. Moisten with 3 cups of scalded milk and 2 cups of hot water in another kettle, stirring until thickened. Season with salt and pepper to taste. Boil once more. Beat 1 egg yolk into ½ cup of cream, with a small pinch of cayenne pepper, and stir into the soup mixture. Serve at once with toasted cheese wafers.

CREAM OF SPRING SOUP   [430]
French style

Cook ¼ cup of chopped onions in 3 tablespoons of butter over a very low heat, stirring frequently until the onion is tender but not brown. Gradually add 1 quart of White or Veal Stock (No. 11) and ½ cup of small pieces of stale bread, and let simmer gently for 35 minutes. Then rub through a fine-meshed sieve into a fresh saucepan, and add 2 cups of scalded thin cream, or undiluted evaporated milk, thickened with 1½ tablespoons of flour blended with 1 tablespoon of sweet butter. Taste for seasoning, let boil gently for 3 minutes, and serve at once, each plate sprinkled with finely chopped parsley.

CREAM OF SQUASH SOUP [431]

Proceed as indicated for Cream of Pumpkin Soup (No. 420), substituting squash for pumpkin, and cook and serve as directed.

CREAM OF STRING BEAN SOUP [432]

Wash 1½ pounds of picked sound string beans, and cut into small pieces. Place in just enough boiling water, about 1½ cups, to have a generous cup of liquid remaining when they are tender, and cook for 15 minutes. Drain, reserving the stock, and rub the beans through a fine-meshed wire sieve into a clean saucepan, moistening with reserved stock to make rubbing easier. Have ready 1 quart of Thin Cream Sauce (No. 346), boiling hot and flavored with 2 tablespoons of onion juice. Gradually stir the cream sauce over the bean purée, stirring constantly over a gentle heat until the mixture boils. Remove from the fire, and strain through a fine-meshed sieve into a clean saucepan. Return to the fire, and heat to the boiling point, adding, while stirring briskly, 3 fresh egg yolks, slightly beaten. Boil once, stirring constantly from the bottom of the pan. Taste for seasoning, and serve at once with a tablespoon of salted whipped cream, flavored with a good amount of finely chopped parsley or chives for each serving.

CREAM OF THRUSH SOUP CHASSEUR [433]
Also called Thrush Bisque Chasseur

This bisque is delicious. It came from a farm in Aveyron Department, France, where the juniper berries are found aplenty and the thrushes have a delicious flavor because they feed on these berries. The original recipe, less classic than the following, was created by a peasant cook. A guest gourmet who tasted this precious soup transmitted the recipe abroad, and today it is very popular during the hunting season. It is the custom to sip a little Madeira wine with this incomparable game bisque. Quails and, in fact, all small wild birds may be prepared in the same way.

Pick, clean, and quickly wash 10 thrushes, and sponge them dry. Heat 3 tablespoons of butter in a soup kettle. Add ⅓ cup of carrot, ½ cup of green celery leaves, ¼ cup of leeks, ¼ cup of onion, all these vegetables cleaned and coarsely chopped, and cook for 15 minutes, stirring frequently. Then stir in ⅓ cup of chopped raw lean ham, and cook for 10 minutes longer, stirring often, over a medium flame. Add the prepared birds, and cook for 12 to 15 minutes, stirring almost constantly. Then sprinkle over 3 tablespoons of uncooked wild rice; 3 or 4 juniper berries, crushed; 1 bouquet garni, composed of 1 large bay leaf, 6 sprigs of parsley, and a small sprig of thyme, tied with kitchen thread; 1 blade of garlic; and 6 freshly crushed peppercorns. Moisten with 2 quarts of Beef Consommé (No. 114). Season with a little salt, cover, and bring to a boil. Reduce the heat, and let simmer gently for 45 minutes. Then stir in 1 cup of black bread crumbs, and cook for 5 minutes longer. Remove the birds, bone thoroughly, and put the meat through a food chopper, using the finest blade, then rub through a fine-meshed sieve. Strain the stock, and stir it into the thrush meat paste. Return to the fire, bring to a rapid boil, and let boil steadily for 15 minutes. Add 1 cup of scalded heavy cream and 3 tablespoons of Madeira wine, beaten with 2 fresh egg yolks. Heat well without letting boil, and serve in hot soup plates, each topped with Croutons (No. 780), substituting black bread for white.

CREAM OF TOMATO SOUP I [434]
Andalouse manner

The exact status of the tomato has been determined by no less an eminent authority than the Supreme Court of the United States, in 1893. The question involved the shipment of a cargo of tomatoes from the West Indies to New York. Under the customs regulations at that time, fruits were exempt from duty, while the tax on vegetables was 10 per cent of their value. The Collector of the Port of New York contended that tomatoes were vegetables; the shipper maintained they were fruits. Technically and botanically, a fruit is that part of a plant which contains the seeds, and tomatoes properly should be classified as fruits. "But," said the court, "in the language of the people, whether sellers or consumers of provisions, all these are vegetables which are grown in kitchen gardens and which, whether eaten cooked or raw, are, like potatoes, carrots, parsnips, turnips, beets, cauliflowers, etc., usually served at dinner in, with, or after the soup, fish, or meats which constitute the principal part of the repast and not like fruits generally as desserts." So now eat your vegetable tomato and not your fruit tomato in this delicious way.

Put in a saucepan 1 quart of strained tomato juice, fresh or canned. Add 1 large bay leaf, 3 thin slices of onion, 1 small clove of garlic, mashed, 2 whole cloves, head removed, 2 fresh leaves of sweet basil, ¼ teaspoon of baking soda, ½ teaspoon of celery salt, a few grains of cayenne pepper, and ¼ cup of well-washed rice. Cook for 20 to 25 minutes, or until the rice is well done, rather on the mushy side. Empty the contents of the saucepan into a fine-meshed sieve, and rub through with a potato masher into a clean saucepan. Bring to a rapid boil, stirring occasionally, then stir in 1 cup of milk, scalded with 1 cup of thin cream, alternately with 2 fresh egg yolks, slightly beaten. Taste for seasoning, and serve in hot soup cups, each topped with a thin slice of orange, topped with a little whipped cream and sprinkled with a little nutmeg.

CREAM OF TOMATO SOUP II [435]
French manner

Peel, quarter, and seed 3 extra large ripe tomatoes, and let stew in their own juice over a gentle flame until soft, stirring occasionally. Rub through a fine sieve, but not through a fine cloth, lest the liquid extracted be only pinkish water. Turn the mixture into a saucepan, and add ¼ teaspoon of baking soda. When the soda has ceased foaming, stir in, bit by bit, 2 tablespoons of sweet butter. Season to taste with salt and pepper, a dash of nutmeg, and a dash of cayenne pepper. Scald 1 quart of rich milk with ⅓ cup of cooked rice, 3 thin slices of onion, 1 large bay leaf, and 1 clove. Rub the mixture through a fine-meshed sieve. To the milk-rice mixture, add 3 fresh egg yolks, one at a time, beating briskly after each addition. Then gradually stir into the tomato mixture, stirring rapidly, while pouring, to prevent the mixture from curdling. Taste for seasoning, and serve in hot soup cups, each garnished with 2 tiny cubes of Tomato Custard (No. 702).

CREAM OF TOMATO SOUP III [436]

Cook 1 quart of tomatoes over a low flame, stirring occasionally. Wash 2 stalks of celery thoroughly, dice, and cook until tender, in another saucepan, with 1 medium-sized onion, sliced, 2 cloves, a bouquet garni composed of 2 sprigs of parsley tied with 1 large bay leaf, and a pinch of paprika, in enough water to cover, for 25 minutes. Combine the tomato and vegetable mixture, and cook for 10 minutes longer. Discard the bouquet garni, and rub through a sieve. Return to the fire, and add 2 teaspoons of brown sugar. Let simmer gently. Prepare the binding of 1 tablespoon of butter mixed with 1 tablespoon of flour over a low fire, and cook until well blended. Stir in 3 cups of scalded rich milk gradually, and boil for 10 minutes longer. Pour the tomato-vegetable purée over this. Finish with 1 tablespoon of butter, and serve with fried Croutons (No. 780).

CREAM OF TOMATO SOUP IV   [437]
Club style

Put 2 cups of canned tomatoes in a soup kettle, and add 1 tablespoon of finely minced onion, 1 tablespoon of chopped celery leaves, and 1 teaspoon of sugar. Cook gently for 15 to 20 minutes, stirring occasionally. Then rub through a fine-meshed sieve into a saucepan. Blend 2 tablespoons of butter and 2 tablespoons of flour over a low flame, stirring constantly. Gradually stir in 1½ quarts of milk, previously scalded with 1 large bay leaf, 4 sprigs of fresh parsley, and 1 whole clove, then strained. Still stirring constantly, let cook until the mixture thickens and boils. Combine with the tomato mixture, then let boil up once or twice. Season to taste with salt and white pepper. Remove from the fire, and stir in 2 well-beaten egg yolks alternately with 1 tablespoon of sweet butter. Serve in heated soup plates, each garnished with 1 tablespoon of salted whipped cream, topped with a little finely chopped parsley or chervil.

CREAM OF TOMATO SOUP V   [438]
Quick method

Melt 3 tablespoons of butter in a large saucepan and sprinkle over 1 tablespoon of flour, stirring constantly to prevent lumping. Blend well. Moisten with 1 quart of scalded milk, stirring meanwhile. Heat 3 cups of tomatoes. Combine with the first mixture. Simmer slowly for 15 minutes. Season with salt and pepper to taste. Remove from the fire, and stir in 2 well-beaten egg yolks. Finish with 1 tablespoon of butter. You may add 1 teaspoon of sugar to the tomatoes, if desired sweet. Serve with Croutons (No. 780).

CREAM OF TOMATO SOUP VI   [439]
Country style

Combine 4 cups (1 quart) of tomatoes with 2 cups of water, 2 tablespoons of sugar, 1 large onion, chopped, and a bouquet garni composed of 1 bay leaf and 1 small bunch of parsley tied together with kitchen thread. Simmer slowly for 25 minutes. Meanwhile, melt 2 tablespoons of butter, and stir in 3 tablespoons of flour. Blend well, and add gradually, while stirring constantly, 1 quart of scalded milk. Combine with the first mixture. Season to taste with salt and pepper. Boil for 10 minutes over a low fire. Remove from the fire, and stir in 2 well-beaten egg yolks. Serve piping hot with a puff of salted whipped cream in each serving.

CREAM OF TOMATO SOUP VII [440]
Austrian style

To the above recipe (No. 439), stir the 2 well-beaten egg yolks into 1 cup of cream before adding to the soup. Garnish each serving with small pieces of cooked macaroni, cooked asparagus tips, and freshly cooked peas. Serve with a side dish of grated Parmesan cheese.

CREAM OF TRIPE SOUP [441]

Boil 1 large veal soupbone, with about 1 pound of meat attached to it, in 2 quarts of water for 2 hours. Remove the bone, and cut the meat into very small pieces. Return to the broth, and add 1½ pounds of fresh tripe, cut in inch squares. Season with salt to taste and 6 slightly bruised peppercorns. Boil together for ½ hour after adding 4 medium-sized potatoes, diced. Blend 3 tablespoons each of butter and flour with a little stock. Stir into the soup, and let boil for a few minutes. Serve with Sponge Dumplings (No. 760).

CREAM OF TURKEY SOUP [442]
An old American pioneer soup

Place in a soup kettle a turkey carcass with the bones cracked, 5 or 6 sprigs of green celery tops, 2 bay leaves, 2 large onions, quartered, 1 clove of garlic, 1 parsley root, grated, and 2 cloves. Cover with 1½ quarts of cold water, and cook for about 2 hours over a low flame. Run both liquid and solid through a sieve, removing all the bones. Return the mixture to the fire, season with salt and pepper to taste, and add 1 pint of scalded thin cream, or undiluted evaporated milk. Cook for 4 or 5 minutes longer, and taste for seasoning. When ready to serve, add 18 small fresh oysters, carefully cleaned and drained, and serve at once with toasted crackers or buttered brown bread.

CREAM OF TURNIP SOUP [443]

Cook 2 generous cups of diced white turnips in 1 quart of Mutton Broth (No. 753) until tender. Strain. Rub the turnips through a fine sieve. Add again to the cooking liquor, and return to the fire. Let boil once. Add 1 cup of fresh scalded cream, and season to taste with salt and pepper. Let boil once more. Remove from the fire, and stir in 2 well-beaten egg yolks. Finish with 1 tablespoon of butter, and garnish with the coarsely chopped white of 2 hard-cooked eggs. A fine and delicious soup!

CREAM OF VEGETABLE SOUP [444]

Peel, clean, wash thoroughly in several cold waters, and dice the following vegetables: 2 large onions, 1 large carrot, 2 large potatoes, ¾ cup of celery, 1 medium-sized turnip, and 1 small parsnip. Wash and clean also by the same method ½ cup of cauliflower flowerets, 1 cup of finely shredded cabbage, ½ cup of fresh peas, and 1 cup of finely chopped leeks. Put all into a soup kettle, and add 2 quarts of water. Add 1 bay leaf, 1 small bunch of parsley, and 2 cloves. Cover, and bring to a boil. Reduce the heat, and let simmer very gently for 1 hour. Wash ½ cup of barley and 1 cup of rice, and add to the soup. Cook for 1½ hours more over a gentle fire. Rub through a sieve, and return to the fire. Season to taste with salt and pepper. Add 1 cup of scalded cream. Boil once more, and finish with 3 table-spoons of butter. Serve with fried Croutons (No. 780).

CREAM OF VEGETABLE SOUP [445]
CISTERCIAN MANNER
Potage à la Crème de Légumes des Cistercians

Here is a potage, the origin of which dates back for more than a thousand years, created by the Cistercian monks of the Abbaye de Citeaux, place of birth of the famous Clos Vougeot Burgundy wine, a wine, it is claimed, before which an entire regiment was ordered to present arms.

For 6 servings, take ½ cup each of dry lima beans and yellow split peas, washed and soaked in cold water overnight; 3 medium-sized potatoes, peeled and cubed small; 2 small carrots, grated, then cubed small; 2 small white turnips, peeled, then cubed small; 3 medium-sized onions, peeled, then chopped very fine, not grated; 2 small leeks, white part only, chopped very fine, and washed in several changes of cold water; ⅓ cup of green celery leaves (tops), chopped very fine, then washed in several changes of cold water; and 1 bouquet garni, composed of 2 large bay leaves, 8 sprigs of fresh parsley, 1 sprig of thyme, 1 sprig or leaflet of sweet basil, tied together with kitchen thread, and soaked in cold water for 20 minutes to enhance the flavor. Place all the above in a squat plump earthenware casserole, or *pot-au-feu* casserole. Pour over 1½ quarts of cold water, add butter the size of a large egg, season lightly with salt and pepper, and let go over a bright flame for about 25 minutes. Then lower the flame, and allow to simmer very gently until the vegetables are tender, or about 1½ hours, covered. Empty the contents of the casserole into a fine sieve, and after removing the bouquet garni, press gently but thoroughly, easing the rubbing with 2 cups of scalded thin cream, into a clean earthenware casserole. Return to the fire, and let simmer gently, after adding more thin cream or rich milk to obtain a soup of the consistency of thin cream.

Have ready ½ scant cup of rice cooked in rich Chicken Broth (No. 25) until each grain is a separate white oval, like snow. Have also ready a dozen sorrel leaves, shredded as for coleslaw, blanched for 3 minutes in butter, and thoroughly drained.

To the simmering cream of vegetables, add 4 egg yolks, one at a time, beating well after each addition. Remove from the fire, and add the snow-white rice and cooked shredded sorrel, and mix thoroughly. Pour into a hot soup tureen, and dust the top with 1 tablespoon of finely chopped chervil, or parsley if chervil is not available. Serve at once. Sherry wine is the usual accompaniment of such a fine soup!

CREAM OF VEGETABLE SHERRY SOUP [446]
A very refreshing spring bisque

Place in a soup kettle 1 cup of ground green celery leaves, 1 medium-sized carrot, ½ medium-sized green pepper, 1 handful of raw young spinach, ½ cup of chopped parsley, 2 medium-sized tomatoes, peeled and seeded, a small lettuce, and 1 large onion. Have the vegetables ground fine, and mix them well. Pour over 1 quart of Chicken Stock (No. 25). Add a bouquet garni, composed of 2 scraped small parsley roots, 1 large bay leaf, 1 sprig of thyme, and 2 whole cloves, and ¼ cup of uncooked rice. Season to taste with salt and pepper, and add 1 clove of garlic, peeled and left whole. Gradually bring this to a boil, and allow to simmer as gently as possible for 35 minutes. Empty the whole contents of the kettle into a fine-meshed sieve, and rub through with a potato masher into a clean saucepan. Return the mixture to the fire, bring to the boiling point, then stir in, off the fire, 2 cups of thin cream, or undiluted evaporated milk, scalded, stirring briskly from the bottom of the pan. Taste for seasoning. When ready to serve, stir in ⅓ cup of sherry wine, to which has been added 2 well-beaten fresh egg yolks. Serve in hot soup plates, each garnished with 2 tiny Chicken Liver Dumplings (No. 717).

CREAM OF WATERCRESS SOUP I [447]
Also called *Potage Valois*

The Romans ate watercress to sharpen their wits, but did so secretly, as the acid taste was supposed also to twitch the nose. This nose twitching has been perpetuated in the botanical name of watercress— *Roripa Nasturtium-Aquaticum.*

Follow the directions for Chilled Cream of Watercress Soup (No. 96), and serve hot instead of cold. When ready to serve, stir in ½ cup of scalded sweet cream, garnished with Croutons (No. 780).

CREAM OF WATERCRESS SOUP II [448]
Farmer style

Clean and peel 2 large potatoes, 2 medium-sized turnips, and 1 large leek (white and green parts). Cut in small pieces, and wash thoroughly, especially the leek. Cook in salted water for 30 minutes. Rub through a sieve. Return to the kettle, and stir in 1 quart of scalded milk, to which has been added 3 tablespoons of butter. Stir well. Bring to a boil. Throw in 3 tablespoons of quick-cooking tapioca, and cook for 15 minutes. Meanwhile, clean and chop finely ½ bunch of watercress. Season the soup with salt and pepper to taste. Add the finely chopped watercress, and finish with 1 tablespoon of butter. Serve with toasted crackers.

CREAM OF WATERCRESS [449]
AND CHEESE SOUP

Melt 3 tablespoons of butter in the top of a double boiler. Stir in 2 tablespoons of flour, and when bubbling, but not browning, stir in 1 quart of scalded milk gradually, stirring constantly, until the mixture has thickened. Then stir in 2 tablespoons each of grated onions, finely chopped green pepper, and finely chopped parsley. Let this boil gently for 2 or 3 minutes, then strain through a fine-meshed wire sieve into a clean saucepan, containing 2 cups of finely ground watercress. Boil steadily for 3 minutes, and then rub the mixture through a fine-meshed wire sieve into a clean saucepan. Beat in 3 fresh egg yolks, adding one at a time, beating well after each addition. Then stir in ½ cup of grated cheese. Let boil once, remove at once from the fire, and season to taste with salt, white pepper, and a few grains of nutmeg. Serve with Croutons (No. 780).

CREAM OF WATERCRESS   [450]
AND CHIVE SOUP

Melt 2 tablespoons of butter in the top of a double boiler over a direct gentle flame. When hot, stir in 1½ cups of finely chopped, carefully washed, and drained fresh watercress and ½ cup of finely chopped chives. Cook for about 5 minutes, stirring almost constantly. Place the pan over hot water, and stir in 3 tablespoons of flour, previously diluted in a little cold milk, and blend thoroughly. Gradually stir in 1 quart of milk, which has been scalded with 1 small bay leaf, 4 sprigs of parsley, 4 thin slices of onion, 1 whole clove, and a grating of nutmeg, and then strained. Stir constantly from the bottom of the pan until the mixture has thickened. Season to taste with salt and white pepper. When ready to serve, stir in, little by little, 2 well-beaten egg yolks. Serve hot.

CREAM SOUP I   [451]
Pioneer method

Place 1½ pounds of spareribs in a kettle of 1½ quarts of cold water over medium heat. When coming to a boil, skim thoroughly, and continue boiling for ½ hour. Then add 3 medium-sized onions, sliced, and ½ cup of tomatoes. Then ½ hour later, add salt and pepper to taste and 6 medium-sized potatoes, diced. Let simmer gently, and 5 minutes before serving, add 1 quart of rich milk, in which has been diluted 1 tablespoon of flour. Finish with ½ tablespoon of finely chopped parsley, and garnish with Ribbles (No. 801).

CREAM SOUP II   [452]
Russian style

Dilute 2 cups of flour with 6 egg yolks, 2 egg whites, nutmeg to taste, and a little pepper from a pepper mill. Have a kettle containing 1½ quarts of boiling milk ready. Let the liquid paste drop by soupspoon into the boiling milk. In sliding from the spoon, it will form a ball. Let cook for 25 minutes, and serve at once, placing a few of the balls in each plate.

CREAM SOUP III   [453]
Saxon style—serves one

According to medical authorities, this soup is very good for a pain in the stomach and is very nourishing.

Dilute 1 tablespoon of rice flour in 1 tablespoon of cold water, stirring well. Have ready on the fire 1 cup of rich milk brought to the boiling point, to which has been added a small lemon peel and a very little stick of cinnamon. Pour over the milk the diluted flour, stirring vigorously. Remove the lemon peel and cinnamon. Let boil once. Sweeten to taste with sugar. Add a dash of salt (no pepper), and finish off the fire with a wineglass of good old port wine. Serve hot.

Chapter Seven

BISQUES

FISH CREAM SOUPS—ALSO CALLED COULIS—INCLUDING FRESH-WATER AND SALT-WATER FISH AND CRUSTACEANS

Above all, a bisque should be smooth, light without being liquid, glossy to the eye, and definite as to taste.

WHAT IS A BISQUE?

MOST PEOPLE AGREE THAT THERE IS SOMETHING WHOLEsome about any kind of soup. This philosophy probably has been handed down from the happy countryfolk who in years past gathered on winter or Lenten nights for chowder parties. But modern cooks also have worked out several variations of the supper soup. Three soups that are closely related to chowders are cream soups, purées, and bisques. Each of these is different, yet each has something in common with the chowders.

Cream soups often are made from a single vegetable, such as peas, corn, carrots, spinach, or asparagus. But several vegetables also may be used together.

A purée is much like cream soup, but it is always made from sieved vegetables and is usually thicker than cream soup.

Bisque is the third variation. It is generally a fish, crustacean, or shellfish soup, as well as tomato, pea, or similar vegetable.

The following bisques serve 6 to 8 persons unless otherwise indicated in the recipe.

CLAM BISQUE I
Manhattan style

Weighted with clams, he comes with weary stride
Across the purple of the clutching ooze,
Beyond the menace of the deepening tide. . . .
OLD FISHERMAN'S BALLADE

Wash 2½ quarts of soft-shelled clams in the shell in several changes of cold water to remove the sand. Put in a kettle, add ½ cup of cold water, cover tightly, and steam until the shells are opened. Strain the liquor through a fine cloth into a clean saucepan, and add 3½ cups of boiling water. Keep hot. Melt 3 tablespoons of butter in a saucepan, blend in 3 tablespoons of flour, and when thoroughly blended without being brown, gradually stir in the hot clam liquor mixture. Bring to the boiling point, and let boil steadily for 3 or 4 minutes. Stir in 1½ cups of hot sweet cream. Season to taste with salt, white pepper, and a tiny pinch of nutmeg and thyme. Let boil once, and set aside. Add 3 egg yolks gradually, while stirring constantly. Serve hot in hot cups sprinkled with a few grains of paprika. Serve a side dish of buttered saltine crackers.

CLAM BISQUE II   [456]
French method from Charente

In 2 cups of cold water, steam 2¾ quarts of soft clams, which
have been carefully scrubbed and rinsed in several changes of cold
water. When opened, strain the liquor into a clean saucepan, and
bring the liquor to a boil. When boiling, stir in ½ cup of well-washed
rice, and cook until tender. Remove the muscles, place the clam
bellies in a mortar, and reduce to a paste with the strained broth
from the cooked rice. Then rub this paste through a fine sieve, and
add 1 cup of heavy cream, scalded with 3 cups of rich milk and 1
large bay leaf. Boil once or twice. Season to taste with salt, pepper,
and a tiny pinch of powdered thyme. When ready to serve, stir in
1 fresh egg yolk, beaten with a little cold milk, alternately with 1
tablespoon of sweet butter. Serve in hot soup plates with Clam
Dumplings (No. 717), each plate sprinkled with a few grains of
paprika.

CLAM BISQUE III   [457]
Corinth

Wash 3 dozen clams, and put them in a soup kettle. Add ¼ cup
cold water, bring to the boiling point, and cook the clams until the
shells open. Lift out the clams, and remove from their shells. Chop
fine, and add them to the liquor in the kettle. Then add 1 medium-
sized onion, coarsely sliced, 1 sprig of parsley, a little blade of mace,
salt, and a few grains of cayenne pepper. Let simmer very gently for
20 minutes. Add to a quart of scalded milk, 2 scant tablespoons of
cornstarch, diluted in 2 tablespoons of cold water or cold milk, and
pour over the clams. Cook for 10 minutes longer. Strain through a
fine cloth. Correct the seasoning, and finish just before serving with
2 egg yolks added gradually while beating constantly. Serve with fried
Croutons (No. 780).

CLAM BISQUE IV   [458]
Mock Clam Bisque

Soak 1 cup of marrowfat beans overnight in water to cover. In the
morning, drain, and put them on the fire in 2 quarts of cold water,
with 1 small onion, chopped fine, a very small pinch of thyme leaves,
a few sprigs of parsley tied with 1 small bay leaf, a few grains of nutmeg, and salt and pepper to taste. Meanwhile, scald 1 cup of cream

with 1 tablespoon of butter kneaded with 1 tablespoon of flour. When the beans are done, add the cream, and rub through a fine sieve. Return to the fire, and let boil once or twice. Correct the seasoning, and finish with 1 tablespoon of butter. Add the coarsely chopped white of 4 hard-cooked eggs. Serve with Croutons (No. 780).

CLAM BISQUE V [459]
Home manner

Cook together in a saucepan 1 medium-sized onion, 1 clove of garlic, mashed, and 3 medium-sized potatoes, pared and sliced thin, in ½ cup of water until tender. Stir in 1 quart of scalded milk with 1 large bay leaf and 1 whole clove, and bring to a boil. Rub the liquid and solid through a fine sieve into a clean saucepan, and stir in 2 quarts of soft clams, chopped very fine. Season to taste with salt, white pepper, and a pinch of nutmeg, and let simmer very gently for 20 minutes. Strain through a fine sieve into a clean saucepan. Stir in ½ cup of scalded heavy cream, and when ready to serve, stir in 2 tablespoons of butter. Serve in hot soup plates with Fried Oysterettes (No. 785), each plate dusted with finely chopped parsley.

CLAM AND OYSTER BISQUE [460]

Clean and pick a pint of small oysters, reserving the liquor. Do likewise with a pint of clams, and chop together very finely. Place in a kettle with the liquor. Add ½ cup of cold water. Bring to a boil. Set aside to simmer very gently for 5 minutes. Pour over 1 quart of milk, to which is added 2 tablespoons of cornstarch diluted in 2 tablespoons of cold milk. Bring to a boil. Season to taste with celery seed, salt, and white pepper, and let simmer for 5 minutes longer. Strain through a fine cloth over another pan. Add 1 tablespoon of butter mixed with 1 tablespoon of flour, and cook for 10 minutes. Finish off the fire with 2 egg yolks, slightly beaten and added gradually while stirring constantly, 1 tablespoon of butter, and a few drops of onion juice. Serve in cups with a teaspoon of salted whipped cream over each cup.

CLAM AND OYSTER BISQUE [461]
SARAH BERNHARDT

Proceed as indicated in the above recipe (No. 460), omitting the whipped cream, and pouring, while boiling violently, 3 fresh eggs beaten through a fine sieve. Serve with caviarette crackers.

CODFISH BISQUE   [462]
Also called Mock Crab Bisque

Soak 1 cup of shredded dry salt codfish in boiling water for 3 minutes, then drain thoroughly, squeezing gently. Put the fish in a saucepan with 2 cups of canned tomatoes, using pulp and liquid, or the equivalent of chopped fresh tomatoes, 1 large bay leaf, 6 thin rings of sliced onion, 1 whole clove, 4 whole peppercorns, gently bruised, and 6 sprigs of fresh parsley. Bring to a boil, lower the heat, and let simmer very gently for 35 minutes, stirring occasionally, the pan well covered. Rub the mixture through a fine sieve into a clean saucepan, and keep hot.

Rub together 3 tablespoons of butter or margarine with 4 tablespoons of flour. Add bit by bit to the bisque mixture, and bring to the boiling point. When boiling, stir in ¼ teaspoon of baking soda and 3 cups of rich milk, scalded. Taste for seasoning, and serve in hot soup plates with a tablespoonful of whipped cream over each serving.

CRAB BISQUE I   [463]
Southern manner

Chop finely 1½ cups of fresh-cooked or canned crab meat; place in a saucepan, and add 2 cups of Chicken Stock (No. 25), or canned chicken bouillon, ½ cup of soft bread crumbs, 3 slices of onion, and 4 sprigs of parsley. Bring to a boil, lower the flame, and let simmer gently for 20 minutes; then add 2 cups of rich milk, thin cream, or undiluted evaporated milk, and continue simmering for 15 minutes longer. Rub the mixture through a fine sieve into a clean saucepan. Season to taste with salt, cayenne, and a few grains of nutmeg, then stir in 2 tablespoons of butter blended with 2 tablespoons of flour. Bring to a boil, let simmer for 5 minutes; remove from the fire, and just before serving in hot cups, stir in 3 tablespoons of good sherry. Serve without garnish.

CRAB BISQUE II   [464]

Proceed as indicated for Crab Bisque I (No. 463) above, adding, when ready to serve, ½ cup of heavy cream, whipped with a few grains of salt and 2 teaspoons of Worcestershire sauce. Cook as directed, and serve in the same way.

CRAB BISQUE III   [465]
Normandy manner

Wash 2 dozen live hard-shelled crabs in several cold waters, and drain. In sufficient White Wine Court Bouillon (No. 79) to generously cover, cook the crabs for 15 to 20 minutes, or until the crabs are red. Allow them to cool in the cooking broth overnight. The next day, drain them, reserving the court bouillon. There should be 5 cups of it, but if not, add either chicken bouillon or fish stock to make the 5 cups. Now pick the meat from the crabs, and either pound it in a mortar with a pestle, or put it two or three times through a food chopper, using the finest blade, meanwhile adding 2 tablespoons of plain boiled rice and moistening the paste with a little of the court bouillon to ease the pounding or chopping. Now place the crab-meat mixture in a saucepan, and add the strained court bouillon. Bring to a boil, then strain again through a fine-meshed sieve or a flannel cloth, and stir in 2 fresh egg yolks, beaten with 2 teaspoons of Calvados or applejack. Return to the fire, and bring to a boil, without boiling. Remove from the fire, and taste for seasoning. When ready to serve, stir in 2 tablespoons of butter, or preferably, shrimp butter, made by pounding finely 6 cooked shelled shrimps, then kneading with 2 tablespoons of salted butter. Serve piping hot without garnish.

CRAB BISQUE A LA MARYLAND   [466]
The recipe of a Baltimore chef

Blend 1 rounded tablespoon of flour with 2 generous tablespoons of butter in the top of a double boiler, stirring constantly. Gradually add 2 quarts of rich milk, scalded with 1 medium-sized onion, thinly sliced, 2 tablespoons each of parsley and celery, finely chopped, and salt, pepper, and nutmeg to taste, stirring constantly. Cook very slowly until the soup thickens a little, stirring frequently, then add 1 pint (2 cups) of picked shredded crab meat. Cook for 10 minutes longer, still over a gentle flame. Taste for seasoning, and serve in individual dishes with a spoonful of whipped cream on top.

CRAYFISH BISQUE I   [467]
Creole method

Soak 2 dozen crayfish in cold water for 30 minutes, and wash thoroughly and carefully, using a brush to remove all the dirt. Place the crayfish in a kettle. Add 5 cups of cold water; 1 medium-sized onion, thinly sliced; 2 small carrots, grated, then thinly sliced; 2 stalks of celery, scraped, then finely chopped; and 4 sprigs of parsley tied with 1 large bay leaf and 1 small sprig of thyme. Bring to a boil, lower the flame, and let simmer gently for 30 minutes. Drain, reserving the broth. Remove all the meat from the heads and bodies of the crayfish. Set aside the heads and bodies, which are to be stuffed. Moisten 6 tablespoons of cracker crumbs with a little milk. Put the crayfish meat through a food chopper, using the finest blade, and combine with the moistened cracker crumbs. Cook in 1 tablespoon of butter, 2 tablespoons of finely chopped onion, 1 teaspoon of chopped parsley, a tiny blade of garlic, finely chopped, and 1 tablespoon of finely chopped onion, for 2 or 3 minutes, stirring constantly, over a low flame. Add the crayfish mixture, season with salt and pepper to taste, and cook for 2 minutes longer. Remove from the fire, cool slightly, and stuff the crayfish heads with this stuffing. Dredge the stuffed crayfish heads in a little flour, and fry in 2 tablespoons of butter until nicely browned, stirring frequently with a wooden spoon. Drain on absorbent paper, and keep hot. Strain the reserved broth through a fine cloth into a clean kettle. Bring to a boil, and stir in, bit by bit, 2 tablespoons of crayfish butter, made by pounding finely 1 large cooked crayfish, or preferably putting it through a food chopper 2 or 3 times, using the finest blade, and kneading with 2 tablespoons of butter. Allow the bisque to simmer gently for 5 long minutes. Taste for seasoning, and when ready to serve, stir in off the fire 1 or 2 fresh egg yolks and the stuffed hot crayfish heads. No other garnishing is needed.

CRAYFISH BISQUE II   [468]
Parisian manner

Clean 2 dozen crayfish as indicated for Crayfish Bisque I (No. 467), remove the head coffers, and keep in ice-cold water. Remove the meat from the tails, and put the meat through a food chopper 2 or 3 times. Add ¾ cup of soft bread crumbs soaked in a little cream, just enough to moisten the crumbs, 1 teaspoon of finely minced parsley, 1½ tablespoons of finely chopped, or preferably grated, onion, 1 teaspoon of finely chopped chives, a tiny blade of garlic, mashed, and salt, pepper, and nutmeg to taste. Cook this mixture in 3 tablespoons of butter for 3 long minutes over a gentle flame, stirring almost constantly. Remove from the fire, and stir in 2 tablespoons of sherry wine. Stuff the head coffers with the mixture, and cook in 3 tablespoons of butter until browned all over. Keep hot.

Melt 2 tablespoons of butter in a soup kettle. Add 1 medium-sized onion, thinly sliced, 2 small young carrots, scraped, then thinly sliced, and 1 large bay leaf tied with 6 sprigs of parsley and 1 sprig of thyme, and cook for 2 minutes over a bright flame, stirring almost constantly. Then add 2 dozen crayfish, carefully washed or rather scrubbed, as well as the trimmings from the first 2 dozen crayfish, and cook until the crayfish are beautifully red. Sprinkle over 2 tablespoons of brandy, mixed with ¼ cup of dry white wine and 2 tablespoons of melted butter, and ¼ cup of well-washed drained raw rice. Stir in 1½ quarts of hot water, bring to the boiling point, lower the heat, and allow to simmer gently for 45 minutes, stirring frequently. Strain through a fine sieve, pressing thoroughly to extract all the juices from the solid parts, into a clean kettle. Return to the fire, and bring to a fast boil. Correct the seasoning, and lastly, stir in ¼ cup of scalded heavy cream. Serve immediately with the stuffed fried heads on the side.

CRAYFISH BISQUE III [469]
Italian style

Prepare, cook, and serve as indicated for the recipe above (No. 468), adding, just before serving, 3 tablespoons of cooked macaroni, cut in small pieces, with a side dish of grated Parmesan cheese and a poached egg for each serving.

CRAYFISH BISQUE IV [470]
The favorite soup of Francis I of France—sixteenth century

The foreign policy of Francis I, who succeeded Louis XII, called the "Father of the people," was on the whole no better than the one of his predecessor, and his internal policy was much worse. Francis was a showy, pretentious man who, by his patronage of artists, architects, poets, and cooks trained in the Italian school, did much to advance French cuisine. He was also ready to dip into the treasury for ambitious building schemes, and he encouraged his rich nobles to do likewise. This was therefore the epoch for the erection of many elegant châteaux—stately residences and palaces, not mere comfortless frowning castles as in the now departed Middle Ages. The region around Tours is to this day dotted with the magnificent buildings which recall a stately and luxurious age. Chambord, Chenonceaux, and Blois are merely random examples of the famous châteaux which were either erected or remodeled in the days of this splendor-loving king, who loved good foods and surrounded himself with masters in the art of good cuisine. The bisque of crayfish, said Mellin de Saint-

Gelais, his chaplain, is more royal than a king and deserves a public homage—a *Culte* of Comus.

The following recipe was created by Vincent de la Chapelle, Francis I's master chef and author of several cook books.

Scrub and carefully wash in several changes of cold water 50 live crayfish. Using a perforated ladle or skimmer, transfer the live crayfish into a soup kettle. Add ⅓ cup each of carrot, onion, and green celery leaves, all finely chopped; 1 bouquet garni, composed of 1 large bay leaf, 6 sprigs of parsley, 1 sprig of thyme, and 2 whole cloves, tied with kitchen thread; salt, pepper, and a pinch of cayenne to taste; and ¼ cup of butter. Cook over a bright flame, stirring almost constantly with a wooden spoon, until the crustaceans are cardinal red. Then moisten with a ladleful of rich chicken bouillon and ¼ cup of Madeira wine. Cook for 2 or 3 minutes longer, then lift out the crayfish with a perforated ladle, strain the small amount of liquid from the kettle, and set aside. When the crayfish are cold enough to handle, remove the meat from the tails, and dice (do not chop) it very small. Put the shells and trimmings of the crayfish in a mortar with ¾ cup of freshly cooked rice, well drained, and pound with a pestle. Transfer this pulp, as is, into a clean saucepan. Add 5 cups of boiling Chicken Bouillon (No. 25) and the strained liquid from the cooking of the crayfish, and let boil once. Strain through a fine cloth. Add 2 tablespoons of sweet butter, taste for seasoning, then stir in ½ cup of scalded thick cream alternately with the crayfish dices. Heat to the boiling point, and serve at once in hot soup plates, each garnished with 4 or 5 small cubes of Crayfish Custard Garnish (No. 689).

FROG'S LEG BISQUE [471]

Wash 2 dozen frog's legs quickly in lukewarm water. Drain well, and place in a saucepan with ⅓ cup of butter, and salt, pepper, and nutmeg to taste, and sauté them for 10 minutes over a bright flame, stirring frequently with a wooden spoon. Lower the heat, and continue cooking for 10 to 15 minutes longer, stirring occasionally. Drain, reserving the butter and juices from the pan. When cold enough to handle, remove the bones, and put the meat through a food chopper twice, then rub to a smooth paste through a fine-meshed sieve with the reserved cooking butter and juice. Stir in 2 cups of thin cream, or undiluted evaporated milk, scalded with 1 large bay leaf, 1 grated root of parsley, chopped, and 1 tablespoon of grated onion. Turn the mixture into a saucepan, bring to the boiling point, and gradually add 3 cups of boiling rich Chicken Stock (No. 25), stirring well. Let the mixture simmer gently for 15 to 20 minutes, and when ready to serve, stir in 3 fresh egg yolks beaten with 3 tablespoons of sherry wine, beating briskly to prevent curdling. Taste for seasoning, and serve very hot, in hot cups, each topped with a little whipped cream forced through a pastry bag with a small fancy tube, and dusted with a little paprika.

HALIBUT BISQUE NEW ENGLAND [472]

To 1½ or 1¾ cups of cooked halibut, boned, cut into small pieces, and rubbed through a fine sieve, add 1 quart of scalded milk, with a blade of mace, 3 or 4 drops of onion juice, a few grains of cayenne pepper, salt to taste, 4 or 5 thyme leaves, and a very tiny bit of bay leaf. Cook over a low fire for 15 minutes, adding 1 tablespoon of butter, kneaded with 1 tablespoon of flour and a very finely chopped green pepper. Just before serving, add one by one, while stirring constantly, 2 egg yolks. Correct the seasoning, and serve with toasted saltine crackers.

LANGOSTINA BISQUE [473]
Spanish style

Note. Langostina are giant or jumbo shrimps, which resemble small lobsters, and are found in great quantities along the coast of Spain, and Mexico, in the southern Pacific, and in the Gulf Stream.

Cook 2 dozen langostina (large shrimps may be used) in 1 cup of white wine (or ½ cup of white wine and ½ cup of Fish Stock, No. 8) for 5 or 6 minutes. Add 1 small onion, finely chopped, 1 small carrot, finely chopped, 1 small bouquet garni consisting of a few sprigs of parsley and 1 bay leaf tied together with kitchen thread, a few thyme leaves, salt and pepper to taste, and a few grains of cayenne pepper. Cook for 15 minutes. Lift out the langostina, shell them, and pound the meat in a mortar to a paste, adding 1 tablespoon of butter, bit by bit, then gradually 4 pieces of toast dipped in the cooking liquor. Moisten the whole with 1 quart of Fish Stock (No. 8), and add to the cooked vegetables in the pan. Let boil once, and set aside to simmer gently for 15 to 20 minutes. Strain through a fine cloth. Return again to the fire. Let boil once. Add ½ cup of thick cream, then gradually off the fire add 3 egg yolks, while stirring constantly. Correct the seasoning. Finish, just before serving, with

1 tablespoon of butter. Serve with a side dish of Jocko Toast (No. 790).

LOBSTER BISQUE I   [474]
A New England recipe

The Roman gourmet, Apicius, is reputed to have set out promptly in search of African lobsters and shrimps when he learned that they were bigger and sweeter than those in his city's ponds. His epicurean journey strengthened the precedent of travelers whose routes are mapped by their palates, and it has modern echoes in the seasonable jaunts of nostalgic American inlanders, whose remembrance of things past or hope of things to come leads them to New England shores and New England sea food every summer. Like Apicius, they eat lobster and shrimp, and fish in general, of course, but mainly they seek out that king of the sea, that royal redhead of the pot—the lobster.

Our own lobster, which has one claw larger than the other, is the world's most delicious, and is found from Delaware Bay northward to Hendley Harbor in Labrador.

From June till September, lobsters reach their greatest size and are most plentiful, but in general they can be obtained all the year round. Ordinarily, the shells of recently caught lobsters are a brownish green, but those trapped on sandy bottoms have a tinge of red. There are exceptions to that usual brownish green. Not infrequently is this gawky crustacean very colorful—red, white, blue, black. The New York City aquarium once had one half black, half red. However, it reaches its full glory—the gorgeous hue of a Chinese wedding chair—only when boiled. There seems to be no limit to the number and the variety of dishes its wet pink and white meat may grace.

Remove the meat from the shell of a 1½-pound cooked lobster (or use canned lobster). Place the pounded shells and trimmings in a soup kettle. Add 1 cup of fish stock, made with a few heads and trimmings of any kind of white-meat fish. Bring slowly to the boiling point, lower the heat, and let simmer gently for 25 minutes. Drain through a fine cloth. Let stand a minute or so to allow the small particles to settle in the bottom of the container. Return the liquid to the fire, bring to a boil, and add 2 tablespoons each of flour and butter rubbed to a cream. Let simmer gently for 10 minutes. Meanwhile, scald 2 cups of rich milk, or thin cream or undiluted evaporated milk, to a boil with the tail meat of the lobster, finely chopped. Let simmer for 10 minutes. Rub through a fine-meshed sieve both the liquid and solid, then combine with the first liquid. Season to taste with salt and a few grains of cayenne pepper. Add the claw and body meat and the coral, rubbed through a sieve and pounded with 2 tablespoons of butter. Taste for seasoning, and when ready to serve, stir in ½ cup of cream, to which has been added 2 well-beaten fresh egg yolks, beaten with 2 or 3 (according to taste) tablespoons of sherry wine. Serve in hot cups, each with 2 small cubes of Lobster Custard Garnish (No. 689).

LOBSTER BISQUE II [475]
Home method

Cook 1 medium-sized onion, finely chopped, in 3 tablespoons of butter, in the top of a double boiler placed over direct heat of low intensity, until softened, but not colored. Stir in 3 tablespoons of flour, and blend well. Then stir in 2 cups of scalded milk mixed with 2 cups of hot Chicken Consommé (No. 25), stirring until thickening just begins. Put over hot water, and continue cooking for 25 minutes, stirring occasionally. Season to taste with salt, pepper, and a few grains each of cayenne and nutmeg. Then stir in 1¾ cups of flaked cooked lobster meat (fresh, canned, or frozen). Continue cooking for 10 to 15 minutes. Rub the mixture through a fine-meshed sieve into a clean saucepan, heat to the boiling point, then stir in ½ cup of scalded cream alternately with 3 tablespoons of sherry wine. Serve in heated cups or soup plates, each garnished with a few Croutons (No. 780).

LOBSTER BISQUE III [476]
Bourgeoise method

In the following delicious bisque, three distinct operations are necessary.

First Operation. Cook 2 one-pound live lobsters for 15 minutes in 1 cup of dry white wine mixed with 1 cup of chicken broth, to which has been added 1 bay leaf, 3 sprigs of parsley, 1 sprig of thyme, 3 slices of onion, and 1 small carrot, scraped and thinly sliced. Season to taste with salt and freshly crushed black pepper. When the lobsters are of a beautiful red hue all over, lift them out. Strain the broth, reserving it, and when lobsters are cold enough to handle, remove the shell from body and claws, and cut the meat into small cubes, but do not chop. Set aside.

Second Operation. Place the cracked tail shell parts in a mortar, and pound with a pestle to a smooth paste with 3 tablespoons of sweet butter. Place this paste in a small saucepan over a very gentle flame, and stir until the butter mixture is melted. Place this red butter in a strong cloth, and twist it over a small vessel containing some ice-cold water. Remove the butter floating on the surface of the water, and set aside.

Third Operation. Pound the remaining part of the shell with ½ cup of cooked well-drained rice, adding, while pounding, the strained hot wine broth. Place in a small saucepan, heat to the boiling point, and strain through a fine cloth into a clean saucepan, to which add gradually the red butter and 1 quart of rich scalded milk alternately with 2 fresh egg yolks, slightly beaten, stirring briskly from the bottom of the pan. When the mixture just begins to boil, add the lobster meat, heat well without allowing to boil, and stir in 3 tablespoons of good sherry wine. Taste for seasoning, and serve in hot soup cups, each with 2 small cubes of Lobster Custard Garnish (No. 689).

MUSSEL BISQUE   [477]

Know ye therefore—so spoke his Highness the Prince—that mussels were known in the days of ancient Rome, that the kings of France were particularly fond of them, and that Louis XVIII prized them so highly that he took special measures to protect and develop them. Of what these special measures consisted seems to have been lost in the mists of time, for it appears that those who operate the greatest mussel beds in France today follow exactly the same method which was first devised seven hundred years ago.

It was in the year 1237, as the story goes, that a ship carrying a cargo of English mutton foundered off the coast of France, not far from New Rochelle. The skipper, an Irishman named Patrick Walton, managed to swim ashore, and soon set about finding a means of living. To his favorite pastime of fishing, he added that of hunting wild birds which, he noticed, flew very low over the water during the night, and which he captured by attaching a large net, washed ashore from his boat, to high sticks placed in the sand at low tide. These sticks were soon covered with hundreds of young mussels which in the new location grew much faster than when left in their usual ocean beds. The fishermen in this neighborhood today get their mussels in exactly the same manner.

Steam 3 pounds of mussels, first carefully scrubbed and rinsed in several changes of cold water, in one cup of white wine, to which have been added 1 medium-sized finely chopped onion; ¼ cup of green celery leaves, chopped; ½ medium-sized green pepper, finely chopped; and a bouquet garni, composed of 1 large bay leaf, 6 sprigs of fresh parsley, and a sprig of thyme, tied with kitchen thread. Do not salt or pepper as yet. When all the mussels are open, strain them through a colander, remove the meat from the shell, and place in a sieve, rubbing this through while easing the rubbing with the twice-strained broth. Transfer this to a saucepan, bring to a boil, and season to taste with very little salt, freshly ground black pepper, and a few grains each of cayenne and nutmeg, and boil once. Again strain through a fine cloth into a clean saucepan to ensure that no sand is left in the broth. Bring to a boil, then stir in 2 cups of scalded thin cream, or undiluted evaporated milk, and allow to simmer gently for 10 minutes. Remove from the fire, and stir in 3 fresh egg yolks beaten with 3 tablespoons of sherry or Madeira wine, beating briskly while pouring. Serve in hot soup plates, each garnished with mussel custard made like Clam Custard Garnish (No. 687), substituting mussels for clams.

OYSTER BISQUE I [478]
Southern manner

Of all children of the Creator, the lowly oyster has long been the most wistful. Born on the ocean bed, doomed to pass his days evading the grasp of more mobile creatures and then only to yield to a grappling hook, loved only for what it can give—a pearl or a first course—the pitiful *Ostrea edulis* has been defenseless, misunderstood.

Put 1 quart of oysters through a food chopper, then rub through a fine-meshed sieve. Heat 2 tablespoons of butter, and add 1 tablespoon of flour, blending well without letting it take on color. Gradually stir in 2 cups of milk, and continue cooking until the mixture just begins to thicken. Place over hot water, and allow to cook gently for 15 minutes, stirring occasionally. Cook ½ cup of finely chopped green celery leaves in 2 tablespoons of butter for 5 minutes over a gentle flame, stirring frequently. Add 1 small green pepper, finely chopped, and continue cooking for 3 or 4 minutes longer, then stir in 2 cups of scalded milk with 3 thin slices of onion. Strain this mixture into the first mixture. Season to taste with salt, white pepper, and a few grains of cayenne, then stir in 2 fresh egg yolks beaten with 1 teaspoon of Worcestershire sauce. Place over a direct flame, and bring to a boil, stirring constantly. Add the oysters, mix well, and serve in hot soup plates, with a side dish of small Croutons (No. 780).

OYSTER BISQUE II   [479]
Parisian method

Clean and pick over 1 quart of oysters, reserving the liquor, and
set aside the soft portions while chopping the harder muscle parts.
In a soup kettle, put 2 cups of rich Chicken Stock (No. 25); 1½ cups
of stale bread crumbs; the reserved strained oyster liquor; 3 thin
slices of onion; 2 small stalks of celery, finely chopped, using both
white and green portions; and 1 bouquet garni, composed of 6 sprigs
of parsley, 1 large bay leaf, 1 sprig of thyme, and 2 whole cloves, tied
with kitchen thread. Cook the whole for 30 minutes. Then strain
the mixture through a fine-meshed sieve, rubbing the solid parts
through. Return to the fire, bring to a brisk boil, and add the reserved soft parts, together with the chopped muscles. Heat thoroughly, and season to taste with salt, white pepper, and nutmeg.
When ready to serve, stir in 4 cups of rich scalded milk, 1 tablespoon of sweet butter, and 3 tablespoons of good sherry wine. Serve
without garnishing.

OYSTER BISQUE CAPUCINE   [480]

Parboil 1 quart of oysters in their own liquor. Strain. Reserve the
liquor, and finely chop the oysters. Add to the liquor 1½ quarts of
White Stock (No. 11), or hot water; 2 small stalks of celery, diced;
2 small leeks, diced; 1 small onion, chopped fine; a small bouquet
garni, composed of 6 sprigs of parsley and 1 bay leaf tied together
with kitchen thread; and a blade of mace. Bring to a boil. Then add
the oysters, ¾ cup of well-washed raw rice, and 2 cups of rich milk.
Bring to a rapid boil, reduce the flame, and let simmer very gently
for 20 to 25 minutes, stirring once in a while to prevent scorching
the rice. Force through a fine sieve over another saucepan. Season
with salt and pepper and a few grains of cayenne pepper to taste.
Finish, off the fire, while stirring rapidly, with 2 egg yolks, added
one by one, and 1 cup of heated cream.

SALMON BISQUE   [481]

Heat ¼ cup of butter in the top of a double boiler. Stir in 2
tablespoons of grated onion, and immediately stir in 2 tablespoons
of flour. Blend thoroughly. Gradually pour in 1 quart of sweet milk,
scalded with 1 large bay leaf, a blade of garlic, 3 sprigs of fresh
parsley, and 1 whole clove, head removed, alternately with 1 pound

can of salmon, flaked, skinned, and carefully boned. Cook over a direct flame, stirring constantly, until the mixture just begins to thicken. Transfer to the boiler, and continue cooking for 15 minutes longer. Empty the entire contents of the pan into a fine-meshed sieve, and rub through into a clean saucepan. Return to the fire, bring to a boil, remove from the fire, and stir in 2 fresh egg yolks, slightly beaten, and ¼ cup of boiled dry rice. Taste for seasoning. Serve in hot soup plates, each garnished with a tuft of whipped cream.

SALMON AND TOMATO BISQUE   [482]
Home method

One of the most prized relics that French archeologists have found in the French Pyrénées is a piece of reindeer bone, carved with a picture of a salmon. This carving, it is believed, was made at least 15,000 years before Christ, at a time when the great ice sheet was retreating from the mountainous region which divides France and Spain. A hundred and fifty centuries passed before Julius Caesar's soldiers discovered this same fish during their victorious march through Gaul. The fish was new to the Romans, who named it *salmo* from their Latin word *salire*, meaning "to leap."

Turn a 1-pound can of salmon without draining into a soup kettle. Add a No. 2 can of tomatoes, or the equivalent of fresh, peeled, coarsely chopped tomatoes, 1 tablespoon of chopped parsley, 1 large bay leaf, and 2 whole cloves. Pour in 1½ cups of Chicken Stock (No. 25), and season to taste with salt, pepper, and a few grains of mace. Bring to a boil, and allow to simmer gently for 30 minutes, stirring occasionally. Meanwhile, cook 1 medium-sized onion, chopped, in 2 tablespoons of butter for 2 or 3 minutes, stirring almost constantly. Blend in 2 tablespoons of flour, then stir in 1 cup of scalded milk with 1 can of undiluted evaporated milk. Cook until the mixture just begins to thicken, stirring constantly. Season to taste with salt and pepper, and add to the salmon mixture. Heat to the boiling point, empty the contents of the pan into a fine-meshed sieve, and rub through. Return to the fire, and let boil once. Remove from the fire, and stir in 2 fresh egg yolks, slightly beaten with 2 tablespoons of heavy cream. Taste for seasoning, let boil again once, stirring constantly from the bottom of the pan. Serve in hot soup plates, each garnished with Garlic Popcorn (No. 786), or serve with a side dish of Garlic Toast (No. 787).

SCALLOP BISQUE I   [483]
French method

Pick 1½ pints of scallops carefully, and reserve ½ cup. Chop the remaining 2 cups or put through a food chopper, using the finest blade. Turn the ground scallops into a saucepan, and add 1 cup of dry white wine, 1 cup of Chicken Stock (No. 25), 1 large bay leaf, 4 thin slices of onion, and 2 whole cloves, and cook gently for 25 minutes, stirring occasionally. Empty the contents of the saucepan into a fine-meshed sieve, and rub through with a potato masher. Return to the fire, bring to a boil, then stir in 2 cups of scalded milk and 1 cup of thin cream, or undiluted evaporated milk. Bring to a boil, season to taste with salt and pepper, and a few grains each of cayenne and nutmeg. Let boil once, remove from the fire, and beat in 2 fresh egg yolks, beaten with 3 tablespoons of sherry wine, beating briskly to prevent curdling. Taste for seasoning, and serve in hot cups, each garnished with 2 tiny Egg Balls (No. 672).

SCALLOP BISQUE II   [484]
Home method

Clean 1 quart of scallops, reserve half, and chop the remainder. Add the latter to 4 cups (1 quart) of scalded milk. Season to taste with salt, pepper, and a few grains of nutmeg. Add a very small pinch of ground clove, 1 small bay leaf, 4 peppercorns, bruised, and 1 small onion, finely chopped, and cook very slowly for 30 minutes. Strain. Thicken with 1 tablespoon of butter and 1 tablespoon of flour kneaded together. Let boil once. Simmer for 5 minutes. Set aside, and add 2 egg yolks, one by one, while stirring constantly. Finish with 1 tablespoon of butter. When ready to serve, parboil the reserved scallops, cut them in quarters, and add to the soup. Serve with freshly made toast.

SHRIMP BISQUE I   [485]
A la Bretonne—the Brittany way

Although the popularity of the shrimp grows constantly, few cooks explore the possibilities of shrimp cookery. Their culinary interests often take them no further than a cocktail, a salad, or an occasional excursion into the realms of the exotic by way of a shrimp chop suey. Yet the canned or fresh varieties can be prepared in as many as 350 other ways. Considering the palatable, economic, and nutritive values of this small shellfish, good American cooks think it worth while to exert great ingenuity in its preparation.

Three kinds of shrimps come to market, but only one in quantity, the "common" shrimp. There is also the grooved shrimp and the sea bob. To bring out the best flavor, shrimps are best boiled in sea water. If this is impossible, use strongly salted water, adding thyme, bay leaf, peppercorns, and a bouquet garni. Bring the water to a rolling boil, quickly drop in live shrimps, cook for 10 to 15 minutes, according to size. Cool, but do not hurry the cooling by a cold-water bath. Peel, and remove the intestinal vein.

Clean and chop 2 pounds of fresh raw shrimps as finely as possible, or put through a food chopper, using the finest blade. Cook over a very low flame for 3 minutes with 4 tablespoons of butter, or prefer-ably with shrimp butter (see below), together with 1 rounded table-spoon of finely chopped carrot and 4 tablespoons of finely chopped fresh mushrooms. Transfer the mixture into a soup kettle. Add 2 cups of strained clear rich Chicken Stock (No. 25), 2 tablespoons of finely chopped celery leaves, salt and pepper to taste, and a few grains of cayenne pepper and nutmeg. Cook for about 15 to 20 min-utes over a gentle flame; then put the mixture through a fine-meshed sieve or a flannel cloth, pressing gently but thoroughly, into a fresh saucepan. Bring to a boil, and let boil for 2 minutes. Remove from the fire, and add 1 cup each of heated dry white wine and parboiled cream. Taste for seasoning, reheat to the boiling point, and serve at once either in hot cups or soup plates, without garnishing.

In some parts of Brittany, 3 tablespoons of heated sherry wine are stirred into the bisque just before serving, and brown bread and butter finger sandwiches are served on the side.

Shrimp Butter. Pound (or grind several times, using the finest blade) 6 cooked shelled fresh shrimps, and cream with 2 tablespoons of salt butter.

SHRIMP BISQUE II [486]
American manner

Clean ¾ pound of cooked shrimps, or 1½ to 1¾ cups of canned shrimps, and cut them in very small pieces. Work 3½ tablespoons of butter to a soft cream, and add the shrimp (all but 3 tablespoons for garnishing the bisque when ready to serve). Mash them with a wooden spoon to a smooth paste, then rub the paste through a fine-meshed wire sieve. Soak 1 cup of soft bread crumbs in 4 cups of hot water for about 5 minutes, or until quite soft, then add the shrimp mixture, salt and pepper to taste, and a generous dash of nutmeg. Stir over a medium flame until the mixture starts to boil. Lower the flame, cover the pan, and let simmer very gently for about 20 minutes, stirring occasionally to prevent scorching. Then add 1 tablespoon of flour, mixed with a little cold milk. Let boil twice, then rub again through a fine-meshed wire sieve into a clean saucepan. Scald 1 quart of rich creamy milk with 3 thin slices of onion, 1 small bay leaf, 1 whole clove, and 3 sprigs of fresh parsley, and strain into a clean saucepan. Add to the milk a dash of baking soda, then the shrimp mixture. Just when ready to serve, beat in 2 fresh egg yolks, adding one at a time and beating well after each addition. Serve in hot soup plates with a very thin slice of lemon in each portion, and sprinkle a few of the reserved chopped shrimps.

SHRIMP BISQUE III   [487]
French manner

Cook 3 ounces of well-washed and drained rice in 1½ pints (3 cups) of milk until soft and mushy. Rub it through a fine-meshed sieve. Keep hot. Cook 1½ cups of fresh shrimps in salted boiling water for 20 minutes. Drain, shell, and put through a food chopper, using the finest blade. Heat 3 tablespoons of butter, stir in the ground shrimps, and cook for 2 minutes. Then moisten with 1 cup of dry white wine, mixed with 1 cup of hot Chicken Bouillon (No. 25), and parboiled with 1 large bay leaf, ¼ cup of ground fresh mushrooms, 1 tablespoon of grated onion, a sprig of marjoram, and a blade of mace. Strain over the ground shrimps. Transfer this to a soup kettle, stir in the rice mush, season to taste with salt and pepper, and a dash each of cayenne and nutmeg to taste, and bring to a boil. Let simmer gently for 20 minutes, covered, then strain through a cloth into a fresh saucepan. Bring to the boiling point, stir in ½ cup of scalded cream mixed with 2 fresh egg yolks, stirring briskly from the bottom of the pan. Taste for seasoning. When ready to serve, stir in 3 tablespoons of Madeira or sherry wine, according to taste. Taste for seasoning, and serve in hot cups, each garnished with 2 tiny cubes of shrimp custard, made as indicated for Crawfish Custard Garnish (No. 689), substituting shrimp for crawfish.

SKATE BISQUE   [488]
English manner

Clean, wash, sponge, and cut into 2-inch pieces 1 skate, weighing 2½ pounds. Save the head, skin, and trimmings, as they are also used. Be sure the fish is strictly fresh, or else reject it. Melt 2 table-spoons of butter in a deep skillet, put in the head, trimmings, skin, and bones, then the meat cut up. Brown lightly over a low flame, turning often. Sprinkle 2 tablespoons of flour over, and stir until light golden brown and well absorbed in the butter. Pour over 2 cups of cold water, stir well, and let simmer for 5 minutes. Turn all into a soup kettle, then pour in another quart of cold water. Season with salt, pepper, and cayenne to taste, and let boil once. Now add 2 small onions, sliced, and 1 small parsley root, finely chopped. Cover, and let simmer for 30 to 35 minutes over a moderately hot flame. Then remove from the fire. If desired, set aside a few pieces of the cooked fish for garnish. Strain through a fine sieve to another kettle, rubbing and pressing a little. Return the soup to the fire, and let boil once. Set aside, and add 1 generous wineglass of good sherry wine and 1 tablespoon of catsup, and finish with 1 tablespoon of butter kneaded with 1 tablespoon of flour. Stir, and let boil again two or three times. Correct the seasoning, and pour into a soup tureen over the reserved pieces of cooked fish, or serve with Croutons (No. 780).

Chapter Eight

CHOWDERS

FISH, GAME, MEAT, POULTRY, AND VEGETABLE,
INCLUDING FISH STEWS CONSIDERED AS SOUP,
AND BOUILLABAISSE

*Clam chowder is one of those subjects, like
politics or religion, that can never be discussed
lightly. Bring it up even incidentally, and all
the innumerable factions of the clambake regions raise their heads and begin to yammer.*

ALAS, WHAT CRIMES HAVE BEEN COMMITTED IN THE NAME OF chowder! Dainty chintz-draped tearooms, charity bazaars, church suppers, summer hotels, canning factories—all have shamelessly travestied one of America's noblest institutions; yet while clams and onions last, the chowder shall not die, neither shall it sink into the limbo of denatured, emasculate, forgotten things.

Clam chowder, mind you, is not a bisque, not a French potage, not a delicate broth for invalids. A certain famed American, Mrs. Malaprop, is credited with saying indignantly when a friend remarked about her daughter's frail physique: "Delicate? Nonsense! My daughter is one of the most indelicate young women in Boston!" And by the same token, clam chowder is essentially one of the most indelicate of our national dishes. It is rude, rugged, a food of body and substance—like Irish stew, Scottish haggis, English steak and kidney pie—a worthy ration for the men and women of a pioneer race and for their offspring.

Whence, you may indeed ask, came the word "chowder"? Do you wonder whether it is perhaps an Indian name like so many others borne by our native dishes, such as samp and succotash? No, the trail in quest of chowder origin leads us over the vast waters of the Atlantic, and begins first in the little fishing hamlets and villages of Brittany, famed fishing villages that originated naturally a community enterprise in the guise of *faire la chaudière*, or "prepare the cauldron."

After a fishing expedition, when the men were back home from the sea with their catch, it became the custom to celebrate with a huge pot or cauldron of soup or stew, to which each man of family contributed some share or ingredient. Some brought fish, others vegetables, still others seasonings and spices, and everything went into the pot—all together and at once. Each family participated equally in this steaming aromatic brew, around which gathered much festivity, quite after our own fashion of a village fair or festival, or perhaps like our first Thanksgiving dinner. And there too were prepared weddings *en masse* during the *pardon*, which continued for several days.

It matters not whether you belong to the milk or to the water party in the chowder cult. Clams and onions and salt pork are the fundamentals on which to concentrate. Much was said about onions in relation to Spanish omelets, and much must be said of onions and clams when chowder is in the balance. "Take a dozen clams and one small onion," says a certain undeservedly popular cook book, taking the name of clam chowder in vain. A dozen clams, forsooth! Take at least three dozen good soft clams if your family is a small one. Men and women of Rhode Island and Massachusetts Bay never sat down to less than a peck of clams apiece. And then take at least three large onions and a good third pound of the finest fat salt pork, and follow up the recipe, Clam Chowder I (No. 502).

Manhattan chowder? Yes, but it came from Gloucester, Swampscott, Nahant, Cohasset, Scituate, all around the Cape, and up and down Narragansett Bay from the Point to Providence. In more spacious days, good trenchermen downed a quart of clams, with lobsters, crabs, bluefish, and green corn, all roasted in steaming seaweed that was banked on superheated rocks. And all the good men who were still conscious finished off with half a watermelon.

They make all the varieties there, no matter what you call them. If you prefer a milk or cream chowder, leave tomatoes out of the recipe, and use only a pint of water, then follow up Clam Chowder II (No. 503).

Many of these French fisherfolk crossed the Atlantic to settle in Newfoundland, bringing, of course, their *chaudière*, or cauldron, along with them. And only a little distance farther, either in New England, or across that narrow link of water called Long Island Sound, each claims to be the original home of the chowder. For by this time, the "big stewpot," or *chaudière*, had been contracted and modified into the Yankeefied "chowder." Naturally the New Englander, with an abundance of sea food at his very doorstep, continued mightily in the chowder tradition. He made it of fish, he made it of clams, he made it of oysters—or he made it of all three—and added another little seasoning tidbit, such as diced salt pork, chopped bacon, thyme, and other fragrances out of the spice cabinet. Now and again he added milk, or still later, and lower down the Middle Atlantic seaboard, he began to add tomatoes. Thus started the famous food controversy, still, if ever, to be settled, as to whether chowder should be made with milk or with tomatoes.

Here is a recipe in verse for clam chowder, dated 1834, and anonymous:

> To make a good chowder and have it quite nice
> Dispense with sweet marjoram, parsley, and spice;
> Mace, pepper and salt are now wanted alone,
> To make the stew eat well and stick to the bone.
> Some pork is sliced thin and put into the pot;
> Some say you must turn it, some say you must not;
> And when it is brown, take it out of the fat,
> And add it again when you add this and that.

A layer of potatoes, sliced quarter-inch thick,
Should be placed in the bottom to make it eat slick;
A layer of onions now over this place,
Then season with pepper, and salt, and some mace.
Split open your crackers and give them a soak,
In eating you'll find this the cream of the joke;
On top of all this, now comply with my wish
And put in large chunks, all your pieces of fish;
Then put on the pieces of pork you have tried.
In seasoning I pray you, don't spare the cayenne;
'Tis this makes it fit to be eaten by men.
After adding these things in their regular rotation
You'll have a dish fit for the best of the nation.

Note. Fish broth and milk are to be added.

The old-fashioned soup tureen is back in style for anyone so fortunate as to possess one. But lacking this, a chowder party can enjoy the dish served in a gayly painted or peasant-type bowl. A large pottery salad bowl is very smart indeed, accompanied by round bowls of capacious size. These chowders serve 6 to 8 persons.

BEAN CHOWDER I [490]
Middle West method

Wash 1½ pounds of red kidney beans thoroughly in several changes of water, and soak overnight in 2½ quarts of cold water. Drain, and cover with 2 quarts of fresh cold water. Add 2 large onions, chopped, 1 large bay leaf tied with 6 sprigs of fresh parsley and 2 whole cloves, ½ teaspoon of thyme leaves, 1 teaspoon of salt, ⅛ teaspoon of pepper, and a No. 2½ can of tomatoes, liquid and solid. Gradually bring to a boil, lower the flame, and cook gently for 1½ hours, or until the beans are tender, but not mushy. Then add 2 cups of small potato cubes, 1 medium-sized green pepper, chopped, and continue cooking for 15 to 20 minutes, or until the potatoes just begin to be tender. Then add 6 frankfurters in ¼-inch slices, and cook for 10 minutes longer. Taste for seasoning, and serve in hot soup plates, each dusted with finely chopped parsley. Any kind of salted crackers may be served as a side dish with this almost-a-meal soup.

BEAN CHOWDER II [491]
Mulligan method

Fry ½ pound of bacon until crisp over a gentle flame. Set aside, and use half of the drippings in the pan or kettle. First make a layer of 2 large sliced potatoes, then a layer of 3 large onions, sliced thin, seasoning with salt, pepper, and thyme leaves (not powdered thyme) as you go along, then a layer of 1½ cups of cooked navy beans, fresh or canned (or any other kind of beans). Top the beans with 1 large green pepper, finely chopped. Repeat these layers of ingredients. Pour over 2 cans of tomato soup or juice. Gradually bring to a boil, lower the flame, and let simmer gently for 1 hour. Taste for seasoning, and serve in hot soup plates, each sprinkled with a little of the crisp bacon, chopped.

BISCAYNE CODFISH CHOWDER [492]

However great the consumption of codfish in the United States, the cod is not exclusively ours. There are many other nations and peoples that depend on it for food and look on that food with favor. Outstanding among these is Portugal, a chowder-lover like ourselves. Perhaps the ancient Portuguese originated chowder—no one knows. But we do know that their modern descendants make a chowder called *caldeirada a pescadora*, a mixture of sliced fish, onions, sorrel, parsley, garlic, olive oil, white wine, and thin slices of bread. And we do know that the Portuguese discovered the delicacy of cod liver when it is sautéed. They take the livers from the cod, roll them in seasoned flour, and sauté them in butter over a gentle flame, like ordinary liver. One such bit from a ten-pound cod makes a royal breakfast or luncheon treat.

Such a treat in Portugal, of course, is always prepared under the guidance of Saint Anthony, who stands, in his wooden or plaster image, on every kitchen shelf. Saint Anthony is also the patron saint of the fisherman, so that the fishwife has good cause to respect him, and to pray to him for a safe voyage home for her men. But not always is he given all the reverence which is his due; for when Saint Anthony has miscalculated the proportion of the ingredients that go into a chowder, or into any other dish, and dinner is a failure, he receives the blame—and sometimes most pointedly. Never, we assure you, is the cook at fault; always it is Saint Anthony, and occasionally an irate wife administers to him a vigorous spanking and a temporary banishment to the well outside, to hang there head down for penance. The next meal is usually a good one.

For six large servings, put in a saucepan the trimmings of a 4-pound codfish, 1½ quarts of cold water, 2 large tomatoes, pounded, 1 large bay leaf, 10 whole peppercorns, 2 whole cloves, and 10 sprigs of parsley. Heat gently until the boiling point is reached, and allow to simmer for 25 minutes. Strain through a fine sieve into a soup kettle, and add the codfish, boned and cut into small pieces, 2 tablespoons of finely chopped onion, 2 tablespoons of finely chopped celery stalk, 1 cup of cooked shrimps, peeled and black veins removed, coarsely chopped, and salt to taste. Bring the mixture to a boil, and let simmer gently for 30 minutes, stirring frequently to prevent scorching. Stir in 1 cup of scalded medium cream sauce, and allow the chowder to boil up once again. Then let it simmer gently while you prepare fish balls.

Fish Balls. Put 1 cup of raw codfish (or any other white-meat fish), free from bones and skin, through the finest knife of the food chopper. Combine the fish paste with 1 fresh egg, slightly beaten, 2 table-spoons of fine bread crumbs, a blade of mace, 1 tablespoon each of finely chopped chives and parsley, a dash of cayenne pepper, and ½ generous teaspoon of salt, more or less, according to taste. Shape this mixture into a dozen and a half small balls. Salt the chowder to taste, and bring it to a brisk boil. Add the fish balls and 2 cups of raw potatoes, cut in small dices, and cover the pan. Simmer for about 20 minutes, or until the potatoes are tender. Correct the seasoning as needed. Serve the chowder with finger-shaped pieces of toast rubbed with garlic butter, after stirring into the chowder 3 tablespoons of sweet butter.

Note. Salmon, halibut, flounder, or turbot may be substituted for codfish in this delicious recipe which is a meal in itself.

BLACKFISH CHOWDER [493]
American

The blackfish is one of the most interesting and venerable of all American fishes. It's a living fossil, the sole surviving species of a once numerous order that lived in very early geologic times. Its survival, unchanged over practically all other forms of life of that time shows that it has remarkable qualities of endurance. The male is marked with a dark spot at the base of the tail. It is known under many aliases, according to locality, such as bowfin, mudfish, lawyer, cotton-fish, speckled cat, scaled ling, grindle, choupiquel, dogfish, and so on, and is in season the year round. Its average size is from one to two feet, the male being smaller than the female.

Dice 4 ounces of salt pork small, and try in a soup kettle until crisp. Lift out the cracklings with a perforated ladle and keep hot. To the fat remaining in the kettle, add 3 stalks of celery, chopped fine, 1 large green pepper, chopped fine and free from seeds and white ribs, 1 small clove of garlic, mashed, and 3 medium-sized onions, peeled and finely chopped. Cook, stirring almost constantly, until the vegetables are just beginning to brown. Then add 4 pounds of cleaned blackfish, washed and skinned and cut into 2-inch pieces. Pour over 1¾ quarts of hot water (or fish stock made from trimmings including the skin); 2 cups of potatoes, diced small; ½ cup of carrot, scraped, then cubed small; 1 bouquet garni, composed of 1 large bay leaf, 6 sprigs of parsley, 1 sprig of thyme, and 2 whole cloves, tied together with kitchen thread; ½ teaspoon of thyme leaves (not thyme powder); 1 teaspoon of salt; and ½ scant teaspoon of black pepper, freshly ground. Bring slowly to the boiling point, and simmer gently for 25 minutes. Stir in 1 cup of scalded cream, and let boil once. Taste for seasoning, and serve at once with the hot cracklings on the side and a tray of Cracker Puffs (No. 779).

Note. Sea or fresh-water bass may be substituted for blackfish in this Middle West recipe.

BURGER VEGETABLE CHOWDER   [494]
Estonian

Beware of buying bargain-price hamburger at any time, at any place. It is usually from the less desirable cuts and may be excessively fat so that it shrinks badly in cooking. Grind the meat yourself, and choose chuck or plate beef for grinding whether for patties, balls, or loaf. Both round and flank steaks are too lean to make juicy hamburger, and the chuck and plate cuts are more economical in price. Ready ground "burger" may contain as much as 25 per cent fat, according to government regulations. Since it's lean meat that counts for protein, it's often more economical in the long run to select a lean piece of meat and have it ground or grind it at home.

Form 1 pound of ground beef into tiny balls about the size of large grapes, after seasoning to taste with salt and pepper. Heat 3 tablespoons of butter or other fat in a soup kettle, and in it brown the burger balls, turning them with a wooden spoon. When delicately brown, add 6 cups of boiling water gradually, stirring constantly. Bring to a boil. Add 2½ tablespoons of washed rice. Reduce the flame, cover, and let simmer gently for about 15 minutes, stirring occasionally. Then add 1 cup of minced onions, 1 cup of potatoes, diced small, 1 cup of fresh or canned tomato pulp, ½ cup of scraped carrots, diced small, 1 large bay leaf, 2 whole cloves, 1 generous teaspoon of salt, a generous dash of pepper, and ½ teaspoon of thyme leaves. Cover, and let simmer gently for 25 minutes, or until the vegetables are tender, stirring occasionally. Then stir in 2 teaspoons of beef essence (commercial), 1 cup of chopped spinach leaves, and 2 tablespoons of minced parsley. Cover, and continue cooking for 5 minutes longer, or until the spinach stems are wilted. Taste for seasoning, stir in 2 tablespoons of butter, and serve in hot soup plates with freshly made buttered toast.

CARROT CHOWDER [495]
American

References to carrots are frequent in records: in China from the thirteenth century on, in Japan in 1712, in India in 1826, in Arabia in 1775, in Europe by nearly all the writers and herbalists since 1536, in Virginia in 1609, in Brazil in 1647.

Eat the raw carrot, said the medical authorities, and you will get all the carotene (from which vitamin A is produced in the liver) it is possible to get. Whether the juice squeezed from raw carrot or that from steamed carrot gives the more carotene isn't known as yet.

Scrub enough carrots to make 2 cups (do not scrape or pare), and cook them with 2 cups of diced potatoes in 1½ cups of Beef Stock (No. 114), or water, reinforced with 1 teaspoon of Pique Seasoning, salt, pepper, and a dash of paprika to taste, for about 20 minutes, or until almost tender. Meanwhile, cook ½ cup of chopped onion in 5 tablespoons of butter very, very slowly until tender, stirring frequently with a wooden spoon, using a large saucepan. Sprinkle the onion with 2 tablespoons of flour, and mix thoroughly. Then stir in 3 cups of hot milk, alternately with the carrot-potato and liquid mixture. Cook over a very low flame for about 15 minutes. Stir in ½ teaspoon of thyme leaves (not powdered thyme). Taste for seasoning, and serve in hot soup plates, each garnished with finely chopped chives, and with a side dish of freshly made whole wheat toast, buttered whole wheat crackers, or heated buttered saltine crackers.

CARP CHOWDER IN RED WINE [496]
Austrian

Although the history of *Cyprinus carpio*—carp's name, officially— is lost in antiquity, its original home was China. Of yellowish tinge on the sides, shading to bronze above, with scales of considerable size—in summer the flesh has a muddy flavor, which is eliminated by keeping live fish in fresh water for a time, or by skinning and soaking in cold water. The winter carp is much preferred, especially during the holidays of those of the Jewish faith. They are never sold "dressed," but in the "round," meaning fish as caught, head on, insides intact.

In Vienna, Prague, and Warsaw, one may find the indolent carp, soft fins moving slowly, in tanks framed in the walls of every little café. For Christmas dinners in these cities, carp is as essential as turkey to an American Thanksgiving. This fresh-water fish is known under different names, according to locality, such as winter carp, buffalo fish, golden carp, and so on. A favorite dish made with this lean fish in Vienna is this chowder.

Chop coarsely 4 slices of bacon, and brown in a soup kettle. Stir in 1 tablespoon of butter creamed with 2 tablespoons of flour, and blend thoroughly; then add a 2-inch piece of parsley root, ½ cup of chopped celery heart, 6 whole peppercorns, freshly crushed, ⅓ cup of chopped onion, 1 large bay leaf, ½ teaspoon of thyme leaves, 3 thin slices of lemon, seeded, 3 cups of fish stock made with the trimmings of the fish, 2 cups of good red wine, and a 4-pound carp, cleaned, skinned, and cut into inch pieces. Season with salt to taste. Bring very slowly to a boil, lower the flame, and let simmer very gently for 40 minutes, covered. Fish out the bay leaf, and taste for seasoning. When ready to serve, stir in 2 tablespoons of sweet butter creamed with 1 scant teaspoon of paprika. Serve in hot soup plates, each sprinkled with a little chopped parsley.

CATFISH CHOWDER [497]
American

> *"Don't talk to me o' bacon fat,*
> *Or taters, coon or 'possum;*
> *Fo' when I'se hooked a yaller cat,*
> *I'se got a meal to boss 'em."*
> THE DARKEY AND THE CATFISH

The catfish has long fleshy feelers (whiskers), smooth scaleless skin, and a small fleshy fin to the rear of the dorsal fin exactly as in salmon and trout. This fresh-water fish consists mostly of head. It's a toothsome morsel when properly cooked. It is of different varieties and aliases, such as bullhead, Easter or Holy Cross, horned pout, channel catfish, blue cat, mud cat, tadpole, mad tom, and so on, and measures from one foot, reaching a weight from one to forty pounds. The smaller the fish, the better.

Fry 3 slices of chopped bacon until brown. Drain the excess bacon drippings, leaving only 3 tablespoons. Stir in 1½ tablespoons of flour, stirring constantly until brown. Add ¾ cup of chopped onion and ¾ cup of small potato cubes, and stir until partly cooked. Season to taste with salt, pepper, and a dash of cayenne pepper. Add 1 scant cup of tomato catsup, ¾ cup of chopped celery leaves, 4 cups of hot water, and 2 teaspoons of Worcestershire sauce. Bring to a boil, then add 1 large bay leaf, 2 whole cloves, and ½ generous teaspoon of thyme leaves (not thyme powder), and let simmer gently for 25 minutes. Then add 3¾ to 4 pounds of cleaned catfish, cut into inch pieces. Cover, bring to a boil, and let simmer gently for 25 minutes. Do not stir, as this breaks the fish pieces, but run a perforated ladle on the bottom of the kettle. Taste for seasoning, and if the liquid is or seems thin, add a little flour paste. Boil for a few minutes. Serve in hot soup plates with corn muffins or hot biscuits.

CAULIFLOWER CHOWDER [498]
American

Early historians placed cauliflower and broccoli in one botanical variety, and it was not until 1724 that broccoli was mentioned separately. It is believed that the Romans knew them both, in which case they have been in cultivation for a considerable period of time, but little is known of their history.

This "cabbage with a college education," as some gourmets call the cauliflower, requires some care when used in cookery. To keep it white and mild flavored, cook it quickly in boiling salted water, uncovered, for 10 to 15 minutes if the flowerets are separated, for 25 to 30 minutes if the head is left whole. Fine quality in cauliflower is indicated by a white or creamy white clean, heavy, firm, compact curd or flower head. The jacket or outer leaves which protect the head should be fresh, firm, and green. A compact clean curd means a minimum of waste, and such a head is easily prepared for cooking. Large and small heads may be equally mature. "Riceyness" is the term used to describe the granular appearance when the flowerets of cauliflower have begun to grow. Yellow leaves may indicate staleness or age, but are not important if the curd is otherwise of good quality. Avoid spotted, speckled, or bruised curd.

Soak 1 medium-sized head of cauliflower in cold water for 25 to 30 minutes, head down to allow any sand or foreign matter to fall to the bottom of a deep pan. Drain, rinse in slightly salted water, and drain again. Break into flowerets in a soup kettle, and add a bouquet garni composed of 1 large bay leaf, 6 sprigs of fresh parsley, 2 sprigs of green celery leaves, 2 whole cloves, all tied with kitchen thread. Cover with

2 quarts of hot water, and cook for 15 minutes. Drain, reserving the broth and the bouquet garni. Return the broth to the fire, and bring to a boil, letting it boil down until reduced to about 3 cups. To the broth, add ½ cup of tiny potato cubes, ½ cup of tiny carrot cubes, ¼ cup of finely chopped onion, and ¼ cup of finely chopped green pepper, and cook for 15 minutes, or until the vegetables are tender. Add the cooked flowerets of cauliflower, 5 whole peppercorns, freshly crushed, ½ teaspoon of thyme leaves, and 1 quart of scalded milk. Let boil once, and taste for seasoning. Just before serving in hot soup plates, stir in 3 tablespoons of butter creamed with 1½ tablespoons of flour. Bring to a boil, and let boil 2 or 3 times. Serve with a side dish of bread and butter finger sandwiches. For effect, you may sprinkle over each plate a little paprika.

CELERY CHOWDER [499]
Swiss

Celery, which belongs to the parsley family, has grown wild and been used as a medicine for hundreds of years. The wild plant is a native of marshy places in European regions extending from Sweden to Algeria, Egypt, and Ethiopia, and eastward to the Caucasus. It was not until 1623 in France that any mention was made of a cultivated variety. The wild variety was called smallage, and it was a herb eaten to purify the blood. In 1686, it was claimed that smallage transferred to culture becomes milder and less ungrateful. In Italy and France, the leaves and stalks are esteemed as delicacies, eaten with oil and pepper.

Scrape enough outer stalks of celery to make 2 cups when finely· chopped. Chop enough leaves of celery, the green ones as far as possible, to make 2 cups. Place the chopped scraped stalks and chopped leaves in a soup kettle. Add 1 large bay leaf, 2 whole cloves, and ½ generous teaspoon of thyme leaves, and 1 peeled large potato, freshly grated. Pour over 3 cups of cold water. Do not salt as yet. Cook over a gentle flame until the celery is tender, stirring occasionally. Meanwhile, blend 2 tablespoons of butter with 1½ tablespoons of flour over a gentle flame, stirring constantly until the mixture just begins to bubble. Gradually stir in 3 cups of scalded milk with 1 cup of cream, stirring constantly from the bottom of the pan until the mixture boils; let boil for 3 or 4 minutes, then season to taste with salt and white pepper. Gradually add to the milk mixture the cooked celery and broth, and bring to a boil. Let boil for 3 or 4 minutes, and taste for seasoning. When ready to serve, stir in 2 fresh egg yolks and the hard-cooked whites of the yolks, finely chopped. Serve in hot soup plates, each sprinkled with finely chopped parsley.

CHICKEN CHOWDER DINNER [500]
Massachusetts method

> New England is my home, 'tis there
> I love the pagan Sun and Moon.
> 'Tis there I love the growing year,
> December and young-summer June.
> PHILIP HENRY SAVAGE

In New England, there is an imperishable quality about the home instinct which has continued through generations—a heritage from the early sturdy pioneers who braved untold hardships in a new land and hewed homes out of a wilderness.

The soil and the sea are ever the important factors in developing the characteristic cookery of a country; and in New England, it is interesting to note the part that sea and farm play in the diet. Here is an old, very old chowder dinner recipe from New England, in fact, from Massachusetts.

This will serve 12 generously. Simmer 1 six-pound fowl in 2 quarts of water until tender, after adding 1 large bouquet garni, composed of 2 large bay leaves, 10 sprigs of parsley, 3 sprigs of green celery leaves, and 1 generous sprig of thyme, 8 peppercorns, gently bruised, and salt to taste. Remove the chicken, and cut the meat into large cubes. Let the broth become cold, remove the fat carefully, then return the chicken cubes to the broth, and let stand in the refrigerator overnight to mellow and get tender.

On the day the chowder is to be served, try out ¼ pound of cubed salt pork. Add 2 medium-sized onions, sliced thin, and sauté slowly in a little chicken fat until light brown. Place pork and onions in the bottom of a large soup kettle. Add 4 cups of hot water; 6 cups of raw potatoes, cubed small; 1 tablespoon of salt; 1 bouquet garni, composed of 2 large bay leaves, 2 small parsley roots, scraped, 1 sprig of thyme, and 2 sprigs of green celery leaves, all tied together with kitchen thread; and 8 peppercorns gently bruised. Bring to a boil, and let simmer gently until the potatoes are tender, but still firm. Bring the chicken stock and meat to the boiling point, then add 1 quart of scalded rich milk, or 2 cups of milk and 2 cups of cream, with 4 tablespoons of sweet butter. Discard the bouquet garni from the potato mixture, and combine the two mixtures. Stir well, and just before serving, stir in ½ cup of freshly cooked rice. If the mixture is not thick enough, stir in a little flour diluted in a little cold milk. Boil for a few minutes. Serve as hot as possible in hot soup plates, each garnished with 2 or 3 small Egg Balls (No. 672).

CLAMS [501]

The clam, which plows its way along sandy bottoms, standing erect on the edge of its shell, is obtained wholly by raking in water of various depths. It is interesting to see the clam digger waiting in silence for the slow retreat of dragging waters from the dripping sand, knowing perfectly well the sea must give consent before his feet may trespass on the bivalved borderland between the gray dunes, while the gull-winged garrulous sea birds watch his labor and wait to get their share of clams, soft or hard.

The quahog, quatog, quahaug, or quohog, as the hard clam is known in New England, is the original name bestowed on it by the Indians who used the purple margin of the shell for making their dark wampum or money. It's the "luxury" clam—firm-textured and sweet—and the chief commercial clam on our east coast, and is abundant from Cape Cod to Florida.

There are hard and soft clams, and the hard ones are classified according to their size. They are also called chowder clams. The middle-sized clams are cherrystones, and the smallest of all are the littleneck clams. These delicious little bivalves are usually served on the half shell or in cocktails, since for them "boiling is spoiling." But they may be substituted for the oyster in many of the traditional baked oyster favorites.

The soft or "steamer" clams are choice morsels, because they have absolutely everything a sea food should have. They are of a different character, having comparatively thin, smooth elongated shells. They remain sunk in the sand of the shore, between tidemarks, with their syphon mouth just at the surface, and when disturbed, they eject a spurt of water as they withdraw to safer depths.

Soft clams or "steamers" are steamed open before being brought to the table. The first step to enjoy a dish of steamed clams is the "bearding" of the clam—that is, removing the black hood from the neck, together with its trailing "veil." The opened soft-shelled clams are usually served on a deep dish or large platter. An oyster or dinner fork is used to remove the clam from the shell and the black cap from the head. At the side of each plate should be a small dish containing melted butter sauce mixed with lemon or onion juice, and hot, and each clam should be dipped into the sauce before eating.

There is no closed season on clams. They really come into their own in summer, or in warm weather when conditions make clam digging easy. Soft clams are seldom seen in the winter, but hard clams are never out of season.

The sand clam is as important on the Pacific coast as the hard clam is on the east coast. It is used especially in chowders. The surf clam, sometimes called jumping clam, is one of the largest bivalves on the Atlantic coast. The California species looks like the littleneck. There are several of this species, which are greatly relished on the Pacific coast, namely the solid surf, the beaked surf, and the mattock surf.

The rosy razor is the common clam of southern California. It is a smooth, pinkish white, flattened, straight tube clam, and its flesh is considered a delicacy along the coast. In flavor it is unsurpassed, especially in chowder.

The giant rock clam, also known as the dweller, Oregon, or Vancouver clam is a large edible clam of the Northwest. It has the general form of the eastern hard-shelled species, and is found in great abundance in the Aleutian Islands and Monterey Bay.

The Morton or trading clam is extensively used for chowders, the young ones serving as littleneck or cherrystone clams. It is very popular on the Florida coast.

The giant Callista clam is found from Cape Hatteras to Texas. It is shaped and painted like a rainbow—blue, lilac, or gray on a pale ground. It is especially abundant on the beach of western Florida and is widely used for chowders and cream soup.

The spotted Callista clam is oval, with a shiny surface, and fawn colored with broken radiating bands of violet brown. It is extensively used for chowders.

The Tiveta, thick-shelled, or three-angled clam is one of the finest as well as one of the largest California species, with the flavor of the surf clam, and is greatly used for chowders and cream soup.

The ribbed carpet clam has a thin podlike shell oval, radially ribbed (hence its name) often marked with chevrons of darker shades. It is found abundantly and used extensively for chowders and cream soup all along the west coast, especially north of San Francisco.

The netted carpet clam is distinguished by the very fine crisscrossing of sharply chiseled lines on its valves. It is found in great quantities on the Pacific coast and used for chowders and cream as well as bisque soup.

The giant Washington clam is the largest of all the surf clams and is found in large quantities on the Pacific coast. It is oblong, rounded at both ends, and is a noble and estimable shellfish, which beats any other clam yet discovered for chowders, clam purée, clam loaf, clam fritters, clam soups, clam pies, and clam sauce. It has nearly the consistency of the oyster as well as its flavor.

CLAM CHOWDER I   [502]
New England manner

"Take a dozen clams and one small onion," says a certain undeservedly popular cook book, taking the name of clam chowder in vain. A dozen clams, indeed! Take 3 dozen good tightly closed clams, if your family is a small one. Then take 3 large onions and ⅓ pound of the finest fat salt pork. Cut the pork into half-inch dice, and brown slowly in an iron skillet; then slice the onions thinly into the pork fat, and let them turn to golden brown rings. Meanwhile, wash the live clams, using a brush to get rid of all sand, and heat them slowly in a pan till the shells open. Save the juice, cut the coarse membrane, then chop half of the clams, not too finely, and keep the rest whole. Put the pork, onions, clam juice, and a quart of boiling water in a soup kettle. Add 3 peeled large tomatoes; 1 bunch of leeks, cut fine; 2 stalks of celery, thinly sliced; 2 young carrots, scraped and diced small; 1 tablespoon of chopped parsley; a generous pinch of thyme leaves; 2 bay leaves; 1 teaspoon of salt; ½ teaspoon of freshly ground black pepper; and a slight grating of nutmeg. Let the mixture boil up smartly, then reduce to the simmering point, and put in 2 large potatoes cut in neat small dices. Prepare a roux by browning 1 tablespoon of flour in 1½ tablespoons of butter, and make it creamy and smooth by stirring in a little broth from the kettle before the potatoes begin to soften. Simmer slowly until the potatoes are just right, then stir in the roux and 2 pilot biscuits, coarsely crumbled, and add ½ generous teaspoon of Worcestershire sauce and a dash of Tabasco sauce.

Sit down and enjoy religiously the real, original New England clam chowder.

CLAM CHOWDER II   [503]
Manhattan manner—so called

Manhattan chowder? Yes, but it came from Gloucester, Swampscott, Nahant, Cohasset, Scituate, all around the Cape, and up and down Narragansett Bay from the Point to Providence. In more spacious days, good trenchermen downed a quart of it as a mere prelude to a peck of clams, with lobsters, crabs, bluefish, and green corn, all roasted in steaming seaweed that was banked on superheated rocks.

And all the good men who were still conscious finished off with a half a watermelon.

They make all the varieties up there, no matter what you call them. All the flavors and seasonings are highly essential, but the pinch—a generous one—is vital, like the pinch of saffron in bouillabaisse.

Proceed as indicated above, but leave tomatoes out of the recipe, and use only a pint of water. When the chowder is ready to serve, bring 3 cups of milk to a boil, and add it to the chowder off the fire, with a cup of rich cream, heated, but not boiled.

CLAM CHOWDER III   [504]
Manhattan manner

This is still another variant of Clam Chowder I (No. 502), which retains the tomatoes, but ¼ teaspoon of soda is stirred in before the milk and cream are added, to prevent curdling, and the color and flavor are effective and satisfying.

Variations to Clam Chowder I, II, III. (a) Two No. 1 cans of minced clams may be used instead of fresh clams. (b) When served in colorful peasant earthenware bowls, you may crumble some crackers in bowls before pouring in the chowder. (c) Canned tomatoes or even tomato juice may be substituted for fresh tomatoes. (d) Shucked clams may be used instead of freshly opened clams. (e) To make the chowder more substantial, especially when it takes the main dish place, the Midwesterners add 1 cup of canned cream-style corn.

CLAM CHOWDER IV   [505]
Pacific Coast manner

Have ready 1½ quarts of rich Beef Stock (No. 114), or use water. Stir in ¾ cup of rich tomato sauce or tomato purée, bring to a boil, and let simmer gently for 15 minutes. Meanwhile, cook 3 or 4 slices of bacon, chopped, until just beginning to take on a nice light brown color. Skim off the pieces of bacon, and in the drippings, cook ¾ cup of chopped onions until tender. Add to the soup kettle, and allow to simmer for 10 minutes. Then add 2 cups of raw potatoes, cubed small, ½ cup of raw carrots, cubed small, and ¾ cup of celery stalk, cubed small. Season to taste with salt and black pepper, a generous dash of Worcestershire sauce, and ½ teaspoon of thyme leaves. Cook gently until the vegetables are tender (about 20 minutes), then stir in 2 cups of fresh clams, chopped, or 2 cups of canned minced clams. Serve very hot with freshly made buttered toast.

CLAM GUMBO CHOWDER   [506]
Creole

The species of okra are numerous. The okra in general use, both in the East and West Indies and in the United States, as an article of food is the *Hibicus esculentus*. Its name in the West Indies is gobbo, and it is an important ingredient of West Indies pepper pot, erroneously called Philadelphia pepper pot. Because okra has long been associated with Creole gumbos, the pods are frequently called gumbo.

To any of the first three clam chowders, add, when ready to serve, 1 cup of canned gumbo or okra.

CLAM AND OYSTER CHOWDER   [507]
Creole

Clean and pick 1 pint of shucked oysters, reserving the liquor. Chop the oysters, and add to the liquor. Clean and pick 1 pint of shucked clams, reserving the liquor. Remove the hard parts, and chop them. Add to the clam liquor, putting aside the soft parts. Combine the oysters and clams, heat slowly to the boiling point, and let simmer for 15 minutes. Meanwhile, cook together 1 cup of small raw potato cubes and 1 cup of small raw carrot cubes until tender. Drain, and add to the oyster-clam mixture, mixing thoroughly. Let simmer gently for 10 minutes. Season to taste with salt, cayenne pepper, and ⅓ teaspoon of thyme. Then pour over 1 quart of rich milk, scalded with 1 large bay leaf and 6 thin slices of onion, discarding the bay leaf and onion slices before adding. When ready to serve, stir in 3 tablespoons of butter creamed with 1 tablespoon of flour. Let boil once, and let simmer gently for 3 or 4 minutes. Serve in hot soup plates, each garnished with a few oysterettes and dusted with a little chopped parsley.

CODFISH CHOWDER I   [508]
Biscayne style

There are two places on the crust of this small bubble, the earth, in which the humble but powerful creature, the codfish, is beatified, if not actually canonized, and they are Portugal—a land peculiarly set apart from the rest of Europe—and Cape Cod—which could be no more insular if it were entirely surrounded by water.

The codfish capital of the world is Gloucester, where "Cape Cod Turkey" is handled by the ton, and all other fish by the pound. The consecrated effigy of the sacred cod is enshrined under the golden dome on Beacon Hill, yet the Cape may well be regarded as the "Land of the Cod," with Boston and environs holding fast to the bean. And never believe that any portion of the Bay State east of the Berkshires despises or rejects the cod, for it is perpetually a staple commodity in every town and village, to the greater glory of Gloucester. There may be two or three Massachusetts Yankees still living who can vaguely remember some doggerel lines that were chanted in the middle of the state about Civil War time, though cause and source must be forgotten:

> "*Barret for beauty,*
> *Petersham for pride;*
> *If it hadn't been for codfish*
> *Dana would have died.*"

Some day the whole history of codfish as a New England asset and institution must be written, and then perhaps the true story of Portuguese influence in the industry may be found out, though it seems always to have been smugly ignored. The beautiful and heroic traditions of New England have been kept singularly free from "foreign" taint by the New Englanders, with rarely more than a brief apologetic reference to an occasional red Indian who came and went, yet a sort of isolated Portuguese colonial life was planted along the strands and among the cranberry bogs of the Cape, and it still survives, strangely enough, with much credit to the sturdy Portuguese stock which has resisted complete assimilation.

And it is significant that codfish is as substantial and important an asset to the Portuguese nation as the celebrated wines of Portugal are, or ever have been. The people of that narrow but populous strip of the peninsula of southern Europe feast on prodigious quantities of sea food, and wash it all down with prodigious libations of good wines. While the grape never got a firm foothold on Puritan soil, it seems logical enough that the immigrant "Portagee" fishermen who swarmed all over the old colony in the early days must have had more than a little to do with the founding of a colossal industry, as well as with the attendant customs and traditions.

Clam chowder and fish chowder most certainly are not of old England, but no New England cook book has ever credited the Portuguese settlers with a finger in the stew. Yet today, across the Atlantic in Portugal, a *caldeirada a pescadora* is made according to our kitchen exploring.

Put in a saucepan the trimmings of a 4-pound codfish, 1½ quarts of cold water, 2 large tomatoes, pounded, 1 large bay leaf, 10 whole peppercorns, 2 whole cloves, and 10 sprigs of fresh parsley. Heat gently until the boiling point is reached, and allow to simmer for 25 minutes. Strain through a fine sieve into a soup kettle. Add the codfish, boned and cut into small pieces, 2 tablespoons of finely chopped onion, 2 tablespoons of finely chopped celery stalk, 1 cup of cooked shrimps, coarsely chopped, and salt and thyme leaves to taste. Bring the mixture to a boil, and let simmer gently for 30 minutes, stirring frequently with a wooden spoon to prevent scorching. Stir in 1 cup of medium cream sauce, and allow the chowder to boil up once again. Then let it simmer gently while you prepare fish forcemeat (fish balls).

Fish Forcemeat or Fish Balls. Put 1 cup of raw codfish (or any other white-meat fish), free from bones and skin, through the finest knife of the food chopper. Combine the fish with 1 egg, slightly beaten, 2 tablespoons of fine bread crumbs, a blade of mace, 1 tablespoon each of finely chopped chives and parsley, a dash of cayenne pepper, and 1 scant teaspoon of salt (more or less, according to taste). Shape this mixture into a dozen and a half small balls. Bring the chowder to a brisk boil, add the fish balls, 2 cups of raw potatoes, cut in small dices, and 1 cup of scalded milk. Cover the pan, and let simmer for about 20 minutes, or until the potatoes are tender. Taste for seasoning, and stir in 2 tablespoons of butter creamed with 1 teaspoon of flour (more or less, according to desired thickness of the broth). Boil once, and serve in hot colorful earthenware soup bowls with finger-shaped pieces of toast, rubbed with garlic and buttered. Salmon may be substituted for codfish in this recipe.

CODFISH CHOWDER II　　　　　　　　　　[509]
Maine manner

So important was the cod in the early history of this country that it was placed on the colonial seal of Massachusetts, and also on a Nova Scotian banknote with the legend, "Success to the Fisheries."

The cod is one of the most prolific of fish. A female thirty-nine to forty inches long produces about three million eggs.

Skin and bone a 4-pound cod, and cut it into 2-inch pieces. Put the head, tail, skin, and backbone of the fish, cut into small pieces, in a saucepan with 2 cups of cold water and 1 bay leaf tied with 6 sprigs of parsley and 3 sprigs of celery greens. Bring this mixture to the boiling point, season to taste with salt and pepper, and allow it to boil gently for 25 minutes. Cut a 1½-inch cube of fat salt pork into small cubes, and render the fat over a gentle flame. Add 3 thin slices of onion, and allow them to cook gently for 5 minutes. Then strain the fat into a large stew kettle, and let it boil for 5 minutes longer. Add the pieces of fish, and after 5 minutes, add 1 quart of scalded milk. Allow the whole to simmer for another 15 minutes, after adding the strained fish broth. Let boil once, stir in 1 table-spoon of butter creamed with 1 teaspoon of flour, and let simmer for 3 or 4 minutes. Taste for seasoning, and just before serving, stir in 3 tablespoons of butter. Serve in hot soup plates with a soda cracker or a pilot biscuit, moistened in cold milk, in each plate.

SALT CODFISH CHOWDER I   [510]
Italian—Zuppa di Baccala

Heat 4 tablespoons of good olive oil in a soup kettle. Add 1 cup of thinly sliced onions, and cook until just beginning to take on color. Then add the chopped white parts of 2 small leeks, and 2 cloves of garlic, mashed, and continue cooking for 5 minutes longer, stirring frequently with a wooden spoon. Then stir in 2 cups of boiling water, 1 bottle (4 cups) of dry white wine, and 1 large bay leaf tied with 6 sprigs of fresh parsley and 2 cloves. Season to taste with salt, 6 freshly crushed peppercorns, and ⅓ teaspoon of thyme leaves. Bring the mixture to a boil, and add 2 cups of small potato cubes, ¾ cup of small carrot cubes, 2 pounds of salt codfish (which has been soaked in cold water overnight, drained, and cut into inch pieces), and 1 small pinch of saffron. Bring to a boil, and let simmer for 25 to 30 minutes. Taste for seasoning, and serve in hot soup plates, after discarding the bouquet garni, with a side dish of grated Par-mesan cheese and freshly made toast.

SALT CODFISH CHOWDER II   [511]
Home style

Cut ⅓ pound of salt pork into small cubes, and render in a soup kettle. Then add ¾ cup of coarsely chopped onions and 5 medium-sized potatoes, pared and sliced thin, and cook for 5 minutes, stirring almost constantly. Add 2 pounds of salt codfish, soaked overnight in cold water, drained, and cut into inch cubes. Pour over 2½ cups of boiling water. Add 1 large bay leaf tied with 6 sprigs of fresh parsley and 3 sprigs of green celery leaves, 2 whole cloves, a thin slice of garlic, and salt, pepper, and thyme to taste. Cover, bring to a boil, and let simmer gently for about 30 minutes, or until the vegetables are tender and the salt cod beginning to thread. Stir in 1 quart of scalded milk. Bring to a boil, taste for seasoning, and serve with a side dish of freshly made buttered toast in hot soup plates, each sprinkled with a little chopped chives. Should the mixture be thin, you may thicken it with a little butter creamed with an equal amount of flour, and boil once or twice before serving.

Aztec Indians utilized cocoa beans by grinding them with corn and dried codfish, then adding water, and seasoning the resultant soup with chili, spices, and herbs.

CODFISH CHOWDER DINNER   [512]
Ouka Russkaia—Codfish and Caviar Chowder

Cut in julienne fashion the white parts of 2 small leeks, 2 medium-sized carrots, 2 stalks of celery, carefully scraped, 1 medium-sized white turnip, and 1 large green pepper. Wash the matchstick vegetables in cold water, and sponge in a dry towel. Heat ⅓ cup of butter, add the vegetables, and cook over a gentle flame for 5 minutes, stirring almost constantly. Pour over 1 quart of Fish Stock (No. 8), made from 2 pounds of fish trimmings or cheap fish, stirring well. Then add 3½ pounds of fresh codfish, skinned, boned, and cut into inch pieces, ⅓ cup of well-washed uncooked rice, 1 large bay leaf, very little salt, pepper and nutmeg to taste, and ⅓ teaspoon of thyme leaves. Cover, bring to the boiling point, lower the flame, and let simmer gently for 20 to 25 minutes. Stir in 2 cups of hot sweet cream mixed with 3 tablespoons of caviar. Bring to a boil, and serve at once, after tasting for seasoning, in colorful peasant earthenware bowls, with a side dish of brown bread and butter finger sandwiches and a hot dish of anchovy fritters.

Julienne of Anchovy Fritters. Wash 1½ dozen anchovy filets in several changes of lukewarm water, to which has been added 3 tablespoons of lemon juice. Drain and sponge dry in a towel. Cut each filet into 3 strips lengthwise, and dip into a fritter batter—*pâte à frire.* Place a few at a time in a wire basket, and when ready to serve, plunge the basket once into clear hot deep fat. Drain, and dress on a folded napkin, then cover with deep fat-fried parsley.

CORN CHOWDER I   [513]
Home style

An old Oregonian game law permits fish to be caught using single kernels of corn as bait, but makes it a misdemeanor to feed fish on canned corn.

Brown lightly ½ cup of salt pork, cut in small dices. Stir in 4 thin slices of onion (more or less, according to taste), and cook for 2 or 3 minutes, stirring frequently. Then add 1 small bay leaf tied with 4 or 5 sprigs of parsley, salt and pepper to taste, and 1 sprig of sage. Stir in 1 cup of raw potatoes, diced small, and 2 cups of hot water, and cook until the potatoes are tender. Thicken the mixture with 3 table-spoons of flour mixed with a little cold water or milk. Then mix 2½ cups of canned or freshly cooked whole kernels of corn with 3 cups of scalded rich milk, and stir this mixture into the first. Bring the whole to a boil, and remove from the fire. Correct the seasoning, adding salt, black pepper, and thyme to taste. Just before serving, stir in 2 fresh egg yolks and 1 tablespoon of sweet butter. Serve in hot soup plates, each dusted with finely chopped parsley or chives, and serve very hot.

CORN CHOWDER II   [514]
Pioneer method

In 1706, twenty settlers' brides, imported from France by the Governor of Louisiana, staged the "Petticoat Rebellion" when they found that corn was to be the principal food item in their new homes.

Try out slowly 1 cup of cubed pork fat back in a frying pan until it is smoking. Add 1 cup of chopped onions, and cook for about 5 minutes, stirring almost constantly. Then add ½ teaspoon of paprika, salt to taste (remembering that the pork is already salted), pepper to taste, and ¼ teaspoon of thyme leaves. Transfer the whole into a soup kettle. Add ½ cup of chopped pimientos, ½ cup of chopped green pepper, 2 well-packed cups of corn, freshly grated from the cob, 2 cups of small cubed raw potatoes, and 3 cups of hot water. Cook for 15 long minutes. Meanwhile, melt 2 tablespoons of butter, and mix in 2 tablespoons of flour. Gradually pour into this butter-flour mixture 2¼ cups of scalded rich milk, stirring constantly until the mixture boils; then pour the whole into the chowder. Cook very gently until the mixture thickens, stirring often. Serve in hot earthenware bowls with old-fashioned New England biscuits or crackers on the side.

When the Bavarians were threatened with famine at the close of the eighteenth century, an American, Benjamin Thompson, saved the day by introducing them to corn meal mush. While grateful, they didn't enjoy the meal in the least.

CORN CHOWDER III   [515]
Michigan method—no milk used

Cut the kernels from 6 large ears of corn. Measure, and set in a
cool place for later use. Now break or cut the cobs into small pieces,
and place them in a soup kettle with 1 quart of cold water. Cover,
and let cook steadily over a gentle flame for 40 minutes to extract
all the minerals and flavor from the cob pieces. Drain, and add to the
liquid 1½ cups of fresh lima beans and the corn pulp, and set
aside. Now add 1 extra large onion, sliced in rings, 1½ cups of
diced raw potatoes, a bouquet garni composed of 1 bay leaf, 8 sprigs
of fresh parsley, and 1 sprig of thyme tied together with kitchen
thread, 1 blade of mace, ½ teaspoon of allspice, and 10 peppercorns.
Cover, and let cook for 25 minutes. Then add 3 tablespoons of
butter kneaded with 2 generous tablespoons of flour. Let simmer
gently for 10 minutes longer. Season with 1 scant tablespoon of
salt. Discard the bouquet garni, and serve hot in bowls with pilot
crackers, split in two and toasted lightly.

Old-fashioned Maine cooks still "thribble the hulled corn," cooking it until the grains are three times their normal size, and serving
it with milk and sugar as a breakfast dish.

CORN CHOWDER IV   [516]
New Jersey manner

Heat ¼ cup of butter. Stir in 1 large onion, sliced thin in rings
and each ring separated, and 1 cup of finely chopped green pepper,
and cook 5 minutes over a very low flame, stirring frequently. When
the onion is transparent, stir in 2 cups of boiling water, boiled with
1 large bay leaf, 1 whole clove, and 1 small whole clove of garlic,
and then strained. Continue cooking for 5 minutes longer, then stir
in ⅓ cup of boiled rice, and season to taste with salt, black pepper,
and ½ scant teaspoon of thyme leaves. Then stir in 2 cups of freshly
scraped corn. Let simmer gently for 10 minutes, then stir in 1 quart
of scalded rich milk. Bring to the boiling point, taste for seasoning,
and serve in hot soup plates, each sprinkled with finely chopped parsley. Pass a side dish of your favorite crackers.

Variation. For seashore flavor, you may add ½ to ¾ cup of cooked
or canned crab meat, carefully boned and flaked.

CRABS

Most hard-shelled crabs are popularly known as blue crabs. They form the basis of the crab-meat industry, coming principally from Louisiana, Florida, Georgia, Maryland, Virginia, North Carolina, and particularly Chesapeake Bay. Those that migrate to fresh waters are called sweet-water crabs.

The fiddler crabs are abundant in Tampa and Key West, Florida. They travel in large schools, often numbering thousands.

Soft-shelled crabs are highly perishable and must be handled with care. In reality, they are the hard-shelled or the blue caught while changing their shells.

The king, giant, or Dungeness crab, found on the Pacific Coast, resembles the hard-shelled species, but is about four times as large.

Oyster crabs are expensive, and only Father Neptune himself would know how many there are to the pound. These pygmies are soft-shelled and come from Maryland and Virginia Cape waters. This little crab is a "sponger"; it takes shelter with the oyster.

The stone or Moro crab is a native of the South Atlantic from Carolina to Florida and farther south. The claws are sold ice-packed.

The hermit crab is known as the fighting crab. It is of the hard-shelled type with its back denuded and concealed in a large empty shell which it drags along.

Deep-sea crab meat is firm and succulent, with a specially pleasing rich tangy or salty flavor. All that is needed to pick over the meat is to slightly separate it from the bones or cartilages, preferably using a silver fork. This is what is called, in many recipes, flaking crab meat. Once the meat is so flaked, it is immediately ready for use in many hot and cold dishes, which number into the hundreds.

The Strange Life Story of the Crab. Fishermen say the crab is "in berry" when the bristles of the underparts of the crab are crowded with red eggs. On the smaller crabs, there may be half a million, but on the aged and full-sized, over two million eggs may be glued or impaled about the protected part of the crab's body.

The incubation takes many months. Not until summer warms up the sea edges will the mother crab begin to brush off her young. The tiny crustaceans will not walk, but swim, looking first like young shrimps, then like lobsters, molting three or four times before sinking to the sea floor, there to walk for the rest of their lives. These myriads of swimming crabs, so small that the sea water is milky with them, are the relished food of countless other fish from sea anemones to whales, hence their millions. Crabs are sea scavengers, turning all fish waste into tender fresh crablets that are food for all other fish and, should they survive long enough, for bird and man also.

The crab's growth is not gradual but by bounds, if not leaps. He puts his skeleton outside his skin for protection, making it so hard that he cannot stretch it, nor can he add to it, as do the oyster and clam. When his armor has become too tight, it must be cast off. This will not happen regularly, but according to the plenitude of food he has found. His molting is a very serious operation and must be done under the shelter of a stone or crevice in the rocks. Before growing, he must reduce, withdrawing all the water possible from his system, softening his muscles. The big shield on his back is loosened at the edges, to be pushed off; such castoffs are often seen on the shore. He draws up his legs and claws from their coverings and is a limp defenseless creature when creeping from the old casing.

While soft, his skin expands, so that the new armor must be larger. He has been carrying lime in solution in greater quantities than usual, and this begins to harden over his tender skin. He may eat the smaller parts of his old skeleton to help in forming the new. He will be a finer fellow when he walks out again, but he is careful not to walk out too hurriedly. His gait seems curious to walkers on two legs. His footless three-kneed legs move sideways, and when he stops, he sits with legs forward and vicious claws before his legs, a defensive and offensive attitude. Should he lose a leg in an encounter, he may have an imperceptible limp until the next molt, when a new joint will appear, repairing former damage.

The ebbing tide may leave him stranded, but that concerns him little. It is a youthful escapade to run from rock to rock or pool to pool in waterless air, as boys play in and out of water. Older crabs are more staid. They keep under water in the ebb-tide shallows. Several lie in an eelgrass pool, sheltered and well fed. One, large as a man's hand, resents disturbance, for underneath she bears more berries than any old bush that ever grew on the hillside.

CRAB MEAT, CELERY, AND EGG CHOWDER [518]

Scrape, then chop fine, enough outer stalks and leaves (tops) of celery to make 4 cups. Wash by placing the chopped celery in a fine sieve, and let cold water run over, shaking well to remove all sand, if any. Have ready a kettle containing 2 cups of boiling water; a bouquet garni, composed of 2 sprigs of thyme, 10 sprigs of fresh parsley, 1 large bay leaf, 1 whole clove, and 2 sprigs of fennel, tied together with kitchen thread; 1 slice of garlic; and ½ cup of chopped onion. Add 1 extra large potato, pared and grated. Bring to a boil, season to taste with salt and pepper, lower the heat, and allow to simmer very gently while making the sauce. In a saucepan, melt 3 tablespoons of butter, blend in 2 tablespoons of flour, and when smooth and bubbling, gradually add 1 quart of scalded milk, stirring constantly until the mixture boils. Turn this sauce into the celery mixture (first discarding the bouquet garni), and bring to a boil. Remove from the fire, and beat in gradually 2 slightly beaten egg yolks. Return to the fire, boil only once, and taste for seasoning. Pour into a heated soup tureen containing 1 cup of canned or cooked crab meat, carefully boned and flaked, 1½ tablespoons of finely chopped chives, 2 hard-cooked egg whites, coarsely chopped, and 1 teaspoon of paprika, all well mixed. Stir well to heat the crab meat, and serve in a heated bowl with saltine crackers.

CRAB MEAT CHOWDER [519]
Home style

Remove the meat from 8 to 10 hard-shelled crabs, and chop fine (or use 1 can of crab meat, boned and flaked, then chopped fine). Place in a soup kettle, and pour over 1 quart of Fish Stock (No. 8), 1 cup of stale bread crumbs, 1 small onion, finely chopped, 1 large sprig of parsley, a pinch of thyme leaves, and 1 small bay leaf. Bring to a boil, then let simmer very slowly for 20 to 25 minutes. Strain, forcing a little, through a sieve. Return to the fire, and add 2 tablespoons of butter kneaded with 2 tablespoons of flour. Bring to a rapid boil. Let simmer 10 minutes after adding 1 cup of cream, and seasoning to taste with salt, white pepper, and a few grains of cayenne pepper. Just before serving, add 1 tablespoon or more of flaked crab meat, or 2 tablespoons of cooked diced shrimps, and 1 tablespoon of butter.

CRAB MEAT CORN CHOWDER [520]
American

Combine 2½ cups of fresh grated corn, or cream-style canned corn, a slice or two of onion, the more the better, and 2½ cups of scalded rich milk. Cook this mixture over boiling water for 20 minutes. Then remove the onion, if you like, and force the rest of the mixture through a coarse sieve. Add 2½ cups Thin White Sauce (No. 346); bring the whole to the boiling point. Stir in 2 fresh egg yolks, one at a time, beating briskly after each addition. Season to taste with salt, white pepper, thyme, and a grating of nutmeg. Then stir in 3 cups of scalded rich milk. Just before serving, stir in 1 cup of flaked crab meat, either freshly cooked or canned, and 1 tablespoon of butter. Serve very hot with salted crackers.

CRAB MEAT AND SHRIMP GUMBO [521]
CHOWDER
Creole

Sauté 1 cup of minced onions, ¾ cup of minced celery (using stalk and leaves), 1 clove of garlic, minced, and 3 tablespoons of green pepper in ¼ cup of butter or bacon drippings in a heavy soup kettle, stirring frequently for about 4 or 5 minutes. Stir in 3½ cups of strained cooked or canned tomatoes and 2 cups of hot water. Season to taste with salt, black pepper, ½ scant teaspoon of thyme leaves, and a few grains of cayenne pepper. Add 1 bouquet garni, composed of 1 large bay leaf, 8 sprigs of fresh parsley, and 1 sprig of tarragon leaf, tied together with kitchen thread, and cook for 20 minutes over a gentle flame.

Wash ½ pound of okra, trim the stems, and slice the pods ½ inch thick. Cook in 2 cups of water in a covered pan for 15 minutes, and add to the first mixture. Bring to a boil, and let simmer for 10 minutes. Then add ¼ pound of cooked, shelled, and chopped shrimps, ½ pound of cooked, fresh, or canned crab meat, flaked and free from any cartilage, and ¼ cup of cooked rice. Taste for seasoning. Discard the bouquet garni, and when ready to serve, stir in 1 cup of milk mixed with 1 cup of cream, scalded with a tiny piece of cinnamon. Serve in hot soup plates, each sprinkled with chopped parsley. Serve a side dish of crackers and of freshly made toast.

DRIED BEEF CHOWDER [522]
American woodman's

The buccaneers were not originally pirates, but sailors who deserted their ships in the West Indies and dried the beef of stolen cattle into buccan, which is prepared the same as the biltong of the South African Boers.

It is interesting to know how dried beef is prepared. The meat for it comes from the ham of the beef, which is divided into three parts. It is first treated with a mild pickling process and followed with sugar curing before it is smoked over hickory and maple wood. Dried beef prepared in this way is fine in texture, rich red in color, and has a wonderful nutlike flavor.

In preparing the dried beef, one should determine its saltiness before putting it into a dish. Taste it, and if there seems to be too much salt, pour boiling water over and drain it off immediately. The beef is then ready to be converted into various dishes, such as this delicious chowder which our woodmen know so well.

Brown ½ cup of minced onions in 3 tablespoons of bacon drippings, or still better, cook over a gentle flame 4 slices of bacon, chopped, until just beginning to brown. Add the chopped onions, and when just beginning to brown, stir in 2 cups of small raw potato cubes, ½ cup of finely chopped green celery leaves, ½ cup of small raw carrot cubes, and ¼ cup of chopped green pepper. Pour over 4 cups of boiling water, then add 1 large bay leaf tied with a 2-inch piece of scraped parsley root and 1 sprig of thyme (or ⅓ teaspoon of thyme leaves) and 6 freshly crushed peppercorns. No salt at all. Bring to a boil. Lower the flame, and let simmer gently for 25 minutes, or until the vegetables are tender, but not mushy. Then stir in a No. 2 can of corn, 1 can of evaporated milk, and ¾ pound of dried beef. Cover, and let simmer for 15 minutes longer. Taste for seasoning, being careful with the salt. Discard the bay leaf bundle, and serve at once with your favorite crackers.

EEL AND RED WINE CHOWDER [523]
Bouillonnée d'Anguilles

The eel, this amphibian which creeps on the soil and swims in the water, is thus a "Jekyll and Hyde." It has two existences, two homes, two regimens. In the rivers, it lunches on small fish; in the meadows, in the evening and especially during the night, it dines on insects. The eel is the undine of the rivers. It slides, gets away, comes back, undulates, steals away anew, is ever sliding and disappearing. The more it is held, the less it is held, and when one thinks one holds it, it is free. The eel is emblematic of deception, but it is not a deception when, as a dish, it is placed on the table.

The eel is perhaps one of the most savory of the fish inhabiting the vivacious and running waters. The mud of the pool is its undoing, as it needs the clear spring. The uninitiated assume that its snow-white and fat flesh is indigestible. Nonsense!

There are still some old mills in Great Britain, operating under ancient leases, that pay a part of their rent for water rights with eels. The old practice is carried out as a mere formality, and only a few of the wigglers are handed over as token payment. Some of these agreements, if strictly adhered to, would require millowners to gather as many as 1000 eels a year.

When the leases, granted by the towns, were first written, eels were plentiful, and millowners scooped them out of their sluices by the hundreds. But with eels currently drawing prices of $2500 a ton in England, millowners would be hard put to it if they were required to adhere strictly to the terms of some of the old contracts.

Eels belong to the Apodes family and are found all over the world in both fresh and salt water. They ascend the rivers and live there for the most part, returning to the depths of the sea in the autumn, or they may bury themselves in mud during the winter.

The eel has minute scales imbedded in the skin. The upper part of the body is blackish in color and the lower is yellowish when the eel is found in muddy water, but the back is a beautiful olive green and the belly a silver white if the habitat is clear water.

The reproduction of the eel has excited the attention of naturalists since the day of Aristotle. Where the eggs are laid is not yet known, whether at the bottom or near the surface of the water. From five to twenty million eggs are laid by each female, and the eel dies after once spawning.

The average length of an eel is two feet, maximum five feet. Its average weight is from one to two pounds, with a maximum weight of ten pounds. The shoestring eel averages one-quarter pound.

Like lobsters, crabs, clams, and oysters, eels should always be bought alive or freshly killed, and skinned at once. Make an incision on the skin, near the head, turn back a little of the skin, hold the head with a dry towel, and pull down the skin bluntly. Clean and wash in several changes of cold water, removing all the blood from along the dorsal bone by passing the finger along the bone.

Take 2¾ pounds of freshly killed eel, skinned, washed, and cut into pieces of about 2 inches. Season with mixed salt, black pepper, a dash of nutmeg, and a dash of thyme. Cook in ¼ cup of heated olive oil (the original recipe calls for walnut oil), with 1 cup of tiny small white onions, peeled and left whole, 2 onions stuck with a whole clove, a 2-inch piece of scraped parsley root, 1 large clove of garlic, mashed to a pulp, 1 large bay leaf, and 3 thin slices of lemon, seeded, until the pieces of eel are browned, stirring almost constantly with a wooden spoon over a bright flame. Transfer the entire mixture into a soup kettle. Add 3 cups of red wine, 2 cups of Fish Stock (No. 8), ¾ cup of fresh mushrooms, peeled and sliced, using stems and cups, and 3 tablespoons of raw rice, well washed and drained, and bring to a boil. Let simmer gently for 25 to 30 minutes, or until the eel pieces begin to blister and flake and the rice is tender but not too soft. Remove from the fire, taste for seasoning, and discard the parsley root and bay leaf. Then stir in 3 tablespoons of brandy, slightly heated. Serve in hot soup plates, each garnished with half of a hard-cooked egg white, coarsely chopped, then sprinkled with finely chopped chervil or parsley. Serve with fresh rye bread generously buttered.

EEL CHOWDER I [524]
Great South Bay method

Technically, fish is flesh, old sayings and obdurate appetites notwithstanding. But a number of people are apparently refusing to abide by the technicalities. King Neptune's bottomless larder is chockfull of edible material. Out of that bountiful monarch's salty realms, or out of fresh-water lakes or streams, fishermen can, if it is necessary and remunerative, haul in enough provender to defy the worst meat shortage that ever was or ever could be. It's not enough nowadays for cook to learn about piscatorial anatomy, physiognomy, physiology, psychology, and philosophy (if any) in the kitchen. We admit that chronic meat eaters (as aren't we Americans nearly all) are a difficult crew to convert. Most of us make shift to do without when the goose flies so high as to be out of reach, and when the cow and the steer jump over the moon, leaving nary rib nor roast for human consumption. Yet let us detect one trace of fowl or flesh (not the fishy kind), and the caveman in us re-emerges with hungry fangs, heading for the butcher shop whence emanates the irresistible lure, or we dispatch our cooks there in a hurry, carrying hopeful market baskets.

Clearly we need re-education, especially about the goodness and nutritive values of more than 800 edible fish found in American fresh and salt waters.

Eels were considered a supreme delicacy in the days before the supermarket and the machine age took the place of the well-stocked cellar and attic. Fifty years ago when the winter country diet of salt meat got monotonous, father would put on his rubber boots, heavy mackinaw, and ear muffs, take his long-handled spear and ax, and call to mother that he was "goin' eelin' down to the pond." There, like as not, he would find several of his neighbors already on the thick ice, jigging their spears through small chopped holes in the soft mud bottom where the big Kneeshaw or silver eel hibernates.

Put ½ scant pound of sliced salt pork in an iron kettle, and let fry until the salt pork is nicely browned on all sides. Wash 2½ pounds of freshly killed eel, skinned, and cut into 2-inch pieces, well in slightly salted water, then rinse in fresh cold water. Wipe dry, and dredge in salted, peppered, and thymed flour. Put the eel pieces in the hot salt pork fat to brown quickly over a bright flame, stirring frequently with a wooden spoon. Add 2 cups of small raw potato cubes mixed with 1 cup of small raw carrot cubes. Then add water enough to cover generously, with 1 bouquet garni, composed of 1 large bay leaf, 8 sprigs of fresh parsley, 2 sprigs of thyme (or ⅓ teaspoon of thyme leaves), 2 sprigs of green celery leaves, and 2 whole cloves, all tied together with kitchen thread; 3 or 4 gently bruised peppercorns; salt to taste; and 1 small clove of garlic, mashed to a pulp. Slowly bring this to a boil, and allow to simmer gently for about 25 to 30 minutes, or until the potatoes and carrots are tender and the meat comes off the bones of the eel pieces easily. Serve in hot soup bowls, each sprinkled with finely chopped parsley.

This old-time recipe was used for the annual dinner of the Long Island fishermen and boatmen.

EEL CHOWDER II   [525]
Netherlands

> "A youthful eel resided in a tiny tidal pool;
> He was lithe as gutta-percha, and as pliable;
> From his actions and contractions he appeared to be a fool,
> But his virtue was completely undeniable."
>   CARRYL

The Hollander housewife thinks of her kitchen as a sanctuary, and her culinary art is a distinctively national and characteristic one. She excels in soup making, and of the hundreds of soup recipes, her eel chowder seems to be the best.

Heat 4 tablespoons of butter, and stir in the white parts of 3 small leeks, thinly sliced, and ½ cup of chopped onions, cooking until the mixture just begins to take on color, and stirring almost constantly with a wooden spoon, over a gentle flame. Gradually pour over 4 cups of rapidly boiling water, and add 1 bouquet garni, composed of 1 large bay leaf, 2 sprigs of green celery leaves, 6 sprigs of fresh parsley, 1 sprig of thyme, and 1 or 2 blades of tarragon leaves, tied together with kitchen thread; 8 whole peppercorns, freshly crushed; a generous pinch of nutmeg, mace, and sage; and salt to taste. Now add 2½ pounds of freshly killed eel, skinned, washed, and cut into 2-inch pieces. Bring to a boil, and let simmer gently for 25 to 30 minutes, or until the eel pieces are tender and the meat comes off easily. Using a perforated skimmer, lift out the eel pieces, remove the bones, and keep hot. Discard the bouquet garni. Strain the broth through a fine sieve, rubbing well to extract all the pulp possible from the leek and onion. Keep the broth hot.

Clean ¼ pound of spinach, removing the stems, and chop fine. Do likewise with a small head of lettuce, and cook both in 3 tablespoons of butter for about 5 minutes, stirring often. Moisten the spinach-lettuce mixture with a little of the broth, then stir in ½ cup of stale bread crumbs. Let simmer gently for 10 minutes, then add the remaining broth, and continue simmering for 15 minutes longer. Remove from the fire, then stir in 2 fresh egg yolks, one at a time, alternately with 1 cup of scalded sweet cream, stirring briskly after each addition. Add the flaked eel pieces, taste for seasoning, and just before serving, stir in 1 tablespoon of sweet butter. Serve in soup plates, each garnished with a few Croutons (No. 780).

French, Scandinavian, and Italian cooks know the tender sweetness of eel meat and they too make the most of it, especially during winter. But American cooks muff their chance for enjoying this delicacy by calling eels snakes and looking superior and shivery if one so much as mentions the slithery things.

FINNAN HADDIE CHOWDER [526]
Scotch—Smoky Chowder

Finnan haddie—haddock smoked and salted—takes its name from the town of Findon, Scotland, where it was first prepared. It was formerly called Findon haddie.

Parboil a 3-pound piece of finnan haddie in 1 pint of water for 5 minutes; drain off the water, and save. Place the fish in a shallow pan, and cover with milk. Add 1 large bay leaf, 2 cloves, 3 thin slices of onion, and 1 or 2 thin slices of lemon. Let simmer for 20 minutes. Drain, reserving the milk, and skin and bone the fish. Keep hot.

Cut ½ pound of fat salt pork into small cubes, and try out over a low flame. Add the reserved parboiling water, and let simmer gently for 15 minutes. Transfer the mixture into a soup kettle. Add 2 cups of small raw potato cubes, 1 cup of chopped onions, ¼ cup of finely chopped green celery leaves, very little salt, and pepper and thyme to taste, and let simmer gently for 15 minutes. Then add the flaked finnan haddie and the strained reserved milk, and continue cooking until the potato and carrot cubes are tender. Stir in 1 cup of scalded milk, taste for seasoning, and when ready to serve, stir in 2 fresh egg yolks, slightly beaten. Let boil once, and serve in hot soup plates with a side dish of crackers, each plate sprinkled with finely chopped chives.

Part of the enormous catch of haddock of the Grand Banks each year undergoes salting and smoking to become finnan haddie. The fish needs almost no preliminary treatment to be turned into more than a hundred delicious dishes. Haddie is sold by the piece or in filets.

FISH CHOWDER [527]
Home method

Wipe 2½ pounds of any uncooked white-flesh fish (cod, haddock, halibut) with a damp cloth, and place in a kettle with 5 cups of cold water and salt to taste. Slowly bring to a boil, and let gently simmer 20 to 25 minutes. Strain the fish, and return the broth to the kettle. Skin and bone the fish. Set aside, and keep hot. Fry a 1½-inch cube of salted fat pork with 2 onions finely chopped, and add to the broth with 2 cups of diced raw potatoes. Cook until the potatoes are done (about 15 minutes), and return the fish to the kettle. Add 2 cups of strained scalded milk, with a pinch of thyme leaves, 1 small bay leaf, 1 crushed clove, and a sprig of parsley. Season to taste with salt and pepper and a few grains of nutmeg. Add 1 tablespoon of finely chopped parsley. Let heat through, and just before serving, add 1 tablespoon of butter. Serve in hot soup plates, each containing a toasted cracker and a bit of minced parsley.

FISH ROE CHOWDER [528]
Russian

Chop coarsely 2 medium-sized leeks, and cook in 1 tablespoon of butter over a low fire for 10 minutes, stirring often. Sprinkle over 2 tablespoons of flour. Blend well, and cook for 3 minutes longer. Pour over 1 quart of hot water and 1 cup of white wine. Season with a very little pepper and a piece of parsley root (the size of a hazelnut), finely chopped. Let simmer very gently for 25 to 30 minutes. Strain, pressing a little. Return to the heat, and let continue simmering. Meanwhile, remove the skin and filaments of 1 pound of fish roe (any kind desired), well cleaned and washed, parboiled in salt water, rinsed in cold water, and well drained. Chop very fine to obtain a kind of semolina, and throw into the rapidly boiling broth. Cook for 5 minutes longer, steadily boiling. Reduce the fire, and let simmer for 5 minutes. Off the fire, add slowly, one by one, 3 egg yolks, stirring constantly. Just before serving, finish with 1 tablespoon of butter. Correct the seasoning, and serve with a side dish of brown bread and butter finger sandwiches.

FLOUNDER CHOWDER [529]
French Potage Bagration

For 6 generous servings, take 4 filets of flounder (save heads, bones, and skins for later). Sprinkle them lightly with mixed salt and white pepper, and steam them in ¼ cup of butter mixed with ¾ cup of light Beef Consommé (No. 114), or Chicken Bouillon (No. 25), or use canned bouillon, for about 5 minutes. Then stir in 2 more cups of beef or chicken bouillon, previously scalded, 1 cup of dry white wine, ½ cup of chopped mushroom trimmings (canned or fresh), and let this bubble gently for 30 minutes, stirring occasionally. Meanwhile, place the bones, heads, and skins of the fish in a saucepan. Add 1 generous tablespoon of chopped onion, 1 generous teaspoon of chopped shallots, 1 bouquet garni composed of 8 sprigs of fresh parsley and 1 bay leaf tied together with kitchen thread, 4 whole peppercorns, crushed, *no* salt at all, and pour over 3 cups of cold beef or chicken bouillon. Cook for 15 minutes over a very bright flame. Strain through a fine sieve, pressing well with a wooden spoon to extract all the pulp from the solid parts. Add this to the flounder mixture, let boil once or twice, then strain through a fine-meshed sieve into a clean soup kettle, rubbing well to obtain the pulp of the solid parts. Return to the fire, stir in 1 tablespoon of butter kneaded in equal parts of flour. Season with salt and white pepper to taste. Let boil again once or twice, and when ready to serve, stir in, off the fire, 3 egg yolks beaten with ½ generous cup of scalded heavy cream and a few grains of nutmeg. Again strain through a fine-meshed sieve. Stir in either ½ cup of cooked chopped shrimps or crayfish, or a dozen poached small oysters, if in season. A side dish of small Croutons (No. 780) is usually served with this delicious chowder.

FROG'S LEG CHOWDER or SWAMP [530]
PIGEON CHOWDER
French

Frog's legs, the gourmet's delight, a dish fit for the gods, make their appearance on May 1, and continue through September, supplanting oysters on the menu.

There are hundreds of ways to prepare this dish of dishes, but an old French Canadian gave this recipe, which is popular, though seldom presented in this way:

"Now, you take nice, fat bullfrog an' cut off hin laigs," the old guide instructed. "Skin heem, soak heem in saalt water, an' parboil heem. Den you rohl heem in corn meal, or maybe you lak de fine cracker crumbs. After dat you fry heem brown in buttaire, an'—an' I just 'zactly soon have cheekeen!"

Bring 2 cups of rich milk to a boil, and keep hot. Heat 3 tablespoons of butter, and blend in 2 tablespoons of flour until the mixture bubbles, stirring constantly. Gradually stir in the hot milk, stirring constantly from the bottom of the pan. Then season to taste with salt, mignonnette pepper (freshly ground coarse black pepper), and a grating of nutmeg, and bring to a boil. When boiling briskly, add 1 medium-sized onion peeled and stuck with 1 whole clove, 1 small clove of garlic, peeled and left whole, and 1 bouquet garni composed of 1 large bay leaf, 6 sprigs of fresh parsley, 6 sprigs of chives, and 1 sprig of thyme, all tied together with kitchen thread. Let simmer gently for 20 minutes, then strain through a fine sieve into a clean soup kettle. Return to the fire to simmer gently for 10 minutes longer. Then add ¾ cup of small raw potato cubes, ½ cup of raw carrot cubes, and ½ cup of finely chopped celery stalk, which have been cooked for 5 minutes in 4 tablespoons of butter and well drained; 3 cups of dry white wine, scalded; 2 tablespoons of finely chopped green pepper; and 8 to 10 pairs of large raw frog's legs, boned and the meat flaked. Bring to a boil, and let simmer gently for 30 minutes, stirring occasionally. Taste for seasoning, and when ready to serve, stir in briskly 2 fresh egg yolks, slightly beaten, stirring constantly. Serve in hot soup plates, each garnished with 2 or 3 tiny Watercress Dumplings (No. 763).

The Chinese farmer, strangely enough, discovered a very long time ago that the frog was a valuable ally, for the frog is the mortal enemy of the mole cricket, a dangerous threat to the farmer's rice crop. Some idea of what the Chinese think about the frog can be realized from the fact that they long ago canonized him, adding a frog god to their temples. We do not go to that extreme, preferring to canonize him in our kitchen.

## GREEN CORN CHOWDER					[531]
Middle West manner

When the tassel's on the corn, the home manager may be sure of at least one vegetable which will meet with the approval of all the family and guests. And while corn on the cob is an A-1 popular choice with men and boys, corn off the cob provides many additional informal family dishes with that distinctive and delicious corn flavor. The green or uncooked kernels should be cut off with a sharp knife, so that the woody fibrous scales are left behind on the cob, or the use of a kitchen grater will be sure to remove only the tips of "milk" pulp of the kernel. In this cut or pulpy form, corn becomes the chief ingredient of a long array of American entrée or main dishes, as well as the many accessory fritters, pancakes, puffs, and so on, without forgetting the famous Middle West green corn chowder.

Dice ⅓ pound of fat salt pork into small cubes, and fry in a soup kettle over a gentle flame, stirring occasionally. When only tiny cracklings are left, add 1 cup of thinly sliced onions, and cook until the onions are delicately brown, stirring often. Scald 1 cup of pared sliced potatoes with boiling water, and drain at once; then add to the onions and pork cracklings. Pour over 1 pint of boiling Beef Broth (No. 114), and bring to a boil, then let simmer gently for 10 minutes. Add 1 medium-sized green pepper, coarsely chopped and free from seeds and white ribs, 3 cups of strained chopped fresh tomatoes, or strained canned tomato pulp. Season to taste with salt and pepper, a generous ¼ teaspoon of thyme leaves, a dash of nutmeg, cloves, and mace, and 1 small ·clove of garlic. Bring again to a boil. Allow the mixture to simmer gently for 10 minutes, then add 3 cups of freshly scraped green corn and 2 cups of scalded milk to which has been added a pinch of baking soda. Heat to the boiling point, taste for seasoning, and serve in colorful peasant earthenware bowls, each topped with a pat of butter.

GREEN CORN AND CLAM CHOWDER [532]

Melt ¼ cup of butter or bacon drippings, and blend in 3 tablespoons of flour. Stir in 1½ quarts of milk, scalded with 1 large bay leaf and 2 whole cloves, then strained. Then stir in 2½ cups of freshly scraped green corn pulp, and bring to the boiling point. Remove from the fire, and stir in 1 cup of raw chopped clams, or use the canned kind. Season to taste with salt, pepper, and a generous ¼ teaspoon of thyme leaves. Stir in 1 tablespoon each of finely chopped chives and parsley.

Variation. Cut-up mussels may be substituted for clams, if desired.

FLUKE CHOWDER DINNER [533]
New England manner

Approximately 600,000,000 pounds of sea food are caught by the New England fishermen each year, and 85 per cent of the catch represents only ten species of fish, among them the fluke, a small flounder also called craig fluke, an all-around fish weighing from ¼ to 4 pounds, frequently sold under the name of filet of flounder, or even filet of sole.

In a heavy kettle, or Dutch oven preferably, try out ½ pound of diced-small salt pork over a gentle flame with ½ cup of hot water. Skim off the cracklings, and keep hot. To the fat, add ¾ cup of thinly sliced onions; ½ cup of finely chopped green pepper; 1 large bay leaf and a 2-inch piece of scraped parsley root, chopped; celery root, the size of a hen's egg, finely chopped; 1 cup each of small raw potato cubes and carrots; 1 small clove of garlic, mashed; ⅓ teaspoon of thyme leaves; 8 whole peppercorns, freshly crushed; salt to taste; a tiny pinch each of clove and nutmeg; and 2 cups of fish stock, made from the trimmings of the fish or from 1 pound of cheap white-flesh fish, bones, and all after cleaning. Bring to a boil, let boil gently for 15 minutes, then add a 3-pound piece of fluke. Cover, bring to a boil, lower the flame, and let simmer very gently for 30 minutes. Lift out the fish, and bone and flake it. Return the flaked fish to the kettle or Dutch oven. Stir in 2 cups of thin cream to which has been added 2 fresh egg yolks, well beaten. Let boil once, taste for seasoning, and serve in hot soup plates or bowls, each garnished with a 5-minute boiled egg, carefully shelled. Serve with pilot crackers.

HADDOCK STEW A LA BRETONNE [534]
Chaudronnée d'Aiglefin

The haddock, which is closely related to the cod family, weighs considerably less than the cod, averaging about four pounds, and is like it in appearance and habits. It is easily distinguished by the black lateral line and by the spot above each pectoral fin. Haddock is extremely popular as a food fish and is found only in the North Atlantic. It is dark gray above, whitish below. For some years it abounds, while in others it is very scarce, the cause of which is not understood.

In England, where it is even more popular than in America, a pretty legend is attached to the haddock. It is said to be the fish for which Saint Peter received the tribute money. Indeed, on some large haddocks have been seen finger marks, according to the legend, attributed to that saint. Be that as it may, the fisherman believes firmly in the legend.

Clean, wash, bone, but do not skin, and slice a 4-pound piece of haddock. Dice small ¾ pound of bacon, and cook until crisp; remove the cracklings, and keep them hot. In the bacon fat left in the soup kettle, removed from the fire, arrange first a layer of fish, sliced small, then a layer of potatoes, sliced thin, using about ¾ pound. Season each layer with salt, pepper, nutmeg, and a few grains of cayenne pepper to taste. Over the potatoes, place a bouquet garni, composed of 2 large bay leaves, 12 sprigs of fresh parsley, 3 sprigs of green celery leaves, 4 blades of fresh tarragon herb, 1 generous sprig of thyme, and 2 leaves of mace, tied with kitchen thread. Repeat with a layer of fish, then a layer of potatoes. There should be three layers of fish and potatoes, seasoned as you go along, topping with a layer of thinly sliced onions, for which use about 1 pound of onions. The kettle should be full up to 3 inches from the top. Now pour enough white wine, mixed in equal parts with tomato sauce, barely covering the mixture. Adjust the lid, return the kettle to the fire, bring to a boil, lower the flame, and let simmer gently for 30 minutes. Then lift the cover, and add 1 cup of white wine and tomato sauce mixed in equal parts. Cover, and let continue to simmer gently for another 25 to 30 minutes. Again lift the cover, slip in gently a dozen strictly fresh eggs, and poach them. In a few minutes, the eggs are poached with the full flavor of the fish, vegetables, wine, and tomato, as well as the seasonings, and the chowder is ready to serve in heated soup plates.

This will serve 12 persons. For less, reduce the quantities of ingredients accordingly.

Do not stir the mixture while cooking, as gradually it will settle down a little and the top will be soupy. A fine dish to be served right from the kettle on the beach or in the garden. Each year, invariably, the fishermen of Brittany serve this chowder or stew on the 11th of August, feast day of Saint Suzanne, when the *chaudronnée Bretonne* or *chaudronnée d'aiglefin* (a cauldronful of haddock), is served with many bottles of sparkling cider.

HADDOCK CHOWDER [535]
American

Busy barbers of Brittany in the sixth century served haddock platters to waiting customers. A patron who was cut received his shave free, plus a small flask of wine or a large one of cider, for damages.

Place a 3-pound piece of haddock in 3 cups of boiling water with a bouquet garni, composed of 1 large bay leaf tied with 6 sprigs of parsley and 1 sprig of thyme. Season to taste with salt and 6 bruised whole peppercorns, and cook until the fish flakes or separates from the bones, or about 25 to 30 minutes. Drain, reserving the fish stock, and flake the fish, removing all the bones carefully. Meanwhile, fry slowly until crisp ⅓ cup of finely chopped salt pork in a frying pan.

Add to this ½ cup of finely chopped onion and 1 clove of crushed garlic, and cook for 4 or 5 minutes, stirring frequently over a low flame. Add this to the reserved strained fish stock with 3 cups of raw potatoes, diced very small or sliced very thin, 1 quart of sweet milk, previously scalded, and salt, pepper, and nutmeg to taste. Bring to a rapid boil, reduce the flame, and let simmer gently for 25 to 30 minutes. Discard the bouquet garni, add the flaked fish, and taste for seasoning. Let boil up once or twice, and serve immediately with soda crackers, soaked in milk for a minute, then puffed in a very hot oven, and dusted with finely chopped parsley or paprika.

The chowder family is as full of surprises as a grab bag at a country fair, but a chowder is always nourishing and full of flavor, no matter what turns up in it.

HADDOCK FISH-BALL CHOWDER   [536]
German

Clean, skin, and bone a 3-pound haddock. Make a fish stock with the bones, skin, and trimmings, which after the first boil let simmer gently on a low fire for 25 minutes. Meanwhile, chop the raw fish meat, then pass through a meat chopper. Mix well with 6 rolled saltine crackers, salt, pepper and nutmeg to taste, 2 tablespoons of melted butter, and 1 beaten egg, and again pass the mixture through the meat chopper. Shape in small balls. Fry 2 tablespoons of fat salt pork with 4 or 5 slices of onion for 5 or 6 minutes over a low fire, and add to the strained fish stock (there should be 2 cups). Then add the fish balls and 1 cup of raw potatoes, diced small, and cook until the potatoes are tender. Scald 1 quart of milk, or 3 cups of milk and 1 cup of cream, with a pinch of thyme leaves, 1 small bay leaf, 1 sprig of parsley, and 2 tablespoons of butter kneaded with 2 tablespoons of flour. Boil this for 10 minutes over a low fire, and add to the fish stock. Correct the seasoning. Let boil once or twice, and serve very hot with a side dish of brown bread and butter finger sandwiches. There should be 2 small fish balls for each serving.

HALIBUT CHOWDER   [537]
American—baked chowder

> *"Oh, the rare old Whale, mid storm and gale*
> *In his ocean home will be*
> *A giant in might, where might is right,*
> *And King of the boundless sea. . . ."*
>   OLD WHALE SONG

In the ocean where might is right, the halibut is now mightiest of all, not only in the number of his kin afloat, but in his value to fishermen as well. It is the growing respect for vitamins among civilized people that is putting the deep-sea villain on top. The flat fish with a snow-white belly lives on the bottom of the sea, where he stores up vitamins A and D more quickly than any other fish in the ocean. His vitamin content will be the most valuable in the day forecast by science, when meals will be eaten without plates by the gulping down of little capsules. His abundance may in that day conceivably wipe out restaurants, waiters, cooking, kitchens, pots, pans, silverware, and similar utensils.

Try out ½ pound of salt pork, cubed small, until crisp and brown over a gentle flame, stirring occasionally. Meanwhile, cut 1½ pounds of halibut into small pieces; peel and cube 4 medium-sized potatoes into small cubes; peel and cut into very thin slices 3 medium-sized onions, and separate the rings; and chop fine enough green celery leaves to make a scant cup. Place a layer of potato cubes in the bottom of a soup kettle; cover the potato cubes with a layer of onion rings, then a layer of chopped green celery leaves; and top with a layer of fish. Repeat, seasoning each layer with mixed salt, pepper, thyme, and mace to taste, and a layer of pork cracklings. Pour over 1½ quarts of cold milk, or equal parts of undiluted evaporated milk and water, and dot the top of the chowder with ¼ cup of butter, added bit by bit. Cover the kettle, and bake in a moderate oven (350° F.) for 25 to 30 minutes. Serve very hot with a side dish of toasted bread sticks.

Toasted Bread Sticks. Cut bread into slices ¾ inch thick. Trim off the crusts, and cut into strips ½ inch wide. Have ready 1 cup of crushed flaked cereal mixed with ¼ cup of ground nut meats. Put ½ to ¾ cup of sweetened condensed milk into a shallow dish, and dip the strips of bread in it, turning them so that each side is coated with the milk. Next, dip and roll them in the crushed cereal. Place on a greased baking sheet or shallow pan, and bake in a moderate oven (325°-350° F.) until they are delicately browned. Remove from the baking sheet as soon as done, and let cool before serving. These toasted bread sticks keep well when packed in a container, and may also be served with green or fruit salad.

HALIBUT CHOWDER WITH SAFFRON [538]

Cut into serving pieces 2 to 2½ pounds of fresh halibut, previously cleaned, and washed quickly in cold running water. Now place the fish in a saucepan, and barely cover with boiling hot White Wine Court

Bouillon (No. 79). Place the kettle over a low flame, and let simmer very gently for 8 to 10 minutes, covered. Meanwhile, sauté until light brown, in 3 tablespoons of butter, 1 medium-sized onion, finely chopped, and 1 clove of garlic, mashed. Add to the fish 1 cup of fresh tomatoes, peeled and gently pressed to remove the seeds, then chopped, and a bouquet garni made with 1 small bay leaf, 4 or 5 sprigs of fresh parsley, 2 sprigs of green celery tops, 1 sprig of thyme, and 1 whole clove, tied with white kitchen thread. Season to taste with salt, white pepper, and a small pinch of nutmeg, and let continue simmering very gently over a low flame for about 25 minutes.

Strain through a fine sieve into a fresh saucepan; carefully remove the bones from the pieces of fish, keeping the meat hot. Place the strained broth over a gentle flame, and as soon as it boils add a small pinch of saffron and 1 quart of rich creamy scalded milk, or 2 cups of milk and 2 cups of undiluted evaporated milk. Let boil up once, let simmer 5 minutes, remove from the fire, return the pieces of fish to the stock, and taste for seasoning. Serve very hot, with a piece of fish in each plate and a side dish of fresh toast spread with parsley sauce.

Parsley Sauce. To 1 cup of hot Béchamel Sauce (No. 348) or Cream Sauce (No. 346), add and blend thoroughly an infusion of 3 tablespoons of parsley leaves, strained. Taste for seasoning, and just when ready to serve, stir in 2 tablespoons of finely chopped parsley and a few drops of lemon juice. For the parsley infusion, proceed as if making tea. Especially appropriate for almost any kind of fish cooked in any style.

LA BOUILLABAISSE MARSEILLAISE [539]
Marseilles Fish Chowder

Cook books and recipes are the ruination of novices, because people will not learn that a recipe is not a prescription. A good recipe should suggest, but never govern. A French cordon bleu has his recipes, but his soup or sauce becomes *magnum opus* when he sticks his thumb in it and tastes, then works magic with his array of essences and herbs.

Thackeray's *The Ballad of the Bouillabaisse* is a pretty good recipe if you are blessed with a cook's imagination and instincts, and it is a help to know that the term *bouillabaisse* is interpreted as "When it boils, it's done!" Boil your fish one minute too long, and it becomes a paste.

Thackeray inhaled and absorbed his *bouillabaisse* in the Rue Neuve des Petits Champs, meaning "New Street of the Little Fields," in Paris, and it's likely enough that the Sainted Terre used good codfish or haddock with his

"Green herbs, red peppers, mussels, saffron,
Soles, onions, garlic, roach and dace."

Roach and dace filled out a line and a rime for the balladier rather
neatly, but he failed to add a stanza to warn the world that one breath
too much of peppers or garlic would ruin the whole structure.

No wine or liquor enters into the concoction of this original and
delightful chowder or stew—whatever it may be called—which was
first prepared in Marseilles. The original recipe calls for twelve different kinds of fish, the list of which follows with corresponding names
in English, and the fish which may be substituted for those not available in any part of America.

Rascasse: Unknown in America; sea bass may be substituted.

Sard: Unknown in America; substitute haddock or codfish.

Langouste: Spiny lobster.

Grondin: Red gurnard.

Galiente: Unknown in America; substitute grouper.

Dorade: Dory, also sometimes called John Dory.

Baudroie: Frogfish, also sometimes called sea devil.

Congre: Conger, or conger eel.

Turbot: Turbot, often erroneously called halibut; *turbotin,* a young
        turbot.

Merlan: Whiting.

Fielan: Unknown in America; small eel may be used.

Rouquier: Unknown in America; eel may be used.

Assuming you have all the necessary fish or substitutes, which must
be of a firm flesh, the procedure is as follows:

Take about 6 pounds of the above-mentioned fish or their substitutes in approximately equal amounts for each variety. Cut the large
fish into pieces; leave the small ones whole. Place in a pan a generous
½ cup of good olive oil, and add to it 4 ounces (about ⅓ cup) of
minced onions, 2 ounces of leeks (about 2 young leeks, white part
only), 2 medium-sized fresh tomatoes, pressed, peeled, and slightly
crushed, 4 cloves of garlic, crushed to a pulp, 1 generous teaspoon of
finely chopped parsley, 1 generous pinch of saffron (drugstore)
powder, 1 large bay leaf, 1 small sprig of common savory, 1 generous
pinch of the top of fresh fennel, and salt and pepper to taste.

Place all the above ingredients in the pan with the exception of the
whiting and the red gurnard, which being very tender should be added
when the bouillabaisse has been boiling from 8 to 10 minutes. The
bouillabaisse is ready! Taste for seasoning. Dress up some slices of
plain bread, not toasted or fried, but plain slices, on a hot deep

platter, preferably round. Pour the liquid over these slices, and on another hot platter, dress up the fish, surrounding the whole with pieces of langouste, or spiny lobster.

This Provençal chowder owes its characteristics first to the kind of fish used, then to the garlic and the saffron flavorings. Garlic is a blessing in disguise! In garlic are vitamins and minerals galore. Iodine, calcium, potassium, and phosphorus represent its mineral content. Garlic is also one of nature's greatest internal antiseptics.

It was after tasting bouillabaisse that the famous Jean Henri Fabre, distinguished French entomologist (1823-1915) and poet at the same time, wrote in Provençal the following ode to garlic.

> "Horaça, se l'avies tastado,
> Ben luen de l'ave blastémado,
> L'auries douna toun amitié,
> Auries mies estima ta testa courounado
> D'un rez d'ayet que de lauzié. . . ."

Which translated into English means:

> "Horace, had you tasted it,
> Far from speaking ill of it,
> You would have been better adorned
> And might have been better on friendly terms
> With a chain of garlic instead of laurels."
>
> FABRE

From time immemorial, garlic has been used in cookery, and until the middle of the eighteenth century, many Siberian villages paid taxes in garlic—fifteen bulbs for a man, ten for a woman, five for a child. This member of the lily family has power and authority, as you may see and taste. It is most healthful, and according to the ancients "its heat is very vehement."

LA BOUILLABAISSE PARISIENNE [540]
Parisian Fish Chowder

Into the preparation of bouillabaisse, Parisian style, the following fish enter: *moules* (mussels), *rouget* (red gurnard), *grondin* (a specie of red gurnard), *sole* (unknown in America, unless imported, lemon sole or flounder may be substituted), *vive* (unknown in America, except a short weever, eel may be substituted), *merlan* (whiting), *congre* (conger eel), and *langouste* (spiny lobster).

Place in a large kettle 6 tablespoons of good olive oil, and add 2 large onions, finely chopped, and 2 small leeks, using white parts only, finely minced. Cook over a hot flame, taking care not to color, and stirring almost constantly. Then add 1 fifth bottle of good dry white wine. Season to taste with salt and pepper. Add a small pinch of saffron; 1 bouquet garni, composed of 1 large bay leaf, 6 sprigs of fresh parsley, and 1 sprig of thyme, tied with kitchen thread; 3 medium-sized fresh tomatoes, peeled, pressed, then crushed, or use the equivalent of thick tomato purée; and 2 small cloves of garlic, mashed. Bring to the boiling point, then reduce the flame, and cook gently for 15 to 20 minutes longer.

Having selected the fish, allow 1 pound of fish for each person, and in approximately equal amounts from each variety. Place 6 tablespoons of olive oil in a kettle, add the fish, well cleaned, washed quickly, sponged, and cut in 2-inch pieces, mussels included, after being scraped and well washed but not removed from the shells (in other words, "shell and all"). Sprinkle over 1 tablespoon of finely chopped parsley, and cook about 5 minutes, tossing the kettle once in a while. Then turn into the hot broth. Boil for 10 minutes over a bright flame, and set aside. Thicken the liquid with 1 generous tablespoon of butter kneaded with 2 teaspoons of flour. Stir gently, while simmering for a few minutes. Dress the fish pieces on a hot round platter with a little of the broth, serving the remainder aside. Serve with a side dish of Jocko Toast (No. 790).

LA BOUILLABAISSE A LA NIMOISE [541]
Fish Chowder Nîmoise Style

Into the preparation of bouillabaisse, Nîmoise style, the following fish enter: *anguille* (eel, cut into inch pieces, and half cooked in fish stock), *rouget* (red gurnard, almost cooked, and cut into inch pieces), *sole* (substitute lemon sole or flounder, raw, and cut into inch pieces), *pagel* or *pageau* (unknown in America, substitute sun-fish, raw, and cut into inch pieces), *dorade* (dory, sometimes called John Dory, raw, and cut into inch pieces), *homard* (lobster, tail only, raw, the tail cut into two pieces, using lobsters weighing no more than 1 to 1½ pounds each), and *lotte* (eelpout, raw, using only the liver, which is cooked separately, as indicated further, and used for thickening the chowder).

Heat ½ cup of olive oil to the smoking point, then add the prepared fish, all mixed together. Season to taste with salt and pepper; a pinch each of saffron and powdered fennel; 1 bouquet garni, composed of 2 large bay leaves tied with 8 sprigs of fresh parsley, 1 small leek, white part only, cut in quarters lengthwise, 2 sprigs of green celery leaves, 1 large sprig of thyme, and 2 whole cloves; 2 cloves of

garlic, peeled, then crushed; ½ cup of chopped onions; and 3 whole
shallots, peeled. Pour over enough fish stock (made with cheap fish
and strained) to generously cover; then pour in ½ generous cup of
Madeira wine. Bring to a boil. Let boil steadily and furiously for 8
minutes. Remove from the fire, and taste for seasoning. Dress the
fish into a hot deep dish. Strain the stock into a clean kettle or
saucepan, and stir in the liver of a small eelpout, which has been
cooked a few minutes in a little fish stock, pounded or rubbed
through a fine sieve, then beaten with 3 fresh egg yolks and 4 tablespoons of slightly heated olive oil. Strain this binding over the fish,
garnish the platter with small triangles of white bread fried in butter, and serve at once.

Note. Certain professional chefs from the Nîmes region add 1 teaspoon of grated orange rind to the chowder at the time of adding
the saffron. This is optional. All the surplus of the strained stock
may be served aside to replenish the plates of guests, and extra fried
triangles of bread should be served aside.

LA BOUILLABAISSE DE BRUSSARD   [542]
New Orleans Creole

Now we are in the presence of a Cajun born in the Acadian
settlement where Evangeline sleeps awaiting the Judgment Day.
Annually, Brussard has made a pilgrimage to Europe in search of
something to tickle New Orleans palates. Supreme is his bouillabaisse.

Into the preparation of this bouillabaisse the following fish enter:
bar de mer (sea bass), *bass rayé* (striped bass), *happer rouge* (red
snapper), sole (substitute gray sole or flounder), *crevettes* (shrimps),
homard (lobster), *crabes durs* (hard-shelled crabs), and *huitres* (oysters).

The fish (sea bass, striped bass, red snapper, and sole) should be
quickly washed, sponged, then cut into pieces 1½ inches thick, seasoned with mixed salt and pepper to taste, and let drain for 15 minutes. Strain 2 quarts of tomatoes (use canned or stewed tomatoes,
not tomato juice). Brown 3 large onions, 3 large sweet peppers,
sliced thin, in ½ cup of olive oil. Add to the tomatoes, and cook
for 15 minutes. Then season with a generous pinch of powdered
thyme and 2 large bay leaves. Lay the fish in the mixture, then the
boiled shelled left-whole shrimps (1 pound), two 1½-pound lobsters,
and the meat from 4 cooked hard-shelled crabs. Add 2 cloves of
garlic, peeled, then crushed, 3 cups of dry white wine, 2 tablespoons

of olive oil, and a pinch of saffron, and continue cooking for 15 to 20 minutes over a low flame. Now add 24 fresh oysters, fresh or canned, as well as their own liquor, which should be strained through a fine cloth, and let cook for 5 minutes longer. Serve with freshly made dry toast, cut finger length, each serving dusted with finely chopped parsley.

International travelers revel in Brussard's specialty, and when enjoying the dish with just the right wine, they agree with Thackeray who, after praising bouillabaisse as he ate it in Paris, said, "In New Orleans you can eat a bouillabaisse the like of which was never eaten in Marseilles or Paris!"

LA BOUILLABAISSE DES PECHEURS [543]
French Fishermen's Bouillabaisse

For 12 generous servings; for less, reduce the amounts of ingredients accordingly.

Cut off the heads of 1 pound each of dory, flounder, red gurnard, and gilthead, and 2 pounds each of sea bass and whiting. Then cut the fish into 2-inch chunks. Sprinkle with salt to taste and plenty of freshly crushed peppercorns, and set aside to drain. Cut in two, crosswise, a dozen crabs, and clean; dust with salt, and add to the fish. Cut in 2-inch pieces 2 live 1½-pound lobsters. Wash the pieces in water to which has been added a little lemon juice, and season to taste with salt and pepper. Add these pieces also to the fish. Shell 2 quarts of mussels, saving the liquor, and season with salt, but not pepper. Set the mussels and the strained juice aside—not with the fish.

Into a good-sized soup kettle, put 4 cloves of garlic, peeled, then crushed; 3 large onions; ½ generous cup of parsley; ¼ cup of chives; ¼ cup of celery green tops, all chopped; and 3 large sprigs of fennel, fresh or dried. Over this scented garden, pour ¾ cup of good olive oil. Cook about 4 to 5 minutes, stirring constantly; then sprinkle with 1 scant teaspoon of powdered saffron (more or less, according to taste). Scatter the fish and crabs and lobster over this mixture, but not the mussels; and pour over the whole 2 quarts of dry white wine and 2 quarts of boiling water. Bring this mixture to a boil, and allow it to boil for 8 to 10 minutes. Then add the mussels and the liquor. Boil for 4 or 5 minutes longer, not more than 15 minutes in all. Then pour the bouillon—golden in color—over a mountain of bread slices, each rubbed with garlic. The fish pieces and mussels are served separately.

LA BOUILLABAISSE DE PROVENCE [544]
Bouillabaisse of the Provence Region

In the Provence region of France, famous for its highly garlicked fare, bouillabaisse has a manner of its own, quite different from that of the bouillabaisse of Marseilles.

Bring together 1½ pounds each of whiting, striped bass, small eels, conger eel, dory, and frogfish; 3 pounds each of halibut and sea bass; and 3 rock lobsters of 1 pound each. Cut and split the heads of all the fish, and boil the heads for 20 minutes in 3 quarts of water, slightly salted. Cut the live lobsters into 6 pieces each, and sauté the pieces for 10 minutes in ⅓ generous cup of olive oil which has been poured into a flat-bottomed pan. Shake the pan constantly. Strain over the lobster mixture the stock made with the fish heads; bring to a rapid boil, then let simmer gently for 10 minutes.

In the meantime, chop 2 large onions, 6 fresh tomatoes, peeled, and 3 large cloves of garlic. Place these in a large soup kettle, adding 1 sprig of thyme, 1 large bay leaf, 8 sprigs of fresh parsley, and 2 sprigs of green celery leaves, all tied together with kitchen thread. Sprinkle over the whole 1 teaspoon of saffron (more or less, according to taste), and pour over all 1 scant cup of pure olive oil. Season to taste with salt and freshly ground pepper. Cut the fish into 2-inch chunks, and arrange over the mixture. Allow this kettle of fish to stand, covered with a clean towel, for 30 minutes to 1 hour. About 20 minutes before serving, pour the lobster mixture over this fish *mélange*, and place the kettle and contents over a bright flame. Allow to boil briskly for 10 minutes. Lay from one to several dried (not toasted) untrimmed slices of French bread in each deep soup plate. Lift the fish chunks from the bouillabaisse onto a hot deep platter. Pour the bouillon, unstrained, over the bread slices. And so serve La Bouillabaisse de Provence.

LA BOUILLABAISSE DU PAYS DE [545]
CORNOUAILLES
Also called Land's End Bouillabaisse

French Brittany—La Bretagne—also has its bouillabaisse. It was at the Hotel du Minou, located in the old fortress of Minou-en-Plou-zané, in the department of Finistère, where all roasts are made over wood fire, that this writer enjoyed and learned how to make this famous bouillabaisse.

For 10 generous servings, cut 5 leeks into thin slices, using the white parts only. Drop the slices into lukewarm water, and let stand for 15 minutes. Peel and cube small 2 pounds of potatoes. Peel, halve, and squeeze out the juice and seeds of 5 medium-sized fresh tomatoes, then chop them coarsely. Peel and slice very thin 3 large celery hearts. Drain the leek slices, and place in a large earthenware soup kettle with all the remaining vegetables with 2 quarts of cold water. Add salt, pepper, and thyme leaves to taste, 2 large bay leaves, 2 small cloves of garlic, peeled and mashed, and ⅓ cup of chopped fresh parsley. Gradually bring this to a boil, and let simmer gently for 25 to 30 minutes. Then add 6 to 7 pounds of fish, cleaned and cut into 2-inch chunks, the fish approximately in equal amounts from the following varieties: red gurnard, sea bass, whiting, mackerel, flounder, eelpout, and fresh tuna fish. Let this cook for 15 minutes.

Beat 3 fresh egg yolks slightly, then beat them into 1 cup of scalded heavy cream. Taste for seasoning, pour the chowder into a large heated soup tureen, and just before serving, scatter over 1 cup of small bread croutons, fried in foaming butter. Serve on the side large colorful earthenware peasant bowls of cool hard cider. And after the soup is enjoyed, it is the custom to serve a pony glass of Calvados to help digest this really delicious chowder.

LA BOURRIDE PROVENÇALE   [546]
French Chowder Provençal Manner

The following kind of chowder, a combination of a stew and fish soup at the same time, is very rich. It's a meal-in-one, a meal strongly flavored with garlic.

Pound 6 cloves of garlic to a pulp, then stir in, as in making mayonnaise, 1 fresh egg yolk. When thoroughly blended, stir in ¾ cup (more or less) of good olive oil, drop by drop at first, then when the mixture begins to get a little thick, raise the amount of oil, and stir without stopping until the mixture resembles mayonnaise. Season to taste with salt and black pepper, and set aside.

Wash, cut into 2-inch chunks, wash again, then sponge well, 2 pounds each of three or four different varieties of white-fleshed fish, such as sea bass, whiting, and conger eel, or any other kind of lean fish available; but there should be at least three different varieties. Line a generously oiled large flat-bottomed saucepan with 1 extra large or 2 medium-sized onions, thinly sliced, the rings separated. Add a bouquet garni, composed of 1 generous sprig of fennel, 2 large bay leaves, 1 generous sprig of thyme, and a 2-inch by ½-inch dried orange peel, all tied together with kitchen thread (you may also tie in 2 cloves, but this is optional). Lay over the well-dried and mixed fish chunks. Pour over 1½ quarts (6 cups) of hot water. Bring to a boil, and let boil steadily for about 12 to 15 minutes, or until the fish chunks are done.

Note. In some parts of Provence, notably at Saint-Juan-les-Pins, and Monte Carlo, a dash of saffron is added with the hot water, but the original formula doesn't mention this ingredient.

Season to taste with salt and pepper. Arrange 2 slices of bread, from which the crusts have been removed, in the bottom of each of the six soup plates, and pour over them enough hot fish stock, just enough to moisten them. Set aside.

In a saucepan, put 8 fresh egg yolks and stir in 6 tablespoons of the garlic mayonnaise (*aioli* in Provençal), mixing thoroughly; place the saucepan over a gentle flame, and gradually stir in the strained hot fish stock, stirring constantly from the bottom and sides of the pan until this garlicky sauce coats the wooden spoon. Be sure not to let boil, lest the mixture curdle. Just proceed as if making a custard sauce. It is advisable to stir this sauce over hot water instead of the flame. Taste for seasoning, and immediately pour this really delicious, but garlicky sauce over the soaked bread slices, covering the slices entirely. Dress the fish onto a hot deep platter, after discarding the onion slices and bouquet garni, and serve immediately with the remainder of the garlic sauce aside in a sauceboat.

The usual accompaniment of this chowder-stew-soup dish is an extra dish of bread slices and several chilled bottles of dry white wine.

LA CAGOUILLE DE POISSON DU MONASTERE [547]
Fish Stew in the Monastery Manner

This recipe was created more than one hundred years ago in the monastery of the Benedictines at Fécamp, where the famous Benedictine liqueur originated. It has been modernized since and is still made today in Normandy.

Place in the bottom of a soup kettle 3 thin slices of salt pork, cubed small, and try out until the cracklings are delicately browned. Then stir in 3 medium-sized onions, thinly sliced; 3 medium-sized fresh tomatoes, peeled and coarsely chopped; 1 clove of garlic, peeled and left whole; ½ large green pepper, coarsely chopped and free from white seeds and ribs; and 1 bouquet garni, composed of 1 large bay leaf tied with a 2½-inch piece of scraped parsley root, 1 sprig of thyme, and 3 sprigs of very green celery leaves. Continue cooking, stirring frequently over a gentle flame, for about 7 or 8 minutes. Then pour in 2 cups of dry white wine and 2 cups of boiling water. Add 1 scant teaspoon of salt, 8 peppercorns, freshly crushed, and 1 leaflet or 2 of dill. Bring to a boil, lower the flame, and let simmer gently for 20 minutes. Now add 2 pounds of fresh salmon, wiped with a damp cloth, cut into inch chunks, and carefully boned; 1 cup of fresh shrimps, shelled and coarsely chopped; 1 cup of raw small potato cubes; ½ cup of raw small carrot cubes; and ½ cup of raw small celery root cubes. Continue cooking gently for 20 minutes.

Place in a bowl 1 tablespoon of flour, and dilute with 1 cup of hot mussel broth, provided from 1 pound of carefully cleaned mussels cooked with 1 cup of water until the mussels open. Remove the mussels from their shells, and set aside for garnishing the chowder. Stir the flour mixture into the chowder, stirring constantly. Let simmer for a few minutes, taste for seasoning, and just before serving in colorful peasant earthenware bowls, add the cooked shelled mussels. Top each bowl with a pat of sweet butter.

LA CHAUDRONNEE D'AIGO SAOU PROVENÇALE   [548]

Sea-Salt-Water Chowder in the Manner of Provence

Aigo saou, meaning in Provençal, "cooked in salt water," is a remote variation of the famous Bouillabaisse Marseillaise, and is in great favor among the fishermen families along the Mediterranean Sea. This chowder has the advantage that it may be made with almost any kind of small fish, and right on the beach, if desired.

Cut into 2-inch chunks 5 pounds of any kind of mixed salt-water fish, the more composite the better, but only fish, no crustaceans or shellfish. Sprinkle with mixed salt and pepper, and let stand for 25 to 30 minutes to draw the water. Put in a large soup kettle 1 extra large onion, finely chopped; 2 large fresh tomatoes, peeled and cut into small pieces; 1 large bay leaf, tied with 1 large sprig of thyme, 8 sprigs of fresh parsley, and 2 whole cloves; ½ cup of celery stalk, chopped very fine after being scraped; and salt and freshly crushed black pepper to taste. Add 2 quarts of sea-salt-water. Bring to a boil, and let boil gently for 25 minutes, then add the prepared fish, and boil violently for 12 to 15 minutes. Remove from the fire, and taste for seasoning. Carefully lift the fish from the broth with a perforated ladle, and keep hot, after covering it with 6 slices of bread, untrimmed, each slice sprinkled with olive oil then with as much black pepper as liked.

Have ready a garlic mayonnaise (*aioli*, as it is called in Provence), made as indicated in the first paragraph of the recipe, La Bourride Provençale (No. 546).

Place the bread slices covering the fish into hot soup plates, one in each plate. Pour over the strained fish bouillon. Serve the fish separately with a side dish of garlic mayonnaise and extra slices of bread, sprinkled with olive oil then with plenty of freshly crushed black pepper. The soup and the fish are eaten at the same time, the fish with the garlic mayonnaise, the *aioli*.

LA CHAUDRONNEE DE CARRELET   [549]
LORIENTAISE

Flounder Chowder in the Manner of Lorient—a formula of the Hôtellerie of Perros Guirec

Experts at camouflage could take a lesson from the flounder. Its ability to adjust itself to background for protection is unsurpassed. Sensory impressions received through the eyes of fish change the color of flounder, but camouflaged or not, he is really delicious as prepared by the Norman cooks and Breton cooks.

Wash 2 pounds of flounder filets, and cut into 2-inch chunks. Season to taste with mixed salt and pepper and a few grains of nutmeg to taste, and let stand for 25 minutes. Wash, skin, and remove the black veins from 1 pound of fresh shrimps. Season to taste with salt and pepper, and set aside over the flounder filet chunks. Drain 2 dozen oysters, reserving the liquor. Set aside, but do not mix with the flounder and shrimps. Wash, scrape carefully, and remove the beard from 2 dozen fresh mussels. Put in a saucepan with 1 cup of cider and 2 tablespoons of finely chopped green pepper, 1 tablespoon of finely chopped shallots, and as much of chopped parsley. Cover closely, and let cook over a moderately brisk flame for about 10 minutes, or until the mussels are open, discarding those which are not. Remove the mussels from the pan with a perforated ladle, and when cold enough to handle, remove the mussels from their shells. Strain the mussel broth through a fine cloth, reserving the broth, which add to 1 cup of scalded cream, and keep hot.

Melt ⅓ pound of sweet butter, and blend in 1 tablespoon of flour. Pour in 1 quart of cider, stirring constantly until well mixed. Then add 1 large onion, thinly sliced and the rings separated; 1 cup of finely shredded young spinach, using only the leaves; ½ cup of finely shredded lettuce, using only the leaves; ½ cup of scraped young carrot, cubed very small; ½ cup of finely chopped green celery tops; 1 bouquet garni, composed of 1 large bay leaf, 1 sprig of thyme, 8 sprigs of fresh parsley, 1 sprig of fennel, and 2 whole cloves, all tied with kitchen thread; salt and pepper to taste. Bring to a boil, then let boil gently for 20 minutes. Now add the strained mussel-cream mixture, let boil violently for 1 minute, then add the flounder and shrimps, and cook briskly for about 12 minutes. Remove from the fire, stir in the mussels and oysters with their strained liquor, taste for seasoning, and discard the bouquet garni. Serve in hot soup plates, each topped with 1 teaspoon of sweet butter creamed with 1 scant teaspoon of finely chopped chives.

LA CHAUDRONNEE D'ECREVISSES DE LA MARNE [550]
Crayfish Chowder As Made in the Marne Region

The fishing season for crayfish is very short, opening in August and closing September first. During this period, crayfish are the culinary craze for gourmets, and crayfish festivals take place or are staged to open the season. Mounded platters of this Lilliputian crustacean, with deep dishes of buttered toast and chilled white wines of all denominations, are served, especially this famous crayfish chowder made according to an old formula of the Marne.

Take 4 dozen nice live crayfish, and wash them in several changes of cold water, letting them stand in the last change for 20 minutes, while preparing the broth.

Heat ⅓ cup of sweet butter in a large soup kettle. Add 1 large onion, peeled, then thinly sliced, the rings separated; 3 young carrots, scraped, then cubed very small; 2 stalks of celery, scraped, then finely chopped; 1 clove of garlic, mashed; 3 tablespoons of shallots, chopped; and 1 bouquet garni, composed of 1 large bay leaf, 12 sprigs of chives, 1 sprig of thyme, 1 sprig of fennel, 1 leaflet of tarragon herb, and 2 whole cloves, heads removed, all tied with kitchen thread. Cook for 5 minutes, stirring frequently over a gentle fire. Then stir in ½ cup of finely chopped lean cooked ham, and pour over 1 fifth bottle of Chablis wine and 2 cups of rich chicken broth, clear of any fat. Season with salt and pepper to taste, bring to a rapid boil, then let boil gently for 20 minutes. Add the prepared crayfish, and cook for 12 to 15 minutes, or until the Lilliputian crustaceans are a beautiful red. Using a perforated ladle, remove the crayfish, and when cold enough to handle, cut off with kitchen scissors the little legs, the shells from the tails, the extremities from the large legs, and the tips of the noses. Place the trimmed crayfish in a hot deep platter, and pour over 4 tablespoons of good brandy, set aflame, tossing the crayfish with a wooden spoon until the flames are extinguished. Discard the bouquet garni, return the crayfish to the stock, and stir in 1 cup of heavy cream, scalded and beaten with 3 fresh egg yolks. Heat to the boiling point, but do not allow to boil. Serve at once in hot soup plates, each sprinkled with finely chopped chervil, or parsley if chervil is not available, and a side dish of freshly made buttered toast aplenty. It is the custom to drink a brandy pony of fine champagne when the plate is half emptied, and another when the plate is empty.

LA CHAUDRONNEE DE LAPIN COMME LE FONT LES GARDES-CHASSES [551]
Rabbit Chowder in the Manner of the Gamekeeper

The hare or rabbit's Greek name is *Oryctolagus cuniculus*, which literally translated means "an excavator" or "an animal that digs canals in the earth." Moreover, it is a member of the order Rodentia and is an ineducabilian, placental, diphyodont mammal! All of which in simple English says that this prolific meat and fur producer is a rodent belonging to the largest order among the mammals, closely related to the squirrel and twenty other families of gnawers, such as the rat, mouse, chinchilla, beaver, and guinea pig; that it has only limited mental capacity; that it bears its young in the usual animal manner; that it has two sets of teeth; and that it belongs to the highest order of animals, those having a spinal column and suckling their young. Despite its reputation for docility, the hare or rabbit has a vicious temper and is quick in anger with its own kind and other small animals. However, this ill nature is seldom displayed toward human beings, and hares or rabbits are easy enough to handle when you go about it right. They quickly respond to kind treatment and appreciate caressing probably as much as a cat, and like the cat, they resent having their fur rubbed the wrong way. Their willingness to be petted is taken advantage of in Mohammedan countries, where tame rabbits and tame hares, called "harem kittens," are given to the women of the seraglios for personal pets. It is likely that Scheherazade, that famous bedtime storyteller, dreamed up her clever neck-saving tales in the privacy of an overstuffed Oriental apartment while fondling a fluffy rabbit or hare, probably an Angora. Yes, rabbits can be housebroken just like cats, but they belong in hutches in the back yard, to be raised for delicious stews, roasts, civets, in sweet or sour cream, en casserole, in red wine, jugged, or in chowder as made by the gamekeeper.

With the leftover of a roasted rabbit or hare, the meat scraped from the carcass then set aside, the carcass broken into small pieces, and a 2-pound piece of beef shin, you may prepare a delicious chowder. Reserve the scraped rabbit or hare meat as a garnish.

Put the broken carcass and the beef shin in a large soup kettle containing ⅓ pound of fat fresh pork with the rind left on and downside. Add 1 medium-sized onion, chopped; 2 small carrots, scraped and chopped; ¼ cup of chopped green celery leaves; 1 small leek, quartered, carefully washed, using the white and green parts, tied with 1 large bay leaf, 1 sprig of thyme, and 2 whole cloves; and 1 small clove of garlic, mashed. Pour over 1 quart of cold water. Do not add salt and pepper as yet. Bring to a boil, covered, and let boil steadily until the liquid is almost evaporated. Then pour in 1½ quarts of light beef consommé or water and 2 cups of dry white wine. Bring to a boil, and let boil gently over a medium flame until the liquid is reduced to 1½ quarts (6 cups). Strain this through a fine cloth into a clean soup kettle. Season to taste with salt, pepper, and a few grains of nutmeg. Then add 1 cup of small carrot cubes; ¾ cup of finely chopped celery stalk, previously scraped; 2 tablespoons of finely chopped green pepper; 3 tablespoons of uncooked, broken small vermicelli; and 2 tablespoons of uncooked rice, carefully washed. Cook this for 20 minutes, then add 1 cup of small potato cubes, and continue cooking for 10 minutes, or until the potatoes are tender, but not mushy. Taste for seasoning. Stir in 1 cup of the reserved rabbit or hare meat, cut into small cubes or shredded. Taste for seasoning, and serve in hot soup plates, each garnished with 2 small Liver Dumplings (No. 742).

Note. Should your chowder be too fat, a few lettuce leaves, placed in the soup before adding the meat and the dumplings, will absorb the grease. Remove the lettuce leaves as soon as they become coated with the fat.

You may make chowder in this way with almost any kind of game, furred or feathered.

LA CHAUDRONNEE DE PETITS POIS SECS AUX MARENNES [552]
Split Pea Chowder with Oysters

This French chowder has an American story which is worth repeating. James B. Regan of the once famous Knickerbocker Hotel, at Forty-second Street and Broadway, where I was head chef, boasted that anybody could get any food he wanted in his hotel. He gave an order that on every ship leaving a French port a consignment of Marennes oysters should be shipped. After two weeks, he stopped one day, flanked with Malnatti, his maître d'hôtel, at his oyster counter, which was then headed by Dennis Sullivan as head shucker. By that time, baskets of Marennes oysters had begun to clog the hotel's cold-storage space.

"Dennis," he said to Sullivan, "how are those French Marennes going?" "They ain't going, Mr. Regan," he heard. "What do you mean? How many have you sold?" "Mr. Regan, during the whole two weeks you been getting them, we've sold just two orders."

And that was why for several days patrons of the "Forty-second Street Country Club," as Frank O'Malley had christened the hotel bar, had split pea chowder with Marennes oysters for free lunch, my having received the order to use these French oysters in my best way, and following a formula used for scores of years in Marennes. This chowder was found so delicious and unusual that I had to feature it every Friday on the bill of fare of the old Knickerbocker. Regan never imported any other Marennes, but used the famous Long Island oysters instead.

Now for the recipe. For six servings, soak 1½ pounds of green split peas in cold water for 4 hours. Drain. Put in a soup kettle. Add 3 quarts of unsalted chicken broth and 1 knuckle of smoked ham, with 1 large bay leaf tied with 8 sprigs of fresh parsley and 1 sprig of thyme, and slowly bring to a boil. Meantime, sauté 1 medium-sized onion in 1 tablespoon of butter, and as soon as the pea mixture starts to boil, stir the onion into the mixture. Add 8 whole peppercorns, freshly bruised, and let gently boil for 2 long hours, stirring occasionally to prevent the peas from scorching. When done, force the peas through a fine sieve, and season with salt and pepper to taste. Return the chowder to the fire. Add ¼ pound of butter, ½ cup of picked freshly cooked or canned crab meat, and ½ cup of peas, freshly cooked or canned. When ready to serve, add ¾ cup of cooked small, very small potato cubes, and 18 fresh oysters, carefully picked, and cooked in 2 tablespoons of butter until the edges curl. Serve in hot soup plates, each sprinkled with finely chopped chives.

Note. You may sauté the oysters, and instead of putting them in the chowder, place 3 oysters in each plate, then fill the plates with the pea chowder. Lentils may be prepared in the same way, also navy beans, or other kinds of beans.

LA CHAUDRONNEE DE MORILLES A LA [553] SOLOGNOTE

Morel Chowder in the Solognote Manner

There can scarcely be any doubt that morels (*genus Morchella*) are practically without equal as edible fungi, and in regions where they are common, they are sought avidly by mushroom enthusiasts. In flavor and texture, they surpass both the common cultivated species and most other wild mushrooms, and attempts have been and still are being made to grow them commercially—so far without success. One year they'll be found in abundance on certain hillsides, but they may not reappear there for years. They seem to come up readily in some burned-over areas, and it is said that at one time the residents of some parts of France, Germany, and Belgium made such a practice of burning the woodlands to encourage the growth of morels that they had to be restrained by law. Morels appear for a short time only, usually in the early spring, the season in the northern United States being at its peak during May. There are several species, but they are all enough alike to be described as one. The cap is conical, from three to four inches high and from one to two inches wide at the base. The surface is tan and is indented with large irregular pits or cavities, so that the plant resembles an animal sponge. The stem is white and very delicate and brittle in texture, breaking readily when handled, and averages about one inch in thickness and two or three inches in length. Both stem and cap are hollow.

In France, where morels are abundant, they are used for making this delicious chowder.

Morels usually contain some sand in the cavities of the caps and should be thoroughly washed in several changes of lukewarm water and rinsed by placing them in a colander, letting cold water run over them, and lifting them with the fingers of both hands. They must not remain long in water, lest they lose their fine flavor.

Separate the stems and caps from 1 pound of morels, and wash as indicated above. Strain, and drain well. Chop the stems and caps coarsely. Place them in a pan containing ¼ cup of sweet butter, ¼ cup of unstrained lemon juice, and 1 cup of dry white wine. Cook over a brisk flame for 5 minutes, or until the mixture has boiled once. Remove from the fire, and keep hot.

Heat 2 tablespoons of butter, blend in 2 tablespoons of flour, and cook until the mixture begins to bubble, stirring constantly over a gentle flame. Do not let get colored. Gradually stir in 1½ quarts of clear chicken consommé, fresh or canned, and cook until the mixture is smooth and has boiled for 5 minutes, stirring occasionally. Then add 1 bouquet garni, composed of 1 large bay leaf, 8 sprigs of fresh parsley, 1 sprig of thyme, and 2 whole cloves, heads removed, all tied with kitchen thread. Season to taste with salt, pepper, and a grating of nutmeg. Bring to a boil, then let simmer for 20 minutes. Discard the bouquet garni, add the morels and their liquid and a whole clove of garlic (left whole), and bring to a boil. Remove at once from the fire. Fish out the garlic, and discard it. Stir in 1 cup of heavy scalded cream, to which has been added 3 fresh egg yolks, slightly beaten, ¾ cup of cooked or canned crab meat, picked and flaked, and 18 small fresh oysters, uncooked, which have been marinated in ¼ cup of sherry wine, adding the sherry wine too. Serve in hot soup plates, each containing 3 of the oysters.

LA MARMITEE DE POISSON A LA MANIERE DE TOURS [554]
Fish Chowder in the Manner of Tours

The following chowder is an old formula of the Inn of the Cloister of Psalette, a cloister of the fifteenth century, which is the object of an annual pilgrimage by the faithful. The original recipe calls for wine of Vouvray, but this wine is unavailable in this country, as it is a bad traveler; dry white wine has been substituted.

Cut into 2-inch chunks 1 pound each of the following fresh-water fish: small eels (previously skinned), perch, pickerel, and brook trout. Place the fish chunks in a colander, and rinse quickly under cold water, then drain, and sponge dry. Turn the fish chunks into a deep porcelain platter, and sprinkle over ⅓ cup of sherry wine, cover with a cheesecloth, and let stand for an hour.

Place the heads, trimmings, eel skin, and 1 pound of cheap fish, cut into small pieces, in a saucepan. Add 1 medium-sized onion, chopped; 2 tablespoons of green pepper, chopped and absolutely free from white seeds and white ribs; 1 medium-sized carrot, scraped, then thinly sliced; and 1 large bay leaf, tied with 1 sprig of fresh parsley, 1 sprig of fennel, 1 sprig of thyme, 2 sprigs of green celery leaves (tops). Season to taste with salt and freshly crushed black peppercorns. Pour over 3 cups of dry white wine and 3 cups of cold water. Bring to a boil, and let boil steadily until the liquid is reduced to one quart (4 cups). Strain through a fine sieve into a clean kettle. Add ½ cup each of raw carrot, celery root, and white turnip, cubed small, and of leek, thinly sliced and carefully washed, using the white parts only. Bring to a boil, and let boil steadily for 5 minutes. Then add the fish chunks and the marinade and ½ cup of raw potato cubes. Boil steadily for 12 to 15 minutes. Remove from the fire, stir in 1 cup of heavy scalded sweet cream, mixed with 4 fresh egg yolks, stirring constantly with a wooden spoon; return to the fire. Bring to a boil, but do not let boil. Taste for seasoning. Serve the fish chunks separately on a hot platter covered with small slices of toast, rubbed with garlic, then sprinkled generously with black pepper from the mill, and serve the chowder in soup plates, each garnished with 1 teaspoon of herb butter made as follows:

Blanch in a little salt water for about 5 minutes 1 tablespoon each of watercress leaves, spinach leaves, chervil, parsley, chives, and fennel. Drain, refresh in cold water, place all together in a cloth, and twist well to extract all the moisture. Pound or put through a food chopper, then rub through a fine-meshed sieve. Knead these herbs with 3 tablespoons of sweet butter until thoroughly blended. This butter is really delicious over freshly broiled fish or steaks.

LA POTEE DE MOULES A LA MANIERE DE BAGNOLLES [555]

Mussel and Tomato Chowder in the Manner of Bagnolles —a formula of the Auberge du Vieux Moulin de Chantepie

This most excellent mussel chowder is made in three distinct operations.

(1) Place in a saucepan 4 large tomatoes, peeled, seeded, then cut into eighths, 2 dozen small white onions, peeled and left whole, 1 large bay leaf, 3 sprigs of dill, 1 sprig of thyme, and 2 cloves. Pour over 1 cup of dry white wine. Do not salt or pepper as yet. Cook gently over a medium flame for about 35 minutes, stirring occasionally with a wooden spoon. Rub the mixture through a fine-meshed sieve into the clean top of a double boiler. Then stir into the mixture 1 tablespoon of meat extract (commercial), and keep hot over hot water.

(2) In 1 quart of rich beef stock, cook ½ cup each of raw small potato cubes, raw small carrot cubes, celery stalks, scraped, then finely chopped, and leeks, thinly sliced and carefully washed, using the white parts only, for about 15 to 20 minutes, or till the vegetables are tender. Then add ½ to ¾ cup of small raw potato cubes, and continue cooking until the potato cubes are tender, or about 10 to 12 minutes. Keep hot.

(3) Soak 3 dozen mussels in salted cold water for 30 minutes, then scrape them with the greatest care, pulling out all weed, or beard, gathered between the shells, and wash in 3 or 4 changes of cold water. Drain. Put the mussels in a saucepan with salt and black pepper to taste and 2 tablespoons each of finely chopped onion, green pepper, and parsley. Set the pan over a brisk flame. Add 1 cup of dry white wine and ¼ cup of Madeira wine, and cook, jumping them once in a while to bring up those at the bottom, which under the influence of the heat open more quickly. As soon as they are all open, remove the pan from the fire, strain the broth through a fine cloth, and add it to the beef stock mixture. Remove the shells from the mussels, and keep them hot in a little beef stock.

Now combine the tomato-onion mixture with the beef stock and vegetable mixture, bring to a boil, and let it boil once or twice. Remove from the fire, taste for seasoning, and stir in ¼ cup of sweet butter kneaded with 1 tablespoon of finely chopped chives. Stir well, add the mussels, and serve in large colorful earthenware peasant bowls, each topped with a poached egg yolk dusted with finely chopped chervil, or parsley if chervil is not available. Serve a side dish of brown bread and butter finger sandwiches.

LA PAUCHOUSE BOURGUIGNONNE   [556]
Fresh-Water Fish Chowder in the Manner of Burgundy

From time immemorial, Burgundy wines have been produced on the hillsides of Burgundy (Bourgogne) extending from Dijon in the department of the Côte d'Or (Golden Hill). But also, from time immemorial, good foods have come from Burgundy, among the most popular being fish soups, chowders, stews, such as this famous *pauchouse*, which varies slightly from place to place, but the basic foundation is fresh-water fish.

For 10 persons, cut into 2-inch chunks 1 pound each of the following fish: carp, perch, small live eel, skinned, tench, and pike. Lay the fish chunks in a shallow earthenware platter, and flame with 3 generous tablespoons of good brandy. Melt ½ cup of butter in a heavy copper or earthenware kettle with 2 large cloves of garlic, mashed to a pulp, and a bouquet garni, composed of 7 or 8 sprigs of parsley, 3 sprigs of green celery tops, 1 large bay leaf, 1 sprig of thyme, and 2 whole cloves, heads removed, all tied with kitchen thread. Cook 3 tablespoons of finely chopped onion in this mixture until the onion begins to color, and then lay over it the fish. Season to taste with salt and freshly ground pepper, and add enough red

Burgundy wine barely to cover. Bring to a quick boil, then reduce the heat, and let simmer gently for 15 to 20 minutes, or until the fish chunks are nearly done, that is, a little firm.

In the meantime, melt 2 tablespoons of butter, and add 1 cup of cubed lean fresh pork preferably from the breast, previously par-boiled and drained, 2 dozen small white onions, also parboiled and drained, and an equal amount of small peeled mushroom caps. Cook over a gentle flame for 15 to 20 minutes, or until the ingredients are tender, stirring occasionally with a wooden spoon. Drain the pieces of fish, and add them to this mixture. Cover, and keep hot.

Reduce the stock to half its volume. Taste for seasoning, adding salt and pepper if needed. Stir in 1 tablespoon of equal parts of butter and flour kneaded together, and allow the mixture to boil up once. Strain over the fish mixture, cover the pot, and allow to simmer gently for 10 minutes, or until the fish is done. This fish stew is more a chowder than a stew, and may be served in a deep hot platter or in heated individual casseroles, dusted with finely minced parsley or chervil and garnished with small triangles of bread fried in foamy butter.

LA SOUPIERE DE FRUIT DE MER [557] SAFRANEE BEAU RIVAGE
Tureen of Sea Food with Saffron Beau Rivage Manner

For something very special, prepare the following sea food chowder.

Cube small enough cooked fresh or canned lobster to make 2 cups, and combine with 1 scant cup of cooked or canned crab meat, care-fully picked and flaked, 1 cup of cooked sea scallops, quartered, and ¾ cup of cooked, carefully boned, and skinned whiting, flaked in a shallow porcelain dish. Sprinkle over ½ cup of good sherry wine, toss the sea food well, and cover with a clean cloth. Set aside for about 20 minutes, tossing the fish occasionally to keep it constantly moistened with the sherry wine.

Very slowly scald 6 cups of rich milk over hot water, with a bou-quet garni, composed of 1 large bay leaf, 1 fresh sprig of fennel, 1 sprig of thyme, 12 sprigs of chives, and 2 whole cloves, heads re-moved, tied with kitchen thread. This steeping should last for about 20 minutes.

Meanwhile, cook in chicken stock separately until tender ½ cup each of very small cubes of artichoke bottoms (neatly cubed), scraped celery stalks, young carrots, and potatoes. Drain the vegetables when tender, and combine them.

Melt 4 tablespoons of butter in a soup kettle. Stir in ½ cup of fresh mushrooms, peeled and thinly sliced, and 1 tablespoon each of finely chopped shallots and onions. Cook for 5 short minutes over a gentle flame, stirring frequently, then stir in the strained scalded milk, and bring to a boil. Add salt, pepper to taste, and a tiny pinch of saffron. Mix well, and add the sea food, sherry, and the mixed vegetables. Bring to a boil, and let simmer gently for 10 minutes; then, off the fire, stir in 1 cup of scalded sweet cream mixed with 4 fresh egg yolks, slightly beaten. Taste for seasoning, and pour the entire contents into a heated soup tureen, which has been rubbed slightly with garlic. Serve at once with bread and butter toasted sandwiches, cut in finger lengths.

LA SOUPIERE DE TRIPE A LA NORMANDE [558]
Tureen of Tripe Chowder Normandy Manner

(*Formula of the fifteenth-century-old Hôtellerie du Grand Cerf, Louviers, Eure, France*)

Tripe is not only the dish delicious, but a favorite of the gourmet the world over; it's in fact one of the shining stars in the firmament of gastronomy. On account of its pepsin content, it is easily digested and is recommended for those whose digestive tracts are not equal to such well-prepared delicacies as lobster à la Newburg, Hungarian goulash, rich ragouts, or marinated aged venison. And, we may add, who doesn't remember tripe à la mode de Caen, tripe and onions in cider, served in a chafing dish, honeycomb tripe à la Banus, Béchamel tripe and oysters in patty shells, and tripe pepper pot of fame, the stuff of heroes of Valley Forge.

There are folks who set their faces resolutely against tripe, because it's the stomach of the cow. Nine times to ten the contemptuous have never tasted this honeycombed meat from the inside. They may know nothing of tripe's preparation, yet look askance at the devotees who buy such queer stuff. What about kidneys, brains, livers, lungs? Aren't they meat from the inside? And what about the crabs, the lobsters? Speak up Hype Igoe, Selmer Fougner, Oscar of the Waldorf, and you Master Escoffier!

Bring 1 quart of milk to the scalding point with 1 large bay leaf, 1 sprig of thyme, and a 2-inch piece of parsley root, scraped and halved in two lengthwise. Cover, and let steep for 20 minutes. Heat 2 tablespoons of butter, stir in 2 tablespoons of grated onion, and cook for 1 short minute. Do not let brown or take on color. Gradually stir in the strained milk, stirring until smooth. Keep simmering over hot water.

Have ready 2 cups of veal broth, made by simmering for 2 long hours a large veal soupbone, cracked, with vegetable soup, and the usual herbs, hot and strained through a fine cloth, and seasoned highly with salt, pepper, a dash of cayenne, and a dash of nutmeg. Stir in the milk mixture, and cook gently for 25 minutes over a low flame, stirring occasionally. Strain again through a fine sieve into a clean soup kettle. Add 1½ pounds of fresh honeycomb tripe, cut into inch squares, and boil gently for 15 minutes. Then add ½ cup each of very small cubes of carrots, potatoes, the tips of fresh asparagus, and celery stalks, carefully scraped, and boil gently and steadily for 15 minutes longer, or until the vegetables are done and the tripe is tender. Let simmer gently while preparing sponge balls.

Sponge Balls. Put 2 fresh egg whites in a cup, fill the cup with cold milk, and pour the contents into a saucepan. Stir in 1 scant cup of flour, sifted with ½ teaspoon of salt, a dash of cayenne, and a dash of nutmeg, alternately with 2 tablespoons of melted butter. Stir well over the fire until the batter is thick and smooth. Set it to cool, after which add 2 egg yolks, mixing thoroughly. Drop in scant teaspoons into the chowder, which has been brought to a boil, and cook for 7 or 8 minutes.

Just before serving in a heated soup tureen, rub the tureen with a little cut clove of garlic, and taking ½ cup of the liquid broth from the kettle, beat in 3 fresh egg yolks, and pour into the tureen. Pour over the chowder after tasting for seasoning, and serve at once, after dusting the top of the tureen with finely chopped chervil, parsley, or chives.

LIMA BEAN CHOWDER [559]
American

The delicious and distinctive flavor of the lima bean comes from the presence of cyanide, the deadly poison used as gas in execution chambers. But the amount of cyanide in commercially grown limas is in no way injurious. Lima beans of all colors from red to black grow throughout the world. One type of lima, in Peru, requires a nine-month growing period. But those lima beans need some encouragement to appear at their best. No bean wants just to be a bean and never grow up. Season the little fellows when serving them as a vegetable with a little minced parsley and minced chives.

Cook in a soup kettle ¼ cup of finely chopped salt pork for 3 or 4 minutes. Add 1 large onion, finely chopped, and cook until soft, but not brown, stirring frequently. Pour over 1 quart of either meat or chicken stock or hot water, boiling, stirring while pouring. Add 1 bouquet garni, composed of 1 large bay leaf, 1 sprig of thyme, 7 or 8 sprigs of fresh parsley, 2 sprigs of green celery tops, and 2 whole cloves, tied together with kitchen thread. Add 1½ cups of canned lima beans, 2 cups of raw carrot cubes, 2 cups of raw potato cubes, and 1 cup of thinly sliced fresh mushrooms. Season to taste with salt, pepper, and nutmeg, and add 1 whole clove of garlic, left whole. Cover, and cook for 20 minutes over a gentle flame. Then stir in 1 pint of milk and 1 pint of thin cream, or undiluted evaporated milk. Cook for 5 minutes longer, after stirring in 2 tablespoons of butter creamed with 2 scant tablespoons of flour. Taste for seasoning, discard the bouquet garni, and serve at once with finger lengths of brown bread and butter sandwiches. Dust each plate with finely chopped chives.

LOBSTER CHOWDER CANCALAISE [560]
French

Remove the meat from a 2-pound boiled lobster, and cut into small cubes. Make a lobster-butter-crumb mixture by creaming 1 generous tablespoon of butter with the lobster coral and the liver (the green part) and 3 or 4 tablespoons of fresh bread crumbs. Set aside. Now cook all the lobster pieces for 10 minutes in a generous cup of water or, still better, fish stock, and strain into a soup kettle. Add the lobster meat, the lobster-butter-crumb mixture, and 1 bouquet garni, composed of 7 or 8 sprigs of fresh parsley, 1 extra large bay leaf, the white part of 1 small leek, thinly sliced lengthwise, and carefully washed, and 1 sprig of thyme, all tied with kitchen thread. Then season to taste with a pinch each of mace and sage, and salt and pepper to taste. Pour over the mixture 1 quart of scalded milk and 1 cup of heavy cream, also scalded. Blend thoroughly, and add 1 rounded teaspoon of paprika. Bring this mixture to a boil very slowly, and allow to simmer very slowly for 20 to 25 minutes. Discard the bouquet garni, and taste for seasoning. When ready to serve, stir in 1 generous tablespoon of sweet butter and ¼ cup of cooked or canned crab meat, carefully boned and flaked. Serve at once with a side dish of French bread, cut very thin, toasted Melba style and, if you wish, rubbed with garlic to taste. You may stir in, just before serving, 3 or 4 tablespoons of sherry wine. If a richer chowder is desired, you may add ½ cup each of raw cubed small carrots, potatoes, celery, and thinly sliced white part of leek, washed, then cooked separately until tender in either fish stock or plain water, and well drained.

LOUISIANA CRAB GUMBO CHOWDER [561]

Okra, the great summer vegetable of the Creoles, is the vegetable mucilaginous that will thicken a chowder, a gumbo, a soup, or a stew. Their devotion to okra, also called gumbo, may have something to do with the freshness of the vegetable as it is peddled through the street. "Okraiee! Okraiee! They fresh an' they fine. Yes, am Madame. They fresh and they fine. Jis' from the field. Yes, am Madame."

Of this chowder, 2 platefuls make a meal for the Creoles of Louisiana. This will serve 12 persons generously. For less, reduce the amounts of ingredients accordingly.

Wipe 3 pounds of okra with a damp cloth to remove the misty fuzz, and cut into thin round slices.

Immerse 6 large live crabs in boiling water for a few seconds; then remove the shells, and quarter the crabs. Set aside in a covered pan until ready to use, saving the shells.

Wash 2 pounds of fresh (not canned) shrimps thoroughly; peel and set aside, saving the shells. Put the shells of the crabs and those of the shrimps in a large soup kettle. Cover with 3 quarts of cold water. Add a large bouquet garni, composed of 2 large bay leaves, 12 sprigs of fresh parsley, 2 sprigs of thyme, and 3 or 4 sprigs of green celery tops, tied together with kitchen thread, and 1 clove of garlic, mashed. Let boil for 40 minutes. This stock will be used for the chowder after straining through a fine cloth.

Heat ¾ cup of lard (no other shortening to be used) in a large saucepan or kettle. Add the sliced okra and 2 medium-sized onions, chopped, and cook until the okra is browned, but not to excess, stirring frequently with a wooden spoon. Season to taste with salt, pepper, and a grating of nutmeg; then add the crab meat and cook for 5 minutes, stirring frequently over a gentle flame. Gradually stir in the strained shell stock, and bring to a boil. Then stir in 1 tablespoon of tomato paste or thick tomato purée and 2 cloves of finely chopped garlic. Cook gently for 1 long hour over a medium flame. Now add the shrimps, 3 tablespoons of finely chopped parsley, and 2 tablespoons of finely chopped chives. Continue cooking for 2 hours longer, always gently, stirring occasionally. Finally, add 2 cups of raw potato cubes, and continue cooking for 15 minutes longer. Taste for seasoning, and when ready to serve, stir in ½ cup of cooked rice and 2 cups of scalded sweet cream.

MARTHA WASHINGTON'S CRAB MEAT CHOWDER   [562]

Boil 8 hard-shelled crabs for 25 to 30 minutes in salted water; pick out carefully the crab meat, then flake. Mash 2 hard-cooked egg yolks with a fork, and blend with 1 tablespoon of flour and the grated rind of 1 small lemon, moistening with 1 teaspoon (more or less) of Worcestershire sauce, and seasoning to taste with salt and white pepper. Scald slowly 5 cups of milk with 2 large bay leaves, a few thin slices of onion, 1 sprig of thyme, and 2 whole cloves. Strain, then stir in the egg yolk paste slowly and gradually, stirring constantly. Return the milk mixture to a soup kettle, and bring to the boiling point, stirring occasionally. Add the picked flaked crab meat, and let simmer gently for 5 long minutes. Then stir in 1 cup of scalded heavy sweet cream alternately with ½ cup of sherry wine. Taste for seasoning, and serve at once with toast or toasted crackers.

MUSHROOM AND POTATO SOUR CREAM CHOWDER   [563]

Preserve the distinctive but delicate flavor of fresh mushrooms by careful handling. Do not wash, but peel them, and remove any dark spots. Use the stems down to the joint or knuckle. The peelings, after being washed quickly, may be added to soups or sauces for extra flavor. Canned mushrooms need not be peeled. Dried mushrooms are washed, then soaked for 20 to 25 minutes in warm water before using. Don't throw away the flavorful liquid from canned mushrooms.

Heat 4 tablespoons of butter; stir in ½ pound of fresh mushrooms, peeled and coarsely chopped, and ½ cup of chopped onion. Cook until tender, or for about 6 or 7 minutes, stirring frequently over a gentle heat. Gradually stir in 1 cup of boiling water and 1 cup of small potato cubes, and cook until the potatoes are tender, or about 12 to 15 minutes. Season to taste with salt, pepper, a dash each of nutmeg, mace, and cloves, and ¼ teaspoon of thyme leaves (not powder). Gradually stir in 2 cups of scalded milk, and bring to a boil. Remove from the fire, and gradually add 2 well-beaten egg yolks, beaten with ¼ cup of sherry wine and 2 cups of sour cream. Return to the fire. Bring to a boil, taste for seasoning, and serve at once in heated soup plates, containing small bread cubes, fried in butter and well drained, and each plate dusted with finely chopped parsley.

MUSSEL CHOWDER I [564]
New England manner

As one of nature's most easily digestible foods—equal or superior to either clams or oysters—sea mussels are cheap, easily taken, and accessible to the markets. The quantity of actual nutriment contained in the edible portions is slightly greater than in clams or oysters, and mussels, therefore, contain at least as much food, pound for pound, as is found in related shellfish in common use. Mussels may be cooked in the same ways as oysters and clams, and in other ways distinctly their own.

Wash, thoroughly scrub, removing carefully the beard, then drain, and steam 60 mussels until opened. Remove the mussels from their shells, and save the liquor separately, straining it through a fine cloth. Cook 3 medium-sized onions in 3 tablespoons of butter until just beginning to color, stirring almost constantly. Stir in the mussel liquor or broth, let simmer for 5 minutes, or until the onions are tender. Season to taste with salt, pepper, a dash of nutmeg, and as much of powdered thyme. Then stir in 6 cups of scalded milk and thin cream in equal parts. Bring to a boil. Add 1 cup each of cooked carrot cubes, cooked potato cubes, and cooked finely chopped celery stalks. Let boil once, remove from the fire, taste for seasoning, then add the reserved mussels. Turn the chowder into a heated soup tureen. Sprinkle with 1 cup of fine cracker crumbs, and serve immediately with toasted ship biscuits.

MUSSEL CHOWDER II [565]
Fisherman's manner

This chowder is a one-meal dish, very popular among the New England fishermen and often served for dinner.

Wash ½ peck of fresh mussels, scrub thoroughly, removing the beard carefully, rinse in plenty of cold water, and let stand for 30 minutes. Drain, place in a kettle, and steam until opened. Remove the mussels from the shells, reserving the liquor, which should be strained through a fine cloth and kept hot. Cut ⅓ pound of salt pork into small dices, and fry in a soup kettle until the cracklings are crisp; then add 3 medium-sized onions, thinly sliced, and cook until tender, but do not allow to brown. Sprinkle over 1 teaspoon of flour, and stir well until the flour is blended. Then pour over the cracklings the strained hot mussel liquor and the same amount of hot water.

Let come to a boil, then add 3 medium-sized potatoes, thinly sliced. Let boil slowly for 5 minutes, then season to taste with salt (remembering that mussels are a little salty), white pepper, a generous dash of nutmeg, and ¼ teaspoon of thyme leaves. Continue boiling gently until the potato slices are tender. Just before serving, stir in 1 pint of scalded milk, and serve with pilot crackers.

MUSSELS A LA MARINIERE [566]

It is a well-admitted fact that any kind of fish, crustacean, shellfish, and the like, when prepared with a certain amount of liquid, is professionally considered as soup in all the acceptation and meaning of the word. The fish or crustacean or shellfish, having left all its flavor and nourishing parts in the liquid, besides being more or less out of shape, becomes more or less unimportant as a fish; and furthermore the gastronomic value lies in the liquid much more than in the fish or pieces of fish proper.

Take 3 quarts of mussels, which should be and must be strictly fresh —that is, heavy and with the shells tightly closed, rejecting all those which are open as unfit to eat. Wash them thoroughly, scraping the shells with a knife and changing the water several times. Place them in a large saucepan, and add 1 generous cupful of dry white wine and 1 generous teaspoon each of finely chopped shallots and parsley. You may also add the same amount of finely chopped chives, if desired. Add salt and pepper to taste and a few grains of cayenne pepper. Cover tightly, and steam over a brisk flame until all the shells are open, care being taken that they are not overdone, lest they get tough. Now turn the whole into a colander placed over a large bowl to receive the liquid, which reserve preciously, and strain into a sieve. Remove half the shell of each mussel, leaving those with the fish in them. Arrange these in the dish in which they will be served, and keep hot. Now pour the liquid part into a saucepan, taking care not to mix the sediment which has deposited at the bottom. Reduce this liquid to 1 cup, and to this, add 2 tablespoons of good butter. Correct the seasoning, adding more salt and pepper if necessary, and pour over the mussels. Sprinkle minced parsley over the whole, and serve as hot as possible.

OATMEAL CHOWDER [567]

Quick-cooking oatmeal is not precooked. It is exactly the same as the regular, each single oat kernel is rolled in one large flake. In processing the quick-cooking kind, each grain is cut into pieces and rolled in thin flakes. The starch of these smaller flakes is more rapidly swollen and ruptured because the thinness permits quick penetration by steam. Both the regular and quick-cooking oatmeal are whole grain foods with only the chaffy husk removed. The bran of the oats is entirely retained. The oat kernels are steamed for a few minutes at atmospheric pressure to soften them before rolling. But this mild heat treatment does not constitute precooking, and it in no way alters the fine food value of the original grain.

It was forty centuries ago that oats stepped into the kitchen. Some time in the Bronze Age, 3500-1000 B.C., the oat plant was first developed as a domestic crop. In early America, oat for the table was imported from Scotland and was sold in drugstores as a remedial agent.

Melt ¼ cup of lard, add ½ cup of chopped onions, and cook until the onion just begins to turn yellow. Turn the mixture into a soup kettle. Add 1 quart of scalded milk, and season to taste with salt, pepper, and a generous dash of thyme leaves. Add 1 cup of cooked carrots and 1 cup of cooked potatoes, cut into fine dice, ⅛ teaspoon of soda, and 2 cups of canned tomatoes. Cook for 15 minutes, stirring frequently, then stir in 1½ cups of cooked oatmeal. Heat to the boiling point, and serve in hot soup plates, each sprinkled with finely chopped parsley. Serve with toast, toasted crackers, or oysterettes.

ONION CHOWDER [568]

I am small, but I am mighty; they speak of my virility and strength. I am known from ocean to ocean as the giver of health and happiness. I provide for earth its first beautiful mantle in the spring. I am hardy, yet mild. Women shun me, yet love me, while men glory in my friendship. I bless the sleepless eye with the kind caress of slumber, while often I am smothered with heat and flame. Some weep for me; all desire me, yet denounce me when among friends. I travel round the globe, yet often I am content to live my life in some lone sequestered spot. I was the sustaining power and inspiration to those who reared the pyramids. I helped the doughboys win the war, although they dried me and confined me in boxes. To be sure I'm the truest friend of the poor, yet I'm in the favor of mighty kings, emperors, and dictators. The fragrance of my spirit pervades alike the humble log cabin, the mansion, and the palace. I'm as old as the world's history, but my youth bursts forth each spring to a waiting and expectant multitude. I'm derided and made a jest, yet I'm loved by the universe. What am I? I'm an onion.

Never take liberties with an onion. It will get back at you. Peel them under running cold water, else, if you have tears to shed, prepare to shed them now. If you want to bring a chowder to a sharp point, to be sure, you'll concentrate on the onion.

Brown ¼ cup of diced raw bacon in a soup kettle; then add 2½ to 3 cups of coarsely chopped onions, and continue cooking until the onion is golden in hue. Add 2 cups of scalded sweet milk and 3 cups of potatoes, cubed small. Cook for 15 to 20 minutes. Combine 2 cups of scalded sweet milk and 1 cup of scalded heavy cream, and stir this mixture into that of the onions. Bring the whole to a boil, and allow it to simmer very gently, as gently as possible, for 5 to 8 minutes, stirring occasionally with a wooden spoon so as not to mash the potato cubes. Just before serving, stir in 1 tablespoon of flour which has been blended with 1 tablespoon of cold water. Bring the chowder to a boil, and let boil steadily, but not briskly, for 3 or 4 minutes. Season with salt and pepper to taste, a dash of cayenne pepper, and 1 teaspoon of Worcestershire sauce. Serve with toasted salted soda crackers.

For a richer soup, stir in, when adding the flour diluted with the water, 2 fresh egg yolks.

OYSTER CHOWDER [569]

Cook in its own fat ½ generous cup of diced salt pork until crisp, over a gentle flame, stirring occasionally. Stir in ¼ cup of chopped onions, and cook until the onions are slightly browned. Then stir in ½ generous cup of chopped celery stalks and 1 generous cup of small carrot cubes, and continue cooking for 2 or 3 minutes, stirring almost constantly. Transfer the mixture into a large soup kettle, and add 2 cups of boiling water. Cook for 20 minutes, or until the celery and carrots are tender. Pour in 1 quart of scalded milk, and bring to the boiling point. Do not season as yet. Now add 1 pint of oysters, which have been cooked in their own liquor until the edges curl. Season to taste with salt and pepper. Bring to the boiling point, and serve at once with pilot crackers.

If served in a soup tureen, place the pilot crackers in the bottom of the tureen, and pour the hot chowder over them, using a cracker for each serving.

OYSTER CHOWDER A LA MIRABEAU [570]

The oyster has been sung by J. Rouyer, called the poet-cook, who was chef of cuisine to the Marquis de Mirabeau, deputy under Louis XVI, famous for his answer to the king's order to evacuate the Chamber of Deputies. "Tell the king," said he to the Comte de Brézé, "that we are here by the will of the people, and that we will not leave our places except at the point of the bayonet."

It was the chef-poet Rouyer who created this oyster chowder, a culinary masterpiece, and a meal in itself, in honor of Mirabeau.

For 6 generous servings, heat ¼ cup of sweet butter. When the butter is foaming, remove the pan from the heat. Stir in 1 pint of well-drained freshly opened small oysters, reserving the liquor, and immediately skim off the oysters, and keep hot. Into the butter remaining in the pan, stir in 1 cup of peeled thinly sliced fresh mushroom caps, and cook for 2 minutes over a gentle flame, stirring constantly. Pour the butter and mushroom slices over the oysters, and keep hot.

Melt 2 tablespoons of butter, but do not allow it to sizzle, in a saucepan over a low flame; blend in 2 tablespoons of flour, and when bubbling, stir in 1 pint of rich scalded milk, stirring and beating well until the mixture just begins to boil. Let boil for 3 or 4 minutes, stirring frequently, then remove to hot water. Stir in 1 cup of ground fresh oysters, liquid and all. Add 1 bouquet garni, composed of 1 large bay leaf, tied with 1 sprig of thyme, 1 whole clove, and a 2-inch piece of scraped parsley root. Let simmer gently for 25 minutes, stirring occasionally, over hot water. Meanwhile, in a separate small saucepan, cook until tender, with just enough salted water to barely cover, ⅓ cup of finely chopped celery; ⅓ cup of thinly chopped green pepper; ¾ cup of tiny potato cubes; ½ cup of tiny carrot cubes; ¼ cup of chopped onion; and ⅓ cup of thinly sliced, rings separated, white part of small leeks. When the vegetables are tender, add liquid and all to the milk-oyster mixture.

Strain the oyster liquor through a fine cloth, and pour into a bowl. Add 3 fresh egg yolks, and beat well. When well blended, beat in 2 cups of thin cream, scalded, beating well and briskly to prevent curdling. Season to taste with salt and white pepper and a tiny dash of nutmeg. Heat well, but do not let boil.

Arrange the whole oysters and mushroom slices, well drained, in the bottom of a hot soup tureen. Pour over the hot chowder, sprinkle the top with finely chopped chervil, and serve at once with small finger lengths of buttered toast.

OYSTER GUMBO CHOWDER [571]
Creole

Clean, pick over, and parboil in their own liquor 1 pint of shucked or canned oysters until the edges curl. Drain, and add the oyster liquor to 1 quart of Fish Stock (No. 8). Cook 2 tablespoons of grated onion in 2 tablespoons of butter over a low flame, until it just takes on a light color, stirring occasionally. Then add to the stock, butter and all, together with 1 cup of cooked or canned drained okra and 2 cups of tomatoes, cooked or canned (in either case chopped and well drained). Season to taste with salt, pepper, and thyme leaves. Heat to the boiling point, remove from the fire, and stir in the oysters and 2 tablespoons of sweet butter. Serve with toasted crackers or buttered toast.

OYSTER STEW [572]
Belmont style—serves 6, allowing 6 oysters to a serving

Strain off the liquor of freshly opened 6 medium-sized oysters, reserving the liquor. Cook 3 sprigs of parsley, 3 small branches of celery leaves, and 3 thin slices of onion in 2 cups of hot water for 7 or 8 minutes in a large saucepan. Add 1 quart of rich creamy scalded milk, and allow to heat to the boiling point. Remove from the fire, strain into a heated soup tureen, and season to taste with salt and white pepper. Add 3 dozen oysters and the strained oyster liquor, and let stand a half minute. Put 1 tablespoon of butter in each of the six heated bowls, and serve the stew in the soup tureen. Let each guest dust his own serving with a little paprika to taste. Serve with a side dish of hot toasted oyster crackers.

Variation. You may add 2 teaspoons of curry powder to the hot milk before adding to the water and vegetable mixture, after diluting the curry powder in a little cold water.

PARSNIP CHOWDER [573]

All evidence seems to indicate that the cultivated parsnip was known to the ancient Greeks and Romans. The Romans were supposed to have served parsnips boiled with a sauce made with mead or honey wine; and the Emperor Tiberius liked parsnips so much that every year he had them brought from France, where the climate enabled them to be grown to perfection.

Cube small ⅛ pound of salt pork, and try out over a low flame until the cracklings are crisp and brown. Skim off the cracklings with a perforated spoon, and keep hot. To the fat remaining in the soup kettle, add ¼ cup of chopped onions, and cook until the onion just begins to take on color, stirring frequently. Then stir in 3 cups of parsnips, scraped, cut into small dices, discarding the core, which is usually coarse and tough, and 1 cup of small raw potato cubes. Cook 3 or 4 minutes, then pour over enough hot water to barely cover. Add 1 bouquet garni, composed of 1 large bay leaf, tied with 6 or 7 sprigs of fresh parsley, 2 sprigs of green celery leaves (tops), and 1 sprig of thyme; 6 or 7 freshly crushed whole peppercorns; and salt to taste. Cook for 25 to 30 minutes over a gentle flame, stirring occasionally with a wooden spoon. Then stir in 1 quart of rich creamy milk, scalded and mixed with ½ cup of rolled cracker crumbs. Bring to a boil, and let boil for 1 minute. Serve very hot in heated soup plates, each dusted with minced parsley, chives, or chervil.

PERCH CHOWDER   [574]
American camper's manner—a full meal

> *"Perch, like the Tartar clans, in troops remove,*
> *And, urged by famine or by pleasure, rove;*
> *But, if one prisoner, as in war, you seize,*
> *You'll prosper, master of the camp with ease;*
> *For, like the wicked, unalarmed they view*
> *Their fellows perish, and their path pursue."*
>   THOREAU

The perches are among the most singular and interesting of our fresh-water fish, all being of small size and most of them of very brilliant coloration. The two most important species are the yellow and the white perch. The yellow is probably our very best pan and chowder fish.

Melt ¼ cup of bacon drippings or lard in a soup kettle, and add the following vegetables in layers: 2 cups of sliced raw potatoes, well packed; 1 cup of thinly sliced carrots; 1 cup of peas, canned and drained; and 1 cup of cleaned string beans. On top place 2½ pounds of cleaned perch, cut into serving pieces, counting the weight after removing the heads and tails. Pour over enough cold water to cover the vegetables, but leave the fish pieces dry. Add 1 large bay leaf tied with 7 or 8 sprigs of fresh parsley and a generous sprig of thyme, 6 or 7 whole peppercorns, freshly crushed, and 2 teaspoons of salt. Cover the kettle. Slowly, very slowly, bring to a boil. Reduce the flame, and continue simmering until the vegetables are pierceable and the fish is steamed tender. Remove from the fire, and stir in 3 cups of scalded rich milk, or 1 can of undiluted evaporated milk and 1½ cups of boiling water, to which has been added 1½ to 2 tablespoons of flour, previously diluted in a little cold milk. Cover, and return to a very low flame for about 5 minutes, or until the mixture is thickened. At serving time, remove the skin and bones from the fish (which should be on top of the chowder). Flake the fish. Heat to the boiling point, taste for seasoning, and serve at once in heated soup plates or bowls with toasted pilot crackers.

PIKE AND ALMOND CHOWDER [575]
Formula of the royal house of Louis XVIII

Like the coat of arms of the city of Boston, the coat of arms of the city of Kaiserslautern, Germany, was adopted from a fish story of a pike who lived 267 years!!! in the fish pond of Emperor Frederick II (1230-1497).

Called a "standard" fresh-water fish, because it may be found in the market most of the year, is the yellow pike. In texture, it is somewhat like haddock, and all sorts of things may be done to it, such as the delicious pike chowder which used to tickle the palate of Louis XVIII.

Stem, wash in several changes of cold water, the last being lukewarm, and sponge in a dry kitchen towel, the following ingredients, then put through a food chopper, or chop fine, collecting carefully the juices: ½ pound of fresh spinach; 3 large lettuce hearts, free from green parts; the white part of 1 medium-sized leek; 2 medium-sized onions; 1 clove of garlic; ⅓ cup of sorrel leaves; ¼ cup of orach or mountain spinach, if available; ½ cup of stemmed young beet leaves; 2 tablespoons each of chervil and parsley; 12 small fresh leaves of purslane; and 12 marigold petals, carefully freed from ovaries and calyxes, which may give a bitter taste to the stock.

Heat ⅓ cup of butter in a large soup kettle, add the chopped vegetable mixture and juices, and wilt—no more—over a gentle flame. Do not let cook, but wilt them, stirring constantly. Pour over 2 quarts of fish stock, made from cheap white-flesh fresh-water fish and equal parts of dry white wine. Add 1 bouquet garni, composed of 1 large or 2 medium-sized bay leaves, 1 sprig of thyme, and 2 whole cloves, heads removed, tied with kitchen thread, 8 whole peppercorns, gently bruised, and 2 teaspoons of salt. Bring to a boil, lower the flame, and let simmer gently for 30 minutes over a low flame, the kettle partially covered.

Strain through a fine-meshed wire or hair sieve into a clean soup kettle. Bring quickly to a boil. Add 3 pounds of cleaned washed pike, cut into small pieces. Boil very gently, let simmer, let smile, for about 20 minutes, or until the fish pieces just begin to flake or separate from the bone. Skim off the fish pieces with a perforated ladle, and let the court bouillon reduce to about 3 cups over a bright flame. Meanwhile, when the fish pieces are cold enough to handle, carefully remove all skin and bones from them, then flake the flesh. Keep hot.

You'll have cooked separately, in enough salted boiling water to barely cover, the following vegetables: ½ cup of tiny raw carrot cubes, ½ cup of tiny raw white turnip cubes, ½ cup of tiny raw celery hearts, ½ cup of tiny raw artichoke bottom cubes, ¼ cup of tiny raw parsnip cubes, and 1 cup of tiny raw potato cubes. When the vegetables are tender, add liquid and all to the reduced court bouillon, and bring to a boil. Remove from the fire, and stir in the following almond milk:

Almond Milk. Blanch ½ pound of sweet almonds and 3 or 4 bitter almonds, skin them, and put through a food chopper several times, using the finest blade. Add the resulting product to 1½ cups of scalded sweet cream, and let draw for about 15 minutes. Then boil once, and strain through a fine cloth, squeezing both ends, over a clean saucepan. Bring to a boil, and remove from the fire. Beat in, one at a time, 3 fresh egg yolks, beating well after each addition. Stir into the fish stock alternately with ½ generous cup of blanched, shredded, toasted almonds. Taste for seasoning, stir in the flaked fish, and serve immediately in heated soup plates, each sprinkled with a dash of paprika and a little finely chopped chervil or parsley.

PORK SAUSAGE CHOWDER [576]
Gypsy manner

Although Germany has long been considered the home of the sausage, Italy gave it to the world, getting it from the ancient Romans. As early as 100 B.C., according to some archeologists, Rome had many public buffet counters somewhat like the modern frankfurter stands, with a large board displayed over the counter, saying: "Any Roman sellers or peddlers selling adulterated sausage with wheat will be sentenced to hard labor in the mines for life."

Separately cook 2½ cups of tiny raw potato cubes, ½ cup of tiny raw green pepper cubes, ½ cup of tiny raw carrot cubes, ½ cup of tiny raw celery stalk cubes, and ¼ cup of chopped onions in a small amount of salted boiling water until the vegetables are tender, but not mushy, and combine the stock and vegetables in a soup kettle. Shape ½ pound of pork sausage meat into tiny balls, not larger than an ordinary marble, and cook these balls in their own fat over a very

low flame until well browned on all sides, shaking the pan from time
to time. Pour off all the fat from the pan, and add the sausage balls
to the vegetables in the soup kettle. Take 2 tablespoons of the hot
fat, heat well, then blend in 2 tablespoons of flour, but do not let
brown. When the mixture just begins to bubble, stir in 1 quart of
milk, scalded with 1 large bay leaf, 1 sprig of thyme, and 2 cloves, then
strained, and cook gently, stirring constantly. Let this boil once or
twice, then strain through a fine sieve over the vegetables and sausage
balls in the kettle. Season to taste with salt, pepper, and a little nutmeg. Bring to a boil, and pour into a heated soup kettle containing 2
or 3 beaten fresh egg yolks. Mix well and serve at once.

POTATO AND CORN CHOWDER   [577]
Maine manner

> *"Leek to the Welsh, to Dutchmen butter's dear,*
> *Of Irish swains potato is the cheer. . . ."*

This verse by John Gay voices a popular conception. It's surprising,
therefore, to learn that so-called Irish potatoes did not come originally
from Europe or the British Isles, but are native to South America,
where they have been cultivated since at least the time of the Incas.
Here the early explorers found potatoes in cultivation, and one of
them wrote: ". . . the skinne . . . is of earthy colour, but the inner
meate thereof is very white; these are nourished in gardens . . . they
are also eaten rawe and have the taste of rawe chestnuts but are somewhat sweeter. . . ."

In his *Herbal*, published in 1597, Gerarde gives some directions for
the use of potatoes, saying: ". . . that they may be rosted in the
ashes, when they be so rosted, infuse them and sop them in wine, and
others, to give them the greater grace in eating, do boile them with
prunes, and so eate them; and likewise, others dress them, being first
rosted with oile, vinegar, and salt, every man according to his owne
taste and leaking; notwithstanding, however they be dressed, they
comfort, nourish, and strengthen the bodie. . . ."

The white potato, frequently shunned by persons trying to lose
weight, is no more fattening than a large apple or a large orange, and
provides the diet with valuable vitamins and minerals at low cost, says
the U.S. Department of Agriculture, Washington, D.C.

Cut 2 slices of salt pork in small pieces and fry in its own fat until
crisp. Remove the cracklings, and keep hot. Add 1 medium-sized
onion to the fat remaining in the pan, and cook very slowly for five

minutes. Do not allow to brown. Parboil 2 generous cups of potatoes, diced small, for 5 minutes in enough salt water to cover. Then add the potato cubes and whatever there is of potato stock to the onion, adding enough hot water to make 2 cups of liquid. Add 1 large bay leaf tied with 6 sprigs of parsley and 1 sprig of thyme, and cook until the potatoes are tender. Then add 1 cup of canned corn alternately with 1 quart of scalded rich milk. Season to taste with salt and pepper. Stir in 3 tablespoons of butter. Discard the bouquet of bay leaf, parsley, and thyme, pour over 6 soda crackers placed in a soup tureen, and sprinkle the top with the pork cracklings.

POTATO AND STRING BEAN CHOWDER　　[578]
New Jersey manner

Put through a food chopper, using a coarse blade, 2 strips of fat bacon or salt pork, and try out in a soup kettle. Stir in ¼ cup of finely chopped onion, and cook until just beginning to take on color, stirring almost constantly. Then add ½ generous pound of cleaned string beans, broken into small pieces, and cook for 3 or 4 minutes. Pour over 1 cup of boiling water, and cook for 15 minutes. Then add 1 bay leaf, 1 sprig of thyme, and 6 or 7 sprigs of parsley, tied together with kitchen thread, and 2 cups of tiny raw potato cubes. Pour in 1 quart of scalded milk. Season to taste with salt and pepper. Cover, and let simmer gently for 25 minutes. Remove from the fire, discard the bay leaf bouquet, taste for seasoning, and stir in ¾ cup of scalded thin cream. Pour into hot soup plates or bowls, each containing 4 slices of hard-cooked eggs, dust with parsley and a dash of paprika, and serve at once.

SALMON CHOWDER　　[579]
North Pacific manner

From California to Alaska, under the tossing waves of the North Pacific, beneath the blue waters of Puget Sound, and the rolling, swirling surface of the coastal rivers, the miracle of the fall migration of salmon and trout is repeated. As if on orders from some high command, one school after another moves from the sea. First come those who must fight their way the full tortuous length of the great rivers —Klamath, Rogue, Columbia, Campbell, Fraser, Yukon. Then others cross river bars, following currents through the sound and through the straits, to seek out their appointed spawning grounds—bubbling stretches of shallow water, gravel bottomed and lightly silted. There are millions on the move—returning after three, four, five, even eight years in the ocean to the fresh swift waters of their birthplace—steadily swimming toward spawning grounds not yet made ready for them. Rains must come to cool the waters, and make murky shallow streams. Creeks must rise, for many future spawning beds are now dry gravel. Small coastal streams must flood to wash away the sand bars blocking their mouths, admitting those who by appointment to nature's command wait outside. But the recurrent miracle has begun to unfold, and geared to strange instinct, to rain and water, it will continue until the silver-sided millions rediscover their first homes, spawn and die.

Cook without browning 1 large onion, thinly sliced, the slices cut in two crosswise, and each ring separated, in ¼ cup of good olive oil, stirring frequently. Then add 1 large can of tomatoes, 1 small can of tomato paste, and 1 bouquet garni, composed of 1 large bay leaf, 8 sprigs of parsley, 1 sprig of thyme, 3 sprigs of green celery leaves (tops), and 2 whole cloves, all tied with kitchen thread. Do not season as yet. Cook gently, covered, for about 15 minutes, stirring frequently from the bottom of the kettle. Pour in enough boiling water to generously cover, add 1¾ cups of tiny raw potato cubes and ¼ cup of chopped green pepper, and cover. Cook for 15 to 20 minutes longer, or until the potato cubes are almost tender, stirring occasionally. Meanwhile, scald 1 quart of rich milk with 1 small clove of garlic, peeled and left whole. Add to the chowder 2 pounds of fresh salmon cut into 1½-inch squares, and continue simmering for about 15 minutes, or until the fish flakes. Remove from the fire, discard the bouquet garni, and when ready to serve, season to taste with salt, pepper, and a tiny pinch of cayenne pepper. Pour the chowder into a heated soup tureen, containing ¼ cup of good sherry wine, alternately with the scalded milk, from which the garlic has been removed and discarded. Dust the top of the chowder with finely chopped parsley, and serve immediately.

SCALLOP CHOWDER   [580]
Dieppoise manner

What does a scallop look like when it comes from its habitat? A pair of shells, resembling in general that of the cherrystone clam, except that they are fluted more artistically and are of fine coloring and richer markings. About two and a half inches in width or perhaps three is the maximum for an adult bay scallop. The deep-sea scallop prevails in water from five to one hundred feet in depth, the shells being smoother and frequently eight inches in diameter, not fluted or scalloped, rather plain.

What part of the scallop goes to market? Only the great muscle, otherwise the eye, or better, the heart of the bivalve, is kept for the table. The rest of the soft part, which in an oyster would be the belly, is considered nonedible and is discarded. Therefore, what the cook buys is only the muscle of the eye, which the uninformed often mistake for the whole animal. Just the tidbit of the whole shellfish reaches the kitchen.

Heat 3 tablespoons of butter, and blend in 2 tablespoons of flour, stirring almost constantly over a gentle flame. When the mixture just begins to bubble, stir in 1 quart of rich milk, scalded with 1 large bay leaf, 1 sprig of thyme, and 2 leaflets of fresh tarragon herb, then drained. Stir constantly until the mixture starts to boil. Let boil gently for 14 minutes while cooking 3 large onions in salted boiling water until tender. Drain and rub the onions through a fine-meshed wire sieve, and add to the milk mixture, mixing well. Bring to a boil, stir in ¾ pound of sea scallops, which have been washed quickly, drained, then quartered. Lower the flame, and let simmer gently for 15 minutes longer, then add ½ cup each of boiled rice, cooked or canned peas, well drained, small cubes of cooked potatoes, and finely chopped and well-drained red pimiento. Salt to taste, add a generous turn of the pepper mill, and a fresh grating of nutmeg. Keep hot.

Scald 1 cup of rich milk, gradually beat in 3 fresh egg yolks, beating well to prevent curdling, and gradually stir into the chowder. When ready to serve, stir in 3 tablespoons of good sherry wine and 1 tablespoon of butter kneaded with 1 scant tablespoon of finely chopped chervil and 5 or 6 drops of lemon juice. **Serve at once.**

SHRIMP CHOWDER [581]
Southern manner

Whiskered shrimps resemble small editions of lobsters, but are easier to handle—no waving claws to nip at the fingers, no cold and beady eye to bother the conscience as the cook drops them into the boiling cauldron; but there is an art to practice in cooking fresh shrimps, as there is with lobsters or crawfish.

To bring out the best flavor, shrimps are best boiled in sea water. If this is impossible, use strongly salted water, adding thyme, bay leaf, parsley, and the green tops of celery. Then bring the water to a boil quickly, and drop in the live shrimps. Cook for 8 to 12 minutes, according to size. Cool, but do not hurry the cooling by a cold water bath, as by doing so, you throw away the flavor. Peel, and remove the intestinal black vein. They are ready for hundreds of preparations.

Three kinds of shrimps come to market, but only one in quantity, the common shrimp. There is also the grooved shrimp and the sea bob shrimp.

Place 1 pound of fresh shrimps in a colander, and let the cold water run over them, shaking the colander well. Drain well, and place in a saucepan. Add 2 cups of cold water; 2 teaspoons of salt; 1 bouquet garni, composed of 1 large bay leaf, 1 sprig of thyme, 8 sprigs of parsley, 2 sprigs of green celery leaves (tops), and 2 whole cloves, tied together with kitchen thread; ½ medium-sized onion, thinly sliced; and 6 unbruised peppercorns. Cover, bring to a boil, and let boil for 3 or 4 minutes. Then add the shrimps, and let simmer for 8 to 12 minutes, according to size. Allow the shrimps to cool in their own liquor, then shell, being careful to remove the black vein. Meanwhile, cook until tender, 1 cup of tiny raw potato cubes in enough salt water to cover, together with 1 cup of freshly shelled peas, preferably the small kind, and ½ cup each of finely chopped celery stalk and carrots, cubed small, about 15 minutes.

If the shrimps are large, cut them in two, if small, leave them whole. Add them to the cooked vegetables, the vegetable stock included. Keep hot. Blend 3 tablespoons of butter and 3 tablespoons of flour over a gentle flame. When the mixture just begins to bubble, stir in the heated strained shrimp stock, stirring constantly until the mixture begins to boil. Let boil for 3 or 4 minutes, then add the vegetable-shrimp mixture, and blend thoroughly. Scald 1¾ cups of rich milk, thin cream, or undiluted evaporated milk, then stir it into 2 well-beaten egg yolks, and gradually stir this into the chowder. Taste for seasoning, heat well, but do not allow to boil, and serve piping hot, dusted with finely chopped parsley.

SHRIMP AND CRAB MEAT CHOWDER [582]
Moscovite manner

Flake a large can of crab meat or its equivalent of freshly cooked crab meat, removing all cartilage carefully. Mash 3 hard-cooked eggs, or rub through a fine-meshed sieve, and work to a paste 1½ tablespoons of sweet butter and 1 tablespoon of caviar, the grated peel of half a small lemon, and 1 tablespoon of flour, seasoning as you go along with a dash of cayenne, a few grains of white pepper, and ⅛ teaspoon of salt (more or less, according to the saltiness of the caviar).

Have ready 5 cups of milk, scalded with 1 large bay leaf and a few thyme flowers, then strained. Pour the strained milk gradually and slowly, while stirring constantly, over the paste, stirring until smooth over a gentle flame. When the mixture just begins to bubble, add the flaked crab meat and an equal amount of freshly cooked fresh shrimps, cooked as indicated for Shrimp Chowder (No. 581) above. Let simmer for 19 long minutes, remove from the fire, then stir in 1 cup of thin cream, scalded, into which has been beaten 2 fresh egg yolks, stirring briskly, alternately with 4 tablespoons of cold boiled rice and ⅓ cup each of tiny cooked carrot dices and tiny cooked green pepper cubes. Taste for seasoning, and when ready to serve, stir in 2 tablespoons of sherry wine, and serve with blinis.

Blinis (Russian Small Pancakes). Dissolve 1 yeast cake in a little luke-warm milk; stir into 1 cup of warm milk enough sifted flour to make a running pancake batter. Stir in the yeast mixture, and let rise for 2 hours in a warm place, covered with a light clean cloth. Then stir in 2 or 3 egg yolks, one at a time, beating well after each addition, and seasoning, while beating, with a few grains of salt to taste. The batter should be smooth and of a consistency to spread when poured, adding more flour if needed. Lastly, fold in 1 stiffly beaten egg white mixed with ¼ cup of heavy cream, whipped stiff. Cook as you would ordinary pancakes, but have them as small as possible, and as soon as browned on both sides, roll in cigarette fashion.

Just before serving comes the spirit of this delicious chowder, the fragrant saffron. You may rub it to powder, pound it in a mortar, or roast it light till it crumbles, but the last method involves the risk of scorching. Stir it in the chowder, a tiny pinch at a time, till you begin to suspect that you can taste it. Let it not go beyond that suspicion, for the perfect effect is one of delicate aroma, to charm and puzzle the dinner guest.

SHRIMP AND TOMATO CHOWDER [583]
Formula of the Hôtel des Roches Noires, Trouville

Cook 1 pound of large fresh shrimps as for Shrimp Chowder (No. 581), adding 4 thin slices of seeded lemon. When done, let the shrimps cool in their own stock, then shell them, remove the black vein, and cut them in half crosswise. Keep hot in a little hot bouillon.

Meanwhile, in another clean saucepan, containing ¼ cup of sweet butter, cook 6 large tomatoes, peeled, gently pressed from their juice and seeds, then cut into small pieces; 2 large onions, peeled, and cut into thin slices, the rings separated; 1 small clove of garlic, peeled, then mashed; and 1 bouquet garni, composed of 1 large bay leaf, 7 or 8 sprigs of fresh parsley, 1 sprig of thyme, 2 sprigs of green celery leaves (tops), 1 small sprig of fennel, and 2 whole cloves, tied together with kitchen thread. Cook until the mixture is tender, over a low flame, covered, stirring occasionally.

When the tomato-onion mixture is done, discard the bouquet garni, and rub the mixture through a fine-meshed wire sieve into a clean saucepan. Season to taste with salt and cayenne pepper. Place over a medium flame, and cook, stirring almost constantly, until the mixture thickens and a good part of the moisture has evaporated. Do not add any sugar, as is done for tomato soup, because the onions partly remove the acid taste of the tomatoes. Now gradually and gently stir in 3 cups of rich chicken stock, fresh or canned, mixed with 3 cups of the strained shrimp broth, which have been heated together to the boiling point. If you have some *glace de viande*, or meat extract, 1 tablespoon of it stirred into the mixture will not be amiss.

Bring the chowder to a brisk boil, let boil 3 or 4 times, then stir in the cut cooked shrimps. Boil once more, and remove from the fire. Then add 3 tablespoons each of cooked or canned tiny French peas, boiled rice (well in grains), mushroom buttons, halved, cooked in a little butter, and well drained, and canned artichoke bottoms, cubed small, 2 tablespoons of hard-cooked egg whites, chopped, and 2 tablespoons of canned red pimientos, gently squeezed through a cloth to remove excess moisture, and finely chopped. Taste for seasoning, and when ready to serve, pour into a heated soup tureen, containing 1 tablespoon of blanched, shredded, then pounded hazelnuts, creamed with 1 tablespoon of sweet butter. Stir well, dust with finely chopped chives and chervil in equal parts, and serve as hot as possible.

SMELT CHOWDER [584]
Great Lakes manner

Soak 3 pounds of fresh or frozen smelts overnight in salted water to cover. Rinse. This is done to remove the "fresh cucumber" odor. Clean, rinse again, place in a soup kettle, and pour over 1 cup of hot water. Place the kettle in the oven (350° F.) until the smelts are almost tender. Cool slightly, and split the fish in two, removing the backbone and little bones on the edges of each filet. Peel and slice 5 medium-sized potatoes, and place in a soup kettle. Add 6 cups of cold water (not hot). Add 1 cup of chopped onion; 1 bouquet garni, composed of 1 large bay leaf, 2 sprigs of fresh thyme, 2 sprigs of green celery leaves (tops), and 1 whole clove, all tied together with kitchen thread; 1 small clove of garlic, mashed to a pulp; 1½ teaspoons of salt; and 8 peppercorns, crushed. Bring to a boil.

Add 3 tablespoons of butter kneaded with 1½ tablespoons of flour, bit by bit, and 1 cup of scalded heavy cream. Boil once more, taste for seasoning, and remove from the fire. Add the flaked smelts, discard the bouquet garni, and serve at once in heated soup plates or bowls, each containing 1 teaspoon of finely chopped parsley.

SNAPPER CHOWDER [585]
Pensacola manner

Of all the snappers, the red snapper is by far the most important and best known. It reaches a length of two to three feet and a weight of ten to thirty-five pounds. It is known everywhere as the red snapper. To the Spaniards, it is the *pargo colorado*, while in the Havana market it is the *pargo guachinango*, or Mexican snapper because it is brought to that city from the Mexican coast. When the red snappers are spawning, they often are so abundant around a fishing smack as to color the water. The intensity of color of the red snapper varies much with the locality. Specimens from Puerto Rico have a paler general color and the black lateral blotch more persistent.

The red snapper is very much liked in Florida, where they make this delicious chowder.

Cut off the head of a red snapper weighing about 4 pounds. Split the fish in two lengthwise, and remove the dorsal bone. Place the head and bone in a soup kettle with about ¾ to 1 pound of cheap fish (any kind). Cover with 2 cups of cold water and 2 cups of dry white wine. Then add 1 large bouquet garni, composed of 2 bay leaves, 2 sprigs of green celery leaves (tops), 10 sprigs of parsley, 1 sprig of thyme, and 3 whole cloves, all tied with kitchen thread. Add 1 medium-sized carrot, scraped, then sliced thin; 1 small clove of garlic, mashed; 1 small leek, cut into quarters lengthwise, carefully washed, then folded, and tied with kitchen thread; and 2 or 3 thin slices of lemon, seeded. Gradually bring this to a boil. Season with salt and pepper to taste, and allow to simmer gently for 30 minutes. Strain through a fine sieve, and keep this fish stock hot.

Cut the prepared red snapper into small pieces. Rub each piece with a little mixed salt and pepper, then add the pieces to the fish stock, which has been brought to a boil. Let simmer very gently for 20 minutes. Then add 2 cups of tiny raw potato cubes, 1 cup of tiny raw carrot cubes, ½ cup of tiny raw turnip cubes, and ½ cup of coarsely chopped onions. Continue cooking gently for 20 minutes longer, or till the vegetable cubes are done.

Cream 3 tablespoons of butter with 2 tablespoons of flour, and add bit by bit to the chowder. Cook for 5 minutes longer, and taste for seasoning. When ready to serve in hot soup bowls, stir in 1½ cups of thin cream, scalded and mixed with 3 beaten egg yolks. Heat well, but do not allow to boil, and serve with Melba Toast (No. 791).

STURGEON CHOWDER [586]
Northwestern Canadian manner

An almanac of 1760 mentions that the Delaware River abounded with sturgeon, and the colonial fathers ate plenty of caviar and sturgeon. Then all of a sudden this delicate fish disappeared. Today we rely on Canada, which ships annually around 30,000 pounds —much of it is smoked and sold for the delicatessen market. It is richer than salmon. However, those who can find some fresh sturgeon, properly cooked, enjoy a prime delicacy. At its best, sturgeon meat, a bit firmer than halibut and of a better flavor than swordfish, is popular along the Atlantic seaboard, and is a supreme delicacy. With the end part, the Northwestern Canadians make a fine chowder.

Wipe with a damp cloth a 3-pound piece of sturgeon taken from the side tail. Pour over 3 cups of fish stock, made with 1 pound of cheap fish in the usual way, and 3 cups of dry white wine. Add 1 small carrot, thinly sliced; the white part of a small leek, thinly sliced; 2 small hearts of lettuce, thinly sliced; 1 large bay leaf; an inch piece of parsley root, scraped and thinly sliced; 1 sprig of thyme; 2 whole cloves; 1 good-sized blade of garlic; and 6 thin slices of onions. Season to taste with salt and black pepper, freshly ground, and slowly bring to a boil. Let boil for 1 or 2 minutes, lower the flame, and allow to simmer gently for 30 minutes. Remove the fish from the court bouillon, and strain the stock. When the fish is cold enough to handle, remove all bones, returning the fish to the stock as you go along. Then add ½ cup of boiled rice, ½ cup of canned or freshly cooked peas, and ½ cup of cooked celery root, diced small. Simmer the mixture while preparing herring soft roes as follows:

Wash quickly 6 herring soft roes, place in a shallow pan, cover with milk, and blanch for 5 minutes, counting the time when the milk boils. Drain, discarding the milk. Arrange the soft roes in 4 tablespoons of hot butter, and cook for 5 minutes on both sides. Take a ladleful of the liquid from the chowder, pour it over the roes, and let them simmer gently for 5 to 8 minutes, the time depending on the size of the roes. Pour the roes and liquid into a heated soup tureen, and keep hot.

Beat 3 fresh egg yolks with 1 tablespoon of parsley and 2 table-spoons of Madeira wine until thoroughly blended; then pour over, gradually and slowly, beating briskly all the while, 2 cups of scalded thin cream or evaporated milk. Beat this into the chowder off the fire. Taste for seasoning, and pour over the roes in the soup tureen. Serve with cheese croutons.

Cheese Croutons. Cover 3 slices of bread with thin slices of American or Swiss cheese. Toast under a low flame in the broiling oven until the cheese is entirely melted. Quickly sprinkle with paprika, then more rapidly cut each slice into 9 squares with a sharp knife dipped in hot water.

TOMATO CHOWDER [587]
Beauvilliers manner

Cut enough salt pork as finely as possible to make 5 tablespoons of it. Place it in a soup kettle with 1 clove of garlic, minced very fine, and fry until crisp. Then add 3 medium-sized onions, sliced very thin, and 1 whole green pepper, removing the white ribs and seeds, and cutting it julienne fashion. Cook for 4 to 5 minutes, stirring almost constantly with a wooden spoon. Now add 1 cup of small cubes of raw potatoes, 1 cup of thinly sliced leeks, using white and green parts, and enough cold water to cover generously. Bring to a boil. Add 1 large bay leaf, tied with 6 or 7 sprigs of parsley, 1 sprig of thyme, and 2 whole cloves with heads removed. Lower the flame, and allow to simmer gently until the potatoes are done, but a little on the firm side. Moisten ¼ teaspoon of baking soda with a few drops of cold water. Add to the soup with 3½ to 3¾ cups of fresh raw tomatoes, peeled, seeded, and cut into small pieces, and salt, pepper, and a touch of cayenne. Continue simmering for about 20 minutes longer. At this point, the water should be almost evaporated. Pour in, stirring constantly, 2½ cups of scalded milk and 2½ cups of scalded thin cream (undiluted evaporated milk may be used, if desired). Bring to a boil, set the soup kettle aside, and skim off all the fat possible. Thicken the soup with 2 tablespoons of butter and 1 tablespoon of finely chopped parsley or chervil. Return to the fire, boil up once or twice, and taste for seasoning. Serve in hot soup plates, each containing 5 or 6 thin slices of frankfurters, skinned. Serve with American soda biscuits, toasted after being soaked in milk.

TURKEY CHOWDER   [588]

It isn't just the leftovers of a previous meal that go into a second, even a third day, dish. Imagination is one of the chief ingredients, and imagination is not mentioned in the cook books, to captivate discriminating tastes. For instance, don't throw out the turkey carcass, the scraps of skin or dibdabs of dressing, until you've first extracted their goodness for the soup kettle.

By the way, do you know how our holiday bird was named? One explanation (there are several) is that Luis de Torres, a member of Columbus's crew, named the bird *Tukki*, Hebrew for peacock. Through usage, *Tukki* became turkey.

Let simmer, covered, all the bones and skin of roast turkey in 2 quarts of cold water, with 1 large bay leaf, tied with 7 or 8 sprigs of fresh parsley, 1 sprig of thyme, and 2 whole cloves, for 1½ hours. Strain through a fine sieve into a clean kettle. Let cool, and when cold, skim off the cake of fat from the top. Return the turkey stock to the fire. Add 1 cup of tiny raw potato cubes, ½ cup of tiny raw carrot cubes, ¼ cup of finely chopped green pepper, free from seeds and white ribs, ⅓ cup of coarsely chopped onion, 1 whole clove of garlic, left whole, and 2 sprigs of marjoram. Cook until the vegetables are tender, and season to taste with salt and black pepper. Stir in 2 cups of scalded milk mixed with 2 beaten egg yolks. Taste for seasoning, and just before serving, stir in 1½ tablespoons of sweet butter. Serve very hot with toasted buttered crackers.

You may stir in, just before serving, 2 or 3 tablespoons of sherry wine, about ½ to ¾ cup of chopped cooked turkey, and 2 hard-cooked eggs, chopped.

TURTLE CHOWDER   [589]
Philadelphia manner

The turtle, like the oyster, stands in a class of its own. It has a specialized public, and most people believe a specialized season, beginning with Christmas and extending through winter. But turtle soup cannot be relegated to a seasonal category. The initiated know it's a soup epicurean for a midsummer dinner. It's not heavy, it's not heating, a rare stimulant and nutritious. Turned into a chowder, it's almost a complete delicious meal, especially if flavored with sherry wine, which releases some subtle essences in the flesh of the turtle that, uniting with the wine, miraculously blend with it into the savor of things Parnassian, that primal and refreshing snack of the

Castalian spring that recaptures for the aging epicurean youth's keenness of appetite.

For a delectable soup, use the turtle flippers, which also make a delicious stew.

Cut into small pieces 4½ pounds of turtle flippers, with the bone in, to lend its extra goodness to the chowder. Rinse in cold water, then in lukewarm water. Place the drained pieces in a soup kettle, containing 3½ quarts of lukewarm water. Add a bouquet garni, composed of 2 large bay leaves, 1 sprig of thyme, 10 sprigs of fresh parsley, 2 sprigs or leaflets of sage, 2 sprigs or leaflets of rosemary, and 2 sprigs or leaflets of savory, all tied together with kitchen thread. (Should you not be able to get the fresh herbs, use the dried ones tied into a small muslin bag.) Season lightly with salt, and add 1 dozen bruised peppercorns. Slowly bring to a boil, and let boil steadily, but gently, for 5 minutes, skimming off the scum. When no more scum appears on the surface, add 2 small carrots, scraped and quartered; 1 large onion, coarsely chopped; 2 celery stalks, scraped, then coarsely chopped; 2 small leeks, halved, the green parts folded with the white parts and tied together; 1 small white turnip, quartered; and ½ cup of fresh mushrooms, peeled, then coarsely chopped. Cover, and let simmer gently for 3 hours. Empty the whole kettle into a colander, then strain the stock through a fine cloth, and let it cool overnight. Fish out from the colander the pieces of turtle flippers. When cold enough to handle, pick all the meat from the bones. Keep in the refrigerator overnight.

Next day, skim off all the fat from the stock, which will be in a form of a cake. Reserve it for other use. Divide the stock in two, using one part for the chowder, the other part for hot or jellied turtle bouillon some other day.

Put the unreserved part into a clean saucepan over a bright flame, and let it reduce to half its volume, or about 3½ cups. Add 1 cup of the chopped turtle meat; 1 cup of dry white wine; ⅓ cup each of boiled rice, cooked tiny cubes of raw carrots, and tiny cubes of cooked (a little on the firm side) tiny potato cubes; 1 tablespoon of cooked minute tapioca; and 2 tablespoons of hard-cooked chopped egg whites. Bring to a boil, let simmer for 5 long minutes, and taste for seasoning. Just before serving, stir in 1 cup of scalded heavy cream, mixed with 3 beaten fresh egg yolks, the egg yolks beaten with 3 tablespoons of dry sherry wine. Then pour into a heated soup tureen, containing a half shad roe, parboiled, then drained. Dust the top with a little finely chopped parsley, and serve at once with a side dish of Boston brown bread and almond-butter finger sandwiches, the almond butter made as follows:

Special Almond Butter. Blanch 1 dozen almonds, drain, then pound into a mortar, or put several times through a food chopper, using a fine blade. Add while pounding or grinding a few drops of cold water to prevent the almonds from turning oily. Then cream the almond paste with 2 tablespoons of sweet butter and 1 teaspoon of finely chopped chervil. When thoroughly blended, rub the mixture through a fine sieve, and chill well before using.

Chapter Nine

MISCELLANEOUS SOUPS

"Soup is cuisine's kindest course. It breathes reassurance; it steams consolation; after a weary day, it promotes dinner sociability as successfully as the five o'clock cup of tea."

BRILLAT-SAVARIN

Have you ever thought about the opportunity we have here in the United States to learn about all the hundreds of delectable soups from the different countries in the world? Consider for instance the vast amount of intermarriage which has gone on for at least 150 years in America until, as a consequence, an American family of today might reasonably have on one day French onion soup, the next bortsch from Poland and Russia, or Indian mulligatawny. And, again Mexican chick pea soup, English mutton broth, Italian minestrone, or our own Philadelphia pepper pot. And let us not forget for a Friday night's treat a steaming bowl of New England clam chowder.

This adaptation, then, of unfamiliar and strange soups invading the American home, and widely adopted, is a phenomenon that exists in the formative years of all countries. However, it has been strengthened in America by the tremendous number of foreigners who have married John or Mary Smith, Ludwig or Anna, José or Conchita, Naomi or Isaac, Lorraine or André, to such an extent that even the Jewish dish, gefülte fish, has actually found its way to an Irish table on Friday.

The exchange of recipes among women friends or neighbors with different national backgrounds has helped the American family to become world-wise in the culinary art and to have a balanced and varied diet. An enterprising homemaker may add a bit of this or that to a soup that was a prize possession of a friend's grandmother, and she in turn passes it on to a daughter. After being handed down from one generation to another, it is unlikely that the first woman who brought the cherished soup recipe with her to this country would recognize it.

In all countries, among developed nations and those that seek the benefits of modern civilization, the most enlightened minds are the most fervent worshipers at the shrine of good taste. In confirmation of this, the American homemaker furnishes the most striking example that can be adduced; and if we consider the progress effected in so short a time in the culinary art, and especially in home cookery, in this country, it may be predicted that at no distant period the United States will be numbered among the highest in repute.

These well-known national soups from all over the world are adapted to serve 6 to 8 persons unless otherwise indicated.

BARLEY SOUP [591]
English

Combine in a soup kettle 1 quart of Veal Stock (No. 11) and 2 cups of rich milk. Bring to the boiling point, and cook for 3 or 4 minutes. Heat 1 tablespoon of butter, and blend in 1 tablespoon of flour; stir constantly over a low flame without browning. Now, still stirring, add a cup of the stock-milk mixture, and when bubbling, add to the remaining stock and milk in the soup kettle. Stir until boiling, and add 2½ tablespoons of finely crushed barley. Continue boiling with frequent stirring until the barley is clear and thoroughly cooked. Season to taste with salt and pepper, and serve with fried Croutons (No. 780).

BEATEN SOUP [592]
Armenian Tarbia Chorba

Tarbia chorba doesn't mean much if you don't know Armenian, but perhaps you may have dined at the Omar Khayyam restaurant in San Francisco, then you know that *tarbia chorba* is Armenian for this delicious beaten, thin custardlike soup.

Into 7 cups of rapidly boiling fresh Chicken Broth (No. 25), or canned, seasoned to taste with salt and white pepper, drop rainlike ¾ cup of very fine noodles, and let boil steadily for 25 minutes, or until the noodles are tender. Keep hot. Meanwhile, beat 3 whole fresh eggs until fluffy, then add the juice of a lemon, and beat again, seasoning to taste with salt, white pepper, and a few grains of paprika. Gradually add 1 cup of hot broth from the noodle soup to the egg mixture, beating constantly, then gently, very patiently, so the mixture will not curdle. Serve immediately. Do not allow to boil after the egg mixture has been added to the soup.

BEEF LIVER SOUP [593]
Austrian—a fine nourishing and healthy soup

Remove the skin and tubes from 1 pound of beef liver. Place in a soup kettle, and add 3 quarts of cold water. Cook very slowly for 15 short minutes, then add 1 large can of tomatoes, or the equivalent of fresh chopped tomatoes; 2 medium-sized raw sweet potatoes, peeled and diced small; 2 medium-sized carrots, grated then cubed small; 1 large turnip, peeled then cubed small; 1 stalk of celery, scraped then chopped fine; and ¼ cup of washed rice. Season with 2 teaspoons of salt, ¼ scant teaspoon of black pepper, 1 large bay leaf tied with 10 sprigs of fresh parsley, 1 blade of mace, a small pinch of allspice, and a few grains of cayenne. Cover, and let simmer for 40 long minutes. Then lift out the liver, and cut into small pieces. Rub through a sieve, or put through a food chopper. Return to the kettle, and add ½ pound of salt pork, cubed small, and fried with 1 extra large or 2 medium-sized onions, chopped fine, until lightly browned. Boil once, then let simmer for 15 minutes. Remove and discard the parsley and bay leaf, and serve as piping hot as possible with freshly made toast.

BEEF, OKRA, AND TOMATO SOUP [594]
American style—almost a complete meal

Have 3 pounds of beef shinbone sawed in several pieces instead of splitting it, to avoid splintered bone. Wash the bone quickly with the meat; drain and place in a soup kettle with 2 quarts of cold water. Slowly bring to a boil, and after 5 minutes of hard boiling, reduce the heat, and skim thoroughly. Then add 1 bouquet garni composed of 1 large bay leaf, 1 sprig of oregano, and 8 sprigs of fresh parsley, tied together with white kitchen thread. Continue simmering until the broth is flavorful and the meat nearly tender. Then add 2 cups of sliced okra, 2 cups of diced peeled tomatoes, ½ cup of diced onions, 1 cup of diced string beans, ½ cup of diced celery, which has been scraped carefully, ½ medium-sized green pepper, carefully freed of seeds and white fibrous ribs, ½ cup of diced small raw carrots, ½ teaspoon of salt, and ¼ teaspoon of black pepper. Cover, and let simmer gently for about 45 minutes. Remove the meat from the soup, dice the meat, and return it to the kettle. Cook gently for 10 minutes longer. Taste for seasoning, and serve in heated soup plates with a side dish of plain boiled rice.

BEER SOUP [595]
German method

A fine, strengthening, nourishing soup, and a good pick-me-up.

Bring to a boil 2 bottles of beer. Dilute 1 scant tablespoon of cornstarch with a little extra beer, using ¼ cup. Add 3 tablespoons of granulated sugar (more if desired sweet), the grated rind of half a large lemon, and a 1-inch stick of cinnamon (no ground cinnamon). Allow to infuse for 20 minutes, covered, over a very low flame. Strain through a fine cloth, and when ready to serve (if desired), beat in, one at a time, 4 egg yolks, stirring and beating rapidly after each addition. Serve in glass cups or bouillon cups with slices of buttered rye bread.

BLACK BEAN SOUP   [596]
American home style—serves 10 persons

Heat ¼ cup of sweet butter. Stir in ¼ cup of chopped onion and ⅓ cup of chopped carrots, and cook over a low flame until the mixture just begins to brown. Add 2½ quarts of hot water mixed with ½ cup of Pique Seasoning; then 1½ pounds of black beans, which have been soaked in water overnight and well drained; and 1 bouquet garni, composed of 1 small bay leaf, 1 sprig of thyme, and 1 sprig of very green celery leaves, tied together with kitchen thread. Season to taste with pepper only. Bring slowly to a boil, lower the flame, and let simmer gently for 2¼ to 2½ hours, or until the beans are tender. (The exact time cannot be determined, it depends on the age and quality of the beans.) Discard the bouquet garni, rub the liquid and solid through a fine sieve into a fresh soup kettle, and stir in 1 quart of cream of chicken soup. Taste for seasoning, adding salt and black pepper as needed. Heat to the boiling point, and when ready to serve, stir in 1 cup of scalded heavy cream, 2 tablespoons of sweet butter, and 2 hard-cooked eggs, finely chopped. If desired, garnish each serving with a thin slice of seeded lemon.

BORTSCH POLONAISE   [597]
Hot or cold

A very luxurious and expensive soup, but how good.

Roast a whole cleaned domestic duck of about 6 pounds in a hot oven (450° F.) until well browned (seared). Drain, put it in a soup kettle with 1 pound of beef bone and ¼ pound of bacon in one piece. Add 3 quarts of cold salted water; the pulp of 12 medium-sized fresh beets; the pulp of 2 small carrots; 5 small leeks, carefully washed and passed through a food chopper; 1 bouquet garni, composed of 1 large bay leaf, 12 sprigs of fresh parsley, and 1 large sprig of thyme, tied together with kitchen thread; 2 stalks of celery, scraped and chopped; 2 medium-sized onions, quartered, 2 quarters being stuck with 2 cloves each; 1 large clove of garlic; 12 whole peppercorns, gently bruised; and a grating of nutmeg. Bring slowly to a boil, skimming off all scum carefully. When boiling, lower the flame, let simmer gently, covered, over a very low flame for about 4 hours without disturbing. When done and tender, strain the bouillon through a fine-meshed sieve or fine cheesecloth into another soup kettle. Add 3 egg whites and their crushed shells, and gradually bring to a boil, stirring and beating at the same time gently but thoroughly. When the boiling point is reached, let simmer very gently for 12 to 15 minutes, but do not stir or beat any more. Strain through a fine cheesecloth over a sieve, taste for seasoning, and serve either very hot or very cold, but always with plenty of rich sour cream on the side. When served cold, sour cream whipped with a few grains of salt may be forced through a pastry bag with a small fancy tube to decorate the top of each cup.

Note. You may if desired cut the duck meat into small cubes, and serve in the soup. Polish peasant women usually use goose or chicken fat instead of the diced duck meat, and add barley and caraway seeds.

CALF'S BRAIN SOUP WITH NOCKERLS [598]
Hungarian Velöhaluska Leves

Blanch a pair of calf's sweetbreads. Rinse thoroughly in cold water, then rub through a fine sieve. Slice very fine 1½ dozen fresh mushrooms, and cook in 2 generous tablespoons of butter, with 1 tablespoon of minced parsley, for 5 short minutes over a low flame, stirring almost constantly to prevent scorching. Sprinkle the mushrooms with ½ tablespoon of flour, and add the calf's brain. Stir well, and gradually, while stirring constantly, pour over 1½ quarts of good Beef or Chicken Stock (Nos. 114 and 25). Now add ½ cup of grated raw carrots, and let simmer gently for 25 long minutes. Season to taste with salt, pepper, and a generous teaspoon of paprika. Serve very hot over a slice of freshly made toast placed in each soup plate. You may dust with chopped parsley if desired. Delicious.

Calf's Brain Nockerls or Dumplings. Blanch ½ calf's brain in salted water. Drain and rinse well in cold water. Then rub through a fine sieve, discarding all the nerves and tubes. To the sieved brain, add 1 generous cup of bread crumbs, soaked in milk, then squeezed and tossed to lighten. Place in a saucepan in which 1 generous tablespoon of butter has been melted, but not browned, and cook very slowly for 2 minutes, stirring constantly. Stir in 4 whole eggs, well beaten, with 2 tablespoons of flour, and seasoned highly with black pepper and salt, stirring until the mixture is of handling consistency. Take dough the size of a walnut with a teaspoon and drop into the soup. Cover and let boil for 10 long minutes.

CALF'S HEAD SOUP   [599]
Virginia method

Wash and scald 1 calf's head. Put it into 4 quarts of cold water, and let simmer gently for 4 to 4½ hours, skimming off all scum as it rises. Add, during the last hour, 1 large onion, quartered; 1 bouquet garni, composed of 2 bay leaves, 3 sprigs of green celery leaves, about 15 sprigs of fresh parsley, 1 large sprig of thyme, and 3 or 4 sprigs of marjoram, all tied together with kitchen thread; 1 tablespoon of peppercorns; 4 whole cloves; and salt to taste. Remove the head. Strain the stock through a fine sieve into a saucepan, and keep hot. Reserve the rest of the calf's head for an excellent entrée.

Take about 1 pound of the meat from the head, and with it make small forcemeat balls. Fry them in butter until delicately browned. Place the balls in a heated soup tureen. Pour 2 quarts of the head stock, seasoned to taste, over them. Stir in ½ cup of good sherry wine or Madeira wine, and serve as hot as possible, each plate garnished with a thin slice of lemon, topped with a little finely chopped parsley. Serve a side dish of chopped hard-cooked eggs and plenty of toast.

CANADIAN PEA SOUP   [600]
Soupe aux Pois à l'Habitant

The cuisine of the Canadian shows its spiritual descent from French gastronomy by its rich and recondite sauces, by its slow simmerings—to extract all the nourishing parts of the foods—and by the refinements which make a meal an act of delicate sensuality.

To make the genuine Canadian pea soup, the soup of the habitant, soak 2 cups (1 pound) of washed dried whole green or yellow peas overnight in 1½ quarts of cold water. Next day, discard the water, and rinse the peas several times in cold running water. Turn them into a soup kettle with 6 cups of fresh cold water, and add 2 small onions, each stuck with a whole clove; ½ pound of salt pork; 8 whole peppercorns, slightly bruised; 1 generous teaspoon of salt; and the real *herbes salées*, or if the latter is unobtainable, a bouquet garni, composed of 8 sprigs of fresh parsley, 2 sprigs of green celery tops (leaves), 1 large bay leaf, and 1 sprig of thyme, tied together with kitchen thread. Gradually bring these to a boil, reduce the flame, and allow to simmer very, very gently for 2½ to 3 hours, the kettle being only half covered with the lid. Remove the salt pork, and keep it hot. Then turn the contents of the kettle into a fine-meshed sieve, and rub till all the liquid, peas, and onions have been forced through into a fresh soup kettle. Return the soup to the fire, and taste for seasoning. Reheat to the boiling point, then serve in hot soup plates, dropping into each plate a small square of the salt pork and a few Croutons (No. 780).

CARAWAY SEED SOUP [601]
Austrian Kümmel Suppe

Melt 4 tablespoons of butter in a saucepan, stir in ¼ cup of flour, and cook over a gentle flame until the mixture becomes a golden brown, stirring almost constantly to keep from burning. Mix in 1 teaspoon of caraway seeds. Gradually stir in 3 cups of boiling water, and let simmer for 30 minutes. Season to taste with salt and pepper. Strain through a fine-meshed sieve. If desired, add a handful of cooked macaroni, broken into inch lengths; or have fried Croutons (No. 780) floating on top of each serving.

CAULIFLOWER SOUP [602]
Norwegian Blomkaalsuppe

Select a nice medium-sized cauliflower, wash and break it into flowerets, and cook in boiling salted water. Reserve the water for later use. Keep the flowerets hot. There should be about 2 cups (1 pint). Now melt 1 tablespoon of butter in a soup kettle, blend in 1½ tablespoons of flour, and cook over a gentle flame until the mixture becomes a golden brown. Stir in gradually 1½ quarts of good Beef Stock (No. 114) and the reserved cauliflower liquid. Cook for 10 minutes. Just before serving, beat together 1 egg yolk and ½ cup of cream, and add to the soup. Do not let the soup boil again. Now place a few of the cauliflower flowerets (hot) in each plate, and pour over them the soup sprinkled with paprika.

CHEESE SOUP [603]

Chop fine 1 large onion, and fry until slightly goldened in 2 tablespoons of butter or bacon drippings. Stir in 2 tablespoons of flour alternately with 2¾ cups of hot Beef Stock (No. 114), stirring almost constantly until thickened. Then add 1 can of undiluted evaporated milk, which has been scalded. Heat almost to the boiling point, and stir in 1¾ cups of grated American cheese, stirring until the cheese is melted. Season to taste with salt, pepper, and a few drops of cayenne pepper, and add 1 teaspoon of Worcestershire sauce. Serve at once.

CHESTNUT SOUP AUVERGNATE MANNER [604]
French

Wash and dry 1¾ pounds of sound chestnuts, then crisscross the rounded sides of their shells with a sharp-pointed knife, and roast the nuts for 12 to 15 minutes on a pan containing 1 tablespoon of good cooking oil in a very hot oven (450°-475° F.), shaking the pan occasionally. Remove the chestnuts from the oven, and when cool enough to handle, peel them; the inner skin should come off with the outer one. Place the chestnuts in a saucepan, and add a bouquet garni, consisting of 3 sprigs of green celery tops, 8 sprigs of fresh parsley, 1 large bay leaf, 1 sprig of thyme, and 2 whole cloves, all tied together with kitchen thread. Pour over the nuts enough boiling salted water to cover, then let them boil gently for 20 to 25 minutes, or until tender. Discard the bouquet garni, drain the chestnuts thoroughly, and rub them through a ricer into a fresh soup kettle, easing the rubbing by adding a few tablespoons of thin cream or undiluted evaporated milk. Measure the resulting chestnut purée; there should be 4 generous cups.

Add to the purée 1 quart of rich Chicken Broth (No. 25). Season to taste with salt, white pepper, and a few grains of paprika, and bring to the boiling point. Stir in 1 cup of scalded cream, seasoned with a tiny pinch of dry mustard and a pinch of salt. Let the soup boil once, remove it from the fire, and stir in a generous ⅓ cup of sherry wine. Divide the soup among 6 heated bouillon cups, and top each cup with meringue. For this, beat 2 egg whites very stiffly with a few grains of salt, and fold into them 3 tablespoons of coarsely ground nut meats. Set the cups under the flame of the broiling oven 5 inches from the flame, and delicately brown the meringue. Serve at once.

> *He's like a brother of his wares,*
> *Brown-shelled, and burred with bristle.*
> *His only advertisement is*
> *A steam-escaping whistle. . . .*
> *He'll pull your chestnuts from the fire,*
> *No extra charge for burns,*
> *So let Pierre roast you some—*
> *He gives more than he earns.*

'Round the corner, down the street
The whistle's growing fainter—
He'll never know that he has been
A model for a painter.
            L. P. De Gouy, "The Chestnut Man"

CHICKEN SOUP A LA RUSSE   [605]
Russian—elaborate, but delicious and nourishing

Place a 4-pound fowl, cleaned, singed, and trussed in a large soup kettle with ½ pound of beef marrow bones. Cover with 2 quarts of cold water. Add 2 carrots, grated then quartered; 2 stalks of celery, grated, washed, then cut into small pieces; 1 large onion, quartered; a bouquet garni, composed of 1 large bay leaf tied with 10 sprigs of parsley and 1 sprig of thyme, using kitchen thread; and 1 small clove of garlic. Season with salt and pepper to taste, bring to a rapid boil, then reduce the flame, and continue boiling very gently for 1 long hour. Lift out the fowl and all the fat appearing on the surface of the liquid, and continue boiling for 30 minutes. Now strain the stock first through a fine sieve, then through a fine cloth. Keep warm, removing whatever fat may appear on the surface. Keep the vegetables, but discard the bouquet garni.

Melt in a saucepan ¼ cup of butter, and into it put 10 small pieces of parsley root, a root of celery, 1 medium-sized onion, and 2 cucumbers, cut into strips. Cover, and let simmer slowly for 10 minutes. Then add 1 cup of flour diluted in just enough cold water to make a running paste, and stir constantly until thoroughly blended and the mixture is thickening. Then add 1 generous cup of dry white wine, the strained stock set aside, and the vegetables. Now add 4 salted cucumbers, cut in strips, and 3 tablespoons of cucumber juice 10 minutes before serving. When ready to serve, stir in 3 egg yolks, well beaten, beating rapidly to prevent curdling, and ½ generous cup of heavy cream. Correct the seasoning, and add 1 tablespoon of lemon juice, if the mixture is not sour enough to the taste.

CLAM AND WINE SOUP A LA VENDEENNE [606]

After having cleaned 2 dozen large clams with a stiff brush and rinsed them in several cold waters, place them in a heavy kettle with ½ to ¾ cup of good dry white wine, 2 large bay leaves, a sprig of parsley, and 8 sprigs of green celery tops (leaves), 6 crushed peppercorns, 1 whole clove, and 1 small clove of garlic. Place the kettle over a bright flame, and as soon as the clams are opened, remove from the fire, and remove the clams from the shells. Strain the juice into a clean kettle, and put the celery leaves through a food chopper. Have ready 1 generous quart of fish stock made from inexpensive fish or trimmings of fish. Add this fish stock to the clam-wine juice, and place over a bright flame. As soon as the mixture boils, add 2 cups of raw potatoes, diced very small, ½ cup of fresh peas, and ¼ cup of finely chopped onion. Cook about 20 minutes, or until the potatoes and peas are tender. Then add 1 cup of dry white wine and the chopped clams, and cook for 5 minutes. Set aside, taste for seasoning, and when ready to serve, add the chopped whites of 2 hard-cooked eggs and 1 tablespoon of finely chopped chervil.

COCKALEEKIE SOUP   [607]
Original English recipe

Put into a soup kettle 2 quarts of Chicken Broth (No. 25), and bring to a boil. Let simmer gently while preparing the other ingredients. Wash very carefully, in several changes of water, 8 small leeks, roots and outside leaves trimmed off, and halved lengthwise. Drain, then blanch in boiling water to cover. Drain again, and dry. Then add to the chicken broth with 2 tablespoons of washed uncooked rice. Bring slowly to a boil, lower the flame, cover, and let simmer gently for 35 to 40 minutes. When ready to serve, add 1 cup of small chicken cubes, using the chicken meat from the broth. Heat well and serve, topping each portion with a little finely chopped parsley.

COCONUT SOUP   [608]
Potage à la Noix de Coco

Soak 4 ounces of grated fresh coconut in 1 cup of chicken stock for at least 1 hour. Put in a soup kettle 7 cups of Chicken Stock (No. 25). Add a generous dash of mace, the coconut and liquid, 1 bay leaf, 2 whole cloves, and 6 thin slices of onion. Bring to a boil, and let simmer gently for 1 hour. Mix 2 tablespoons of flour (rice flour if available) with a little cold water, and stir into the soup mixture together with 4 tablespoons of raw washed rice, 2 tablespoons of chopped raw vermicelli, and 1 tablespoon of quick-cooking tapioca. Bring to a boil, and let simmer, uncovered, for 25 to 30 minutes, stirring occasionally. By this time the liquid should be slightly reduced. When ready to serve, taste for seasoning, and stir in 1 cup of coconut milk, which has been scalded. Turn the soup into a heated soup tureen, and serve at once, each serving sprinkled with 1 tablespoon of grated cheese and 1 teaspoon of chopped cooked spinach.

CUCUMBER SOUP IN SOUR CREAM [609]
Russian

Have ready cooked about ½ cup of white chicken meat, cut into shreds. Place the chicken meat in a saucepan, cover with 1 cup of hot Chicken Broth (No. 25), and keep hot. Cream ¼ cup of butter with 2 teaspoons of finely chopped chives and ½ teaspoon of dried tarragon herb. Place this butter in a soup kettle, and when hot, stir in ½ cup of chopped scallions. Cook for 3 minutes over a low heat, then stir in 1¼ cups of pared, seeded, diced raw cucumber. Cook for 2 minutes longer, then add the chicken and chicken stock, 2 cups of scalded milk, 1 large bay leaf, salt, pepper to taste, and a dash of cloves. Bring to a boil. Let simmer very gently for 15 minutes, discard the bay leaf, and stir in 2 cups of thick sour cream, scalded. Taste for seasoning, and just before serving, stir in 2 hard-cooked eggs, finely chopped. Serve in heated colorful bowls, dusted with chopped parsley, after tasting for seasoning.

DUMPLING SOUP A LA RUSSE [610]

This potage is as popular in Russia as bortsch.

Dilute 1 cup of flour with 6 fresh egg yolks, 2 stiffly beaten egg whites, and freshly grated nutmeg and freshly ground pepper to taste, adding a little cold bouillon to make the mixture run from the spoon like heavy cream. Have ready 2 quarts of rich Beef or Chicken Broth (Nos. 114 and 25) boiling rapidly. With the finger, push tablespoons of the paste into the boiling liquid, holding the spoon high, and making a slight rotation with the spoon when the paste is dropped in. In dropping, the paste will form a small ball, either round or oval. Let this boil very gently for 25 minutes, and serve at once in soup plates.

EGG AND CARAWAY SEED SOUP VIENNESE [611]

Melt 2 generous tablespoons of lard or bacon drippings, and blend with an equal amount of flour. Do not brown. Gradually add 1½ quarts of rich Beef Stock (No. 114) and 1 generous tablespoon of caraway seeds. Season with salt and pepper to taste, and 1 generous tablespoon of paprika. Cook for 5 long minutes. Remove from the fire, and gradually beat in 6 whole eggs, one at a time, beating vigorously after each addition. Serve sizzling hot.

Note. The addition of ½ cup of diced or cubed cooked chicken is a great improvement.

FRIMSEL SOUP [612]
Hebrew

Add a little salt to 3 eggs, and beat in as much bread flour as needed to make a dough sufficiently stiff to roll out as thin as a wafer. Divide it into 3 strips. Set aside until thoroughly dry, then place the strips one above the other, and shred very finely in vermicelli fashion. Bring to a rolling boil 1½ quarts of rich Beef Stock (No. 114), gradually add the shredded strips of frimsel, and let simmer very gently for 20 minutes, skimming carefully to obtain a clear broth. Taste for seasoning, and serve boiling hot in hot soup plates.

GARBANZO SOUP [613]
Mexican Chick Pea Soup

Put 1½ quarts of ham or tongue liquor in a soup kettle. Add 4 medium-sized potatoes, peeled and cubed small; 1 large onion, grated; 1 small clove of garlic, peeled and mashed; 1 large bay leaf tied with 6 sprigs of fresh parsley, using kitchen thread; and a No. 2 can of garbanzo beans (also called Spanish beans or chick peas). Cook until slightly thick, and the potatoes are very tender. Taste for seasoning, and when ready to serve, stir in 3 tablespoons of sherry wine (optional). Serve in hot soup plates, each dusted with finely chopped parsley or chives.

GARLIC SOUP MADRILENE [614]
Spanish

One of the most famous soups in Spain, and each province has its own and special way of making it. This is how it is made in Madrid.

Fry for each person 1 clove of garlic in a little olive oil over a gentle flame until it begins to take on color, stirring occasionally. Then add 1 thin slice of bread, and season to taste with salt and pepper. Pour over ¾ cup of boiling water, let boil for 1 minute, and serve, after stirring into it 1 well-beaten egg.

GULASCH SOUP [615]
Hungarian Guyla Sleves

Shred 6 medium-sized onions, and cook them in 6 tablespoons of hot melted butter, or other fat, in a soup kettle until of a golden hue. Add 2 pounds of beef, cut in inch pieces; 2 fresh tomatoes, chopped; 2 red or green pimientos; salt and pepper to taste; and 2 tablespoons of paprika. Let simmer for 45 minutes, then add 1½ quarts of hot water gradually. Cover, and let simmer for 2 hours longer. Add 3 potatoes, peeled and quartered, 30 minutes before done. About 10 minutes before serving, place 2 smoked Hungarian sausages on top of the soup. When done, cut in serving portions, place in soup plates with pieces of meat, and pour soup over.

Note. The onion and paprika flavors predominate, the kind of meat may differ, but the method of preparation is always the same.

HOCHEPOT BELGE [616]
A variation of the French pot-au-feu

A meal in itself, because the soup or stock is served in the soup tureen at the same time as the meat—as a separate course—but at the same time.

Put 1½ pounds of brisket of beef, 1½ pounds of shoulder and breast of mutton in equal parts, 1½ pounds of shoulder of veal, 1½ pounds of cleaned pigs' feet, ½ pound of pigs' tails in a large deep earthenware casserole called a *pot-au-feu*. Cover with cold water, bring very slowly to a boil, and skim thoroughly. When the scum has ceased to rise and the stock is quite clear, add the following vegetables, coarsely chopped: ¼ pound of carrots; 4 leeks; 2 small turnips; 3 celery stalks; 1 dozen small white onions, left whole, 2 of which are each stuck with 1 whole clove; and 1 small head of green cabbage, cut into quarters. Season to taste with salt and pepper. Add a bouquet garni, composed of 1 large bay leaf, 8 sprigs of fresh parsley, and a sprig of thyme, all tied together with white kitchen thread. Lastly, add 1 dozen (2 per person) small chipolata sausage, or lacking them, 1 pound of hard sausage. Cover, and let simmer very, very gently for 3 hours. If using soft sausages, add them only ¾ hour before serving. When ready to serve, put the meats and sausages on a hot dish in the center. Drain the vegetables, garnish the meat platter with them, and pour a little of the strained stock over them, and the meat after tasting for seasoning. Serve the broth in the soup tureen with a side dish of very coarse salt.

HOPPING JOHN BLACK BEAN SOUP [617]

Among the "lucky" recipes served in various sections of the United States from the beginning of the year down to the end of the Easter holidays is the Hopping John. This is a simple dish, although a very old one. A ten-cent piece is added to the big bowl of black beans just before it is brought to the table. The person finding the dime in his plate will have good luck all year.

Wash and pick over 1 pound of black beans. Cover with 2 inches of cold water, and let stand overnight. Next morning, add ¾ pound of cubed salt pork, salt, a bouquet garni composed of 1 bay leaf and 6 sprigs of parsley tied together with kitchen thread, and 8 to 10 whole peppercorns. Cook steadily at the simmering point for about 3 hours. While the beans are cooking, wash 1 cup of rice, and drop rainlike into 2½ quarts of boiling salted water. Cook till tender, but not mushy. Drain the rice in a colander, reserving the liquid.

The beans being tender, fish out the bouquet garni, and discard it. Taste for seasoning. Make a mound of rice in the center of hot soup plates, burying in one a 10-cent piece. The person finding it will have good luck the whole year. Dish over the rice the beans, liquid and solid, to which has been added half of the rice water. Sprinkle with chopped parsley, and serve sizzling hot. It is more a dish than a soup, yet it's so soupy that it is called soup.

HOTCHPOTCH A L'ANGLAISE   [618]
English mutton pot-au-feu

Cut 2 pounds of neck of mutton into neat little pieces. Put them in a soup kettle with 2 quarts of cold water and 1 teaspoon of salt; bring slowly to a boil, and skim well. Meanwhile, shred a good head of lettuce finely, taking care to shorten the filaments by cutting them across. Cut off the stalks of a small cauliflower, and break the head into small flowerets. Cut half a white turnip, 1 medium-sized carrot, and 1 medium-sized onion into cubes. The meat having been simmering for 30 minutes and carefully skimmed, add 1 generous bouquet garni, composed of 1 bay leaf, 1 sprig of thyme, 8 sprigs of fresh parsley or a 2-inch piece of scraped parsley root, and 2 sprigs of green celery leaves (tops), all tied together with white kitchen thread; 2 cloves; half a clove of garlic, peeled and left whole; and 8 whole peppercorns. Let simmer gently for 30 minutes longer, covered, over a gentle heat. Then add the prepared vegetables, and let simmer gently for another 30 to 35 minutes. Half an hour afterward, add 1 cup of shelled fresh green peas, cover, and continue simmering for 30 minutes longer, or until all the vegetables are tender. Discard the bouquet garni, and taste for seasoning. Then stir in 1½ tablespoons of chopped parsley, and serve at once in heated soup plates, each having a toasted round of bread sprinkled with 1 generous tablespoon of grated Stilton cheese.

LENTIL SOUP ARMENIAN STYLE [619]
Also called Potage Esaü—a 3500-year-old recipe

This recipe is probably Arabic in origin, for it is the main dish throughout North Africa and Arabia. They keep the stockpot on the fire, throwing in with the lentils whatever vegetables they have in season, with chunks of goat meat or mutton, but never, never any pork. This potage is warmed up as many times as necessary until it is all eaten, and we find that we like it better when warmed up than we do the first time, though it is extra delicious the first time. The following recipe is from Armenia, and is very popular in America.

Pick over carefully, and wash 1 generous cup of lentils, and soak overnight in ½ pint of cold water. Heat 1 tablespoon of ham or bacon drippings, and in it cook ¼ to ⅓ cup of finely chopped onions until delicately brown, stirring almost constantly. Turn the onion and fat into a soup kettle. Add 1 bouquet garni, composed of 1 bay leaf, 8 sprigs of fresh parsley, and 1 sprig of thyme, tied together with kitchen thread, then the soaked lentils, and whatever water is left with them. Gradually bring to the boiling point, cover, lower the flame, and let simmer very gently for 1½ to 1¾ hours, or until the lentils are tender, but not mashed. Taste for seasoning, and discard the bouquet garni. About 4 or 5 minutes before serving, stir in 3 tablespoons of finely chopped parsley and 5 or 6 fresh mint leaves, also finely chopped. Serve in heated soup plates with crackers, and if desired (this is not Armenian) garnish each plate with 4 or 5 slices of frankfurters, slightly heated in beef broth.

LETTUCE SOUP REFORM CLUB [620]

Lettuce, from the Latin, *lactuca*, referring to the milky juice, is greatly used for making delicious soup in France. The native country of the lettuce is unknown, and from what species the garden varieties originated is merely conjectural. According to Herodotus, it was in use 550 years B.C. Pliny says the ancient Romans knew but one sort. In his time, it was cultivated so as to be had at all seasons of the year, and even blanched to make it more tender. The following soup was created by no less than the famous French chef, Alexis Soyer, who was chef at the Reform Club in London.

Shred a fairly large head of Cos lettuce as finely as possible. Cream ¼ cup of sweet butter until light and lemon colored. Gradually add to it 1 thin slice of garlic, finely chopped, 1 teaspoon of finely chopped

tarragon herb, and ½ teaspoon of dried parsley. Cream well. Heat
this butter in a soup kettle. Add 3 tablespoons of finely chopped onion
and 2 tablespoons of finely chopped green pepper. Cook for 2 minutes,
stirring almost constantly. Chop 1 bunch of green watercress, and add
to the butter, together with the shredded Cos lettuce. Cook for 3 or 4
minutes, stirring constantly. Pour over 1 quart of boiling Beef Stock
(No. 114), or canned bouillon, and cook for 20 minutes. Season to
taste with salt and pepper, and continue cooking for 15 minutes longer.
Remove from the fire. Stir in 1 cup of scalded milk alternately with 1
cup of heavy sweet cream, also scalded. Taste for seasoning, and just
before serving, stir in 3 egg yolks, slightly beaten. Serve very hot with
toasted rolls spread with anchovy butter.

LIMA BEAN GUMBO SOUP GEORGIA   [621]

A very nourishing soup, which may be considered as a complete
meal when served with a side dish of green salad and one of those
delicious peach desserts in which the Georgia women excel.

Place in a large heavy soup kettle 1 large ham bone (which may
be from a leftover cooked ham); 3 large onions, minced fine; 12 whole
peppercorns, gently bruised to allow their pungent flavor to go out
during the cooking process; 1 bouquet garni, composed of 1 large bay
leaf and 12 sprigs of fresh parsley, tied together with kitchen thread;
1 pound of dried lima beans, soaked overnight; and 2½ quarts of
water, using the water in which the beans have been soaked. Cover,
and place over a low flame. Simmer for 3 long hours, stirring occasionally to prevent scorching. Take from the kettle 1½ cups of cooked
lima beans. Turn the rest, liquid and all, into a fine sieve, after removing and discarding the bone and the bouquet garni. Rub well so that
everything passes through the sieve. Now return the purée to the fire,
and add 1 cup of chopped raw carrots, ½ cup of chopped green
pepper, and 2¾ cups of tomato juice. Cover, and let simmer gently
for 35 minutes. Then add the reserved 1½ cups of cooked lima beans
and the meat from the ham bone, ground. Season to taste with salt
and 1 teaspoon of Worcestershire sauce. Serve in soup plates with a
side dish of fried Croutons (No. 780). Dust each serving with finely
chopped parsley.

MILK AND BREAD-CRUMB SOUP   [622]

Brown 1 cup of whole wheat bread crumbs in the oven or in a
skillet over a hot fire, stirring constantly to prevent burning. Scald

1½ quarts of good milk with 4 slices of onion, 2 sprigs of fresh parsley, 1 bay leaf, and 1 clove. Strain the milk infusion over a double boiler alternately with the bread crumbs. Now set aside, and gradually beat in 2 egg yolks, already beaten together, beating hard and rapidly. Season to taste with salt and white pepper, then stir in 3 tablespoons of good butter. Serve in soup plates, having in each 1 slice of crisp toast sprinkled with grated American cheese. Children and adults love this soup.

MILK SOUP VERMICELLI [623]

Fine for children's supper, and for grownups, too.

Scald 1½ quarts of rich milk with 1 tablespoon of onion juice, 2 whole cloves, a bouquet garni composed of 1 small bay leaf and 3 sprigs of parsley, and salt and white pepper to taste. Place on top of a double boiler, over direct flame, and boil for 12 long minutes. When ready to serve, add 3 tablespoons of cooked rice, and stir in 2 egg yolks, already beaten together, and 3 tablespoons of good butter. Serve in soup plates without any accompaniment.

MILLEFANTI SOUP [624]

This delicious soup should not be confused with Consommé Millefanti (No. 58). Of Italian origin, it is very popular on the other side of the Alps, and in America among the Italian colony. It has the advantage of being rapidly made.

Mix in a large bowl 1 cup of bread crumbs, freshly made, and the same amount of grated Parmesan cheese, and blend with 2 whole eggs. When ready to serve, pour over this mixture 2 quarts of boiling rich consommé (any kind), beating rapidly with a wire whisk. Boil briskly for 5 minutes, stirring almost constantly, and serve at once with the traditional side dish of grated Parmesan cheese, olives, and Italian bread.

MINESTRONE MILANESE [625]

As in America, soups and their innumerable "trimmings" in the way of ravioli, gnocchi, spaghetti, and all manner of appetizing delicacies are very popular in Italy. Each province, each city, small town, or even village, seems to boast of its own particular soup or of some special and characteristic accompaniment to it. Minestrone soup is the great spring and summer soup, made with fresh young vegetables, and it may be served hot or cold. In any case, this soup should be very thick.

Put 1½ quarts of good Beef Stock (No. 114) in a large saucepan. Bring to the boiling point, and add ¼ pound of salt pork, cut in inch lengths; ½ pound of fresh kidney beans; ½ pound of new peas; 1 stalk of celery, scraped and diced; ½ pound of young cabbage, shredded; ⅓ pound of fresh spinach, stemmed, the leaves shredded; 1 small onion, thinly sliced; ¼ cup of chopped carrots; 2 medium-sized fresh tomatoes, peeled and chopped; 1 sprig of sage; ¼ cup of un-cooked rice; and salt and pepper to taste. Bring again to a boil, lower the flame, and let simmer very gently, as slowly as possible, until the vegetables are tender and have nearly absorbed the beef stock. Taste for seasoning, add 2 or 3 cups of hot beef stock, and serve in heated soup plates or bowls, passing a dish of grated Parmesan cheese on the side.

Variations. You may add, before cooking the vegetables, ½ cup of uncooked macaroni, spaghetti, or vermicelli, broken small. It is also served with a kind of loose dumpling, called Pesto (No. 797).

MULLIGATAWNY SOUP   [626]

Mulligatawny, which means "pepper water," is an East Indian soup —a one-dish meal—greatly relished in India, in which curry plays a leading role, giving to the soup punginess, body, and substance. This seasoning may be raised or diminished according to taste. An East India chef gave this recipe to me when I was chef on a yacht during a cruise around the world. Several versions or variations are made, but they far from rivalize with this original recipe.

Cut up a 2½-pound chicken as for fricassée. Sponge with a damp cloth. Melt 1 tablespoon of butter in a deep skillet. Add ¼ pound of diced salt pork, and brown lightly, then add the cut-up chicken. Fry lightly over a low flame until beginning to color, turning the pieces very often, almost constantly to ensure an even coloring. Then sprin-kle 1 tablespoon of flour mixed with 1 generous teaspoon of curry powder (more if desired) over the whole. Continue cooking, stirring and turning the pieces of chicken often until the meat is firm, but not quite done. Turn this into a soup kettle. Then add 2½ quarts of Veal Stock (No. 11), ½ cup of diced carrots, ¼ cup of diced onions, 1 bay leaf, 2 whole cloves, 6 peppercorns, slightly bruised, and salt, pepper, and a few grains of cayenne pepper to taste. Bring to a rapid boil, reduce the heat, and let simmer very gently, as slowly as possible, for 1 long hour. Taste for seasoning, correcting if necessary. Now add the following garnishings: 3 tablespoons of cooked rice; ½ cup of eggplant, diced and slightly sautéed in butter after being parboiled; ½ cup of leek, cut diamond shape, then sautéed in butter; and 1 generous cup of diced cooked chicken meat (from the chicken pieces). Cook for 10 minutes longer, or until the garnishings are cooked. Serve piping hot with a side dish of hot plain boiled rice.

MUSHROOM SOUP [627]
Gypsy manner—a velvety and supremely delicious soup

Clean and wash ½ pound of fresh mushrooms. Drain well. Place in a saucepan, and barely cover with equal parts of cold water and lemon juice, seasoning to taste with salt. Cover, and cook gently over a low flame, shaking, not stirring, the pan until tender. Remove from the fire, drain, then rinse in cold water. Sponge dry, and put the mushrooms through a food chopper, using the finest blade. Have ready 2 cups of cream sauce, made from 2 tablespoons of butter, 2 tablespoons of tapioca flour, and 2 cups of sour cream, then seasoned to taste with salt and white pepper. Stir into it the ground mushrooms. Bring to a boil, and gradually stir in 1 quart of good Chicken Stock (No. 25), stirring until the mixture thickens. Skim off the froth which may appear on the surface. Set aside, and one by one, beat in 2 fresh egg yolks, beating rapidly after each addition. Season to taste with salt and white pepper, and serve in soup plates, each sprinkled with paprika then with finely chopped parsley. Serve with a side dish of freshly made finger toast.

ONION SOUP ARGENTINA [628]
As served at the Rivadavia night club in Buenos Aires

Pliny said that the Romans used onions to cure the sting of serpents and other reptiles, that they made poultices of onions and barley for those who had watery eyes because onions clear the sight by the tears they draw, and that onion juice was given to those who suddenly became speechless.

Heat ⅓ cup of olive oil in a soup kettle. When smoking, throw into it 4 large red onions, thinly sliced and rings separated, and 1 clove of garlic, mashed to a paste. At once lower the heat, and let simmer gently until the onions begin to take on a pale yellowish color. Then stir in 2 large green peppers, finely shredded and free from seeds and white ribs, and continue cooking until the onions turn a light yellow, stirring constantly. Then stir in 1½ quarts of rich Beef Stock (No. 114), or use the concentrated canned beef consommé, as slowly as possible, stirring all the while. Season to taste with salt, pepper, and a fresh grating of nutmeg, and allow to simmer very gently, covered, for about 20 minutes.

Meantime, fry in olive oil 1½ cups of small croutons until crisp, almost dry. Drain on absorbent paper, and keep hot.

Beat 4 egg yolks until light, and gradually stir in 3 tablespoons (or more, according to taste) of good sherry wine in a soup tureen. Take some of the liquid from the soup, and stir it into the beaten eggs, beating briskly with a rotary beater or a wire whisk. When ready to serve, pour the onion soup over the beaten egg mixture, and float the croutons over it. Serve at once with a large side dish of grated Parma cheese. The custom is to serve a glass of sherry wine right after the soup. A meal in itself, which is usually served at the wee hours before retiring.

ONION SOUP AU GRATIN PARISIENNE   [629]

Charles Dickens, in *A Christmas Carol*, reminded us of this fondness for onions when he wrote: "There were ruddy, brown-girthed Spanish onions, shining in the fatness of their growth like a Spanish friar." We would not be so bold as to say that Bernard Shaw likes onions, but in *Candida* he announces, "Maria is ready for you in the kitchen, Mrs. Morell, the onions have come."

Cook in 4 tablespoons of sweet butter, over a gentle flame, 3 large onions, finely sliced, until golden brown, stirring frequently. Sprinkle over them 1 tablespoon of flour, if the soup is desired thick. Gradually stir in 2 quarts of Beef Stock (No. 114). Season to taste with salt and pepper; cover, and let cook gently for 20 minutes. Serve in heated soup plates or individual earthenware marmites if available, for real French style, each garnished with a toasted round of French bread topped with grated Swiss, Parmesan, or American cheese, browned under the flame of the broiling oven. Serve at once.

In the fourteenth century, Finnish women rubbed their skin with freshly cut onions and drank two quarts of onion soup daily—all for beauty's sake.

OXTAIL SOUP [630]

This is the original recipe for real English oxtail soup, as made in County Kent and over England generally, and graciously given to the writer by an old English chef and innkeeper, established for more than fifty years and famous for his fine old English recipes. It consists of several operations each distinct from the other and the directions must be carefully followed if a good result is to be obtained.

Initial Operation. Prepare Beef Consommé (No. 114). Meanwhile, prepare the ingredients for the second operation: 2 oxtails, strictly fresh, cut in pieces 1½ inches long, the thickest pieces split in two lengthwise, well washed, and then sponged.

Place the cut-up oxtails in a soup kettle. Cover with water, bring to a boil, strain, and discard the water (the purpose of this operation being to lessen if not remove entirely the tallowlike odor peculiar to all animal tails).

Second Operation. Sponge the pieces of tail, and brown them in a skillet with 3 tablespoons of butter. Strain the butter, set it aside for later use, and place the meat in a fresh soup kettle. Add 1 bouquet garni, composed of 1 small bunch of fresh parsley, 1 sprig of thyme, and 1 large bay leaf, all tied together with kitchen thread; 2 cloves; 1 onion, cut in quarters; 10 peppercorns; and a pinch of cayenne pepper.

Cover the above ingredients with 2 quarts of the strained beef consommé made in the initial operation, setting aside the vegetables for later use. Set the soup kettle in a moderately hot oven for 2 hours without disturbing whatsoever, seeing that it is tightly covered. Remove then from the oven. Lift out the pieces of oxtail, place in a strainer, and drain well. Heat 1 generous cup of good Madeira wine, and place in it the well-drained pieces of oxtail. Stir well. Cover, and keep hot.

Strain the broth again, and add the butter set aside from the skillet of the second operation, straining through a fine cloth or fine sieve, the cloth previously wrung out in cold water. Let stand a while (10 minutes). Remove the fat from the surface, and pour into a deep saucepan 1½ quarts of the strained beef consommé. Bring to a violent boil, and add rapidly 2 teaspoons of arrowroot diluted in a little cold bouillon. Stir, and let simmer gently over a low fire for 15 minutes. Meanwhile, cut in julienne style, matchlike, or dice the vegetables from the beef consommé set aside as indicated. Place these vegetables in the soup tureen. Add the oxtails and Madeira wine. Pour over the broth simmering. Correct the seasoning. Serve. No apologies will be needed for your soup course.

During the Terror in Paris in 1793, many of the nobility were starving. It was the custom those days for the *abattoirs* of Paris to send their hides, as soon as the animals were killed, to the tanneries without cleaning them, even leaving on the tails, subsequently discarded during cleaning. One of the nobles asked for a tail, which was willingly given him, and with it he created the first oxtail soup. Hearing of this, the tanners, annoyed by the great and constant demand for oxtails, put a price on them.

OYSTER SOUP AU GRATIN [631]

The oyster is, to the average mind, a formless mess of succulent tissue, shaped by benign Providence to descend with ease "into the eager and expectant tomb." That is because we are accustomed to meet the oyster only at mealtime. As a living creature it is wonderfully made, and is wonderfully good.

Scald 1½ quarts of rich milk with 6 slices of thinly sliced medium-sized onion, 1 blade of garlic, and 3 slices of green pepper, thinly sliced. Add 3 tablespoons of butter, and let stand for 5 minutes off the fire. Then strain into a clean saucepan, and add 1 scant teaspoon of celery salt and 1½ cups of crushed unsalted crackers. Bring to a boil, remove from the fire, drop in 3 dozen cleaned picked small oysters, a few at a time, and add the liquor, strained through a fine cloth. Transfer at once into a deep earthenware bean pot. Sprinkle over ½ generous cup of coarse fresh bread crumbs mixed with equal parts of grated American cheese. Put in a hot oven (450° F.), or place under the flame of the broiling oven until the top browns and milk bubbles over the crumb mixture. Stir, let brown again, and then a third time, after sprinkling over the top small cubes of bread, fried in butter, then rolled in grated cheese. When the top is golden brown, serve immediately.

PEANUT BUTTER CORN SOUP [632]
Middle Western manner

Cook 2 cups of corn kernels, freshly scraped from the cob, for 15 minutes with 2 tablespoons of grated onion and 3 cups of Beef Stock (No. 114), and rub through a sieve. Heat 3 cups of milk in a double boiler to the scalding point. Mix together 2½ tablespoons of peanut butter, 2 tablespoons of butter, and 2 tablespoons of flour, and stir into the scalded milk. Cook until the mixture is thickened, stirring all the while. Combine the milk mixture with the corn mixture. Let boil once. Season to taste with salt, pepper, and paprika. Serve with a tablespoon of whipped cream to each serving.

PETITE MARMITE [633]
French Little Pot—serves 10 to 12 persons

Place in a 10-quart earthenware pot 2 pounds of lean beef plate, a 5-pound young fowl, and about 5½ to 6 quarts of cold water with salt to taste. Bring very slowly to a boil, lower the flame, and let simmer very gently until tender, or about 3 to 3½ hours, the longer the better, skimming off all scum as it rises to the surface. Then add 2 medium-sized leeks, carefully washed and cut into inch strips; 3 or 4 medium-sized carrots, cut into inch pieces; 2 white turnips, quartered; 3 stalks of celery, scraped, then cut into inch pieces; half a very small green cabbage, quartered; and 1 medium-sized onion, halved, each half stuck with 1 clove, and slightly browned in a little fat to impart color to the bouillon, and give it a delicate flavor. Season to taste with salt and black pepper. Finally, add 1 bouquet garni, composed of 1 large bay leaf, 8 sprigs of fresh parsley, and 1 sprig of thyme, tied together with white kitchen thread. Allow the whole to cook slowly for 1½ hours longer, removing the beef and chicken after half an hour of this further slow cooking. Cool slightly, then cut the meat into cubes or strips (except the chicken legs, which may be used otherwise). Return to the kettle, and continue cooking till the vegetables are tender. Just before serving, add 8 slices of raw beef marrow and 1 generous teaspoon of minced chervil or parsley. Discard the onion, and serve in individual earthenware soup tureens, with a side dish of toasted bread and grated cheese. The remainder of the soup keeps well for a week in the refrigerator.

PHILADELPHIA PEPPER POT [634]

Pepper-y pot, piping hot! In colonial days, the pepper-pot vendor plodded Philadelphia's twisting streets and alleyways chanting the pepper-pot call:

> *"All hot! All hot!*
> *Pepper pot! Pepper pot!*
> *Makes back strong,*
> *Makes live long,*
> *All hot! Pepper pot!"*

The vendor and her cart have gone, but pepper pot lives on as one of America's favorite soups in midwinter and even in the spring, in this old American colonial recipe.

Cook 2 pounds of honeycomb tripe the day before using. Wash thoroughly, place in a kettle, and cover with cold water. Bring to a boil, and let simmer gently for at least 8 hours. Remove the tripe, and when cool, cut into pieces about ½ inch square. Next day, wash 1 veal knuckle in cold water. Cover with 3 quarts of cold water, gradually bring to a boil, and skim off very carefully all scum as it rises to the surface. Add 1 bouquet garni, composed of 2 bay leaves, 10 sprigs of parsley, and 2 sprigs of green celery leaves, tied together with white kitchen thread. Let simmer gently for 3 hours, adding, after 2 hours, 1½ teaspoons of salt and 12 peppercorns, slightly bruised. Remove the meat from the bones, and cut into small pieces. Strain the broth, and return to the kettle, then add 2 medium-sized onions, each stuck with 1 whole clove. Simmer for 1 hour, then add 4 medium-sized potatoes, peeled and cubed, also the meat and tripe pieces. Taste for seasoning, and let simmer gently while making the following dumplings:

Suet Dumplings. Combine 1 cup of beef suet, previously put through a food chopper, 2 cups of flour, ½ generous teaspoon of salt, and enough ice-cold water to allow rolling the dough into dumplings about the size of marbles. Flour well to prevent sticking, and drop into the simmering soup. Cook about 8 to 10 minutes. Stir some chopped parsley into the soup, and serve in heated soup plates with brown bread and butter finger sandwiches.

POTAGE BONNE FEMME   [635]
Good Woman's Soup

This potage is supposed to be a creation of Madame de Pompadour when she played the farmerette in the garden of the Petit Trianon.

Wash and shred a white heart of lettuce finely. Cut a small cucumber into quarters, reserve ¾, and cut ¼ into thin slices, matchlike. Heat 3 tablespoons of sweet butter, and stir in the lettuce and cucumber sticks. Fry for 2 or 3 minutes, then add 2 leaves of tarragon herb and 1 teaspoon of finely chopped chervil, and continue cooking for 1 minute longer. Then stir in 5 cups of White Stock (No. 11), and add the reserved ¾ cucumber. Boil gently for 15 minutes, or until the vegetables are tender. Beat the yolks of 2 eggs, add to them ½ cup of heavy sweet cream, and blend thoroughly. Remove the soup from the fire, and gradually stir in the egg-cream mixture, stirring vigorously, and seasoning to taste with salt, pepper, and a tiny dash of freshly grated nutmeg. Serve at once in heated soup plates, each sprinkled with a little finely chopped chervil, or parsley if chervil is not available.

POTAGE BRESSOIS [636]

This soup is an example of what the French chefs and cooks can make with a fowl.

To a fine fowl, weighing 3½ to 4 pounds, thoroughly cleaned, and 2 marrow bones of beef, add 2 quarts of cold water, and bring to a boil, skimming frequently. After boiling for 5 minutes, add 2 medium-sized carrots, quartered; 2 leeks, halved, well washed, folded, then tied together; 2 medium-sized onions, halved, each half stuck with a whole clove; 1 bouquet garni, composed of 1 bay leaf, 6 sprigs of parsley, and 1 sprig of thyme, all tied together with kitchen thread; 1 small clove of garlic, 1 small heart of celery, grated and chopped; 1 piece of parsnip the size of an ordinary egg; and salt to taste (no pepper yet). Boil for 1 hour, skimming the fat as it appears on the surface of the stock. Fish out the chicken from the stock, and continue to boil gently for an additional 30 minutes. Strain the stock through a fine sieve, and keep it hot, again removing whatever fat appears on the surface. Melt in a saucepan ¼ cup of butter, and put in 6 small pieces of parsley root, a celery heart, 1 small onion, quartered, and 1 large cucumber, cut in strips. Smother slowly for 7 or 8 minutes, and add ¾ cup of flour (12 tablespoons). Blend well, and let simmer for 5 minutes to remove the raw taste of the flour; then add 2 cups of dry white wine, and pour the strained chicken stock over it. Bring to a boil, reduce the heat, and allow to simmer until the vegetables are tender. Strain through a fine sieve, and thicken with 2 or 3 egg yolks. Taste for seasoning, adding salt, white pepper, and a fresh grating of nutmeg. Just before serving, stir in 2 tablespoons of sweet butter. Serve very hot with a side dish of Croutons (No. 780).

POTAGE A LA CONDE [637]
Red Kidney Bean Soup

Soak overnight in cold water to cover 3 cups of washed picked red kidney beans. Next day, transfer the beans, which should be almost dry, to the soup kettle. Add 3 medium-sized onions, quartered; 2 small carrots, quartered; 1 bouquet garni, composed of 1 bay leaf, 6 sprigs of parsley, and 1 sprig of thyme, tied together with kitchen thread; 2 whole cloves; and salt to taste. Barely cover with cold water, and bring to a boil. Then add 2 cups of red wine, and let simmer gently until the beans are tender, the time depending on the quality of the beans. Discard the bouquet garni, then rub the liquid and beans through a very fine sieve into a clean soup kettle. Taste for seasoning, adding salt and white pepper to taste, and when ready to serve, stir in 2 tablespoons of sweet butter. Serve with Croutons (No. 780).

POTAGE DE FAISAN RAMBOUILLET   [638]
Pheasant Potage Rambouillet Manner

Cut the remainder of carcasses of two pheasants into small pieces. Cut ¼ pound of calf's liver into thin slices, and 4 slices of bacon or an equal amount of ham into small cubes. Heat 2½ tablespoons of butter in a soup kettle, add the chopped carcasses, the calf's liver, and bacon or ham, and sear on all sides until brown, stirring almost constantly with a long-handled wooden spoon. Then pour in 2 quarts of hot chicken stock, freshly made with the carcass and bones of a roasted or boiled chicken, and ½ pint of dry white wine. Then add 1 bouquet garni, composed of 1 bay leaf, 1 sprig of sweet basil, 1 sprig of marjoram, 1 sprig of thyme, and 8 sprigs of fresh parsley, all tied together with kitchen thread. Season with 2 teaspoons of salt, a generous pinch of cayenne pepper or ⅛ teaspoon of sweet red pepper, 2 cloves, 1 small clove of garlic, a pinch of juniper berry powder, and a good pinch of mace powder. Bring to a boil, skimming carefully the scum, lower the flame, and allow to simmer very gently for 1½ hours. Strain through a fine-meshed sieve, and discard the bouquet garni and the garlic and cloves. Put the meat of the pheasant and the liver twice through the food chopper, using the finest blade, then rub through a fine-meshed sieve.

Heat 2 tablespoons of butter in a saucepan, stir in 1 tablespoon of flour until well browned, but not burned, and gradually stir the flour into the hot stock. Let it boil 3 or 4 times, and stir in the sieved pheasant and liver paste alternately with ¼ cup of good sherry wine. Taste for seasoning, and when ready to serve, pour into a heated soup tureen containing 3 tablespoons of well-cooked fluffy rice. Serve immediately.

POTAGE OF FROG'S LEGS AND CRAB   [639]
MEAT ROMANA
Italian

Cook until tender in 2 quarts of salted water 6 pairs of frog's legs, together with 1 bouquet garni, composed of 1 large bay leaf, 1 sprig of thyme, 8 sprigs of fresh parsley, and 2 sprigs of green celery leaves, tied together with kitchen thread; 1 medium-sized onion, chopped; ¼ cup of butter; 2 whole cloves; 1 clove of garlic, peeled and left whole; 8 peppercorns, gently bruised; and 2 teaspoons of salt. Discard the bouquet garni. Strain through a fine-meshed wire sieve into a clean saucepan. Remove the meat from the frog's legs, and put it through a food chopper together with 2 cups of cooked or canned crab meat, carefully picked and shredded. Add this to the strained broth. Bring this to a boil, and let boil gently for 2 or 3 minutes. Taste for seasoning, and when ready to serve, add ¼ cup of sherry wine. Serve in heated soup plates, each dusted with chopped parsley, and pass a side dish of Melba Toast (No. 791).

POTAGE DE FROMAGE A LA FRANÇAISE [640]

History said that this cheese soup used to be the favorite of Victor Hugo.

Melt 3 tablespoons of butter in a heavy saucepan. Blend in 3 tablespoons of flour, and season with salt to taste and a dash each of cayenne pepper and nutmeg. Then stir in 1 cup of sweet milk, which has been scalded with 1 small bay leaf, 4 thin slices of onion, 4 sprigs of fresh parsley, and a blade of garlic, and strained through a fine-meshed wire sieve. Stir constantly until the mixture bubbles, and continue cooking, stirring continually from the bottom of the pan, until smooth and thick. Stir in 1 cup of grated Gruyère cheese alternately with ½ cup of dry white wine, to which has been added 1 teaspoon of Worcestershire sauce and 1 teaspoon of prepared mustard. Bring to a boil, and serve in a heated soup tureen into which has been placed 2 tablespoons of finely chopped chives and 2 egg yolks, slightly beaten and well mixed with the chives. Lastly, and just before serving, fold into the potage 2 stiffly beaten egg whites. Serve in heated soup cups or plates with Jocko Toast (No. 790), which is dunked in the soup.

POTAGE LOMBARD [641]

Put 3 times through a food chopper, using the finest blade, 2 ounces of beef suet, 2 raw cleaned chicken livers, 1 lamb's sweetbread, and 2 tablespoons of peeled fresh mushrooms, adding gradually, while grinding, 1 whole slightly beaten fresh egg. Season this mixture to taste with mixed salt, pepper, and a little nutmeg, then rub through a fine-meshed hair sieve. Now blend in 1 teaspoon of finely chopped (not ground) black truffle. Divide this forcemeat into 3 equal parts. To one, add 1 tablespoon of cooked ground lobster eggs and a few drops of red vegetable coloring. Color the second part with a little cooked ground spinach and a few drops of the red coloring. Leave the third part plain. Shape into small balls the size of a marble, and poach them all together in a little clear boiling beef stock. Drain. Place the little dumplings (or *quenelles*, as they are called in French culinary terms) in a heated soup tureen. Add 12 cooked asparagus tips (tips only) and ¼ cup of cooked little green peas. When ready to serve, pour over, as gently as possible, 2 quarts of rapidly boiling clear beef stock. Dust the top with finely chopped chervil or parsley, and serve immediately in hot soup plates.

POTAGE AUX OEUFS BRETONNE　　　　　　[642]
Egg Potage Brittany Manner

Beat 8 fresh eggs well. Gradually add ¼ cup of flour, and continue beating until the mixture is smooth and free from lumps. Now beat in briskly, a little at a time, 1½ quarts of Beef Broth (No. 114), adding, with the last addition, 1 tablespoon each of finely chopped chives and onion juice. Bring this to a boil, remove from the fire, and season to taste with salt and pepper and a fresh grating of nutmeg. Stir well, serve in a soup tureen, the bottom of which has been lined with toasted bread squares, and sprinkle over each serving some grated cheese, preferably Gruyère.

POTAGE OF RICE AND TURNIPS BRETONNE [643]

Cut 6 medium-sized white turnips into thin slices. Place them in a large plate or platter, sprinkle with 1 teaspoon of salt, cover with another plate or platter, and let stand for 2 hours to draw the water, which should be discarded. Drain well. Place the turnip slices in a large skillet containing ¼ cup of butter, sprinkle with a little pepper, and very slightly brown the turnips, being careful not to let them stick to the skillet, stirring frequently. When brown, stir in 1½ quarts of concentrated Beef Broth (No. 114), made by reducing 3 quarts of beef broth to half its original volume. Season to taste with salt, pepper, and a fresh grating of nutmeg, and let boil for 15 minutes as gently as possible, after adding 1 cup of well-drained boiled rice. Rub the mixture through a fine-meshed wire sieve into a clean saucepan. Beat in, one at a time, 3 or 4 fresh egg yolks, return to the fire, and heat through. Strain through a fine sieve into a heated soup tureen containing small balls (the size of a marble) of twice-ground lean raw beef mixed with a little parsley and chives, finely chopped. Serve in heated soup plates with very fresh brown bread and butter finger sandwiches.

POTATO SOUP MEXICAN METHOD [644]
Sopa de Papas

Mexican cooking is not all beans, chili, tortillas, and tamales. Our ancient Oaxacan Indian *criada* taught us a few of her very Mexican dishes, which are today very favorably accepted by American gourmets.

Mix 2 cups of hot smoothly mashed potatoes, 1 cup of Chicken Broth (No. 25), 1 cup of Beef Broth (No. 114), and 2¾ cups of scalded sweet milk in a soup kettle. Add a small bouquet garni, composed of 1 bay leaf, 1 sprig of oregano, and 6 sprigs of fresh parsley, tied together with white kitchen thread. Cook the mixture very, very gently for 20 minutes. Strain through a fine-meshed wire sieve into a clean soup kettle. Thicken with 1 tablespoon of butter creamed with 2 teaspoons of flour, 1 teaspoon of finely chopped chives, and 1 generous teaspoon of finely chopped parsley, added bit by bit to the hot soup. Return to the fire, and let come to a boil. Put at once in a heated soup tureen, the top dusted with a little paprika, and serve in heated soup plates, each sprinkled with a few Croutons (No. 780).

RED CABBAGE SOUP FLAMANDE [645]

This healthy and nourishing soup is essentially and typically Flemish and is fully appreciated in Lower Flanders and throughout Belgium. It is particularly popular in the southern part of Holland.

Place 1½ pounds of red cabbage, finely shredded then sprinkled with 1 tablespoon of vinegar, in an iron soup kettle. Earthenware or enameled will answer, but do not use an aluminum or copper kettle as the acid of the cabbage will turn all into a black mass. The purpose of adding vinegar to the cabbage is to prevent its discoloring or acquiring a violet hue, which detracts from the appearance of the dish. Add 2 cups of peeled sliced potatoes, and pour over 3 cups of good Beef Consommé (No. 114). Water will answer the purpose, but the soup will not be so rich. Season to taste with salt and pepper, and place over a very low fire to cook for 1½ hours. Strain, and return the broth to the fire. Let boil once. Set aside, and add ½ generous cup of good red wine. Serve in soup plates, each having a piece of toasted French bread in the bottom before pouring the broth.

RED CHERRY WINE SOUP [646]
German Rote Kirschen Suppe

This German soup may be served hot or cold according to season or taste. If cold, no egg yolks are added; if hot, 3 egg yolks are added one by one, while stirring rapidly and briskly to prevent curdling.

Stone 1 generous pound of well-ripened red cherries, and place in a saucepan, being careful not to use aluminum or copper (an enameled one will do). Add 1 generous cup of red wine, an inch stick cinnamon (do not use cinnamon powder), and place over a low flame to cook slowly for 10 minutes. Meanwhile, pound or grind the stones with 3 generous tablespoons of fine bread crumbs, moistening gradually with 2½ cups of boiling water, and stirring well while pounding or grinding at the same time. Strain through a very fine cloth, and add the cherries and wine mixture. Sweeten to taste with granulated sugar, and add 2 more cups of red wine, which has been heated. Let simmer gently for 10 long minutes, or until a white foam appears on the surface. Then serve. If served hot, add, off the fire, the egg yolks as indicated above.

RICE AND CHEESE SOUP [647]

Scald 1½ quarts of milk with 1 tablespoon of chopped onion, 1 blade of mace, 1 bay leaf, and 4 sprigs of parsley. Melt 3 tablespoons of butter in a saucepan, and blend with 2½ tablespoons of flour, stirring constantly. Strain the milk, and stir gradually into the butter-flour mixture, stirring until the mixture thickens. Then stir in ¾ cup of grated American cheese until thoroughly melted. Season to taste with salt and white pepper, then gradually stir in 2 whole eggs, well beaten, stirring rapidly. Serve at once in soup plates with 1 or 2 tablespoons of hot boiled rice in each.

SCOTCH BROTH [648]

Combine the following ingredients in a soup kettle: 1¾ pounds of lean beef, left whole; ¾ cup of pearl barley; 4 medium-sized onions, whole, 2 stuck with 1 clove each; 1 cup of diced carrots; 1 cup of diced turnips; 1 cup of green peas; 3 quarts of boiling water; and salt and whole peppercorns to taste (about ½ generous teaspoon of peppercorns). Cover the kettle with a tight-fitting lid, and bring to the boiling point. Reduce the heat, and allow to simmer gently for 3 hours. Remove the meat, and keep for other use, or cut up in small pieces in the broth. Serve hot with crackers or biscuits. This fine nourishing and healthy soup may be kept in a cool place and reheated as needed.

SCOTCH BUTTERMILK SOUP [649]
A very old recipe

Take 2 quarts of day-old buttermilk, and let it come to a boil, stirring frequently from the bottom of the kettle lest it burn. Then add 1 cup of uncooked oatmeal, 1 teaspoon of salt, 1 tablespoon of sugar, or more to taste, and a generous dash of white pepper, *stirring constantly* for 10 to 12 minutes.

Should there be any left over, don't fret. It is just as good cold. Sprinkle a little cinnamon over it, and add sugar to taste for that sweet tooth.

You may want to dress up this soup, so throw in about 12 small dumplings. They are made with 1½ cups of flour, ½ teaspoon of salt, and enough sweet milk to make a stiff dough. The mixture should be smooth too. The day-old buttermilk usually has in it little pieces of butter, and these take care of the shortening. Just one important thing: *Don't let the soup boil again*, but just let it simmer gently when dropping in the little dumplings. When they come to the top, they are done.

SCOTCH MUTTON BROTH [650]

Separate the meat from the bone from a 3-pound piece of mutton. Place the bone in a soup kettle, and add 3 quarts of water, 2 medium-sized onions, halved, 1 bouquet garni composed of 1 bay leaf and 6 sprigs of fresh parsley tied together, 2 whole cloves, 12 whole peppercorns, and 2 tablespoons of fine barley, stirred with 1 tablespoon of flour and a little cold water. Season to taste, and allow this to simmer gently for 2½ hours, stirring frequently. In the meantime, cut the meat into small cubes, place it in a kettle, and cover with water generously. Add 1 small carrot, cubed small; one large leek, cubed small after thorough washing, using green and white parts; and 1 small knob of celery, peeled and cubed small. Season to taste with salt and pepper, bring to the boiling point, reduce the heat, and let simmer slowly for 2 hours. Remove the bones from the first kettle, and add the barley and liquid to the second kettle. Boil this steadily for 15 to 20 minutes to reduce and condense the broth to a rich stock. Skim off all the fat from the top, and serve immediately.

Important Note. For invalids, cook the bones and meat together and very slowly for 4 hours. Taste for seasoning before serving.

SOUR CREAM AND BEER SOUP   [651]
Palatinate—for dinner parties, serves 14 to 16

Bring 12 cups (3 quarts) of light beer to a boil. In another sauce-pan, cream 1 generous tablespoon of butter, and work in 1 generous tablespoon of flour, and 4 egg yolks, one at a time, creaming thoroughly after each addition. Season to taste with salt and pepper (a few grains of cayenne will not be amiss). Gradually pour over the mixture 4 cups (1 quart) of sour cream, beating thoroughly until smooth. Gradually stir this mixture slowly into the boiling beer, stirring rapidly and constantly. Serve in soup plates with grated Swiss cheese sprinkled over a piece of Jocko Toast (No. 790).

SOUR CREAM, POTATO, AND   [652]
RYE BREAD SOUP
Hungarian

Peel ½ dozen or so of medium-sized potatoes, and cut into small cubes. Place them in a saucepan, and cook in just enough salted water to cover, until tender. Pour over 1½ quarts of hot Beef Stock (No. 114) free of grease. Add 5 slices of rye bread, trimmed of crust and cubed small; 1 bouquet garni, composed of 1 large bay leaf, 1 sprig of thyme, 8 sprigs of fresh parsley, and 1 sprig of green celery leaves (tops), tied together with kitchen thread; 2 tablespoons of chopped onions; and 2 tablespoons of finely chopped lettuce. Cook this over a gentle heat until the liquid is reduced to about 1 quart. Discard the bouquet garni. Then rub the liquid and solid through a fine-meshed wire sieve into a clean saucepan. Season to taste with salt, pepper, and a fresh grating of nutmeg. Bring to a boil, stir in 1½ cups of sour cream, and let boil once. Serve in a heated soup tureen, and float over 6 thin slices of salami, cut into small pieces after removing the skin, and dust with finely chopped parsley and a little paprika.

SPINACH AND MUSHROOM SOUP   [653]

Thoroughly wash 2½ pounds of fresh spinach. Drain well, and put through a food chopper. Place in a large soup kettle. Do likewise with 1½ pounds of fresh peeled mushrooms, using stems and caps, and add to the kettle. Pour over 1 cup of rich Meat Stock (No. 114), to which is added 1 tablespoon of onion juice, salt, pepper and a blade of mace, a pinch of allspice, and 2 whole cloves. Cover tightly, and bring to a rapid boil, then simmer for 20 minutes over a gentle fire. Lift the cover, and pour over 2 cups (1 pint) of scalded milk and 2 cups of undiluted evaporated milk. Boil once, correct the seasoning, adding more salt if necessary, and serve in soup plates over 1 tablespoon of hot cooked rice for each serving.

SPLIT PEA SOUP DANISH MANNER [654]
Gule Arter

Put 3 pounds of brined pork spareribs, carefully washed in several changes of cold water, in a large kettle. Bring to a boil, and drain. Repeat the parboiling 3 times to remove all excess brine from the meat. Do not trim the excess fat from the ribs. After parboiling 3 times, place the ribs in a large soup kettle, bring to a boil, and skim the scum carefully. Allow to boil steadily for 25 minutes. Then add 1½ pounds of washed, picked, and soaked overnight yellow split peas; 2 stalks of celery, scraped and cut into inch pieces; 3 medium-sized carrots, scraped and quartered; 4 medium-sized leeks, trimmed, the first outside leaves discarded, the root cut, the leeks halved lengthwise, carefully washed in several changes of cold water, and then cut into ½-inch slices; 1 parsnip, peeled and diced; 1 bouquet garni, composed of 2 bay leaves, 1 sprig of thyme, and 10 sprigs of fresh parsley, tied together with white kitchen thread; 10 peppercorns, and very, very little salt. Cook gently until the mixture is the consistency of porridge, or about 3½ to 4 hours. Remove the ribs, chop the meat, discard the bones and bouquet garni, and return the chopped meat to the soup. Taste for seasoning, and serve immediately in heated soup bowls.

Note. The very same soup is also made with smoked mutton instead of salted pork ribs, but the meat is not returned to the pot. It is served aside with *Äggekage* or pork pancakes and mushroom sauce.

TOMATO AND LENTIL SOUP GASCONNE [655]

Wash and soak 1 cup of lentils for 12 hours. Drain. Cut 4 tablespoons of lean raw ham finely. Chop 1 medium-sized onion, 1 medium-sized carrot, ½ white turnip, 1 small leek, and 3 fresh tomatoes, peeled. Heat 3 tablespoons of butter in a soup kettle, and put in the ham and all the vegetables, except the tomatoes and lentils. Cover closely, and smother for 2 or 3 minutes, shaking the kettle frequently. Then add the tomatoes and drained lentils, cover closely, and steam for 20 minutes, shaking the kettle frequently. Now pour in 1½ quarts of Beef Stock (No. 114); 1 bouquet garni, composed of 2 bay leaves, 8 sprigs of parsley, 1 sprig of thyme, and 1 sprig of green celery leaves (top), tied together with kitchen thread; 2 whole cloves; 1 small clove of garlic, mashed; and salt and pepper to taste. Let simmer very gently, tightly covered, for 2½ hours, or till the lentils are tender. Discard the bouquet garni, thicken the soup with a little flour diluted in a little cold water, and bring to a boil. When boiling, stir in 2 cups (1 pint) of thin cream, undiluted evaporated milk, or the top of the milk in the bottle. Heat well, taste for seasoning, and pour at once into a heated soup tureen containing some fried Croutons (No. 780). Serve at once, each serving sprinkled with a little chopped chives.

TURKEY SOUP WITH ALMONDS [656]
Soupe de Dinde Amandine

In a large soup kettle, place all the cracked turkey bones from the carcass and scraps of meat and skin; 1 bouquet garni, composed of 12 sprigs of fresh parsley, 4 sprigs of celery leaves (tops), 2 large bay leaves, 1 sprig of thyme, 2 whole cloves, tied together with kitchen thread; 8 peppercorns, bruised; 1 sprig of marjoram; 2 small carrots, grated and quartered; 2 medium-sized onions, quartered; 2 leeks, halved, carefully washed, using green and white parts; 1 small white turnip, peeled and quartered; and 2 teaspoons of salt. Cover with 2 quarts of water mixed with 2 cups of dry white wine. Very slowly bring to the boiling point, then reduce the heat as low as possible, and allow to simmer gently for 2 long hours, with the lid of the soup kettle tilted slightly. Discard the bouquet garni. Strain into a clean kettle, and let cool, uncovered. When cold, skim off very carefully all the fat, heat the stock to the boiling point, then strain through a fine cloth. Heat to the boiling point again, and let boil until the liquid is reduced to 2 quarts (scant) to condense the flavor. When ready to serve in cups, stir in 4 or 5 tablespoons of toasted ground almonds, and dust the top of each cup with a tiny pinch of paprika.

Note. This stock also makes a good foundation for black bean, kidney bean, navy bean, lentil or green or yellow pea soup. You may also substitute Brazil nut meats, toasted, then ground, for almonds. Goose, guinea hen, duck, or several carcasses of squabs may be prepared in the same way.

HOW TO PREPARE AND COOK TURTLE   [657]

Very few homemakers, and cooks for that matter, know how to prepare turtle. This is so simple, so easy, that a novice, after reading the following paragraphs can execute the work with the ease of an accomplished fishman.

To soften and dissolve the foreign matter attached to the flesh or the shell, plunge the live turtle into a pan containing sufficient water to allow it to swim easily, renew the water several times, and allow the turtle to remain thus for about 1 hour. Then scrub thoroughly with a brush, and immediately plunge the turtle into *unsalted* water, boiling rapidly, until the skin of the head and feet becomes white and may be removed easily by rubbing with a dry clean towel.

Cook the turtle in plain *unsalted* water, or it may be steamed, the time will vary according to size, although more than ¾ hour should not be necessary for an ordinary-sized turtle, the cooking point being determined when the feet are soft under pressure of the fingers. Any turtle of ordinary size requiring more than ¾ of an hour to cook is probably of inferior quality and should be set aside, as the meat, although acquiring tenderness through long cooking, is liable to be stringy and of poor quality, except for soup.

Once cooked to the required point, the turtle is set aside to cool. Then the nails are pulled from the feet, the under shell is cut close to the upper shell, and the flesh is carefully removed. The feet are separated from the body, cut in small pieces, and set aside. The upper shell is emptied, and the gall bladder is discarded. Any small particle of the gall bladder remaining in the meat will impart a bitter flavor to the dish. The sand bag, heart, tail, and intestines are also discarded, as well as the white muscles of the inside.

The eggs are carefully removed and set aside with the feet and liver. These are immediately sprinkled with salt and coarse black pepper, and placed in a kettle with the turtle meat. Cover with cold water, and add a few slices of carrots and onions, a bouquet garni composed of 1 large bay leaf and 10 sprigs of fresh parsley tied together with kitchen thread, and 2 whole slightly bruised cloves. The covered kettle is set on the range for 20 minutes to boil rapidly, then moved into a moderately hot oven, still covered, and the cooking process is continued for another 20 or 25 minutes.

The turtle is then ready for soup, a terrapin dish, or any of the delicious preparations which may be made with this reptile, such as terrapin à la Maryland, Baltimore, epicure, New Orleans, à la Newburg, or Delmonico—on toast or patty shells.

This truly American delicacy, be it the green turtle, snapping turtle, terrapin, or its numerous relatives among the edible turtles, is now available in handy cans in first-class grocery stores and delicatessens.

TURTLE SOUP [658]
Home style

Wash a turtle as indicated above, and cook as directed. Cut the skin loose from the under shell, skin the legs and neck, and remove all the fat. Save the liver. Cut the meat into small pieces. Place in a large soup kettle with ½ cup of fresh peas, 1 tablespoon of well-washed barley, ½ small bunch of celery, chopped, 1 large carrot, scraped then diced, 1½ cups of tomato pulp, and 1 large onion, chopped. Season with salt and pepper to taste, and add also a bouquet garni composed of 1 large bay leaf and 8 sprigs of fresh parsley, tied together with kitchen thread, 1 clove, and ½ teaspoon of allspice. Cover, and cook to the boiling point, then reduce the flame, and let simmer for 25 minutes, or until the vegetables are tender. Drop in 12 small Egg Dumplings (No. 728). Cook 10 minutes longer over a brisk flame. Remove from the fire, add 2 tablespoons of either Madeira or sherry wine, and serve.

MOCK TURTLE SOUP I [659]
Country style—using calf's head

That versatile viand, veal, masquerading around the civilized world in chicken croquettes and salad, game pasties, galantine of turkey, turtle soup, terrapin stew, and even, it is charged, in pâté de foie gras, is a mystery meat throughout its brief career. Lamb is so much like mutton—young pig so much like pork—but it's always hard to realize that a pale veal cutlet would have been in a few more months a ruddy and rugged beefsteak and that the calf's head will masquerade as turtle soup.

Scald a calf's head with the skin on, split it, and take out the brains and bones of the nose (the butcher will do it for you). Blanch it well in several waters. Place in a large kettle, and cover with cold water. Bring it to a boil, and skim as often as any scum rises. When the head has boiled gently till tender, take it out, and when cool enough to handle, cut off the skin and fat parts, and cut some of the fleshy parts into cubes 1½ inches square. Peel the tongue, and cut it up in the same way.

Meanwhile, put the broken bones and trimmings back into the water they were boiled in, with 1 pound of lean beef and some knuckle of veal (about half a knuckle) with only a little of the meat left on (but not cooked bones). Let it stew for 4 consecutive hours as slowly as possible. Now strain through a fine cloth into an earthenware container, and when quite cold and the fat has formed a cake, remove the fat carefully. If the directions have been followed, the stock will be a stiff jelly, or nearly so. Put this jelly again into a soup kettle with 1 dozen small white onions, first sliced and browned in a little butter. Thicken with a little mixed flour and butter as needed. Season highly with white pepper, cloves, cayenne, mace, and basil, sage, and lemon thyme or lemon peel to taste. When all are well cooked together, strain through a fine-meshed wire sieve into a fresh pan. Add the meat, ¼ cup of Madeira wine or sherry (more or less, according to taste), about 2 dozen Chicken Forcemeat Balls (No. 671), as many Egg Balls (No. 672), and the juice of a large lemon, strained. Serve at once.

MOCK TURTLE SOUP II [660]
Soupe Fausse Tortue à la Française—using calf's feet

This wonderful soup or potage is the creation of the French chef, Bertrand Guegan, author of the famous *Almanach de Cocagne*, a cook book dedicated to the real gourmands and *francs buveurs*— good drinkers—of the entire world.

Place in the bottom of a thick soup kettle 1½ tablespoons of butter; 1 medium-sized onion and 2 medium-sized carrots, finely chopped; 1 veal knuckle of about 1 pound and 2 pounds of shin of beef, both cut into portion size, using bones and meat; and 2 calf's feet (preferably the black ones, as they resemble in flavor the turtle flesh more than the white ones), previously split in two, then blanched. You can see there's no calf's head used in the French method. But if you use cooked calf's head instead of calf's feet, you *must* add 1 extra pound of calf's knuckle. At any rate, the French do not use the calf's head to make this rich, nourishing, delicious, and inimitable soup.

When the mixture begins to get color, pour over 2 cups of hot water, cover the kettle, and allow the mixture to simmer gently till there's almost no more liquid in the kettle, stirring frequently to prevent scorching, which will spoil forever this soup. Then pour over the almost-dry mixture 4 quarts of good Beef Bouillon (No. 114), or hot water. Add 2 whole cloves, 10 whole peppercorns, tenderly crushed, 1 large bay leaf, and a tiny pinch of salt. Cover, and let simmer gently for about 1½ hours, the meat being tender, but not in shreds. Remove the calf's feet very carefully, and let them cool under a heavy weight. The remaining meat may be used for another meal, either in *miroton* (hash) or salad. Strain the bouillon through a fine sieve or *chinois* (a fine strainer in the shape of a cone), and keep hot after skimming off very carefully all the fat. This soup must be very lean.

In a small saucepan, place 2 teaspoons of butter and equal parts of flour, and blend over a low flame till the mixture begins to bubble; then moisten with 2 cups of the hot strained bouillon, blend thoroughly, and strain into another clean saucepan. Allow this blending to simmer very gently while preparing what we call the turtle sauce. In a clean small saucepan, place 1 large shallot, finely chopped, and 1 generous blade each of powdered thyme, sage, savory, sweet basil, and rosemary. This is called in French culinary terms *herbes à tortue* or turtle herbs. Pour over 8 tablespoons of the best Madeira wine you may have; but please, re-please, do not use the so-called cooking Madeira wine or sherry, but real Madeira. Cover the saucepan and allow the mixture to infuse for 5 minutes over the lowest flame possible, without letting it boil.

Meantime, cut the meat from the pressed cold calf's feet into very small squares (the size of a large pea, but square). Place the meat in a saucepan. Add 2 generous tablespoons of tomato paste (commercial) to the Madeira infusion. Stir well, and pour it over the calf's feet squares. Then add ⅓ cup of cooked mushrooms, cut the same size as the calf's feet meat.

Finale. Again strain the bouillon through a fine, very fine, strainer, or a muslin cloth, into a clean kettle. Taste for seasoning, adding whatever salt is needed, then stir in cayenne pepper the size of a lentil, moistened with a little bouillon. Now combine together the bouillon, the thickening (butter and flour), and the Madeira wine mixture, and finally 5 hard-cooked egg yolks, finely chopped. Serve as hot as possible, and at once.

WHITE TURNIP AND CABBAGE SOUP   [661]
Also called Potage Franc-Comtois

Peel 2 large white turnips, scoop into small balls the size of a large pea, and cook in enough beef stock to cover, until tender but not broken, and keep hot. There should be 1 cup. Heat 1½ quarts of Beef Consommé (No. 114). Stir in 2 cups of finely shredded cabbage, 1 cup of small raw potato cubes, and 1 cup of freshly shelled green peas, and cook for 15 minutes, then add the cooked "turnip peas." Season to taste with salt and pepper, and when ready to serve, stir in ½ cup of vermicelli, which has been cooked in a little beef stock, 4 tablespoons of cooked rice, and 1 tablespoon each of finely chopped parsley and chives. Stir in 2 tablespoons of sweet butter, and serve in a heated soup tureen.

WILD RABBIT SOUP [662]
Hunter style

During the autumn and winter, the cottontails provide some of the most delightful and interesting sport available to American hunters, because they are abundant everywhere. Wild rabbits are an important item of food supply, and their meat can provide tasty variation to any meal, and a very delicious soup.

Wash a young wild cottontail rabbit, and if it is to be served separately, keep it whole, and truss for boiling; if not, cut it into small joints, and remove the liver, kidneys, and like parts. Then wash carefully and quickly in several changes of cold water, the last with a scant teaspoon of soda in a little lukewarm water. Drain, and place the rabbit pieces in a soup kettle together with ½ pound of salt pork, previously parboiled to remove excess salt, cut into cubes, then tried out over a low flame to remove excess fat, having the cubes a little on the crackling side. Cover the rabbit pieces and pork cracklings with 2½ quarts of cold water. Bring slowly to a boil, skimming carefully and thoroughly. Then add 1 large bay leaf, a 2-inch piece of scraped parsley root, celeriac, the size of a hen's egg, coarsely chopped, and 7 or 8 peppercorns, finely crushed, but no salt. Continue simmering for 30 to 35 minutes longer. Then add 2 medium-sized onions, 1 medium-sized white turnip, 1 large leek, quartered, carefully washed, folded in three or four, and tied with white kitchen thread, and also ¼ cup of uncooked washed rice. Continue cooking very gently over a low heat for about 35 to 40 minutes. Now remove the pieces of rabbit from the soup kettle. Remove the meat from the bones, cut it into small cubes, and return it to the broth to be reheated. Season to taste with salt, and bring to a boil. Remove from the fire, and stir in ¼ cup of the best Madeira wine you can get. Serve with toast in heated soup plates.

Chapter Ten

BALL GARNISHES
FOR SOUPS

❦

*Early eighteenth-century Spaniards in Mexico
ornamented their plates and tables with hibiscus. They even used the flower to garnish meats
and served a condiment of vinegared hibiscus.*

I N SERVING MEALS, THE APPEAL TO THE EYE IS FULLY AS IM-
portant as the appeal to the stomach. Indeed, a finicky or
laggard appetite may be stimulated, or a very commonplace dish
made appetizing by the use of a garnish which offers the interest of
color and design as a relief to the monotony of a plain roast, fish,
soup, pudding, or cake. Some garnishes are almost solely decorative,
but others, such as dumplings, alimentary paste, tiny food balls, or
the like, may constitute a nutritive addition to the menu.

Depending both on the character of the dish and of the materials
employed, the garnish may be arranged as a border, in the form of
small clusters, in balls, in stripes, or dotted over the entire surface.

The beauty and effectiveness of a garnish is largely dependent on
color contrast. A touch of green is always refreshing with meats and
fish, used alone or in combination with one or more brilliant-hued
vegetables cut in fancy shapes, and there are any number of substitutes for the sadly overworked parsley. A wide variety of pleasing
combinations can be selected from the garnish recipes found in this
chapter.

COLOR INFLUENCE IN GARNISHES [664]

Colors have had a part in history and food, for instance:

Red. Since the days of ancient Greece and Rome, red has been
deemed sacred to Mars, the god of war, and therefore was formerly
employed for military uniforms. Red is particularly associated with
danger, passion, power, and adventure—danger lights in traffic, warn-
ings, and war itself. In its element of suggesting power, red finds a
place on many national flags, and in all mythologies, red is the
symbol of passion. It is worthy of notice that after the fall of Con-
stantinople, the last great center of natural purple dye production,
Pope Paul II introduced scarlet for cardinals' robes, and during the
Renaissance, Venice was the principal trade center for scarlet dyes.

In garnishes for meat, fish, or poultry, sliced red beets, raw cranberries, currant jelly, pimientos, radishes, red cabbage, tomatoes, and
anchovies are very appropriate. As part of the meal and as garnishes,
they should always be chosen for flavor, texture, and general appearance.

Green and Gray. These colors were at one time the colors of pov-
erty and at another of richness. Charlemagne decreed green as the
color "for the working people and the farmer." And as food gar-

nishes for meat, fish, game, or poultry, we have asparagus tips, Brussels sprouts, carrot tops, chives, dandelion, dill pickle, midget gherkins, green pepper in slices or rings, lettuce, mint, parsley, chervil, sorrel, spinach, and watercress.

White. This is the color of innocence and immortality, and its association with sanctity was promoted by the early Christians who used rough undyed fabrics to symbolize integrity and virtue. Lady Godiva rode a white horse; Sir Galahad was clad in white armor, and when Undine was given the kiss of immortality, her gown "turned lily white."

White is also associated with some negative qualities. In China, the "coldness of death" is symbolized by white flowers, and it is sometimes the color of mourning. White, in the legends of Europe and America, is the costume of those ghosts that haunt ancestral homes and lonely graveyards, presaging death. With the Renaissance, white became a "color of elegance and luxury," and was often embroidered with gold threads.

In food garnishes, we have celery curls, coleslaw, cream cheese balls, egg white, onions, white turnip balls, chicken slices or strips, grated coconut, whipped cream, and cream or white sauce.

Brown. In ancient Rome, brown was sacred to Ceres, the earth goddess, and for many centuries has been the favored color for the clothes of people familiar with the soil. During the Middle Ages, brown was the typical peasant color. Franciscan friars in brown hat and habit walked through Europe in the service of humanity. Even today, brown attire is closely associated with life in the country.

In food garnishes, we have all the fried foods and the brown sauces.

Yellow. The color of the sun rising in the east was the sacred color of imperial China, and was worn for mourning to symbolize the "return of the soul to the sun." In the West, however, yellow is the sign of spring, bringing primrose, daffodils, and crocuses. In the commercial use of the common crocus lies the story of yellow dyes. Nearly four thousand years ago, the Egyptian saffron crocus was used to dye the bindings of mummies, and the earliest known figure subject in fresco painting is the "Saffron Gatherer," for in ancient time, the saffron crocus was used as an herb to flavor and as a drug to cure, as well as a dye.

In food garnishes, we have egg yolk, cooked fresh, or hard-cooked, kumquats, lemon, orange peel and slices, apricots, crystallized ginger, tiny tomato plums, and yellow turnip.

A cook today thinks of a dish as an artist does of his oils. His pictures would lack life and interest if he did not use a variety of color to give highlights and lowlights. A poor color combination, for example, would be creamed tuna, mashed potatoes, cauliflower, and white bread.

Flat surfaces are uninteresting. It is the valleys, hills, and mountains, in combination with the meadows, that make scenic beauty even in a dish, which should have color, form, flavor, texture, balance, arrangement, consistency, temperature. This is what is called "eye appeal" in cookery.

Garnishing food is a very commendable habit at any time, but garnishing can be overdone. Keep the garnish simple and edible; never give a dish a worked-over look. Food which appears to have been handled a great deal in preparation is unappetizing. And most people are wary of food which looks too unusual.

ALSATIAN BURGER BALLS   [665]

A delicious way to use a leftover cooked meat. These little balls are appropriate for almost any kind of hot soup, clear or thick.

Season highly, with salt, cayenne pepper, a few grains of curry powder, a dash each of nutmeg, sage, and thyme, ¾ cup of leftover cooked meat (any kind). Shape in tiny balls the size of a marble. Roll in seasoned flour, and fry in hot fat until delicately brown on all sides, shaking the pan almost constantly. Serve hot.

CALF'S BRAIN AND EGG BALLS   [666]

Very appropriate for mock turtle, oxtail, and vegetable soups or vegetable chowders.

Mash 3 hard-cooked egg yolks to a paste with ½ teaspoon of Worcestershire sauce, a dash of Tabasco sauce, and a little salt, pepper, and paprika to taste. Mix in 2 tablespoons of boiled, skinned, and mashed calf's brain, mixing thoroughly, adding last 1 teaspoon of sherry wine (optional). Shape into tiny balls, the size of a large marble, and roll in seasoned flour. Drop in the soup 5 minutes before serving.

Sweetbread Balls. Substitute cooked sweetbreads for the calf's brain.

BURGER BALLS WITH MARJORAM   [667]

Appropriate for beef, vegetable, oxtail, or clear soup.

To ½ pound of finely ground lean raw meat (beef, lamb, mutton, pork, ham, or veal), add 1 teaspoon of grated onion, ½ teaspoon of grated lemon rind, ¼ teaspoon of dried marjoram, salt, pepper, and nutmeg to taste, and sufficient moistened crackers to bind. Mix thoroughly, roll into balls the size of a small walnut, and 10 minutes before serving, drop them into gently boiling soup (clear or otherwise). Cook for 10 minutes, and serve at once.

BURGER CHEESE BEEF BALLS   [668]

Appropriate for beef, vegetable, oxtail, or clear soup.

Mix ½ pound of ground fresh lean beef with ½ scant cup of soft bread crumbs, ¼ cup of grated cheese (any desired kind), and 1 tablespoon each of finely chopped parsley and chives, and season to taste with salt, pepper, and nutmeg, mixing thoroughly. Shape into tiny balls, the size of a large marble by rolling in the palm of hands. Drop into the simmering soup, a few at a time, stirring to separate them, and let simmer gently for about 15 to 20 minutes. Serve hot in the soup.

CRACKER SPICY BALLS   [669]

Appropriate for almost any kind of hot soup, clear or thick, including chowders.

Sieve enough cracker crumbs to make a half cup. Mix together 2 eggs, 3 tablespoons of butter or margarine, 2 teaspoons each of finely chopped parsley, onion, and chives, and add to the sieved crackers, then season to taste with salt, pepper, nutmeg, and mace. Lastly moisten with enough catsup to make a mixture hard enough to handle. Shape into small balls the size of a large marble, and drop into simmering soup 10 minutes before serving.

CRUMB MARROW BALLS   [670]

Leftover bread can be made into all sorts of tasty dishes. There is no excuse for the wasteful habit of throwing it out. When thoroughly dried, broken up, and rolled into crumbs, then sieved, it can be used for coating croquettes or topping scalloped dishes. Bread not quite so dry can be crumbed and mixed with other ingredients to make delicious meat loaves, filling or stuffing for meat, poultry, or fish, or to make delicious balls for garnishing a soup, clear or thick.

Mix 3 tablespoons of sieved dry bread crumbs, 1½ tablespoons of beef marrow, 1 scant teaspoon of grated lemon rind, salt, pepper, and nutmeg to taste, and 1½ teaspoons of finely chopped parsley. Add just enough unbeaten egg white to moisten. Form into tiny balls the size of a marble, drop into hot soup, and cook until the balls rise on the surface of the soup. Serve immediately.

CANADIAN CHICKEN FORCEMEAT BALLS   [671]

Appropriate for chicken consommé or bouillon and any kind of chicken soup.

Put through a food chopper 2 raw chicken breasts, then pound, and rub through a fine sieve. This will make about 1 scant cup of raw chicken meat. Season to taste with salt, white pepper, and a few grains of nutmeg. Scald 1 cup of dry white bread crumbs with 1 cup of thin cream, or undiluted evaporated milk, and a pinch of mace. Remove from the heat, and add to the bread crumb mixture 3 tablespoons of butter, then stir in the pounded chicken meat. Lastly, mix in 2 egg whites, stiffly beaten with a few grains of salt to taste, mixing thoroughly. Form into small balls the size of a large marble. Roll the balls in the beaten egg yolks, seasoned to taste with salt and pepper, then in sieved bread crumbs. Fry in hot deep fat until nicely browned. Drain on absorbent paper or a towel, and serve in hot soup.

These balls also may be served as a main dish over mashed potatoes, spinach, macaroni, noodles, spaghetti, or any kind of cooked green vegetable.

EGG BALLS   [672]

Appropriate for consommé and any kind of clear soup.

Rub 2 hard-cooked eggs through a fine sieve, season with a few grains each of salt, white pepper, and nutmeg, and mix with ½ teaspoon of melted butter and enough raw egg yolk (about one) to make of handling consistency. Shape into small balls the size of a marble. Roll in seasoned flour, and sauté in butter until delicately brown all over, rocking the pan almost constantly. Add 2 or 3 balls to each serving.

Note. You may plunge the balls in hot deep fat for a short minute, instead of sautéing them in butter. Instead of moistening with raw egg yolk, you may use egg white (raw and unbeaten). Cook the same way.

FRANKFURTER BALLS [673]

Appropriate for all clear or thick soups, except chowders and fish and cream soups.

Mix thoroughly the following ingredients: ¾ cup of sieved bread or cracker crumbs; 3 skinned and ground frankfurters; 1 whole fresh egg and 1 fresh egg yolk; 1 tablespoon and 1 teaspoon of melted bacon or ham drippings, butter or margarine; and salt, pepper, nutmeg, and paprika to taste. Moisten with enough cold bouillon, tomato juice, or water to hold the mixture together, about 1 generous tablespoonful. Form into tiny balls the size of a marble, and let stand aside for about 30 minutes to mellow and ripen. Drop the balls into boiling soup, and cook about 12 to 15 minutes.

MIGNONNETTE or PUFF BALLS [674]

Appropriate for any kind of clear soup, including fish.

Bring 5 teaspoons of rich milk and 2 teaspoons of butter or margarine to the boiling point. Add ½ cup of flour, sifted with a pinch of salt and a few grains of cayenne and nutmeg, all at once, and stir briskly until the mixture is smooth and leaves the sides of the saucepan. Remove from the fire, and cool to lukewarm; then add 2 unbeaten eggs, one at a time, beating briskly after each addition. Drop small pieces of the dough from the tip of a teaspoon into hot deep fat, and cook until nicely browned. Drain on absorbent paper, and add to the soup, just before serving, or pass them on the side and as hot as possible.

VEAL BALLS [675]

Very appropriate for any kind of clear or thick soup, except chowders and fish soups.

Combine thoroughly ½ cup of cooked ground veal, ¼ cup of soft bread crumbs, and 1 whole unbeaten fresh egg, and season with salt, pepper, and a generous pinch of poultry seasoning. Shape into tiny balls the size of a marble. Roll in seasoned thin cream or undiluted evaporated milk, then in seasoned flour, and brown in 2 or 3 tablespoons of butter or margarine. Serve hot on a side dish.

Note. Any kind of cooked meat, game, or poultry, as well as fish, may be prepared in the same way.

Chapter Eleven

CUSTARD GARNISHES FOR SOUPS

"If you've got the TOUCH—*mark you. I only say if—but if you've anything like the genuine* TOUCH, *you're provided for for life. An' further . . . you 'old your neighbours, friends and employers in the 'ollow of your 'and. . . . Everything which a man is depends on what 'e puts inside 'im. . . . A good* COOK's *a King of men —besides being thunderin' well off if 'e don't drink. It's the only sure business in the whole round world."*

His Gift, KIPLING

Fine feathers may not always make fine birds, but fine garnishes can go a long way toward making a soup, as well as any other kind of dish. Let us consider the custard. First of all, it has ingredients which we absolutely need in our daily diet, and surely no more delightful way of consuming milk and eggs can be found than the custard, be it for dessert or garnish. These custard garnishes are never sweetened, but simply seasoned with salt, pepper, nutmeg, or any other seasoning used in cookery. Their variations are many, but the base is always eggs, milk, cream, or meat, fish, poultry, game, or vegetable stock.

The common causes of custard failure are cooking too long and cooking at too high a temperature. The custard should be set in a pan of hot, but not boiling, water and baked in a slow oven (250°–275° F.) only until it is firm, or set, when a silver knife inserted in it comes out clean (about 15 to 20 minutes). The water around it must never boil during the baking. You may even take the custard out when there is a thick jelly on the knife if the shallow buttered pan is thick enough to retain heat, which will finish the cooking. Furthermore, to avoid having a custard curdle during the cooking, be sure that the liquid used is thoroughly heated, then always add the hot liquid to the beaten eggs, and strain through a fine cloth to remove any foam which may be found after beating the mixture. When cold, unmold, and cut into fancy shapes.

For custard garnishes to keep their extreme *délicatesse*, it is important to follow exactly the directions as regards the amount of ingredients indicated, which are tested and retested to ensure solidification.

These special custards also may be served as a main dish, especially during the Lenten season, by doubling the amount of ingredients so as to serve 6 persons. Serve the hot or cold custard, cut in individual portion size, with your favorite sauce, such as tomato, mushroom, brown, or cream sauce. Custards will keep well for a whole week in a good refrigerator, and thus can be made in advance.

Never add the custard to the soup until ready to serve. It should be very firm, clear, and not spongy.

ALMOND CUSTARD GARNISH [677]

Combine ½ cup of soft cooked rice with 4 tablespoons of almond milk, made by grinding, then pounding or rubbing through a fine sieve 12 almonds, freshly blanched, with 3 tablespoons of thin cream, or undiluted evaporated milk. Season to taste with a few grains of salt, and beat in 4 fresh egg yolks, slightly beaten, then strain through a fine cloth. Turn the mixture into a shallow buttered baking dish, and bake as indicated.

ARTICHOKE BOTTOM CUSTARD GARNISH   [678]

Mash 4 ounces of canned drained artichoke bottoms, and rub through a fine sieve with 3 tablespoons of heavy cream. Season to taste with salt and white pepper. Then beat in 4 fresh egg yolks, slightly beaten, and again rub through a fine sieve, adding, while rubbing, ½ cup of white sauce. Turn the mixture into a shallow buttered baking dish, and bake as indicated.

ASPARAGUS CUSTARD GARNISH   [679]

Drain a 1-pound can of asparagus tips. Remove the buds, reserving the stalks for other use, and rub the buds or tips through a fine sieve with ¾ cup of rich cream sauce, highly seasoned with salt, pepper, and nutmeg to taste. Again rub through a fine sieve. Then beat in 4 fresh egg yolks, slightly beaten. Turn the mixture into a shallow buttered baking dish, and bake as indicated.

BEET CUSTARD GARNISH   [680]

A fine and lovely ruby-colored garnish to look at, and very tasty too.

Drain half a can of red beets, sliced or whole, and rub through a fine sieve. Divide the beets into two parts, reserving one for future use. Place the other half in a fine cloth and squeeze out all the extra juice, which add to the remaining half. Again rub the squeezed beet pulp through a fine sieve with ¾ cup of scalded cream, hot white sauce, hot cream sauce, or hot Béchamel sauce. Season to taste with salt, white pepper, and a dash each of nutmeg and mace. Then beat in 4 fresh egg yolks, slightly beaten. Turn the mixture into a shallow buttered baking dish, and bake as indicated.

CALF'S BRAIN CUSTARD GARNISH   [681]

Take 4 ounces of blanched cleaned calf's brain, and rub through a fine sieve with ¾ cup of scalded cream sauce. Season to taste with garlic salt, white pepper, and nutmeg. Then beat in 2 fresh eggs, beaten with 1 fresh egg yolk. Turn the mixture into a shallow buttered baking dish, and bake as indicated.

Sweetbreads Custard Garnish. Substitute cooked sweetbreads for calf's brain, and bake as directed.

CARROT CUSTARD GARNISH [682]

Smother very gently, in 2 tablespoons of butter, 3 ounces of grated red of raw carrots with a small piece of bay leaf, stirring frequently until tender. Then stir in ¼ cup of strained carrot juice alternately with ½ cup of hot cream sauce. Cook for 5 minutes over a gentle flame. Strain through a fine cloth, then beat in 1 fresh egg beaten with 2 fresh egg yolks. Turn the mixture into a shallow buttered baking dish, and bake as indicated.

CELERY CUSTARD GARNISH [683]

Put through a food chopper, using the finest blade, enough celery (green tops and stalks) to make ½ cup, and cook very slowly in 2 tablespoons of butter until tender, stirring frequently. Drain well, stir in ¾ cup of thin cream, undiluted evaporated milk, or a thin cream sauce, and bring to the boiling point. Strain through a fine sieve or cloth, pressing well, then beat in 3 fresh egg yolks, slightly beaten; season to taste with celery salt, a few grains of cayenne, and a dash of nutmeg, and turn the mixture into a shallow buttered baking dish, and bake as indicated.

CHERVIL CUSTARD GARNISH [684]

Infuse 2 teaspoons of chopped chervil in ¾ cup of boiling Beef Consommé (No. 114) for 10 minutes. Strain through a fine cloth, then gradually pour the hot minted consommé over 1 fresh egg, beaten with 2 fresh egg yolks, and seasoned to taste with salt and white pepper, beating briskly while pouring. Strain again through a fine cloth into a shallow buttered baking dish, and bake as indicated.

CHESTNUT CUSTARD GARNISH [685]

Combine ¼ cup of thick chestnut purée with ¾ cup of hot rich Veal Broth (No. 11), and rub through a fine sieve. Season to taste with salt and white pepper and a good pinch of granulated sugar, and beat in 1 whole fresh egg and 2 fresh egg yolks, slightly beaten.

Turn the mixture into a shallow buttered baking dish, and bake as indicated.

CHICKEN CUSTARD GARNISH [686]

Put through a food chopper, using the finest disk, a cooked breast of chicken. Then rub through a fine sieve with ¼ cup of hot rich Chicken Bouillon (No. 25), fresh or canned, alternately with ½ cup of hot Cream Sauce (No. 346), Béchamel Sauce (No. 348), or heavy fresh cream. Beat in 3 fresh egg yolks, slightly beaten. Season to taste with salt and white pepper. Turn the mixture into a shallow buttered baking dish, and bake as indicated.

Chicken and Tomato Custard Garnish. Use the same ingredients, plus 2 tablespoons of tomato paste, added alternately with the beaten egg.

Meat Custard Garnish. Substitute the same quantity of cold cooked meat, any kind, but lean meat only, for the chicken, and bake as directed.

CLAM CUSTARD GARNISH [687]

Drain enough canned clam purée to make ⅓ of a cup, reserving the remaining purée for other use. Rub the ⅓ cup of clam purée through a fine sieve with ⅓ cup of clam juice mixed with ½ cup of scalded heavy cream, hot cream sauce, or hot Béchamel sauce. Beat in 4 fresh egg yolks, slightly beaten. Season to taste with celery salt, a few grains of cayenne and nutmeg, and a pinch of powdered thyme. Turn the mixture into a shallow buttered baking dish, and bake as indicated.

Oyster Custard Garnish. Substitute oysters for the clams, and add to the beaten eggs 1 teaspoon of strained liquid from horseradish. Bake as directed.

CORN CUSTARD GARNISH [688]
Individual

Press the purée from ½ can of corn. Beat 2 whole eggs and 1 egg yolk, add ¼ teaspoon of salt and a dash of pepper, and 3 table-spoons of cream, and mix thoroughly with the corn purée. Turn into floured buttered small individual molds. Set these in a pan on several sheets of paper, surround the molds with hot water, and bake as indicated.

CRAYFISH CUSTARD GARNISH   [689]

Put through a food chopper ¼ pound of shelled cooked crayfish, and rub through a fine sieve with 2 tablespoons of cold heavy cream, 2 tablespoons of strained broth in which the crayfish were cooked and ½ cup of hot rich Cream Sauce (No. 346). Season to taste with celery salt, and a dash each of cayenne, paprika, and nutmeg. Then beat in 3 fresh egg yolks, slightly beaten. Turn the mixture into a shallow buttered baking dish, and bake as indicated.

Lobster Custard Garnish. Use the same amount of cooked lobster meat, and bake as directed.

Fish Custard Garnish. Use any kind of cooked fish, lean or fat, carefully boned and skinned, in the same amount as the crayfish, and bake as directed.

Game Custard Garnish. For game soups, substitute the same amount of cooked feathered or furred game meat, and bake as directed.

CREAM CUSTARD GARNISH   [690]
Basic recipe

Beat together 1 small fresh egg and 3 fresh egg yolks, as for omelet. Then stir in ¾ cup of scalded thin cream, or undiluted evaporated milk. Season to taste with salt, a dash of white pepper, and a dash of freshly grated nutmeg. Strain through a fine sieve or cloth. Turn the mixture into a shallow buttered baking dish, and bake as indicated.

Peanut Custard Garnish. Add 2 tablespoons of finely ground roasted peanuts, smoothed with a few drops of undiluted evaporated milk, or thin cream.

Rice Custard Garnish. Add 2 generous tablespoons of cold plain rice, well grained.

GARLIC CUSTARD GARNISH   [691]

Blanch 3 cloves of garlic in a little water. Drain, and rub through a fine sieve with ¾ cup of hot Béchamel sauce. Season to taste with garlic salt, a dash of cayenne, and nutmeg, and strain again through a fine sieve or cloth. Turn the mixture into a shallow buttered baking dish, and bake as indicated.

GOOSE LIVER CUSTARD GARNISH   [692]

Clean 1 goose liver, and parboil in a little salt water. Chop coarsely, and put through a food chopper with 1 teaspoon of finely minced parsley and ½ cup of bread crumbs, seasoning with salt, black pepper, and nutmeg to taste as you go along. Cream 2½ tablespoons of butter, and combine with the liver mixture, mixing thoroughly. Add 1 teaspoon of onion juice, and put once more through the food chopper, this time with 3 egg yolks. Beat the whites of the 3 eggs to a froth, and fold them into the mixture. Now turn the mixture into a buttered shallow pan, and bake as indicated in a moderate oven (300°-325° F.).

GREEN PEPPER CUSTARD GARNISH   [693]

Scald 1 large green pepper, and remove the outer thin skin; cut open and remove the seeds and white ribs carefully. Put the green pepper through a food chopper, then rub it through a fine sieve with ¼ cup of cold strained veal broth and ½ cup of hot rich cream sauce. Beat in 4 fresh egg yolks, slightly beaten. Season with garlic salt, white pepper, and nutmeg to taste. Turn the mixture into a shallow buttered baking dish, and bake as indicated.

HAM CUSTARD GARNISH   [694]

Put enough lean cooked cold ham through a food chopper to make ¼ cup. Rub through a fine sieve with ¼ cup of strained veal broth alternately with ½ cup of rich cream sauce. Season to taste with salt, white pepper, and a dash of clove. Then beat in 3 fresh egg yolks, slightly beaten. Turn the mixture into a shallow buttered baking dish, and bake as indicated.

LEEK CUSTARD GARNISH   [695]

Put through a food chopper, using the finest disk, ⅓ cup of chopped white part of leeks, and cook over a gentle flame in 1 tablespoon of butter for about 3 minutes, stirring constantly, but do not let brown. Stir in 4 tablespoons of cold cream sauce, and continue cooking for 5 minutes longer, after the cream comes to a boil, stirring frequently. Rub through a fine sieve with ½ cup of scalded thin cream, or undiluted evaporated milk. Season to taste with salt, white pepper, and a dash of nutmeg. Then beat in 1 whole fresh egg and 2 fresh egg yolks, slightly beaten. Turn the mixture into a shallow buttered baking dish, and bake as indicated.

MINT CUSTARD GARNISH   [696]

Appropriate for lamb soup and any kind of fruit soup.

Infuse 4 fresh mint leaves, bruised, or the equivalent of dried mint leaves in ¾ cup of boiling chicken bouillon for 10 minutes. Then strain through a fine cloth, and gradually stir the strained broth over 1 whole fresh egg, beaten with 2 fresh egg yolks, stirring briskly. Season to taste with salt and a few grains of cayenne pepper. Turn the mixture into a shallow buttered baking dish, and bake as indicated.

ONION CUSTARD GARNISH [697]

Rub ½ cup of cooked onions (cooked in strained beef stock with a blade of garlic) through a fine sieve with ⅔ cup of scalded undiluted evaporated milk, or thin cream. Season to taste with salt, pepper, a dash of nutmeg, and a tiny pinch of powdered thyme. Beat in 4 fresh egg yolks, slightly beaten. Turn the mixture into a shallow buttered baking dish, and bake as indicated.

PATE DE FOIE GRAS CUSTARD GARNISH [698]

Rub 2½ ounces of pâté de foie gras through a fine sieve with 2 table-spoons of hot Béchamel sauce. Then beat in ½ cup of thin cream, or evaporated milk, alternately with 1 whole fresh egg and 2 fresh egg yolks. Season to taste with a few grains of salt and white pepper, then rub again through a fine sieve. Turn the mixture into a shallow buttered baking dish, and bake as indicated.

Liverwurst Custard Garnish. Substitute the same quantity of liverwurst, and bake as directed.

PEA CUSTARD GARNISH [699]

Rub through a fine sieve 3 tablespoons of freshly cooked peas with 3 tablespoons of strained hot veal stock, sweetened with a tiny pinch of sugar. Stir in ½ cup of hot rich milk. Season to taste with salt and white pepper. Then beat in 1 whole fresh egg, slightly beaten with 2 fresh egg yolks, and a drop or two of green vegetable coloring. Again rub the mixture through a fine sieve into a shallow buttered baking dish, and bake as indicated.

PIMIENTO CUSTARD GARNISH [700]

Rub through a fine sieve 2 drained canned red pimientos with 3 tablespoons of cold thin cream. Beat in ½ cup of scalded rich milk alternately with 1 fresh egg, beaten with 2 fresh egg yolks. Season to taste with salt, white pepper, and a dash of nutmeg. Turn the mixture into a shallow buttered baking dish, and bake as indicated.

SPINACH OR SORREL CUSTARD GARNISH   [701]

Rub 3 tablespoons of cooked sorrel leaves through a fine sieve with 3 tablespoons of cold thin cream, or evaporated milk. Then stir in ½ cup of hot rich milk alternately with 1 whole fresh egg, beaten with 2 fresh egg yolks, and colored with a drop or two of green vegetable coloring to emphasize the green hue. Again rub the mixture through a fine sieve into a shallow buttered baking dish, and bake as indicated.

TOMATO CUSTARD GARNISH   [702]

Rub 3½ tablespoons of tomato purée or tomato paste through a fine sieve with 3 tablespoons of strained veal stock. Then stir in ½ cup of scalded thin cream, or undiluted evaporated milk. Season to taste with salt, pepper, and a tiny pinch of powdered dill. Then beat in 4 fresh egg yolks, slightly beaten. Rub again through a fine sieve into a shallow buttered baking dish, and bake as indicated.

TRUFFLE CUSTARD GARNISH   [703]

Pound 2 ounces of black truffles with 1½ teaspoons of meat extract and 3 tablespoons of hot Béchamel sauce. Then rub through a fine sieve with ½ cup of scalded rich milk. Season to taste with a few grains of salt and black pepper, then beat in 1 whole fresh egg and 2 fresh yolks, slightly beaten. Turn the mixture into a shallow buttered baking dish, and bake as indicated.

Chapter Twelve

DUMPLING GARNISHES
FOR SOUPS

The world's best culinary art has its roots in the cookery of peasants who evolved marvels in their tireless efforts to make plain food savory, to avoid waste, to secure nourishment. And, boiled dumplings are one of the best examples. They not only garnish the soup, but add nourishment, and are one of the best "extenders" known.

THE WORLD'S BEST CULINARY ART HAS ITS ROOTS IN THE cookery of peasants who evolved marvels in tireless efforts to make plain food savory, to avoid waste, to secure nourishment. And one universal habit of cooks has been to wrap up choice morsels in leaves, dough, or puff paste, or to mix them in a batter, to be popped into hungry mouths without loss of juices, flavor, or aroma.

Hence we have *dolmas* of Greece and the Levant, *tamales* and *empanadas* of Hispanic peoples, *koldunys* of Poland, *kaldomars* of Sweden, stuffed *blinis* of the Slavs and Jews, *ravioli* of Italy, and on a grander scale, the majestic meat, fish, and game pies of Britain, and the *vol-au-vent* and forcemeat of France.

Scarcely one of them is better than another, and not one falls short of lusciousness if you have a cosmopolitan palate, but let us pay homage to the ancestor of them all, the Chinese dumplings which were cooked to the taste of the great khans of Cathay, when the tribesmen of Europe were still tearing meat from the bones of beasts with their teeth and hands. The hearty, exuberant, irrepressible Marco Polo harried all the Italian cooks with his tales of Chinese dumplings when he returned from wandering, and that's why ravioli was born.

Chu-pao-pa and *su-gau*, the Chinese call them, and there are other names in various provinces; and they eat them in soup or with a sauce, just as we eat ravioli. The only difference between the two forms is in the stuffing used by the Chinese and that used by the Italians.

But there are dumplings and dumplings. And here I mean boiled dumplings, the best "extenders" we know. A little soup, meat, stew, ragout, or fricassée will go a long way if served with these little dumplings, which call for simple everyday ingredients.

The following recipes are for soup garnishing only, but if made a little larger, they may be used in stews, pot roasts, fricassées, and the like, or served as a main dish with a sauce.

ALL-BRAN THIMBLE-SIZE DUMPLINGS   [705]

Sift 1½ cups of bread flour once, measure, add 1 scant teaspoon of salt, 3 teaspoons of baking powder, and a tiny pinch of curry powder, and resift into a mixing bowl. Beat 1 large fresh egg until light. Add 1 tablespoon of bacon drippings, melted, and cooled to lukewarm, with ½ cup of All-Bran, alternately with about ¾ cup of cold rich milk. Stir into the flour mixture, blending thoroughly. Drop by scant teaspoons into boiling soup, cover, and cook a few minutes before serving.

BACON DUMPLINGS [706]

Cook ¼ pound of ground bacon for 1 short minute, stirring in the following ingredients: ½ pound of flour; 3 whole eggs, well beaten; salt and pepper to taste; 1 cup of bread crumbs soaked in a little milk or broth, squeezed, then tossed; 1 teaspoon of onion juice; and 1 teaspoon of chopped parsley. Heat thoroughly, but do not brown. Cool. Shape into small balls the size of a small walnut, and add to the soup 10 minutes before serving. The soup should be boiling briskly when dropping in the small dumplings. They may be served separately, if desired. A grating of nutmeg adds to the flavor.

BAKING POWDER THIMBLE-SIZE [707]
DUMPLINGS

Mix and sift 2 cups of all-purpose flour, 4 teaspoons of baking powder, ½ teaspoon of ground cinnamon, and 1 scant teaspoon of salt. Work in 1 tablespoon of bacon or ham drippings. Add 1 scant cup of cold rich milk, and mix lightly. Drop from a teaspoon on top of the soup or stew; or roll very gently on a lightly floured board, shape with a very small biscuit cutter or with a tiny glass, and drop on top of boiling soup or stew. Cover, and cook for a few minutes, or until the dumplings rise.

BAVARIAN MAULTASHEN [708]
Boiled Filled Meat Dumplings

Appropriate for clear consommé or bouillon of beef or game.

Beat 2 fresh eggs with a little salt, pepper, and nutmeg, as for an omelet, in a mixing bowl, and add enough sifted flour to make a stiff dough. Pat, and roll out on a lightly floured board, as thin as possible, and cut into ¼ to ⅓ inch squares. Have ready 1⅓ cups of cooked meat, finely ground, and seasoned to taste with salt, pepper, and a dash of thyme, then moistened with a little meat stock or bouillon. Divide this meat mixture on the squares. Moisten the edges of the filled squares with unbeaten egg white, and seal them in triangles. Have ready some boiling salted water, or meat stock. Drop in the triangles, and boil steadily for 12 to 15 minutes. Drain, and add to the hot bouillon just before serving.

BEEF DUMPLINGS [709]

To ½ scant pound of ground round beef or leftover cooked beef, add ¾ cup of flour, and salt, pepper, and nutmeg to taste. Gradually add enough water or stock (beef, chicken, fish, or vegetable stock may be used according to the kind of soup), or Instant Pique Consommé (No. 24), to make a spongy mixture (about ½ cup). Beat slightly 1 whole egg with another egg yolk, and add to the mixture, blending well. Drop from a moistened teaspoon into boiling soup 5 minutes before serving. There should be about 2 dumplings to each serving, depending on the size of the dumplings, which should not be too large.

BRAN DUMPLINGS [710]

Appropriate for almost any kind of soup, clear, semiclear, or thick, as well as meat and fish stews, and pot roast.

Scald ½ cup of rich milk with 1 tablespoon of butter or margarine. Remove from the fire. Season to taste with salt and a dash of white pepper and nutmeg. Then stir in 1 large well-beaten fresh egg, and mix thoroughly. Now stir in 1 tablespoon each of grated onion, finely minced parsley, and finely chopped chives. Then stir in 2½ cups of finely crushed, then sieved, bran flakes. Mix thoroughly. When cold enough to handle, shape into 1-inch balls. Drop the dumplings into simmering soup, stew, or fricassée. Cover, and let simmer gently for 15 minutes. Serve hot in the soup.

BREAD AND CELERY DUMPLINGS [711]

Appropriate for almost any kind of soup, clear, semiclear, or thick, including fish soup or chowder as well as stews, ragouts, pot roasts, and fricassées.

Chill ¾ cup of rich milk, and stir in 3 cups of soft bread crumbs. Let stand for 15 minutes, then squeeze out excess milk through a dry clean towel. This squeezing renders the dumplings less heavy and less soggy. Heat 2½ tablespoons of butter or margarine. Stir in 3 tablespoons of grated onion with 3 tablespoons of finely ground green celery leaves, and cook for 2 or 3 minutes, stirring frequently, but do not allow to get brown. Then stir in the squeezed bread crumbs, and mix thoroughly. Remove from the fire, and stir into this mixture 2 large fresh eggs, slightly beaten with ½ teaspoon of salt and a pinch of pepper, nutmeg, and thyme. Shape into small balls the size of a large marble. Roll in sieved dry bread crumbs, and drop into hot soup. Cover, and cook about 10 minutes.

BREAD DUMPLINGS [712]

Crumble 6 slices of stale bread, then roll out fine. Add 1 teaspoon of grated onion, and pour over about ½ cup of Beef Stock or Vegetable Stock (No. 114 and No. 10), or Instant Pique Consommé (No. 24). For fish soup, use Fish Stock (No. 8). Then add, and mix well 3 well-beaten eggs, salt and pepper to taste, a grating of nutmeg, and a few grains of cayenne. Drop from a moistened teaspoon into rapidly boiling soup. Cover, and boil for 15 minutes.

BUTTERNOCKERLS [713]
German Butter Dumplings

Appropriate for vegetable or clear chicken bouillon.

Cream ¼ cup of butter until light and lemon colored. Gradually add 1 slightly beaten egg and 1 tablespoon of sweet cream. Season with ½ teaspoon of salt and a good dash each of nutmeg and white pepper. Then add enough sifted all-purpose flour to make a dough the consistency of bread dough. Beat with a wooden spoon until the dough no longer clings to the spoon. Form the dough into little balls the size of a large marble, and drop them into the soup. Let them cook for 5 or 6 minutes. Serve the soup at once after tasting for seasoning. These little balls are fine grained and crumbly, as if they had been made with corn meal.

CALF'S LIVER DUMPLINGS [714]

Appropriate for clear or semiclear soup.

Wash and sponge ¼ pound of calf's liver, grind fine, discarding the tough fiber. Combine with 1 generous cup of bread crumbs soaked in milk, then squeezed and loosened, 1 scant tablespoon of butter, a grating of nutmeg, and salt and pepper to taste. Then grind once more, adding gradually 2 generous tablespoons of flour. Combine with 1 whole egg and 1 egg yolk beaten together, 1 teaspoon of grated onion, and 1 teaspoon of parsley, minced. Shape into small balls the size of a small walnut, and drop into boiling soup 15 minutes before serving. Try these dumplings in Instant Pique Consommé (No. 24). Delicious!

CHEESE DUMPLINGS [715]
Drop method

Appropriate for meat, vegetable, and particularly onion soup.

Chill ¾ cup of rich milk. Stir in 2 well-beaten fresh eggs, and blend thoroughly. Sift 2 cups of bread flour once, measure, add ½ teaspoon of salt, a pinch of freshly grated nutmeg, and 1 level tablespoon of baking powder, and sift over the milk mixture. Blend well to a smooth consistency, then stir in 1 tablespoon of melted butter, 1 tablespoon of grated onion, and lastly 1 cup of grated hard cheese (any kind). The batter should be of heavy cream consistency, and if necessary, add more milk as needed. Drop from a teaspoon into boiling soup. Cover, and cook gently for 10 to 12 minutes.

CHICKEN DUMPLINGS [716]

Appropriate for clear bouillon, consommé, or clear chicken bouillon.

Cook in a little butter 1 teaspoon of grated onion and 1 teaspoon of finely chopped chervil or parsley for about 1 minute, stirring constantly. Do not allow to brown. Cream 3 tablespoons of butter or margarine until light, and combine with ¾ cup of cooked ground chicken, mixed with 2 tablespoons of sieved fine dry crumbs and 1 fresh egg, slightly beaten. Season to taste with salt, pepper, nutmeg, and marjoram, and blend with the cooked onion-parsley, mixing well. When cold enough to handle, shape into small balls the size of a marble, and drop into boiling clear soup. Allow to simmer, covered, for 3 or 4 minutes, and skim off with a perforated spoon. Serve on the side with hot clear Beef Consommé (No. 114).

Burger Dumplings. You may substitute ground cooked meat for the chicken.

CHICKEN LIVER DUMPLINGS [717]
Drop method

Especially appropriate for clear, semiclear, or thick chicken soup.

Sift ½ tablespoon of flour with ½ teaspoon of powdered dry parsley, a pinch each of salt, pepper, and nutmeg, and a few grains of cayenne, into a mixing bowl. Grind ¼ pound of cleaned chicken livers with 3 slices of raw bacon, and add to the flour mixture. Mix in 1 whole fresh egg, and mix thoroughly. The mixture should be moist enough to drop from the tip of a teaspoon. Have ready some salted boiling water or chicken stock, and drop from the tip of a teaspoon some of the mixture. Cook for 2 or 3 minutes, drain, and add to the hot soup just before serving.

Clam Dumplings. Substitute chopped well-drained clams, canned or fresh, for the chicken livers.

CHINESE PORK DUMPLINGS   [718]

Appropriate for any kind of clear, semiclear, or thick soup.

Combine 1 cup of cooked ground pork, 1½ tablespoons of grated onion, 1 tablespoon of cooking oil, 1½ teaspoons of soy sauce, 1 cup of cooked ground cabbage, and the cooked white part of a large leek, ground fine together, and blend well. Season to taste with salt and pepper and a few grains of ground ginger. Sift 1 cup of flour with ¼ teaspoon of salt, and moisten with enough ice-cold water, about 3 or 4 tablespoons, or enough to make a stiff dry dough. Roll very thin, as thin as possible, on a lightly floured board, and cut in 1½-inch squares. Place a little of the pork mixture in the center of each square. Fold over, and seal the edges with a little cold water or unbeaten egg white. Drop into rapidly boiling salted water, and boil about 4 minutes. Drain, and serve on the side with hot soup.

CORN DUMPLINGS   [719]

Appropriate for vegetable soup or corn chowder.

Put ½ can of well-drained canned corn, or 1 cup of leftover corn on the cob, grated, a few grains each of salt, pepper, and nutmeg, and 1 tablespoon of bacon drippings through a food chopper. Put through the food chopper a second time, adding 1 teaspoon of minced onion, 1 teaspoon of minced parsley, 1 egg and 1 egg yolk, beaten together, and ½ scant cup of bread crumbs. Chill for 2 hours in the refrigerator. Drop the mixture by a teaspoon moistened in water into rapidly boiling soup 10 minutes before serving.

CORN MEAL DUMPLINGS   [720]

Appropriate for thick vegetable soups as well as chowders.

Sift ¾ cup of bread flour with ⅓ teaspoon of salt, a few grains of powdered thyme, and 1½ teaspoons of baking powder. Blend in 4 tablespoons of unsifted yellow corn meal, then cut in 1½ tablespoons of shortening. Gradually add about ½ cup of cold milk, and mix enough to moisten the flour mixture. Drop by teaspoonfuls on gently boiling soup. Cover tightly, and allow to boil gently for 12 to 15 minutes.

COTTAGE CHEESE DUMPLINGS [721]
Very fluffy

Appropriate for vegetable soups or stews, or to garnish green vegetable dishes, such as boiled cabbage, spinach, broccoli, or lettuce.

Cream 1½ tablespoons of butter or margarine until light. Gradually add 2 egg yolks, one at a time, and continue creaming until thoroughly blended. Mix in ½ cup of cottage cheese, which has been beaten fine or strained through a sieve and seasoned with salt and a few grains of white pepper to taste, alternately with 2 tablespoons of sieved dry bread crumbs. Mix thoroughly, and lastly, fold in 2 stiffly beaten egg whites. Drop from a teaspoon into rapidly boiling soup, stew, or pot roast. Cover, and cook for 5 minutes.

CRANBERRY DUMPLINGS [722]

Appropriate for hot fruit or wine soup.

Cook 1 cup of picked fresh cranberries in ¼ cup of hot white wine for about 8 to 10 minutes, or until tender. Strain, and add 2 tablespoons of sugar, 1½ teaspoons of butter, ¼ teaspoon of salt, and a few grains of nutmeg. Then blend in about ⅓ generous cup of cracker meal or fine, dry, sieved bread crumbs. Drop by half teaspoon into deep clear fat, and cook until delicately browned. Drain on absorbent paper, and serve alongside soup.

CRAYFISH DUMPLINGS [723]

Appropriate for clear and semiclear consommé, bouillon, broth, or soup, especially chowder and fish soup.

Pound ½ pound of shelled raw crayfish with 2 unbeaten egg whites. Season to taste with salt, pepper, nutmeg, and thyme. Then rub the mixture through a fine sieve into a mixing bowl, and place on cracked ice for at least 2 hours. Then gradually beat in 1⅓ cups (about) of thin cream, or undiluted evaporated milk, until very smooth. Again rub through a fine sieve. Shape into small balls the size of a marble, and drop into gently boiling salted water, or still better, into fish stock. Let boil a minute or two. Skim off the dumplings with a perforated spoon, and drain well before adding to the soup.

Lobster or Shrimp Dumplings. You may substitute raw shelled lobster or shelled fresh shrimp for the raw crayfish.

CREAM OF WHEAT DUMPLINGS [724]

Appropriate for any kind of soup, including fish and chowder, except clear soup, also for meat stew, chicken stew, pot roast, and chicken fricassée.

Cream 1 tablespoon of butter or margarine. Add 1 well-beaten fresh egg, and gradually beat in 6 tablespoons of cream of wheat, mixed with a few grains of salt, pepper, and nutmeg to taste. Now add 1 teaspoon of baking powder and enough sifted flour to make a mixture that can be rolled into small balls with the hands. The dough should be so soft that this is difficult to do, although possible. Drop in salted boiling water or clear stock. Cover, and boil gently for 15 minutes. Do not boil too many balls at a time, as there should be room for all to come to the surface, which is not possible if they are crowded in the saucepan. Serve hot.

CURRIED POTATO THIMBLE-SIZE [725]
DUMPLINGS

Appropriate for meat, fish, or vegetable soup.

Cream 4 tablespoons of butter until light and fluffy. Add 1 slightly beaten egg yolk. Continue creaming and beating at the same time until well blended. Season to taste with salt, grated nutmeg, and ½ teaspoon of curry powder. Then mix in about ¾ cup of cooked riced potatoes (freshly cooked or leftover) alternately with 4 tablespoons of flour. Beat until very smooth and free from lumps. Shape into balls the size of a large marble, and about 8 minutes before serving, drop the dumplings into simmering Meat, Fish, or Vegetable Stock (Nos. 114, 8, 10), depending on the kind of soup. Cover, and simmer very gently for about 6 to 8 minutes. Drain, and serve at once in the soup.

CURRY DUMPLINGS [726]
Yeast method

Appropriate for vegetable and fish soups, chowders, meat, fish, poultry, or game stews, and pot roasts.

Crumble half a yeast cake. Sprinkle over 1 scant tablespoon of granulated sugar, and let stand for 15 minutes. Scald ¼ cup of rich milk, season to taste with salt and a few grains of nutmeg, and stir in 1 teaspoon of curry powder, diluted in a little cold milk. Cool to lukewarm, then stir in the yeast mixture alternately with 1 whole fresh egg, well beaten, and 1¼ cups of sifted bread flour. Beat briskly for 1 long minute, then knead a half minute on a lightly floured board. Put the dough into a small greased mixing bowl. Brush the top with shortening. Cover with a light, clean, dry towel or cheesecloth, and allow the dough to rise to double its bulk. Shape into tiny balls the size of a small marble. Place on a lightly floured board, and let rise again till light. Drop the dumplings into soup or stew, handling very lightly. Cover tightly, and boil gently for about 12 to 15 minutes.

EGG AND CHEESE DUMPLINGS [727]

Appropriate for almost any kind of clear, semiclear, and thick soup, including fish soups and chowders, stews and casserole dishes.

Beat 1 egg white with a pinch each of salt, white pepper, and nutmeg until stiff. Fold in 1 tablespoon of grated hard cheese, and drop from the tip of a teaspoon into gently simmering soup. Cover, and let simmer gently for about 2 minutes. Serve immediately.

EGG DUMPLINGS I [728]
Drop method

Appropriate for almost any kind of clear or semiclear fish soups and chowders, including stews.

Break 2 eggs in a bowl. Beat well. Add ½ generous (more or less) cup of milk, and beat again, alternately with enough flour to thicken until the mixture is a little thicker than batter for pancakes. Season to taste, while beating, with salt, pepper, and a few grains each of nutmeg and cayenne. Drop from a moistened teaspoon into boiling soup or bouillon 8 to 10 minutes before serving.

EGG DUMPLINGS II [729]

Mix and sift together ½ cup of flour, a pinch each of salt, nutmeg and cayenne pepper to taste, and 1 (scant) teaspoon of baking powder. Beat well until thoroughly blended and smooth, adding a few drops of milk if mixture is too stiff. Roll into small balls, the size of a marble, and 5 minutes before serving, drop all at once in boiling soup or bouillon.

Variation. The addition of a tablespoon of finely chopped cooked ham, or still better ground ham, is a great improvement.

FARINA DUMPLINGS [730]

Appropriate for medium-thick or thick soups, fish soups, chowders, and stews.

Scald 1 cup of rich milk with 1 large bay leaf and 1 whole clove. Strain, and gradually stir in ⅓ cup of farina, stirring briskly to prevent lumping, and seasoning to taste with salt and a few grains of white pepper. Cook until the mixture thickens, stirring constantly from the bottom of the pan. Remove from the fire, and stir in 1 whole fresh egg, beaten as for omelet. Form into small balls the size of a marble for soup, and into 6 dumplings for stew or chowder. Drop into boiling salted water for 5 or 6 minutes. Drain well, and add to soup or stew. The dumplings for stew, being larger, require about 8 to 10 minutes of gentle boiling.

FISH DUMPLINGS [731]

Appropriate for any kind of fish soup or fish broth.

Clean, bone thoroughly, then cut in small pieces or flake enough raw white-flesh fish to obtain ½ generous cup when put through a food chopper. Combine with an equal amount of soft bread crumbs, soaked in milk, then squeezed and tossed lightly to loosen, and ¼ cup of good creamed butter. Return all the mixture through the food chopper, adding salt and pepper to taste, 1 teaspoon of grated onion, and a few grains of nutmeg. Shape into small balls the size of a walnut, and 10 minutes before serving, drop into rapidly boiling fish soup or fish broth. Delicious!

FLOUR DUMPLINGS [732]

Appropriate for almost any kind of soup or broth.

Bring 3 generous tablespoons of butter and ½ cup of cold broth (any kind), or Instant Pique Consommé (No. 24), to a rapid boil. Add ½ cup of flour all at once, stirring vigorously. Cook over a low flame, keeping on stirring until the mixture leaves the sides of the pan in a smooth mass, and adding 1 scant teaspoon of onion juice, and salt, pepper, cayenne, and nutmeg to taste, while stirring. Cool. Break 1 whole egg into the dough, and beat thoroughly and hard. Add a second and possibly a third egg until a smooth spongy mixture is obtained. Drop from a moistened teaspoon into rapidly boiling soup (any kind), and when the dumplings rise to the surface, they are done. Serve 2 or 3 dumplings to each serving. They may be made smaller, if desired, by just taking the dough from the tip of a moistened teaspoon, instead of a teaspoonful. These fine dumplings will puff as soon as they come to the surface of the boiling soup.

FLUFFY DUMPLINGS   [733]
Drop method

Appropriate for almost any kind of soup, clear, semiclear, and thick, including fish soups, chowders, and stews, meat stews, chicken stews, and pot roast.

Sift together 1 cup of sifted pastry flour, 1 teaspoon of baking powder, ¼ teaspoon of salt, and a few grains of cayenne, thyme, and cloves, into a mixing bowl. Cut in 1½ teaspoons of butter or margarine, then stir in ¼ cup of cold milk, beaten with 1 fresh egg yolk, mixing quickly. Do not beat until smooth, as this will remove the air bubbles from the mixture and make the dumplings heavy. Grease the top part of a steamer, and place it over rapidly boiling water. Drop this batter by teaspoons into the steamer. Cover closely, and steam for 12 to 15 minutes. Add to soup or stew immediately, and serve at once. Be sure not to remove the cover during the steaming process.

FRENCH DUMPLING STRIPS   [734]

Appropriate for almost any kind of soup, including fish soups, chowders, and stews, meat and poultry stews, pot roasts, and casseroles.

Rub 1 tablespoon of lard into 1 cup of sifted pastry flour, sifted with ¼ teaspoon of salt and a few grains each of nutmeg, cloves, and cayenne pepper. Moisten with ⅓ scant cup of cold water, mixing thoroughly. Roll out on a slightly floured board to about a scant ¼ inch in thickness, and cut in long strips, about ½ inch thick, and then again into about 2-inch pieces. Dust them with flour, and drop into boiling soup, stew, or pot roast. Cook about 10 minutes, and serve at once.

GAME DUMPLINGS   [735]

Appropriate for game soup, and clear bouillon.

Put through a food chopper the raw meat from the breast of a grouse. Cook in a little butter 1 teaspoon of grated onion and 1 teaspoon of finely chopped chervil or parsley for about 1 minute, stirring constantly. Do not allow to brown. Cream 3 tablespoons of butter or margarine until light, and combine with the ground raw breast of grouse, mixed with 2 tablespoons of sieved, fine, dry bread crumbs and 1 fresh egg, slightly beaten. Season to taste with salt, pepper, nutmeg, and marjoram, and blend with the cooked onion-parsley, mixing well. When cold enough to handle, shape into small balls the size of a marble, and drop into boiling soup. Allow to simmer, covered, for 10 minutes, and skim off with a perforated ladle. Serve in soup or as a side dish.

Note. Partridge, pheasant, and almost any kind of game bird may be substituted for grouse.

GIBLET DUMPLINGS   [736]

These delicious and nourishing dumplings may be made with the giblets of any kind of fowl, domestic or wild, and are appropriate for poultry or game soups. They may also be used in chicken, duck, goose, or turkey stews, and in game bird stews. In such case, they should be made larger and cooked twice as long as those used for soup, unless they are desired small, as follows:

Sift 1 cup of sifted flour with 2 teaspoons of baking powder, ¼ teaspoon of salt, and a pinch of powdered marjoram, mace, and thyme, into a mixing bowl. Mix in the cooked giblets of the bird, finely ground with 4 tablespoons of cold milk and 2 tablespoons of good sherry wine. The dough should be soft enough to make a drop dough. Drop from a teaspoon into the soup or on the stew. Cover tightly, and boil gently for about 15 minutes. Serve at once.

HAM DUMPLINGS I   [737]
   Viennese method

Appropriate for lentil, pea, bean, potato, and vegetable soups, also for casserole dishes, such as sauerkraut, duck, goose, poultry, as well as meat casseroles, when made double the size and cooked twice as long as those for soups.

Grind ¼ pound of cooked lean ham with 6 tablespoons of soft bread crumbs, soaked in enough milk to cover, then squeezed almost dry. Then mix with 4 tablespoons of small bread cubes, fried in butter until crisp and thoroughly drained, and 1 large fresh egg and 1 fresh egg yolk, beaten into ½ cup of heavy fresh cream, mixing thoroughly. Season to taste with salt, a dash of powdered thyme and nutmeg, and add enough sifted bread flour to make a dough sufficiently soft to handle and shape into small balls the size of a walnut. Drop the balls into slightly salted boiling water, and boil gently for about 15 minutes. Skim off the dumplings with a perforated spoon, drain well, and serve as hot as possible.

HAM DUMPLINGS II [738]
Quick economical method

Appropriate for vegetable soups, spinach, or lentil soup, as well as stews of fish, meat, and poultry.

Sift together 1½ cups of pastry flour with 2 teaspoons of baking powder, ¾ teaspoon of salt, and a pinch each of pepper and nutmeg, in a mixing bowl. Then mix in about ⅔ cup of cold milk, added to ½ cup of ground cooked lean ham. Shape into small balls the size of a small walnut, and drop into boiling soup. Cover tightly, and boil gently for 15 minutes. Serve hot.

HAM DUMPLINGS III [739]
Home method

Delicious with pea soup.

Cream 5 tablespoons of butter. Add 2 whole eggs first beaten with 2 egg yolks, salt, black pepper, and nutmeg to taste. Mix thoroughly, then put through a food chopper to ensure smoothness, adding, while grinding, 5 ounces of cold ground cooked ham, fat removed, and enough bread crumbs to thicken. Shape into small balls the size of a small walnut. Allow to stand for 1 hour to ripen in the refrigerator, and drop all at once in rapidly boiling soup or stock 8 to 10 minutes before serving.

ITALIAN DUMPLINGS [740]

Appropriate for clear or semiclear consommé.

Heat 1 generous tablespoon of butter over a gentle fire, and sprinkle with 1 generous teaspoon of flour. Blend well, then add 1 tablespoon of thick cream, stirring rapidly until it is a thick paste. Add 2 ounces of cooked and chopped fine macaroni, 2 ounces of grated Parmesan cheese, salt and pepper to taste, and a grating of nutmeg. Beat the mixture over the fire until it is smooth and firm and leaves the sides of the saucepan with the spoon. Mold into small balls the size of a small marble, and 10 long minutes before serving the soup, drop the balls all at once into the boiling soup or broth. For a different treat, try dropping the dumplings into Instant Pique Consommé (No. 24).

KROPPKAKOR or POTATO BALLS WITH PORK [741]
Swedish

These delicious dumplings also may be served as a main dish with cream gravy, or hot as an appetizer. They are very good with almost any kind of vegetable, lentil, noodle, macaroni, pea, or bean soup, when made small and steamed in boiling salted water or meat stock.

Cut ¼ pound of salt pork into tiny cubes, and cook with 1 table-spoon of finely chopped onion. Combine 1 cup of cold mashed potatoes and 1 small fresh egg. Mix well, and season to taste with salt, pepper, and a dash of nutmeg. Mix in ½ cup of sifted flour, blending well, then add a little more flour, also sifted, to make a mixture stiff enough to be rolled into small balls the size of a large walnut. Wrap in each a small portion of the pork and onion mixture. Roll the stuffed balls in seasoned flour, and drop them into rapidly boiling salted water or meat stock. Let them cook gently, uncovered, for about 15 minutes. Serve hot in soup.

LIVER DUMPLINGS [742]

Especially appropriate for consommé, broth, or chicken bouillon.

Mix 1½ tablespoons of grated onion, 1 large fresh egg, ½ pound of beef, calf's, lamb, or pork liver, finely ground together, and season with ½ generous teaspoon of salt and a good pinch of pepper. Lastly, mix in 2 tablespoons of finely minced parsley and 1 cup of soft bread crumbs soaked in milk, then squeezed dry. Knead in enough sifted bread flour (about ¾ cup) to make a stiff mixture. Have 1½ quarts of broth boiling rapidly. Dip a tablespoon into the broth, and then take enough of the dumpling mixture to make small dumplings, and drop into the boiling broth. Continue this process, each time dipping the spoon into the hot broth before making another dumpling. Let boil for 15 minutes, and serve in hot broth, dusting each serving with a little finely chopped parsley.

Oyster Dumplings. You may substitute well-drained chopped oysters for the liver.

MARROW DUMPLINGS [743]

Appropriate for clear and semiclear consommé or vegetable soup.

To 1 egg, well beaten, to which has been added ½ teaspoon of onion juice and 1 teaspoon of minced parsley, add salt, white pepper, and nutmeg to taste, 1 tablespoon of milk, 1 teaspoon of butter, and 2 generous tablespoons of cooked beef marrow. Mix well, then add enough bread crumbs to thicken and a pinch of baking powder. Roll small dumplings the size of a marble into the bread crumbs, and 5 minutes before serving, drop them into the rapidly boiling soup, to which has been added ¼ cup of Pique Seasoning mixed with 1 cup of hot water.

MERINGUE ALMOND DUMPLINGS [744]

Appropriate for hot and cold fruit and wine soups, hot or cold consommé, broth and clear chicken soup, and also for clear fish broth, such as clam or oyster broth.

Heat to the boiling point 1 cup of milk in a small saucepan. Beat 2 egg whites with a few grains of salt until stiff, then fold in 2 tablespoons of blanched ground almonds. Take teaspoonfuls of the meringue mixture, evened off with the blade of a knife, and poach gently in the hot milk. Skim them off with a perforated spoon, and serve hot or cold.

Variations. You may flavor the meringue with curry, nutmeg, mace, paprika, or allspice instead of using almonds. You may use meat, poultry, or vegetable stock instead of milk.

NUTMEG DUMPLINGS [745]

Appropriate for almost any kind of clear, semiclear, and thick soups, including fish soup and any kind of chowder.

Cream ½ cup of butter, margarine, or shortening until light. Add 2 fresh egg yolks, slightly beaten, and continue creaming until thoroughly mixed. Gradually add ¾ cup of sifted flour with ¼ teaspoon of salt, a few grains of cayenne, and a generous grating of nutmeg. Lastly, fold in 1 stiffly beaten egg white, and shape into small balls the size of a small walnut. Drop into boiling salted water or stock appropriate to the soup served. Cover tightly, and let simmer gently for 5 minutes. Serve at once.

Paprika Dumplings. You may substitute 1 teaspoon of paprika (more or less) for the nutmeg.

Onion Dumplings. Insert small white onions, glazed or boiled, in dough the size of a walnut. Seal each carefully, and cook as directed.

ONION AND CHEESE DUMPLINGS   [746]

A very good substitute for croutons, rounds of toast garnished with cheese, for any kind of onion soup.

Cream ¼ cup of butter, margarine, or shortening until light. Gradually add ¼ cup of grated cheese alternately with 2 fresh egg yolks, slightly beaten, mixing well. Gradually add ¾ cup of sifted bread flour with ¼ teaspoon of salt, a few grains of pepper to taste, and a dash of powdered mace. Fold in 1 stiffly beaten egg white, then take dough the size of a walnut, and wrap around a small white onion, glazed or boiled, sealing well with cold water or a little unbeaten egg white. Drop into boiling salted water or stock. Cover tightly, and let boil gently for 6 or 7 minutes. Serve at once.

PARSLEY or CHERVIL DUMPLINGS   [747]

Appropriate for almost any kind of semithick and thick soups, as well as fish soups and chowders, also for stews, chicken fricassées, pot roasts, and the like.

Sift 1 cup of bread flour. Add 2 teaspoons of baking powder, ¼ teaspoon of salt, and a pinch of nutmeg, and sift into a mixing bowl. Mix in 2 tablespoons of finely chopped parsley, and gradually cut in 1½ teaspoons of shortening. Now add enough cold milk (about ½ scant cup) to moisten the dry ingredients. Drop by teaspoons into the boiling soup, stew, or fricassée. Cover tightly, and cook for 5 or 6 minutes, keeping tightly covered. Serve as hot as possible.

Note. Green onion tops or chives may be substituted for parsley or chervil.

PATE DE FOIE GRAS DUMPLINGS   [748]

Appropriate for almost any kind of consommé, clear broth, or chicken bouillon.

Mix the size of a small egg of pâté de foie gras with 1 fresh egg thoroughly. Then add ¼ cup of sieved dry bread crumbs, and season to taste with salt and pepper. Shape into small balls the size of a marble, and drop them into boiling clear beef, chicken, fish, or vegetable stock, appropriate to the soup used. Cook for 1 long minute. Skim off with a perforated ladle, and serve at once.

Note. Liverwurst sausage may be substituted for pâté de foie gras.

PEANUT BUTTER DUMPLINGS [749]

Appropriate for almost any kind of semithick or thick soups, including fish soups and chowders, stews, pot roast, chicken fricassées, and the like.

Sift ¾ cup of bread flour once, add 2 teaspoons of baking powder, ¼ teaspoon of salt, a few grains of nutmeg, and pepper to taste, and sift again into a mixing bowl. Cut in 1 tablespoon plus 2 teaspoons of peanut butter, and 1 tablespoon of butter or margarine. Then moisten gradually with some cold milk, using about a scant ½ cup, or enough to make a drop dough. Drop by teaspoons into boiling soup or on top of stew. Cover tightly, and let boil gently for about 12 to 15 minutes.

PEDROGAS [750]
Boiled and Fried Filled Dumplings

Very appropriate for fruit soups and wine soups, hot or cold, or served with freshly crushed berries. A meal in themselves, so you better make plenty of them, as they'll disappear rapidly. They should be served very hot.

Sift 2 cups of bread flour once, measure, add ¾ teaspoon of salt, 2 teaspoons of baking powder, and if desired, 1 teaspoon of curry powder, and sift once more into a mixing bowl. Add 1 well-beaten fresh egg with 1 fresh egg yolk, to about ½ cup of fresh or sour milk, or enough to make a not too stiff dough. Roll out on a well-floured board to about half an inch thick. Cut into squares. Place a generous teaspoon of this filling on each square:

Cottage Cheese Filling. To one pound of cottage cheese (pressed variety), add 2 unbeaten fresh eggs, and season to taste with salt (a little sugar may be added, if desired) and a dash of cayenne, and mix thoroughly until smooth and thoroughly blended. The mixture should be quite thick.

Fold the squares firmly to form small triangles, after wetting the edges with cold water or unbeaten egg white, and drop the triangles into rapidly boiling water, fruit juice, or white wine. When they rise to the surface, skim them off with a perforated ladle, and drain thoroughly on absorbent paper. While still hot, fry the triangles in butter until golden brown on all sides, and serve them piled on a folded napkin over a hot platter.

POLISH PORK DUMPLINGS   [751]

Appropriate for vegetable, sauerkraut, and split pea soups, also for garnishing main dishes of sauerkraut, white or red cabbage, spinach, and the like.

Take ⅓ pound of lean cooked fresh pork, and grind with ¼ pound of beef suet 3 times through a food chopper, using the finest blade, and adding with the last grinding 3 tablespoons of browned finely chopped onion and 2 tablespoons of finely chopped parsley. Season to taste with salt, pepper, and a few grains of juniper berries. Blend well. Make a dough of flour and water, having the dough rather soft. Roll out very thin over a slightly floured board. Cut some rounds the size of a silver dollar. Place a little portion of the meat mixture in the center of each round. Top with another round, after wetting the edges with cold water or unbeaten egg white, and seal firmly. Drop the rounds in rapidly boiling water or stock, or place on top of the cooking mixture. Cover tightly, and let boil gently for 12 to 15 minutes without lifting the cover.

POTATO DUMPLINGS I   [752]
Using raw potatoes

Appropriate for almost any kind of semithick or thick soups, including fish soups and chowders, also for stews, fricassées, pot roast, and the like, and for sauerkraut, spinach, cabbage, and almost any kind of cooked vegetable dish.

Grate 3 medium-sized raw potatoes, and mix with ¾ cup of bread crumbs, soaked in cold water, milk, or meat or vegetable stock and thoroughly squeezed, 2 tablespoons of grated onion, 1 teaspoon of finely chopped parsley, and salt, pepper, and nutmeg to taste. Lastly, mix in 2 fresh eggs, beaten as for omelet, and form into balls the size of a walnut, then roll in seasoned flour. Drop into salted boiling water or boiling meat, poultry, or vegetable stock. Cover tightly, and cook for 12 to 15 minutes. Serve very hot in the soup, or garnish a food platter with them.

POTATO DUMPLINGS II   [753]
French method—fluffy, using mashed potatoes

Have ready ½ cup of hot mashed potatoes freshly cooked. Beat in 1 tablespoon of butter alternately with 2 fresh egg yolks. Then blend in ½ cup of soft bread crumbs, and season to taste with salt, a dash of pepper, and a dash of freshly grated nutmeg. Lastly, fold in 2 egg whites, stiffly beaten with a few grains of cayenne. Drop from a teaspoon (dipped in hot soup, or if for a dish, dipped in gravy or sauce) into simmering soup, or on top of a stew, pot roast, or vegetable. Cover tightly, and let simmer gently for 12 to 15 minutes.

RIVVLES or LITHUANIAN DUMPLINGS [754]

Appropriate for almost any kind of thick or clear soup, or chowder and fish stews.

Sift 1 cup of flour into a bowl. Make a hollow in the center, and break in a whole unbeaten egg. Sprinkle with about ⅓ teaspoon of salt and a few grains of pepper and nutmeg. Then with the fingers work the flour into the egg until the whole is a crumbly mass of pieces not larger than an uncooked navy bean, adding more flour, if necessary. They are ready to drop into the boiling soup mixture, 10 minutes before serving. Cook covered.

Note. These dumplings may be prepared far in advance and stored in a closed tin for future use. Spread thinly on a tray or board to dry for a couple of days before storing.

SALMON DUMPLINGS [755]

Appropriate for fish broth or soups, especially chowders.

Almost any kind of cooked or canned fish may be used for these dumplings, which are appropriate to garnish any fish platter, fish soup, or chowder. They may be served as a course with cream sauce or Hollandaise sauce.

Flake any kind of cold, cooked, carefully boned, and skinned salmon to make about ½ pound, or 1½ cups. If using canned fish, drain carefully. Melt 1 tablespoon of butter over a low flame. Stir in, blending well, 2 tablespoons of flour, and when bubbling, but not brown, gradually add ⅓ cup of scalded sweet milk, stirring constantly until the mixture boils and thickens. Lower the heat, and let simmer very gently over an asbestos pad, or over hot water in the top of a double boiler, for 5 minutes, stirring occasionally. Season to taste with salt, pepper, and a dash each of nutmeg, clove, and thyme. Cool slightly, then beat in 2 egg yolks, adding one at a time and beating well after each addition. With the last yolk, stir in 1½ tablespoons of good sherry wine, then add the flaked fish alternately with 4 tablespoons of sieved dry cracker crumbs. Shape into 6 large dumplings or 12 small ones, and drop into salted boiling fish stock.

Cook until the dumplings rise to the surface. Drain, and serve at once.

SAUSAGE DUMPLINGS   [756]

Appropriate for consommé, and pea, bean, or lentil soup.

Put 4 tablespoons of fresh pork meat, ground fine, and 2 generous tablespoons of bread crumbs, soaked in a little milk then squeezed and shaken to loosen, with ½ generous tablespoon of butter, and salt, pepper, thyme leaves, and nutmeg to taste, through a food chopper. Add 4 drops of onion juice and 1 teaspoon of finely chopped parsley, and return to the food chopper again. Shape into small balls the size of a very small walnut, then roll sausagelike between the hands, and 5 minutes before serving, drop them all at once into rapidly boiling soup or consommé.

SCOTCH OATMEAL DUMPLINGS   [757]

Appropriate for clear consommé, chicken broth, or fish broth.

Stir together in a mixing bowl ½ cup of uncooked oatmeal, 1 large fresh egg, slightly beaten with ½ teaspoon of salt, a dash of pepper and nutmeg, 1 teaspoon of baking powder, 2 tablespoons of flour, 1 tablespoon of melted butter, and 2 tablespoons of cold meat or poultry stock. Mix thoroughly, and drop from a wet teaspoon into rapidly boiling consommé seasoned with 2 tablespoons of Pique Seasoning, or chicken or fish broth. Boil for 5 minutes, covered, then reduce the heat, and continue boiling gently for 5 minutes longer. Remove from the fire, and keep covered for 10 minutes before serving, to mellow and ripen.

Note. You may add 1 teaspoon of grated raw onion to the mixture before cooking.

SMOKED TONGUE DUMPLINGS   [758]

Very fine with clear soup, or bean, pea, and potato soups.

Cream 4 tablespoons of butter until mushy with a wooden spoon. Break 1 whole egg into the butter, and cream again until thoroughly mixed and blended, then add a second, then a third egg, beating and creaming after each addition. Add likewise 3 egg yolks and 3 tablespoons of finely chopped or ground cooked smoked tongue (fresh tongue may be used but the flavor is quite different). Then add 3 tablespoons of bread crumbs, and season to taste with salt, pepper, nutmeg, and a few thyme leaves. Put through a food chopper to ensure smoothness. Shape into small balls the size of a large marble, and 10 long minutes before serving, drop them all at once into rapidly boiling soup.

SPINACH DUMPLINGS [759]

Appropriate for almost any kind of semithick and thick vegetable soups.

Combine ¾ cup of cooked sieved spinach leaves (sorrel may be substituted) with 1 teaspoon of grated raw onion and 1½ tablespoons of melted butter or margarine, and season to taste with salt, pepper, and nutmeg. Mix in 1 slightly beaten egg alternately with 4 tablespoons of bread flour sifted with ¼ teaspoon of baking powder. Then blend in ½ to ¾ cup of soft bread crumbs, mix thoroughly, stirring lightly but thoroughly. Drop from a teaspoon into a steamer placed over the soup, or on a rack over hot water or stock. Cover tightly, and let steam for 5 minutes. Serve hot.

SPONGE DUMPLINGS [760]

Appropriate for clear consommé or vegetable soup.

Place 2 egg whites, unbeaten, in a saucepan, and add about ⅔ cup of cold milk, 1 scant cup of flour, then 2 tablespoons of melted butter, and stir well over a moderate flame until the mixture is thick and smooth. Cool. When cold, beat in 1 egg yolk, salt, pepper, and nutmeg to taste, and ½ teaspoon of onion juice. Drop by a teaspoon moistened in water into the rapidly boiling soup, 8 to 10 minutes before serving.

STRETCHED FRENCH DUMPLINGS [761]

The stretching to a transparent thinness is the secret, if any, of success. Appropriate for clear consommé, chicken bouillon, or any kind of fish broth.

Sift together 1 cup of pastry flour with ¼ teaspoon of salt and a few grains of nutmeg, then moisten with enough cold, clear, fatless beef broth to the consistency of soft biscuit dough. Divide the ball of dough into four equal parts. Roll each part very thin, using plenty of flour to prevent sticking. Cut the rolled dough into about 2½-inch squares, and stretch to a transparent thinness. Drop the transparent squares into boiling broth, a few at a time, about 2 or 3 each time. Cook for 5 minutes over a gentle flame, and serve at once.

TOMATO JUICE DUMPLINGS   [762]

Appropriate for cream of tomato soup.

Sift 1 cup of bread flour once, return to the sifter, and add ¼ teaspoon of celery or garlic salt and ½ teaspoon of baking powder. Sift
again into a mixing bowl, then stir in 1 well-beaten fresh egg mixed with
5 tablespoons of tomato juice and 2 teaspoons of melted butter. Stir
lightly but thoroughly, or until the flour is all dampened. Drop from
a wet teaspoon into boiling cream of tomato soup. Cover, and let
boil gently for 3 or 4 minutes.

WATERCRESS DUMPLINGS   [763]
Very fluffy

Appropriate for almost any kind of cream or bisque soup, also for
meat and poultry stews, pot roast, and fish stews.

Sift 1 cup of sifted pastry flour with 1 teaspoon of baking powder,
¼ teaspoon of salt, and a few grains of nutmeg. Cut in ½ tablespoon
of butter or margarine, and mix to the consistency of corn meal.
Combine 1 beaten egg yolk, ¼ scant cup of rich milk, and ½ cup of
finely chopped watercress, using the leaves only, and mix quickly
with the flour mixture. Do not beat until smooth. Grease the top
part of a steamer, place over rapidly boiling water, and drop the
dumpling mixture by teaspoonfuls into the steamer. Cover closely,
and cook gently for 8 to 10 minutes without removing the cover.
Place these fluffy watercress dumplings in the soup at once, and serve
immediately.

WHOLE WHEAT DUMPLINGS   [764]

Appropriate for almost any kind of soup, such as cream, bisque,
clear, thick soups, including fish soups and chowders, also for stews,
pot roast, fricassées, and the like.

Sift ¾ cup of bread flour, measure, then add 1¼ teaspoons of
baking powder, ⅓ teaspoon of celery salt, a few grains of pepper and
nutmeg to taste. Then mix in 6 tablespoons of whole wheat breakfast cereal, 1 teaspoon each of grated onion and parsley, and stir in
enough cold milk (about ½ cup) to make a drop batter. Drop by a
scant teaspoon into boiling soup, stew, pot roast, or fricassée. Cover,
and let boil gently for 5 or 6 minutes.

Chapter Thirteen

MISCELLANEOUS
SOUP GARNISHES

Foods colored yellow were highly regarded as luxurious eating in Roman times; they were colored with saffron, one of the most costly products obtainable. Imitations were used by hosts in the lower income brackets—false saffron, which imparted a reddish tint, and marigold.

CHOPPED, BLANCHED, TOASTED ALMONDS ARE THE PERFECT last touch in a cream or chicken soup. Have you tried adding a tablespoonful of salted whipped cream as a garnish for a plate of tomato soup or any cream soup? It adds not only taste but elegance. You may tint the whipped cream with a little paprika or saffron, or a few drops of green vegetable coloring, also a little curry powder. Butter crackers spread with a mixture of butter and a little curry powder or paprika, then heated under the flame of the broiling oven, form an appetizing accompaniment to fish soup, oyster stew, and fish chowder. Add thin little rounds of frankfurters to split pea, lentil, or cream soup by way of an edible garnish. A few rounds of these with squares of browned bread look pretty and appetizing together. Cut bread or pastry dough into short slender sticks, brush with beaten egg white, dust with salt and caraway seeds, and bake quickly. These go well with salad too. Grate American cheese onto salted crackers, dust with paprika, curry powder, nutmeg, or cinnamon, and brown under the flame of the broiling oven. These, too, are fine with salads.

ALMOND STICKS   [766]

Especially appropriate for chicken bouillon and chicken soup.

Remove the crust from as many slices of bread as desired, and cut the slices into finger length strips. Cream 2 tablespoons of butter with ½ teaspoon of brown sugar, and as much of powdered cinnamon, and spread on the bread strips, then sprinkle with blanched chopped almonds generously. Arrange the strips on a baking sheet, and bake in a moderate oven (350°–375° F.) until the almonds are delicately browned. Serve hot.

AVOCADO SLICES OR STRIPS   [767]

Appropriate for hot consommé or hot chicken bouillon.

Peel the fruit only after halving, to avoid handling or marring the smooth exterior. Strip the pliable skin back from the meat of the pear, like the peel of a thin-skinned orange. Paring with a knife loses such valuable assets as appearance, the inviting green color, and nutritive values found close to the skin. Slice just before adding to the hot consommé or bouillon, after sprinkling the slices with a little salt or lemon juice. When floating in the bouillon, sprinkle with a little paprika.

BREAD AND CHEESE WAFERS [768]

Appropriate for almost any kind of clear or thick soup.

Cut stale bread into any desired small shapes. Spread sparingly with butter, and then generously with grated cheese (any desired kind). Arrange on a baking sheet, a little apart, and place in a moderate oven (325°–350° F.) to delicately brown. Serve on the side with soup, very hot and bubbling.

BREAD STICKS [769]

Slice bread ¾ inch thick, remove the crusts, and cut each slice into 3 or 4 finger strips. Arrange on a baking sheet, and dry in a very slow oven (200° F.) until lightly browned throughout.

BRUNOISE [770]

Appropriate for clear consommé or bouillon, including fish bouillon.

Cut assorted vegetables into tiny squares, rounds, or lozenge pellets, then cook them in hot consommé, bouillon, fish bouillon, or broth.

CHEESE CHIPS [771]

Makes about 4 dozen. Appropriate for almost any kind of clear or thick soup, salads, and drinks.

Mix 1½ cups of sifted flour with ½ teaspoon of salt, a few grains of cayenne, and ⅓ teaspoon of paprika, and sift again into a mixing bowl. Cut in ½ cup of shortening with pastry blender or two knives, then add ¾ cup of grated cheese (any desired kind). Mix thoroughly, then add about ½ cup of beer, which should be very cold, or enough to hold the mixture together. Form into a roll of about 1½ inches in diameter. Wrap in wax paper, and chill thoroughly. When ready to use, slice as thin as possible. Arrange on an ungreased baking sheet, a little apart. Brush the tops with milk, or egg yolk diluted with a little milk or beer, then sprinkle with ¼ cup of caraway, celery, or poppy seeds. Bake in a very hot oven (450° F.) for 8 or 10 minutes, or until delicately brown. Serve piping hot.

CHEESE CROUTONS [772]

Appropriate with any kind of clear or thick soup.

Spread 4 slices of bread with softened cheese (any kind), and cover with another slice of bread. Brush with melted butter on both sides, and toast both sides under a medium flame in the broiling oven. Cut the crust from each sandwich, then cut into narrow strips, and the strips into small cubes.

CHEESE POPCORN [773]

Appropriate for vegetable soup, especially onion soup, also cream soup, and fine with green salads.

Chop ¼ pound of soft American cheese, and melt over hot water, stirring frequently. Then pour over 1 quart of popcorn, and stir thoroughly to coat the popcorn. Pour onto a platter or baking sheet, and when the cheese hardens, separate the grains with a fork. These garnishes keep well when stored in a closed container, and need just warming up to be served.

CHEESE ROUNDS [774]

Appropriate for almost any kind of clear or thick soup, including cream, and for fish chowders.

Cut thin slices of bread (any kind) into tiny rounds with a small cooky cutter. Dip quickly in milk, and sprinkle thickly with grated cheese (any kind). Or you may cream 2 tablespoons of butter and add ¼ cup of grated cheese (any kind); season to taste with a dash of mustard, a few drops of Worcestershire sauce, and a few grains of cayenne pepper, and spread rounds with this mixture. Place on greased cooky sheet, and bake in a very hot oven (425°–450° F.) about 5 minutes, or until delicately brown. Serve hot.

CHEESE PROFITEROLLES [775]

These tiny puffs are appropriate for almost any kind of clear or thick soup, including cream, fish, and chowders.

Put ¼ cup of butter or margarine and ½ cup of boiling water in a small saucepan. When the butter is melted, add, all at once, ½ cup of flour, and continue cooking until smooth and the mixture leaves the sides of the pan. Remove from the fire, and season to taste with salt, a few grains of cayenne (curry powder may also be used), and ½ cup of grated cheese (any kind). Mix thoroughly, then beat in 2 unbeaten fresh eggs, one at a time, beating well after each addition, and lastly 1 unbeaten egg white. Beat briskly for 5 long minutes. Shape tiny pearlike balls on a buttered baking sheet, using a pastry bag and small tube, and bake for 2 or 3 minutes in a hot oven (425°–450° F.). Serve hot, warm, or cold.

CHEESE PASTRY STICKS [776]

Appropriate for almost any kind of clear or thick soup, including cream, fish, or chowder.

Mix and sift together 1 cup of sifted flour, ¼ teaspoon of salt, ¼ teaspoon of paprika, and a few grains of cayenne, in a mixing bowl. Chop in ¼ pound of grated cheese (any kind) and ¼ cup of shortening. Add 1 tablespoon of ice-cold water, and blend well. Gather into a ball, turn onto a floured board, and roll to a scant ¼ inch in thickness. Cut into narrow strips, and bake on an ungreased cooky sheet in a hot oven (425°–450° F.) for 8 to 10 minutes. Serve hot or cold.

Variation. You may cut the pastry with a very small pastry cutter about one inch in diameter, and make a hole with a floured thimble.

CHESTNUT TIMBALETTES [777]

Appropriate for consommé and any clear soup.

Have ready ¼ cup of thick chestnut purée (the chestnuts are boiled, skinned, and pressed through a ricer, sieve, or press). Add ¼ cup of thick cream, 3 slightly beaten egg yolks, and a few grains of mace, salt, and cayenne to taste. Turn into very small buttered timbale molds, set in a pan of hot water, and bake in a slow oven (275° F.) until delicately brown. Cool, after removing from the molds.

CHIFFONADE GARNISH [778]

Appropriate for clear consommé or thick soup.

Almost all vegetables except the pods may be used. They may be cut julienne, that is, in thin narrow strips, matchlike. Put in ice-cold water as soon as scraped and cut. Cook in salt water or meat stock, or fish or game stock, until tender yet firm. Keep in lukewarm stock until used. For a different treat, try cooking the vegetables in Instant Pique Consommé (No. 24). The vegetables used for the chiffonade may be of one kind only, or a composite of several kinds, such as lettuce, watercress, romaine, French endive, raw spinach, raw green or red cabbage. As a rule, no more than a teaspoon or thereabouts should be used for each serving.

CRACKER PUFFS [779]

Appropriate for medium and thick soups, fish soups and chowders.

Soak soda crackers in cold water for 15 minutes. Lift out very carefully, using a pancake turner or a perforated ladle, and drain thoroughly. Place on a generously greased baking sheet, far enough apart to allow for expansion. Pour over each cracker 1 teaspoon of melted butter, and bake in a hot oven (400° F.) for about 35 minutes, or until well puffed and delicately brown. Serve hot, and one to a plate.

CROUTONS [780]

These toasted tiny bread cubes are appropriate for almost any kind of soup, clear, thick, fish, cream, and chowder.

Method 1. Remove the crusts from thinly sliced stale bread, cut the slices in tiny cubes, and brown the cubes lightly in a little melted butter, or in bacon or ham drippings, in a frying pan, stirring constantly with a wooden spoon to keep them from burning.

Method 2. Prepare the croutons as above, having the cubes cut into about ¼-inch squares. Dip quickly in and out of milk. Roll in grated dry cheese. Place on a greased baking sheet in a single layer, and bake in a hot oven (425° F.) until the cheese is melted and the croutons are delicately browned, shaking the pan frequently. Or place about 4 inches under the flame of the broiling oven, and brown delicately, shaking the pan frequently, until the cheese is browned.

Method 3. Cut the bread as indicated above, place on an ungreased baking sheet, and brown or toast the cubes under the flame of the broiling oven until they are crisp.

Method 4. Cut the bread as indicated, dip quickly into Pique Seasoning, drain well, place on a dry baking sheet, and brown delicately under the flame of the broiling oven, shaking the pan frequently.

Four or five croutons should be the right amount for each serving. They should be put in the soup only when ready to serve, lest they soak and become spongy.

These croutons may be prepared in advance, stored in a closed tin, and kept in a cool, dry place. They will keep for a fortnight.

DIABLOTINS GARBURE [781]

Vegetable spread on rounds of French bread. Appropriate for clear or thick soups, including fish soups and chowders.

Cook together 2 tablespoons each of chopped carrots, white turnips, and leeks, and 1 tablespoon of shredded cabbage, in a little butter in a covered saucepan. To this, add 2 tablespoons of mashed green peas, freshly cooked or canned, and spread this paste on ¼-inch rounds of toasted French fluted bread or rolls, then sprinkle with grated cheese, and brown under the flame of the broiling oven.

DIABLOTINS GOURMET [782]

Egg and cheese spread on rounds of French toast. Appropriate for consommé or hot bouillon.

Slice long French bread or long French rolls into slices ¼ scant inch thick, and toast. Butter generously, and drop a fresh egg yolk in the center of each round, then top with grated cheese, Swiss or Parmesan or mixed in equal parts, sprinkle with a few grains of cayenne pepper, and toast quickly under the flame of the broiling oven. Serve each round on top of consommé or hot bouillon in a cup or soup plate.

EGG DROPS [783]
French method Bourgeoise

Have ready 2 quarts of chicken or beef broth rapidly boiling. Put 1½ cups of flour in a mixing bowl. Make a hole in the center of the flour with a fork, and drop in 1 whole egg and 1 fresh egg yolk. Add ½ eggshell of cold bouillon, and mix the egg and liquid slightly, then with a circular motion and mixing quickly, stir flour into the egg mixture. The result should be a flaky mixture. Drop this into the boiling broth, stirring with a fork, and boil gently for 10 to 15 minutes. Just before serving, put in ¼ cup of finely chopped chervil or parsley. It adds to the soup.

EGG FLAKES or FILETS [784]

Appropriate for hot consommé or hot bouillon.

Break 2 fresh eggs, and beat as for omelet, seasoning to taste with salt and white pepper. Place in a small colander over rapidly boiling consommé or bouillon, and stir to let the egg mixture drop in flakes into the hot liquid. Serve immediately.

FRIED OYSTERETTES [785]

Six to a plate; appropriate for any kind of fish soups, chowders, and bisques.

Heat some butter or margarine well. Add oysterettes, and sauté them over a gentle flame until brown.

GARLIC POPCORN [786]

Appropriate for cream, clear, and thick soups, and for fish bisque or chowder.

Heat butter or margarine well; stir in 2 or 3 peeled cloves of garlic, and cook very gently over a gentle flame, stirring occasionally, for about 1 or 2 minutes. Discard the garlic, and stir in enough popcorn to serve 6 persons, about 1 to 1½ tablespoons for each serving.

GARLIC TOAST [787]

Appropriate for almost any kind of soup, such as cream, clear, vegetable, and bisque, and for fish soups and chowders.

Heat 3 tablespoons of butter in a frying pan. Add 1 clove of garlic, peeled and halved, and cook gently for a short minute, stirring frequently. Then add 6 thin rounds of French bread or rolls, and fry to a golden brown on both sides. Place a piece of toast in each cup or soup plate, pour on the soup or consommé, and serve at once.

HOMINY CROUTONS [788]
Southern manner

Appropriate for almost any kind of clear or thick soup, including cream, bisque, fish soup, and chowder.

Pack leftover cooked hominy grits in a buttered ½-pound baking powder can or similar can. Chill. Remove from the can. Cut in scant ¼-inch slices, and then cut into small cubes. Dip in sieved bread crumbs, then slightly beaten egg, and again in crumbs, and fry in hot deep fat. Serve hot on the side.

HOP SHOOTS GARNISH [789]

Appropriate for clear consommé, hot bouillon, or fish broth.
In Europe, hop shoots are greatly relished in salad, or in any kind

of recipe applied to asparagus. In soup, they are greatly appreciated by gourmets. However, they need special preparation as follows:

Take each shoot at the end of the root between the thumb and first finger of the left hand. Slide gently the same fingers from the right hand, and bend the shoot by pulling it toward the point. The right part of the shoot is edible; what is left in the left hand is woody and should be discarded. Wash in several changes of water, and cook them in rapidly boiling salted water, slightly acidulated with lemon juice or mild vinegar, until tender yet firm, or about 12 to 15 minutes, the time depending on the size of the shoots. Drain. They are ready for soup garnishing exactly like asparagus tips, or may be served in cream, tomato, or brown sauce.

JOCKO TOAST [790]

Appropriate for almost any kind of clear consommé or thick soup.

Slice a piece of French bread in two, slightly rub with garlic, then toast dry in a moderate oven (325°–350° F.).

In 1695, when *Civilité*, a book of etiquette à la Emily Post, was published, readers were informed that it was no longer good manners to wipe their fingers on the bread.

MELBA TOAST [791]

It is from Escoffier himself that I learned the origin of Melba toast. One afternoon, Mrs. Marie Louise Ritz, the very capable and devoted wife of Cesar Ritz, complained about toast, which was never thin enough to suit her, and asked Escoffier in front of me, "Can't you do something about it?"

As usual, Escoffier and Ritz took such a remark with absolute seriousness. They discussed the problem of thin toast. "Why not," said Ritz, "toast the thin slices of bread once, then cut it through again, and again toast it?" And with Escoffier he retired to the kitchens to see if it could be done. The result was Escoffier's justly famous Toast Melba. When they brought out on the lawn of the Carlton a silver tray full of thin, crisp curled wafers, Escoffier said, "Behold! a new dish, and it is called Toast Marie." But, as Mrs. Ritz ate it, she tried to think up another name. "Marie" was far too anonymous to suit her.

During that year, Nellie Melba, the famous prima donna, had returned from America very ill. She was staying at the Savoy in London, where she was a much-indulged invalid, and Mrs. Ritz had heard Escoffier discuss her *régime* (diet). Dry toast figured in it. "Call it Toast Melba," said Madame Ritz. And so it was done, and the name remains for posterity.

This paper-thin toast may be served as a side dish with almost any kind of soup and salad, or spread with butter, compounded butter, cream cheese, jam, jelly, ground cooked fish (carefully boned), meat, poultry, or game. It may be served hot or cold. To make it, you need a stale loaf of bread—the staler the better.

Slice stale bread, white preferably, as thin as possible, in squares or long pieces, and remove the crusts. Arrange on a dry baking sheet, and bake in a very slow oven (200°–250° F.) until very crisp, of an evenly brown color and crisp on both sides, turning the pieces frequently. The toast may be made in large quantity and stored in a cool dry place in an airtight container covered with waxed paper. Handle with care, as these fragile toasts break easily. It also may be cut in finger lengths or in any fancy shape.

NOODLE SQUARES [792]

Appropriate for almost any kind of hot consommé, chicken bouillon or broth, and fish broth. If cut in inch squares, they may be served as a side dish for lunch or dinner.

Sift enough bread flour to make a cup, add ¼ teaspoon each of salt, nutmeg, powdered thyme, and allspice, and sift again into a mixing bowl. Make a hole in the center of the flour, and drop in 1 large fresh egg, slightly beaten, and enough lukewarm water to make a noodle dough, which should be rather firm. Knead well on a floured board, and roll as thin as possible. Let dry for at least 30 minutes, the longer the better, but without exaggeration, lest the dough should crumble. Then flour the dough well, and cut into long strips (as for noodles). Place in layers of four, and cut as wide noodles, about 5 pieces at a time, then turn and cut into little squares of about a half inch (larger if used as a side dish). Shake apart. When ready to serve the soup, have ready 2 quarts of rapidly boiling consommé, chicken bouillon, broth, or fish broth, seasoned with salt and pepper to taste, and·just 5 minutes before serving, add the little squares, and cook for 3 or 4 minutes, or until all the squares remain on top of the boiling liquid. Drain, and serve aside with hot soup, each guest helping himself to the amount desired.

PANCAKE GARNISH [793]

Mix together 2 tablespoons of flour, 1 whole fresh egg, ½ cup of cold milk, consommé, chicken bouillon, or fish broth, and ½ teaspoon of finely chopped chervil, parsley, or chives. Cook as you would ordinary pancakes. When done, cut in matchlike strips, small squares, rounds, or lozenges, and serve in hot consommé or other indicated bouillon.

PARSLEY BUTTER CRACKERS [794]

Appropriate for almost any kind of clear or thick soup, cream soup, bisque, or fish soup, including fish chowder.

Cream 2 tablespoons of butter or margarine with the same amount of finely chopped parsley. Spread on any kind of cracker, and broil them under the flame of the broiling oven until brown, or about 1 minute or so.

PASSOVER KRAPLACH [795]

These meat-stuffed squares of dough are appropriate for almost any kind of clear soup, such as consommé, chicken bouillon, broth, or fish bouillon.

Sift 2 cups of flour with ⅓ teaspoon of salt into a mixing bowl. Make a hole in the center, drop in a large fresh egg, well beaten, and 1 teaspoon of creamed butter, and blend in the flour mixture, adding just enough cold water or bouillon to make a stiff dough. Roll out on a lightly floured board, as thin as possible (as for noodles). Then cut into 2-inch squares (larger or about 4-inch squares if they are to be served as a side dish).

On the other hand, mix together ¾ pound of chopped boiled beef (any other kind of meat may be substituted, including poultry or game as well as fish), and 1 large onion, grated, and season with 1 teaspoon of salt and ¼ teaspoon of black pepper. Place a small portion of this meat mixture on each of the 2-inch squares of dough, then fold the dough over the meat to make pastry triangles. Close the edges by pinching firmly together after wetting with cold water. Drop on rapidly boiling clear soup or water.

PASSOVER MATZOTH [796]

These matzoth balls are appropriate for clear consommé, chicken bouillon, or fish broth.

Matzoth is the oldest and the simplest bread known to man. It is made by billions of pounds before Passover. The eating of the matzoth is the most symbolic feature of this Jewish festival commemorating the Hebrews' liberation from Egyptian bondage. Fleeing Egypt hurriedly, the Jews had no time to leaven the bread. This they have eaten for thousands of years, remembering it as the bread of affliction.

Soak 6 matzoths in boiling water for a minute, then squeeze them dry, and crumble thoroughly. Heat 2 tablespoons of chicken fat, add 1 medium-sized onion, grated, and brown lightly. Then stir in the crumbled matzoths, and cook for 2 minutes, stirring constantly. Season with salt, a dash of pepper, ¼ teaspoon of ginger, and 1 tablespoon of finely chopped parsley, then stir in 3 egg yolks. Beat all together, and lastly add 3 egg whites, stiffly beaten, with a few grains of salt and pepper. Form into tiny balls, then roll in a little matzoth meal. Drop in boiling bouillon or salted water for 15 minutes, and serve 3 or 4 in each cup or soup plate. Pour over the hot bouillon, consommé, or broth.

PESTO [797]

Appropriate for minestrone soups as well as all sorts of vegetable soups.

Cream 3 tablespoons of butter until lemon colored. Gradually add 3 tablespoons of olive oil alternately with 3 tablespoons of grated Parmesan cheese, mixed with 3 tablespoons of finely minced parsley, 1 small clove of garlic, mashed to a pulp, salt, a few grains of pepper to taste, and lastly 4 tablespoons of heavy cream. Stir the *pesto* into soup, and let boil for 5 minutes. Serve the soup with an additional bowl of grated Parmesan cheese to be lightly sprinkled over each soup plate.

PIMIENTO WHIP [798]

Appropriate for cold or jellied bouillon or soup, or for jellied fish, chicken, meat, or vegetable loaf.

Chill ½ cup of undiluted evaporated milk or thin coffee cream thoroughly overnight, and whip until stiff (as you would heavy cream). Flavor with 2 tablespoons of unstrained lemon juice, then fold in 1 canned red pimiento, well drained and mashed to a pulp. Place 1 tablespoon in the center of each cup or plate, or each serving of jellied meat loaf, salad, or main dish.

PROFITEROLLES [799]

These tiny pearl-like puffs—*pâté à choux*—are appropriate for almost any kind of clear or thick soup, and are used like croutons. The dough is also used for making éclairs and similar puffs.

Bring 1 cup of milk to a boil with 1 cup of butter, ½ teaspoon of salt, and 1 teaspoon of granulated sugar. Add 2 cups of sifted pastry flour, all at once, and mix thoroughly with a wooden spoon until the mixture is smooth and leaves the sides of the pan. Remove from the fire, cool a little, then beat in 4 fresh unbeaten eggs, adding one at a time, beating briskly after each addition. Fill a pastry bag with a tiny tube, and over an ungreased baking sheet, make small balls, the size of a large pearl. Bake in a hot oven (425°–450° F.) for 2 or 3 minutes. May be served hot, warm, or cold. They keep for a long time in a closed tin.

PULLED BREAD [800]

Appropriate for any kind of clear soup, including cream, fish, and chowder soups.

Remove the crusts from French bread, tear (do not cut) thin strips, and bake in a very slow oven (250° F.) until crisp and delicately browned.

RIBBLES [801]

A very old recipe dating from pioneer times, found by the author in the library in Washington, D. C. They are very nourishing and easy to prepare. Appropriate for clear or vegetable soups.

Beat 1 whole fresh egg until light. Sift 2 cups of flour over the beaten egg, and work between the fingers until fine ribbles are obtained. Just 10 minutes before serving the soup, add as many ribbles as will thicken the soup nicely. If any are left over, they will keep nicely in a covered jar for a few days for future use.

SEMOLINA CHEESE SQUARES [802]

Appropriate for clear or thick soups, including fish soups and chowders.

To a cup of boiling milk add as much semolina as the milk will absorb to make a mush, and cook for 15 to 20 minutes, stirring constantly until the mixture is thick. Remove from the fire, and add ⅓ cup of grated cheese (any kind) and 1 tablespoon of butter. Season to taste with salt, white pepper, and a dash of freshly grated nutmeg. Then beat in 2 small eggs or 1 large egg. The mixture should be that of heavy cream, so add another egg if not thin enough. Pour into a greased shallow pan, set in a pan of hot water, and bake in a very slow oven (250° F.) until the mixture begins to leave the sides of the pan. Cool a little, unmold, and cut in desired fancy small shapes. Add to the soup when just ready to serve.

STUFFED PANCAKE GARNISH [803]
Alsatian manner

Appropriate for clear consommé, bouillon, or broth, and semiclear soups.

Combine ⅔ cup of cooked ground pork and enough leftover brown sauce to blend, and season with salt, pepper, nutmeg, and allspice to taste. Set aside.

Make some ordinary pancakes about 3 inches in length, and place a small amount of the pork meat mixture in center and roll up, securing the rolls with toothpicks. Place the rolled pancakes in a colander or strainer and steam over boiling soup for about 10 minutes. Serve aside the soup and as hot as possible.

TORTILLAS [804]
Frying method

The famous *tamal* of Mexico is always rolled in a tortilla before being wrapped in corn husk. The enchilada is also a rolled tortilla, usually stuffed with cheese and onions, and with a chili sauce poured over it. The workingman at lunch uses it as a combination fork and spoon for the transportation of loads of beans from his lunch pail to his mouth. Filled with beans—or almost anything else—rolled, it becomes the *taca* of the higher classes.

Tortillas are the staple national of the Mexican diet. They form the basis of the ordinary menu, and countless other dishes are based upon them. They may be fried or baked.

Tortillas are made from corn or maize and nothing else; their palatability depends on the way they are handled in the making. The corn should be white and is soaked with enough lime to soften the hull. This process takes from five to six weeks. It is then thoroughly washed in clear water, drained, and ground, forming a paste. This is called *masa*. But in the United States you do not have to go through all that trouble, it can be purchased at any Spanish or Italian food store. The following recipe is a simple one adaptable to the American kitchen. In Mexico, tortillas are made of coarse Indian corn ground on the *metate*, a special square stone for the purpose.

Mix 2 cups of sifted corn meal, 1 scant tablespoon of salt, and 1 tablespoon of lard, adding enough cold water to make a thin dough. Roll very thin, and cut about the size of a coffee-cup saucer. Fry in lard or oil deep enough to float the tortillas. Do not allow them to brown; they are done when they begin to blister. Fry one at a time.

> *We may live without poetry, music and art;*
> *We may live without conscience and live without heart;*
> *We may live without friends; we may live without books;*
> *But civilized man cannot live without cooks.*
> *He may live without books—what is knowledge but grieving?*
> *He may live without hope—what is hope but deceiving?*
> *He may live without love—what is passion but pining?*
> *But where is the man that can live without dining?*
>
> Owen Meredith

INDEX

395

A CATALOGUE OF SELECTED DOVER
BOOKS IN ALL FIELDS OF INTEREST

RACKHAM'S COLOR ILLUSTRATIONS FOR WAGNER'S RING. Rackham's finest mature work—all 64 full-color watercolors in a faithful and lush interpretation of the *Ring*. Full-sized plates on coated stock of the paintings used by opera companies for authentic staging of Wagner. Captions aid in following complete Ring cycle. Introduction. 64 illustrations plus vignettes. 72pp. 8⅝ x 11¼.   23779-6 Pa. $6.00

CONTEMPORARY POLISH POSTERS IN FULL COLOR, edited by Joseph Czestochowski. 46 full-color examples of brilliant school of Polish graphic design, selected from world's first museum (near Warsaw) dedicated to poster art. Posters on circuses, films, plays, concerts all show cosmopolitan influences, free imagination. Introduction. 48pp. 9⅜ x 12¼.   23780-X Pa. $6.00

GRAPHIC WORKS OF EDVARD MUNCH, Edvard Munch. 90 haunting, evocative prints by first major Expressionist artist and one of the greatest graphic artists of his time: *The Scream, Anxiety, Death Chamber, The Kiss, Madonna*, etc. Introduction by Alfred Werner. 90pp. 9 x 12.   23765-6 Pa. $5.00

THE GOLDEN AGE OF THE POSTER, Hayward and Blanche Cirker. 70 extraordinary posters in full colors, from Maitres de l'Affiche, Mucha, Lautrec, Bradley, Cheret, Beardsley, many others. Total of 78pp. 9⅜ x 12¼.   22753-7 Pa. $5.95

THE NOTEBOOKS OF LEONARDO DA VINCI, edited by J. P. Richter. Extracts from manuscripts reveal great genius; on painting, sculpture, anatomy, sciences, geography, etc. Both Italian and English. 186 ms. pages reproduced, plus 500 additional drawings, including studies for *Last Supper*, Sforza monument, etc. 860pp. 7⅞ x 10¾. (Available in U.S. only)   22572-0, 22573-9 Pa., Two-vol. set $15.90

THE CODEX NUTTALL, as first edited by Zelia Nuttall. Only inexpensive edition, in full color, of a pre-Columbian Mexican (Mixtec) book. 88 color plates show kings, gods, heroes, temples, sacrifices. New explanatory, historical introduction by Arthur G. Miller. 96pp. 11⅜ x 8½. (Available in U.S. only)   23168-2 Pa. **$7.95**

UNE SEMAINE DE BONTÉ, A SURREALISTIC NOVEL IN COLLAGE, Max Ernst. Masterpiece created out of 19th-century periodical illustrations, explores worlds of terror and surprise. Some consider this Ernst's greatest work. 208pp. 8⅛ x 11.   23252-2 Pa. $5.00

AN AUTOBIOGRAPHY, Margaret Sanger. Exciting personal account of hard-fought battle for woman's right to birth control, against prejudice, church, law. Foremost feminist document. 504pp. 5⅜ x 8½.

20470-7 Pa. $5.50

MY BONDAGE AND MY FREEDOM, Frederick Douglass. Born as a slave, Douglass became outspoken force in antislavery movement. The best of Douglass's autobiographies. Graphic description of slave life. Introduction by P. Foner. 464pp. 5⅜ x 8½.

22457-0 Pa. $5.50

LIVING MY LIFE, Emma Goldman. Candid, no holds barred account by foremost American anarchist: her own life, anarchist movement, famous contemporaries, ideas and their impact. Struggles and confrontations in America, plus deportation to U.S.S.R. Shocking inside account of persecution of anarchists under Lenin. 13 plates. Total of 944pp. 5⅜ x 8½.

22543-7, 22544-5 Pa., Two-vol. set $11.00

LETTERS AND NOTES ON THE MANNERS, CUSTOMS AND CONDITIONS OF THE NORTH AMERICAN INDIANS, George Catlin. Classic account of life among Plains Indians: ceremonies, hunt, warfare, etc. Dover edition reproduces for first time all original paintings. 312 plates. 572pp. of text. 6⅛ x 9¼.

22118-0, 22119-9 Pa.. Two-vol. set $11.50

THE MAYA AND THEIR NEIGHBORS, edited by Clarence L. Hay, others. Synoptic view of Maya civilization in broadest sense, together with Northern, Southern neighbors. Integrates much background, valuable detail not elsewhere. Prepared by greatest scholars: Kroeber, Morley, Thompson, Spinden, Vaillant, many others. Sometimes called Tozzer Memorial Volume. 60 illustrations, linguistic map. 634pp. 5⅜ x 8½.

23510-6 Pa. $7.50

HANDBOOK OF THE INDIANS OF CALIFORNIA, A. L. Kroeber. Foremost American anthropologist offers complete ethnographic study of each group. Monumental classic. 459 illustrations, maps. 995pp. 5⅜ x 8½.

23368-5 Pa. $10.00

SHAKTI AND SHAKTA, Arthur Avalon. First book to give clear, cohesive analysis of Shakta doctrine, Shakta ritual and Kundalini Shakti (yoga). Important work by one of world's foremost students of Shaktic and Tantric thought. 732pp. 5⅜ x 8½. (Available in U.S. only)

23645-5 Pa. $7.95

AN INTRODUCTION TO THE STUDY OF THE MAYA HIEROGLYPHS, Syvanus Griswold Morley. Classic study by one of the truly great figures in hieroglyph research. Still the best introduction for the student for reading Maya hieroglyphs. New introduction by J. Eric S. Thompson. 117 illustrations. 284pp. 5⅜ x 8½.

23108-9 Pa. $4.00

A STUDY OF MAYA ART, Herbert J. Spinden. Landmark classic interprets Maya symbolism, estimates styles, covers ceramics, architecture, murals, stone carvings as artforms. Still a basic book in area. New introduction by J. Eric Thompson. Over 750 illustrations. 341pp. 8⅜ x 11¼.

21235-1 Pa. $6.95

DRAWINGS OF WILLIAM BLAKE, William Blake. 92 plates from Book of Job, *Divine Comedy, Paradise Lost,* visionary heads, mythological figures, Laocoon, etc. Selection, introduction, commentary by Sir Geoffrey Keynes. 178pp. 8⅛ x 11. 22303-5 Pa. $4.00

ENGRAVINGS OF HOGARTH, William Hogarth. 101 of Hogarth's greatest works: *Rake's Progress, Harlot's Progress, Illustrations for Hudibras, Before and After, Beer Street and Gin Lane,* many more. Full commentary. 256pp. 11 x 13¾. 22479-1 Pa. $7.95

DAUMIER: 120 GREAT LITHOGRAPHS, Honore Daumier. Wide-ranging collection of lithographs by the greatest caricaturist of the 19th century. Concentrates on eternally popular series on lawyers, on married life, on liberated women, etc. Selection, introduction, and notes on plates by Charles F. Ramus. Total of 158pp. 9⅜ x 12¼. 23512-2 Pa. $5.50

DRAWINGS OF MUCHA, Alphonse Maria Mucha. Work reveals drafts-man of highest caliber: studies for famous posters and paintings, render-ings for book illustrations and ads, etc. 70 works, 9 in color; including 6 items not drawings. Introduction. List of illustrations. 72pp. 9⅜ x 12¼. (Available in U.S. only) 23672-2 Pa. $4.00

GIOVANNI BATTISTA PIRANESI: DRAWINGS IN THE PIERPONT MORGAN LIBRARY, Giovanni Battista Piranesi. For first time ever all of Morgan Library's collection, world's largest. 167 illustrations of rare Piranesi drawings—archeological, architectural, decorative and visionary. Essay, detailed list of drawings, chronology, captions. Edited by Felice Stampfle. 144pp. 9⅜ x 12¼. 23714-1 Pa. $7.50

NEW YORK ETCHINGS (1905-1949), John Sloan. All of important American artist's N.Y. life etchings. 67 works include some of his best art; also lively historical record—Greenwich Village, tenement scenes. Edited by Sloan's widow. Introduction and captions. 79pp. 8⅜ x 11¼. 23651-X Pa. $4.00

CHINESE PAINTING AND CALLIGRAPHY: A PICTORIAL SURVEY, Wan-go Weng. 69 fine examples from John M. Crawford's matchless private collection: landscapes, birds, flowers, human figures, etc., plus calligraphy. Every basic form included: hanging scrolls, handscrolls, album leaves, fans, etc. 109 illustrations. Introduction. Captions. 192pp. 8⅞ x 11¾. 23707-9 Pa. $7.95

DRAWINGS OF REMBRANDT, edited by Seymour Slive. Updated Lipp-mann, Hofstede de Groot edition, with definitive scholarly apparatus. All portraits, biblical sketches, landscapes, nudes, Oriental figures, classical studies, together with selection of work by followers. 550 illustrations. Total of 630pp. 9⅛ x 12¼. 21485-0, 21486-9 Pa., Two-vol. set $15.00

THE DISASTERS OF WAR, Francisco Goya. 83 etchings record horrors of Napoleonic wars in Spain and war in general. Reprint of 1st edition, plus 3 additional plates. Introduction by Philip Hofer. 97pp. 9⅜ x 8¼. 21872-4 Pa. $3.75

HISTORY OF BACTERIOLOGY, William Bulloch. The only comprehensive history of bacteriology from the beginnings through the 19th century. Special emphasis is given to biography-Leeuwenhoek, etc. Brief accounts of 350 bacteriologists form a separate section. No clearer, fuller study, suitable to scientists and general readers, has yet been written. 52 illustrations. 448pp. 5⅝ x 8¼.   23761-3 Pa. $6.50

THE COMPLETE NONSENSE OF EDWARD LEAR, Edward Lear. All nonsense limericks, zany alphabets, Owl and Pussycat, songs, nonsense botany, etc., illustrated by Lear. Total of 321pp. 5⅜ x 8½. (Available in U.S. only)   20167-8 Pa. $3.00

INGENIOUS MATHEMATICAL PROBLEMS AND METHODS, Louis A. Graham. Sophisticated material from Graham *Dial*, applied and pure; stresses solution methods. Logic, number theory, networks, inversions, etc. 237pp. 5⅜ x 8½.   20545-2 Pa. $3.50

BEST MATHEMATICAL PUZZLES OF SAM LOYD, edited by Martin Gardner. Bizarre, original, whimsical puzzles by America's greatest puzzler. From fabulously rare *Cyclopedia*, including famous 14-15 puzzles, the Horse of a Different Color, 115 more. Elementary math. 150 illustrations. 167pp. 5⅜ x 8½.   20498-7 Pa. $2.75

THE BASIS OF COMBINATION IN CHESS, J. du Mont. Easy-to-follow, instructive book on elements of combination play, with chapters on each piece and every powerful combination team—two knights, bishop and knight, rook and bishop, etc. 250 diagrams. 218pp. 5⅜ x 8½. (Available in U.S. only)   23644-7 Pa. $3.50

MODERN CHESS STRATEGY, Ludek Pachman. The use of the queen, the active king, exchanges, pawn play, the center, weak squares, etc. Section on rook alone worth price of the book. Stress on the moderns. Often considered the most important book on strategy. 314pp. 5⅜ x 8½.   20290-9 Pa. $4.50

LASKER'S MANUAL OF CHESS, Dr. Emanuel Lasker. Great world champion offers very thorough coverage of all aspects of chess. Combinations, position play, openings, end game, aesthetics of chess, philosophy of struggle, much more. Filled with analyzed games. 390pp. 5⅜ x 8½.   20640-8 Pa. $5.00

500 MASTER GAMES OF CHESS, S. Tartakower, J. du Mont. Vast collection of great chess games from 1798-1938, with much material nowhere else readily available. Fully annotated, arranged by opening for easier study. 664pp. 5⅜ x 8½.   23208-5 Pa. $7.50

A GUIDE TO CHESS ENDINGS, Dr. Max Euwe, David Hooper. One of the finest modern works on chess endings. Thorough analysis of the most frequently encountered endings by former world champion. 331 examples, each with diagram. 248pp. 5⅜ x 8½.   23332-4 Pa. $3.50

HOLLYWOOD GLAMOUR PORTRAITS, edited by John Kobal. 145 photos capture the stars from 1926-49, the high point in portrait photography. Gable, Harlow, Bogart, Bacall, Hedy Lamarr, Marlene Dietrich, Robert Montgomery, Marlon Brando, Veronica Lake; 94 stars in all. Full background on photographers, technical aspects, much more. Total of 160pp. 8⅜ x 11¼. 23352-9 Pa. $6.00

THE NEW YORK STAGE: FAMOUS PRODUCTIONS IN PHOTO-GRAPHS, edited by Stanley Appelbaum. 148 photographs from Museum of City of New York show 142 plays, 1883-1939. *Peter Pan, The Front Page, Dead End, Our Town,* O'Neill, hundreds of actors and actresses, etc. Full indexes. 154pp. 9½ x 10. 23241-7 Pa. $6.00

MASTERS OF THE DRAMA, John Gassner. Most comprehensive history of the drama, every tradition from Greeks to modern Europe and America, including Orient. Covers 800 dramatists, 2000 plays; biography, plot summaries, criticism, theatre history, etc. 77 illustrations. 890pp. 5⅜ x 8½. 20100-7 Clothbd. $10.00

THE GREAT OPERA STARS IN HISTORIC PHOTOGRAPHS, edited by James Camner. 343 portraits from the 1850s to the 1940s: Tamburini, Mario, Caliapin, Jeritza, Melchior, Melba, Patti, Pinza, Schipa, Caruso, Farrar, Steber, Gobbi, and many more—270 performers in all. Index. 199pp. 8⅜ x 11¼. 23575-0 Pa. $6.50

J. S. BACH, Albert Schweitzer. Great full-length study of Bach, life, background to music, music, by foremost modern scholar. Ernest Newman translation. 650 musical examples. Total of 928pp. 5⅜ x 8½. (Available in U.S. only) 21631-4, 21632-2 Pa., Two-vol. set **$10.00**

COMPLETE PIANO SONATAS, Ludwig van Beethoven. All sonatas in the fine Schenker edition, with fingering, analytical material. One of best modern editions. Total of 615pp. 9 x 12. (Available in U.S. only) 23134-8, 23135-6 Pa., Two-vol. set **$15.00**

KEYBOARD MUSIC, J. S. Bach. Bach-Gesellschaft edition. For harpsichord, piano, other keyboard instruments. English Suites, French Suites, Six Partitas, Goldberg Variations, Two-Part Inventions, Three-Part Sinfonias. 312pp. 8⅛ x 11. (Available in U.S. only) 22360-4 Pa. $6.95

FOUR SYMPHONIES IN FULL SCORE, Franz Schubert. Schubert's four most popular symphonies: No. 4 in C Minor ("Tragic"); No. 5 in B-flat Major; No. 8 in B Minor ("Unfinished"); No. 9 in C Major ("Great"). Breitkopf & Hartel edition. Study score. 261pp. 9⅜ x 12¼. 23681-1 Pa. $6.50

THE AUTHENTIC GILBERT & SULLIVAN SONGBOOK, W. S. Gilbert, A. S. Sullivan. Largest selection available; 92 songs, uncut, original keys, in piano rendering approved by Sullivan. Favorites and lesser-known fine numbers. Edited with plot synopses by James Spero. 3 illustrations. 399pp. 9 x 12. 23482-7 Pa. **$7.95**

HOUSEHOLD STORIES BY THE BROTHERS GRIMM. All the great Grimm stories: "Rumpelstiltskin," "Snow White," "Hansel and Gretel," etc., with 114 illustrations by Walter Crane. 269pp. 5⅜ x 8½.
21080-4 Pa. $3.00

SLEEPING BEAUTY, illustrated by Arthur Rackham. Perhaps the fullest, most delightful version ever, told by C. S. Evans. Rackham's best work. 49 illustrations. 110pp. 7⅞ x 10¾.
22756-1 Pa. $2.50

AMERICAN FAIRY TALES, L. Frank Baum. Young cowboy lassoes Father Time; dummy in Mr. Floman's department store window comes to life; and 10 other fairy tales. 41 illustrations by N. P. Hall, Harry Kennedy, Ike Morgan, and Ralph Gardner. 209pp. 5⅜ x 8½.
23643-9 Pa. $3.00

THE WONDERFUL WIZARD OF OZ, L. Frank Baum. Facsimile in full color of America's finest children's classic. Introduction by Martin Gardner. 143 illustrations by W. W. Denslow. 267pp. 5⅜ x 8½.
20691-2 Pa. $3.50

THE TALE OF PETER RABBIT, Beatrix Potter. The inimitable Peter's terrifying adventure in Mr. McGregor's garden, with all 27 wonderful, full-color Potter illustrations. 55pp. 4¼ x 5½. (Available in U.S. only)
22827-4 Pa. $1.25

THE STORY OF KING ARTHUR AND HIS KNIGHTS, Howard Pyle. Finest children's version of life of King Arthur. 48 illustrations by Pyle. 131pp. 6⅛ x 9¼.
21445-1 Pa. $4.95

CARUSO'S CARICATURES, Enrico Caruso. Great tenor's remarkable caricatures of self, fellow musicians, composers, others. Toscanini, Puccini, Farrar, etc. Impish, cutting, insightful. 473 illustrations. Preface by M. Sisca. 217pp. 8⅜ x 11¼.
23528-9 Pa. $6.95

PERSONAL NARRATIVE OF A PILGRIMAGE TO ALMADINAH AND MECCAH, Richard Burton. Great travel classic by remarkably colorful personality. Burton, disguised as a Moroccan, visited sacred shrines of Islam, narrowly escaping death. Wonderful observations of Islamic life, customs, personalities. 47 illustrations. Total of 959pp. 5⅜ x 8½.
21217-3, 21218-1 Pa., Two-vol. set $12.00

INCIDENTS OF TRAVEL IN YUCATAN, John L. Stephens. Classic (1843) exploration of jungles of Yucatan, looking for evidences of Maya civilization. Travel adventures, Mexican and Indian culture, etc. Total of 669pp. 5⅜ x 8½.
20926-1, 20927-X Pa., Two-vol. set $7.90

AMERICAN LITERARY AUTOGRAPHS FROM WASHINGTON IRVING TO HENRY JAMES, Herbert Cahoon, et al. Letters, poems, manuscripts of Hawthorne, Thoreau, Twain, Alcott, Whitman, 67 other prominent American authors. Reproductions, full transcripts and commentary. Plus checklist of all American Literary Autographs in The Pierpont Morgan Library. Printed on exceptionally high-quality paper. 136 illustrations. 212pp. 9⅛ x 12¼.
23548-3 Pa. $7.95

"OSCAR" OF THE WALDORF'S COOKBOOK, Oscar Tschirky. Famous American chef reveals 3455 recipes that made Waldorf great; cream of French, German, American cooking, in all categories. Full instructions, easy home use. 1896 edition. 907pp. 6⅝ x 9⅜.   20790-0 Clothbd. $15.00

COOKING WITH BEER, Carole Fahy. Beer has as superb an effect on food as wine, and at fraction of cost. Over 250 recipes for appetizers, soups, main dishes, desserts, breads, etc. Index. 144pp. 5⅜ x 8½. (Available in U.S. only)   23661-7 Pa. $2.50

STEWS AND RAGOUTS, Kay Shaw Nelson. This international cookbook offers wide range of 108 recipes perfect for everyday, special occasions, meals-in-themselves, main dishes. Economical, nutritious, easy-to-prepare: goulash, Irish stew, boeuf bourguignon, etc. Index. 134pp. 5⅜ x 8½.
23662-5 Pa. $2.50

DELICIOUS MAIN COURSE DISHES, Marian Tracy. Main courses are the most important part of any meal. These 200 nutritious, economical recipes from around the world make every meal a delight. "I . . . have found it so useful in my own household,"—N.Y. Times. Index. 219pp. 5⅜ x 8½.   23664-1 Pa. $3.00

FIVE ACRES AND INDEPENDENCE, Maurice G. Kains. Great back-to-the-land classic explains basics of self-sufficient farming: economics, plants, crops, animals, orchards, soils, land selection, host of other necessary things. Do not confuse with skimpy faddist literature; Kains was one of America's greatest agriculturalists. 95 illustrations. 397pp. 5⅜ x 8½.
20974-1 Pa. $3.95

A PRACTICAL GUIDE FOR THE BEGINNING FARMER, Herbert Jacobs. Basic, extremely useful first book for anyone thinking about moving to the country and starting a farm. Simpler than Kains, with greater emphasis on country living in general. 246pp. 5⅜ x 8½.
23675-7 Pa. $3.50

A GARDEN OF PLEASANT FLOWERS (PARADISI IN SOLE: PARADISUS TERRESTRIS), John Parkinson. Complete, unabridged reprint of first (1629) edition of earliest great English book on gardens and gardening. More than 1000 plants & flowers of Elizabethan, Jacobean garden fully described, most with woodcut illustrations. Botanically very reliable, a "speaking garden" of exceeding charm. 812 illustrations. 628pp. 8½ x 12¼.   23392-8 Clothbd. $25.00

ACKERMANN'S COSTUME PLATES, Rudolph Ackermann. Selection of 96 plates from the Repository of Arts, best published source of costume for English fashion during the early 19th century. 12 plates also in color. Captions, glossary and introduction by editor Stella Blum. Total of 120pp. 8⅜ x 11¼.   23690-0 Pa. $4.50

PRINCIPLES OF ORCHESTRATION, Nikolay Rimsky-Korsakov. Great classical orchestrator provides fundamentals of tonal resonance, progression of parts, voice and orchestra, tutti effects, much else in major document. 330pp. of musical excerpts. 489pp. 6½ x 9¼. 21266-1 Pa. $6.00

TRISTAN UND ISOLDE, Richard Wagner. Full orchestral score with complete instrumentation. Do not confuse with piano reduction. Commentary by Felix Mottl, great Wagnerian conductor and scholar. Study score. 655pp. 8⅛ x 11. 22915-7 Pa. $12.50

REQUIEM IN FULL SCORE, Giuseppe Verdi. Immensely popular with choral groups and music lovers. Republication of edition published by C. F. Peters, Leipzig, n. d. German frontmaker in English translation. Glossary. Text in Latin. Study score. 204pp. 9⅜ x 12¼.
23682-X Pa. $6.00

COMPLETE CHAMBER MUSIC FOR STRINGS, Felix Mendelssohn. All of Mendelssohn's chamber music: Octet, 2 Quintets, 6 Quartets, and Four Pieces for String Quartet. (Nothing with piano is included). Complete works edition (1874-7). Study score. 283 pp. 9⅜ x 12¼.
23679-X Pa. $6.95

POPULAR SONGS OF NINETEENTH-CENTURY AMERICA, edited by Richard Jackson. 64 most important songs: "Old Oaken Bucket," "Arkansas Traveler," "Yellow Rose of Texas," etc. Authentic original sheet music, full introduction and commentaries. 290pp. 9 x 12. 23270-0 Pa. $6.00

COLLECTED PIANO WORKS, Scott Joplin. Edited by Vera Brodsky Lawrence. Practically all of Joplin's piano works—rags, two-steps, marches, waltzes, etc., 51 works in all. Extensive introduction by Rudi Blesh. Total of 345pp. 9 x 12. 23106-2 Pa. $14.95

BASIC PRINCIPLES OF CLASSICAL BALLET, Agrippina Vaganova. Great Russian theoretician, teacher explains methods for teaching classical ballet; incorporates best from French, Italian, Russian schools. 118 illustrations. 175pp. 5⅜ x 8½. 22036-2 Pa. $2.50

CHINESE CHARACTERS, L. Wieger. Rich analysis of 2300 characters according to traditional systems into primitives. Historical-semantic analysis to phonetics (Classical Mandarin) and radicals. 820pp. 6⅛ x 9¼.
21321-8 Pa. $10.00

EGYPTIAN LANGUAGE: EASY LESSONS IN EGYPTIAN HIERO-GLYPHICS, E. A. Wallis Budge. Foremost Egyptologist offers Egyptian grammar, explanation of hieroglyphics, many reading texts, dictionary of symbols. 246pp. 5 x 7½. (Available in U.S. only)
21394-3 Clothbd. $7.50

AN ETYMOLOGICAL DICTIONARY OF MODERN ENGLISH, Ernest Weekley. Richest, fullest work, by foremost British lexicographer. Detailed word histories. Inexhaustible. Do not confuse this with *Concise Etymological Dictionary*, which is abridged. Total of 856pp. 6½ x 9¼.
21873-2, 21874-0 Pa., Two-vol. set $12.00

SECOND PIATIGORSKY CUP, edited by Isaac Kashdan. One of the greatest tournament books ever produced in the English language. All 90 games of the 1966 tournament, annotated by players, most annotated by both players. Features Petrosian, Spassky, Fischer, Larsen, six others. 228pp. 5⅜ x 8½.   23572-6 Pa. $3.50

ENCYCLOPEDIA OF CARD TRICKS, revised and edited by Jean Hugard. How to perform over 600 card tricks, devised by the world's greatest magicians: impromptus, spelling tricks, key cards, using special packs, much, much more. Additional chapter on card technique. 66 illustrations. 402pp. 5⅜ x 8½. (Available in U.S. only)   21252-1 Pa. $3.95

MAGIC: STAGE ILLUSIONS, SPECIAL EFFECTS AND TRICK PHOTOGRAPHY, Albert A. Hopkins, Henry R. Evans. One of the great classics; fullest, most authorative explanation of vanishing lady, levitations, scores of other great stage effects. Also small magic, automata, stunts. 446 illustrations. 556pp. 5⅜ x 8½.   23344-8 Pa. $6.95

THE SECRETS OF HOUDINI, J. C. Cannell. Classic study of Houdini's incredible magic, exposing closely-kept professional secrets and revealing, in general terms, the whole art of stage magic. 67 illustrations. 279pp. 5⅜ x 8½.   22913-0 Pa. $3.00

HOFFMANN'S MODERN MAGIC, Professor Hoffmann. One of the best, and best-known, magicians' manuals of the past century. Hundreds of tricks from card tricks and simple sleight of hand to elaborate illusions involving construction of complicated machinery. 332 illustrations. 563pp. 5⅜ x 8½.   23623-4 Pa. $6.00

MADAME PRUNIER'S FISH COOKERY BOOK, Mme. S. B. Prunier. More than 1000 recipes from world famous Prunier's of Paris and London, specially adapted here for American kitchen. Grilled tournedos with anchovy butter, Lobster a la Bordelaise, Prunier's prized desserts, more. Glossary. 340pp. 5⅜ x 8½. (Available in U.S. only)   22679-4 Pa. $3.00

FRENCH COUNTRY COOKING FOR AMERICANS, Louis Diat. 500 easy-to-make, authentic provincial recipes compiled by former head chef at New York's Fitz-Carlton Hotel: onion soup, lamb stew, potato pie, more. 309pp. 5⅜ x 8½.   23665-X Pa. $3.95

SAUCES, FRENCH AND FAMOUS, Louis Diat. Complete book gives over 200 specific recipes: bechamel, Bordelaise, hollandaise, Cumberland, apricot, etc. Author was one of this century's finest chefs, originator of vichyssoise and many other dishes. Index. 156pp. 5⅜ x 8.
23663-3 Pa. $2.50

TOLL HOUSE TRIED AND TRUE RECIPES, Ruth Graves Wakefield. Authentic recipes from the famous Mass. restaurant: popovers, veal and ham loaf, Toll House baked beans, chocolate cake crumb pudding, much more. Many helpful hints. Nearly 700 recipes. Index. 376pp. 5⅜ x 8½.
23560-2 Pa. $4.50

THE COMPLETE WOODCUTS OF ALBRECHT DURER, edited by Dr. W. Kurth. 346 in all: "Old Testament," "St. Jerome," "Passion," "Life of Virgin," Apocalypse," many others. Introduction by Campbell Dodgson. 285pp. 8½ x 12¼.   21097-9 Pa. $7.50

DRAWINGS OF ALBRECHT DURER, edited by Heinrich Wolfflin. 81 plates show development from youth to full style. Many favorites; many new. Introduction by Alfred Werner. 96pp. 8⅛ x 11.   22352-3 Pa. $5.00

THE HUMAN FIGURE, Albrecht Dürer. Experiments in various techniques—stereometric, progressive proportional, and others. Also life studies that rank among finest ever done. Complete reprinting of *Dresden Sketchbook*. 170 plates. 355pp. 8⅜ x 11¼.   21042-1 Pa. $7.95

OF THE JUST SHAPING OF LETTERS, Albrecht Dürer. Renaissance artist explains design of Roman majuscules by geometry, also Gothic lower and capitals. Grolier Club edition. 43pp. 7⅞ x 10¾   21306-4 Pa. $8.00

TEN BOOKS ON ARCHITECTURE, Vitruvius. The most important book ever written on architecture. Early Roman aesthetics, technology, classical orders, site selection, all other aspects. Stands behind everything since. Morgan translation. 331pp. 5⅜ x 8½.   20645-9 Pa. $4.00

THE FOUR BOOKS OF ARCHITECTURE, Andrea Palladio. 16th-century classic responsible for Palladian movement and style. Covers classical architectural remains, Renaissance revivals, classical orders, etc. 1738 Ware English edition. Introduction by A. Placzek. 216 plates. 110pp. of text. 9½ x 12¾.   21308-0 Pa. $8.95

HORIZONS, Norman Bel Geddes. Great industrialist stage designer, "father of streamlining," on application of aesthetics to transportation, amusement, architecture, etc. 1932 prophetic account; function, theory, specific projects. 222 illustrations. 312pp. 7⅞ x 10¾.   23514-9 Pa. $6.95

FRANK LLOYD WRIGHT'S FALLINGWATER, Donald Hoffmann. Full, illustrated story of conception and building of Wright's masterwork at Bear Run, Pa. 100 photographs of site, construction, and details of completed structure. 112pp. 9¼ x 10.   23671-4 Pa. $5.50

THE ELEMENTS OF DRAWING, John Ruskin. Timeless classic by great Viltorian; starts with basic ideas, works through more difficult. Many practical exercises. 48 illustrations. Introduction by Lawrence Campbell. 228pp. 5⅜ x 8½.   22730-8 Pa. $2.75

GIST OF ART, John Sloan. Greatest modern American teacher, Art Students League, offers innumerable hints, instructions, guided comments to help you in painting. Not a formal course. 46 illustrations. Introduction by Helen Sloan. 200pp. 5⅜ x 8½.   23435-5 Pa. $4.00

THE CURVES OF LIFE, Theodore A. Cook. Examination of shells, leaves, horns, human body, art, etc., in "*the* classic reference on how the golden ratio applies to spirals and helices in nature . . . ."—Martin Gardner. 426 illustrations. Total of 512pp. 5⅜ x 8½.   23701-X Pa. $5.95

AN ILLUSTRATED FLORA OF THE NORTHERN UNITED STATES AND CANADA, Nathaniel L. Britton, Addison Brown. Encyclopedic work covers 4666 species, ferns on up. Everything. Full botanical information, illustration for each. This earlier edition is preferred by many to more recent revisions. 1913 edition. Over 4000 illustrations, total of 2087pp. 6⅛ x 9¼.   22642-5, 22643-3, 22644-1 Pa., Three-vol. set $24.00

MANUAL OF THE GRASSES OF THE UNITED STATES, A. S. Hitchcock, U.S. Dept. of Agriculture. The basic study of American grasses, both indigenous and escapes, cultivated and wild. Over 1400 species. Full descriptions, information. Over 1100 maps, illustrations. Total of 1051pp. 5⅜ x 8½.   22717-0, 22718-9 Pa., Two-vol. set $15.00

THE CACTACEAE,, Nathaniel L. Britton, John N. Rose. Exhaustive, definitive. Every cactus in the world. Full botanical descriptions. Thorough statement of nomenclatures, habitat, detailed finding keys. The one book needed by every cactus enthusiast. Over 1275 illustrations. Total of 1080pp. 8 x 10¼.   21191-6, 21192-4 Clothbd., Two-vol. set $35.00

AMERICAN MEDICINAL PLANTS, Charles F. Millspaugh. Full descriptions, 180 plants covered: history; physical description; methods of preparation with all chemical constituents extracted; all claimed curative or adverse effects. 180 full-page plates. Classification table. 804pp. 6½ x 9¼.
23034-1 Pa. $10.00

A MODERN HERBAL, Margaret Grieve. Much the fullest, most exact, most useful compilation of herbal material. Gigantic alphabetical encyclopedia, from aconite to zedoary, gives botanical information, medical properties, folklore, economic uses, and much else. Indispensable to serious reader. 161 illustrations. 888pp. 6½ x 9¼. (Available in U.S. only)
22798-7, 22799-5 Pa., Two-vol. set $12.00

THE HERBAL or GENERAL HISTORY OF PLANTS, John Gerard. The 1633 edition revised and enlarged by Thomas Johnson. Containing almost 2850 plant descriptions and 2705 superb illustrations, Gerard's *Herbal* is a monumental work, the book all modern English herbals are derived from, the one herbal every serious enthusiast should have in its entirety. Original editions are worth perhaps $750. 1678pp. 8½ x 12¼.
23147-X Clothbd. $50.00

MANUAL OF THE TREES OF NORTH AMERICA, Charles S. Sargent. The basic survey of every native tree and tree-like shrub, 717 species in all. Extremely full descriptions, information on habitat, growth, locales, economics, etc. Necessary to every serious tree lover. Over 100 finding keys. 783 illustrations. Total of 986pp. 5⅜ x 8½.
20277-1, 20278-X Pa., Two-vol. set $10.00

THE DEPRESSION YEARS AS PHOTOGRAPHED BY ARTHUR ROTH-STEIN, Arthur Rothstein. First collection devoted entirely to the work of outstanding 1930s photographer: famous dust storm photo, ragged children, unemployed, etc. 120 photographs. Captions. 119pp. 9¼ x 10¾.
23590-4 Pa. $5.00

CAMERA WORK: A PICTORIAL GUIDE, Alfred Stieglitz. All 559 illustrations and plates from the most important periodical in the history of art photography, Camera Work (1903-17). Presented four to a page, reduced in size but still clear, in strict chronological order, with complete captions. Three indexes. Glossary. Bibliography. 176pp. 8⅜ x 11¼.
23591-2 Pa. $6.95

ALVIN LANGDON COBURN, PHOTOGRAPHER, Alvin L. Coburn. Revealing autobiography by one of greatest photographers of 20th century gives insider's version of Photo-Secession, plus comments on his own work. 77 photographs by Coburn. Edited by Helmut and Alison Gernsheim. 160pp. 8⅛ x 11.
23685-4 Pa. $6.00

NEW YORK IN THE FORTIES, Andreas Feininger. 162 brilliant photographs by the well-known photographer, formerly with Life magazine, show commuters, shoppers, Times Square at night, Harlem nightclub, Lower East Side, etc. Introduction and full captions by John von Hartz. 181pp. 9¼ x 10¾.
23585-8 Pa. $6.00

GREAT NEWS PHOTOS AND THE STORIES BEHIND THEM, John Faber. Dramatic volume of 140 great news photos, 1855 through 1976, and revealing stories behind them, with both historical and technical information. Hindenburg disaster, shooting of Oswald, nomination of Jimmy Carter, etc. 160pp. 8¼ x 11.
23667-6 Pa. $5.00

THE ART OF THE CINEMATOGRAPHER, Leonard Maltin. Survey of American cinematography history and anecdotal interviews with 5 masters—Arthur Miller, Hal Mohr, Hal Rosson, Lucien Ballard, and Conrad Hall. Very large selection of behind-the-scenes production photos. 105 photographs. Filmographies. Index. Originally Behind the Camera. 144pp. 8¼ x 11.
23686-2 Pa. $5.00

DESIGNS FOR THE THREE-CORNERED HAT (LE TRICORNE), Pablo Picasso. 32 fabulously rare drawings—including 31 color illustrations of costumes and accessories—for 1919 production of famous ballet. Edited by Parmenia Migel, who has written new introduction. 48pp. 9⅜ x 12¼. (Available in U.S. only)
23709-5 Pa. $5.00

NOTES OF A FILM DIRECTOR, Sergei Eisenstein. Greatest Russian filmmaker explains montage, making of Alexander Nevsky, aesthetics; comments on self, associates, great rivals (Chaplin), similar material. 78 illustrations. 240pp. 5⅜ x 8½.
22392-2 Pa. $4.50

THE EARLY WORK OF AUBREY BEARDSLEY, Aubrey Beardsley. 157 plates, 2 in color: *Manon Lescaut, Madame Bovary, Morte Darthur, Salome,* other. Introduction by H. Marillier. 182pp. 8⅛ x 11.   21816-3 Pa. $4.50

THE LATER WORK OF AUBREY BEARDSLEY, Aubrey Beardsley. Exotic masterpieces of full maturity: *Venus and Tannhauser, Lysistrata, Rape of the Lock, Volpone,* Savoy material, etc. 174 plates, 2 in color. 186pp. 8⅛ x 11.   21817-1 Pa. $4.50

THOMAS NAST'S CHRISTMAS DRAWINGS, Thomas Nast. Almost all Christmas drawings by creator of image of Santa Claus as we know it, and one of America's foremost illustrators and political cartoonists. 66 illustrations. 3 illustrations in color on covers. 96pp. 8⅜ x 11¼.
23660-9 Pa. $3.50

THE DORÉ ILLUSTRATIONS FOR DANTE'S DIVINE COMEDY, Gustave Doré. All 135 plates from Inferno, Purgatory, Paradise; fantastic tortures, infernal landscapes, celestial wonders. Each plate with appropriate (translated) verses. 141pp. 9 x 12.   23231-X Pa. $4.50

DORÉ'S ILLUSTRATIONS FOR RABELAIS, Gustave Doré. 252 striking illustrations of *Gargantua and Pantagruel* books by foremost 19th-century illustrator. Including 60 plates, 192 delightful smaller illustrations. 153pp. 9 x 12.   23656-0 Pa. $5.00

LONDON: A PILGRIMAGE, Gustave Doré, Blanchard Jerrold. Squalor, riches, misery, beauty of mid-Victorian metropolis; 55 wonderful plates, 125 other illustrations, full social, cultural text by Jerrold. 191pp. of text. 9⅜ x 12¼.   22306-X Pa. $6.00

THE RIME OF THE ANCIENT MARINER, Gustave Doré, S. T. Coleridge. Dore's finest work, 34 plates capture moods, subtleties of poem. Full text. Introduction by Millicent Rose. 77pp. 9¼ x 12.   22305-1 Pa. $3.50

THE DORE BIBLE ILLUSTRATIONS, Gustave Doré. All wonderful, detailed plates: Adam and Eve, Flood, Babylon, Life of Jesus, etc. Brief King James text with each plate. Introduction by Millicent Rose. 241 plates. 241pp. 9 x 12.   23004-X Pa. $6.00

THE COMPLETE ENGRAVINGS, ETCHINGS AND DRYPOINTS OF ALBRECHT DURER. "Knight, Death and Devil"; "Melencolia," and more—all Dürer's known works in all three media, including 6 works formerly attributed to him. 120 plates. 235pp. 8⅜ x 11¼.
22851-7 Pa. $6.50

MAXIMILIAN'S TRIUMPHAL ARCH, Albrecht Dürer and others. Incredible monument of woodcut art: 8 foot high elaborate arch—heraldic figures, humans, battle scenes, fantastic elements—that you can assemble yourself. Printed on one side, layout for assembly. 143pp. 11 x 16.
21451-6 Pa. $5.00

THE SENSE OF BEAUTY, George Santayana. Masterfully written discussion of nature of beauty, materials of beauty, form, expression; art, literature, social sciences all involved. 168pp. 5⅜ x 8½.   20238-0 Pa. $2.50

ON THE IMPROVEMENT OF THE UNDERSTANDING, Benedict Spinoza. Also contains *Ethics, Correspondence,* all in excellent R. Elwes translation. Basic works on entry to philosophy, pantheism, exchange of ideas with great contemporaries. 402pp. 5⅜ x 8½.   20250-X Pa. $4.50

THE TRAGIC SENSE OF LIFE, Miguel de Unamuno. Acknowledged masterpiece of existential literature, one of most important books of 20th century. Introduction by Madariaga. 367pp. 5⅜ x 8½.

20257-7 Pa. $4.50

THE GUIDE FOR THE PERPLEXED, Moses Maimonides. Great classic of medieval Judaism attempts to reconcile revealed religion (Pentateuch, commentaries) with Aristotelian philosophy. Important historically, still relevant in problems. Unabridged Friedlander translation. Total of 473pp. 5⅜ x 8½.   20351-4 Pa. $6.00

THE I CHING (THE BOOK OF CHANGES), translated by James Legge. Complete translation of basic text plus appendices by Confucius, and Chinese commentary of most penetrating divination manual ever prepared. Indispensable to study of early Oriental civilizations, to modern inquiring reader. 448pp. 5⅜ x 8½.   21062-6 Pa. $4.00

THE EGYPTIAN BOOK OF THE DEAD, E. A. Wallis Budge. Complete reproduction of Ani's papyrus, finest ever found. Full hieroglyphic text, interlinear transliteration, word for word translation, smooth translation. Basic work, for Egyptology, for modern study of psychic matters. Total of 533pp. 6½ x 9¼. (Available in U.S. only)   21866-X Pa. $5.95

THE GODS OF THE EGYPTIANS, E. A. Wallis Budge. Never excelled for richness, fullness: all gods, goddesses, demons, mythical figures of Ancient Egypt; their legends, rites, incarnations, variations, powers, etc. Many hieroglyphic texts cited. Over 225 illustrations, plus 6 color plates. Total of 988pp. 6⅛ x 9¼. (Available in U.S. only)

22055-9, 22056-7 Pa., Two-vol. set $12.00

THE ENGLISH AND SCOTTISH POPULAR BALLADS, Francis J. Child. Monumental, still unsuperseded; all known variants of Child ballads, commentary on origins, literary references, Continental parallels, other features. Added: papers by G. L. Kittredge, W. M. Hart. Total of 2761pp. 6½ x 9¼.

21409-5, 21410-9, 21411-7, 21412-5, 21413-3 Pa., Five-vol. set $37.50

CORAL GARDENS AND THEIR MAGIC, Bronsilaw Malinowski. Classic study of the methods of tilling the soil and of agricultural rites in the Trobriand Islands of Melanesia. Author is one of the most important figures in the field of modern social anthropology. 143 illustrations. Indexes. Total of 911pp. of text. 5⅝ x 8¼. (Available in U.S. only)

23597-1 Pa. $12.95

UNCLE SILAS, J. Sheridan LeFanu. Victorian Gothic mystery novel, considered by many best of period, even better than Collins or Dickens. Wonderful psychological terror. Introduction by Frederick Shroyer. 436pp. 5⅜ x 8½.   21715-9 Pa. **$6.00**

JURGEN, James Branch Cabell. The great erotic fantasy of the 1920's that delighted thousands, shocked thousands more. Full final text, Lane edition with 13 plates by Frank Pape. 346pp. 5⅜ x 8½.
23507-6 Pa. **$4.50**

THE CLAVERINGS, Anthony Trollope. Major novel, chronicling aspects of British Victorian society, personalities. Reprint of Cornhill serialization, 16 plates by M. Edwards; first reprint of full text. Introduction by Norman Donaldson. 412pp. 5⅜ x 8½.   23464-9 Pa. **$5.00**

KEPT IN THE DARK, Anthony Trollope. Unusual short novel about Victorian morality and abnormal psychology by the great English author. Probably the first American publication. Frontispiece by Sir John Millais. 92pp. 6½ x 9¼.   23609-9 Pa. **$2.50**

RALPH THE HEIR, Anthony Trollope. Forgotten tale of illegitimacy, inheritance. Master novel of Trollope's later years. Victorian country estates, clubs, Parliament, fox hunting, world of fully realized characters. Reprint of 1871 edition. 12 illustrations by F. A. Faser. 434pp. of text. 5⅜ x 8½.   23642-0 Pa. **$5.00**

YEKL and THE IMPORTED BRIDEGROOM AND OTHER STORIES OF THE NEW YORK GHETTO, Abraham Cahan. Film *Hester Street* based on *Yekl* (1896). Novel, other stories among first about Jewish immigrants of N.Y.'s East Side. Highly praised by W. D. Howells—Cahan "a new star of realism." New introduction by Bernard G. Richards. 240pp. 5⅜ x 8½.   22427-9 Pa. **$3.50**

THE HIGH PLACE, James Branch Cabell. Great fantasy writer's enchanting comedy of disenchantment set in 18th-century France. Considered by some critics to be even better than his famous *Jurgen.* 10 illustrations and numerous vignettes by noted fantasy artist Frank C. Pape. 320pp. 5⅜ x 8½.   23670-6 Pa. **$4.00**

ALICE'S ADVENTURES UNDER GROUND, Lewis Carroll. Facsimile of ms. Carroll gave Alice Liddell in 1864. Different in many ways from final Alice. Handlettered, illustrated by Carroll. Introduction by Martin Gardner. 128pp. 5⅜ x 8½.   21482-6 Pa. **$2.00**

FAVORITE ANDREW LANG FAIRY TALE BOOKS IN MANY COLORS, Andrew Lang. The four Lang favorites in a boxed set—the complete *Red, Green, Yellow* and *Blue* Fairy Books. 164 stories; 439 illustrations by Lancelot Speed, Henry Ford and G. P. Jacomb Hood. Total of about 1500pp. 5⅜ x 8½.   23407-X Boxed set, Pa. **$14.95**

THE STANDARD BOOK OF QUILT MAKING AND COLLECTING, Marguerite Ickis. Full information, full-sized patterns for making 46 traditional quilts, also 150 other patterns. Quilted cloths, lame, satin quilts, etc. 483 illustrations. 273pp. 6⅞ x 9⅝. 20582-7 Pa. $4.95

ENCYCLOPEDIA OF VICTORIAN NEEDLEWORK, S. Caulfield, Blanche Saward. Simply inexhaustible gigantic alphabetical coverage of every traditional needlecraft—stitches, materials, methods, tools, types of work; definitions, many projects to be made. 1200 illustrations; double-columned text. 697pp. 8⅛ x 11. 22800-2, 22801-0 Pa., Two-vol. set $12.00

MECHANICK EXERCISES ON THE WHOLE ART OF PRINTING, Joseph Moxon. First complete book (1683-4) ever written about typography, a compendium of everything known about printing at the latter part of 17th century. Reprint of 2nd (1962) Oxford Univ. Press edition. 74 illustrations. Total of 550pp. 6⅛ x 9¼. 23617-X Pa. $7.95

PAPERMAKING, Dard Hunter. Definitive book on the subject by the foremost authority in the field. Chapters dealing with every aspect of history of craft in every part of the world. Over 320 illustrations. 2nd, revised and enlarged (1947) edition. 672pp. 5⅜ x 8½. 23619-6 Pa. $7.95

THE ART DECO STYLE, edited by Theodore Menten. Furniture, jewelry, metalwork, ceramics, fabrics, lighting fixtures, interior decors, exteriors, graphics from pure French sources. Best sampling around. Over 400 photographs. 183pp. 8⅜ x 11¼. 22824-X Pa. $6.00